BEING GIVEN

Cultural Memory

in

the

Present

Mieke Bal and Hent de Vries, Editors

Regis College Library
MARY STREET
TORONTO, ONTARIO, CANADA
M4Y 2R5

BEING GIVEN

Toward a Phenomenology of Givenness

Jean-Luc Marion

Translated by Jeffrey L. Kosky

STANFORD UNIVERSITY PRESS

STANFORD, CALIFORNIA

2002

B
2430
.M283E8313
2002

Stanford University Press
Stanford, California

© 2002 by the Board of Trustees of the
Leland Stanford Junior University.
All rights reserved.

Assistance for the translation was provided by the French Ministry of Culture.
Being Given: Toward a Phenomenology of Givenness was originally published
in French in 1997 under the title *Etant donné: Essai d'une phénoménologie de
la donation,* ©1997, Presses Universitaires de France.

Printed in the United States of America
on acid-free, archival-quality paper.

Library of Congress Cataloging-in-Publication Data

Marion, Jean-Luc
  [Etant donné. English]
  Being given : toward a phenomenology of givenness / Jean-Luc Marion ;
translated by Jeffrey L. Kosky.
    p.   cm. — (Cultural memory in the present)
Includes bibliographical references and index.
  ISBN 0-8047-3410-0 (cloth : alk. paper) —
ISBN 0-8047-3411-9 (pbk. : alk. paper)
  1. Phenomenology. I. Title. II. Series.
B2430.M283 E8313   2002
194—dc21   2002009243

Original printing 2002

Last figure below indicates year of this printing:
11 10 09 08 07 06 05 04 03 02

Typeset by James P. Brommer in 11/13.5 Garamond

CONTENTS

The publication of this book in America has a special importance in my eyes—obviously because, having taught and lectured for more than fifteen years in the United States, I find that many of my conversation partners are located on this side of the Atlantic, but especially because as a professor invited for several years now to teach at the University of Chicago, I wrote a great part of this work in Hyde Park, presented many of the arguments to students in the classrooms of Foster Hall, Swift Hall, or Classics, and discussed it with my friends and colleagues here. I am obliged to thank this great university for having thus accepted me into its great tradition and also my students, who have been as cordial as they are demanding, for having helped me more than they know. Among my colleagues, I want to thank in particular Dan Garber and David Tracy, who, in very different ways, supported me in a work that seems to me, even now that it is done, well above my abilities. Thus, appearing in America, *Etant donné* in some ways returns to its place of origin.

The essential points having been said, I will indulge myself by adding two points of clarification.

It behooves me to emphasize that *Etant donné* is inscribed, today, in a triptych, begun in 1989 with *Réduction et donation: Etudes sur Husserl, Heidegger et la phénoménologie*[1] and completed in 2001 with *De surcroît: Essais sur les phénomènes saturés.*[2] The first work tried to stay within the history of philosophy applied to phenomenology; it was an inquiry into the method actually followed by Husserl and Heidegger, with an eye toward disclosing the possibilities open, for the future, to this school of thought. It succeeded in rethinking the classic operation of the reduction as no longer dedicated only to securing objects (as in Husserl) or disclosing beings (as for Heidegger), but more radically to opening a still more originary determination of the phenomenon—the given. This is summed up in a formula: "So much reduction, so much givenness." It happened that, contrary to all expectation, this formal and methodological work incited much discussion, indeed passionate debate.[3] In any case, it called for clarification and development—which demanded nothing less than passing from a factual and historical inquiry to conceptual and organic research: the phenomenon as given in terms of givenness, the gift itself reduced to givenness, the determinations of the given, the saturated phenomenon as given par excellence, and finally the gifted (the figure of "subjectivity" granted to and by givenness). After ten painful years, *Etant donné*—and, in the wake of its publication, the discussion of even stronger objections followed (Ricoeur, Derrida, Franck, etc.). But this work was still abstract, at least in its presentation of the givenness of saturated phenomena, which were sketched formally and too quickly. Hence a final series of studies, *De surcroît*, designed to go into the details of the saturated phenomena, including the phenomenon of Revelation. This collection aimed to make possible a revival of phenomenology by freeing it from two horizons whose limits had become obvious to me (objectness, Being), without losing the radicality of a method whose fruitfulness was proven throughout the century just ended, a fruitfulness that remains one of the great trump cards held by a philosophy that means to think after and thanks to the end of metaphysics. I hope that others will make greater progress in this direction.

But *Etant donné*—at least it seems to me in retrospect—resumes questions left in suspense by a previous book, *Dieu sans l'être*.[4] There, it was a question of uprooting the question of God not only from metaphysics (and the fate of the "Death of God"), but also from what made possible an investigation that had become as obsessive as imprecise into the "existence of God," namely, the unquestioned horizon of Being as supposedly the sole frame of his presence. The critical portion of this essay was accomplished within the field of philosophy, but I could not, at that time, glimpse its constructive side (access to charity) except through recourse to theology (hence the second part, "Hors-texte"). What was lacking was a nonmetaphysical method of philosophy—phenomenology, but a phenomenology thoroughly secured. It took twenty years for me to hope to succeed, at least in part. And in fact, *Etant donné*, with the inventory of saturated phenomena, completes, in the particular case of the phenomenon of Revelation, a sketch of what *Dieu sans l'être* bluntly intended through direct recourse to theology.[5] I hope thus to shed some light on the relations, at once essential for the future and poorly illuminated in the past, between phenomenology and theology.

There remains the most agreeable obligation of thanking those who made this translation possible. The editor first, Helen Tartar, who took a risk and made the decision to give a new life to this book. The translator next, Jeffrey L. Kosky, who, no beginner in this difficult task,[6] showed exceptional dedication, precision, and virtuosity. I appreciate the extent to which one must oneself be a real philosopher to have rewritten, therefore rethought, a book word for word. In his case, this is proven by his expert examination of the very issues I mention above (the relations between phenomenology and theology) in the case of Emmanuel Levinas.[7] He has my deepest gratitude and most sincere admiration.

JEAN-LUC MARION
Chicago, 10 May 2001

My work on this translation is dedicated to my grandparents: Lillian and Irving Kosky and Sadie and Julius Fialco. Not everything that merits acknowledgment happens in the public eye, and the most important probably never does. I will always remember what we have shared in the still, quiet moments.

JEFFREY KOSKY
Chicago, March 2002

BEING GIVEN

PRELIMINARY ANSWERS

Axiom: we *cannot know anything on our own*;
all real knowledge must be given to us.

—Novalis[1]

Being given... —the phrase seems self-evident.

The untrained understanding readily joins the learned reading to add an article to the first word and thereby read "the being given," considering as it does "[the] being" as a substantive, and so conclude simply that what is, namely the *ens* of the philosophers or, according to an old French word, *l'étant*,[2] is also given: a being—in other words, a given. In short, the phrase would merely state that there is being rather than nothing. Thus the common reading, at once learned and untrained, hears in "being given" only what metaphysics can say about it. In this way, not only does this reading not really read literally; it exposes itself to incoherence. For if one admits that it is the being (in the nominal sense) that is given and nothing more, why not simply and metaphysically say that "the being is," indeed that "the being *is* given"? Why, on the contrary, juxtapose with neither transition, nor article, nor copula the terms "being" and "given"? Is "given" equivalent to a trivial explanation of "is given," as "being" is to an explanation of "being is"? In short, is "being given" merely the gloss of the strange and two-fold tautology "the being—what—is"? If that is all this is about, why not have said, as philosophy has said again and again since Parmenides, being is—*eon emmenai*?[3] And if that's what is at issue, why does the phrase have recourse to "given," seeing as in the gloss with which this reading concludes, this term and it alone disappears as useless and imprecise? In short, the untrained and learned reading of "being given" lets "being" run rampant and entirely forgets "given."

These readings must therefore be abandoned, and "being given" must be read as, upon reflection, it gives itself. Without added article, "being" must be taken for a verb, and a verb that works for an other (an *auxiliary* verb), since it puts into operation that which now proves itself ultimately "given." "Being given" suggests that the given is indeed already and irrevocably given—as "being done" asserts that the deed is done,[4] "being acquired" that the acquisition is definitively acquired, or "being said" that the said has the status of a promise, etc. Here "being" is preparation for "given," which completes it and confers on it the force of a fait accompli. What is more: considered only as an auxiliary, "being," as a verb, topples and disappears in the "given" because it intends only to reinforce it; "being" posits the fact of the "given" and is entirely de-posited therein. "Being given"—the given is given in fact and thus attests its givenness. "Being given" does not reconduct the given to the status of a being not yet adequately named, nor does it inscribe it in supposedly normative beingness. Rather, "being given" discloses it as a given, owing nothing to anybody, given inasmuch as given, organized in terms of givenness and even employing "being" therein. In one and the same move, the given earns its givenness, and Being (verbal being) disappears in its enactment therein. That is, the given verbally unfolds its givenness in it—what I will name the fold of the given—and the auxiliary Being falls into line with givenness, which it serves. "Being given" says the given as given.

"Being given" thus resumes the question I posed in *Réduction et donation: Recherches sur Husserl, Heidegger et la phénoménologie* in 1989. At that time, I thought only to proceed with a simple historical examination of the development of the phenomenological method: the arising of the reduction with objectness in Husserl; its swerve to beingness in view of reaching the Being of beings for the sake of *Dasein* in Heidegger; finally, the possibility of radicalizing the pure reduction to the given as such. This seemed to present itself as something almost trivial in my reading of the classic texts. No doubt, the privilege I finally granted to givenness could have been surprising—but wasn't it after all a mere translation of a term present throughout Husserl (namely: *Gegebenheit*)? As for knowing if one could receive it or not, this question should in principle never have been left to the standards of accepted thought nor to the ideology of good manners, but only to the exigencies of the thing itself. No doubt, the possibility of a "third reduction" was shocking—but if Husserl's transcendental reduction is indeed at play within the horizon of objectness, if Heidegger's existential reduction is deployed within the horizon of Being, shouldn't we, as soon as the reduction is no longer blocked by the object or the being, designate it specifically as the third, ordered to the pure given? I thus thought myself to have been working almost as a historian of philosophy, applying my research to the history of phenomenology.

The debate provoked by *Réduction et donation*, with its positive and negative reactions, happily opened my eyes, since it proved that I had advanced theses of greater importance than I had ever imagined. The agreements, the disagreements, and even the misreadings unambiguously suggest the stakes, but also new difficulties that await a decision. In taking count of them, I would like to express my debt and my gratitude to those who truly pointed them out to me. The present work tries to respond to these questions. (a) First, at issue is the new principle, "So much reduction, so much givenness," more adequate than the other principles proposed for phenomenology because finally last (Book 1, §1).[5] This principle led me to thematize explicitly a new definition, at once broader and more basic, of the phenomenon—no longer as object or being, but as given. This charge motivates the project that deduces and articulates all the characteristics of the phenomenon as such on the basis of its determination as given (Book 3). (b) It was then necessary to reinvestigate the given character of the gift: can it be conceived as gift without annihilating all content, every actor, and all intrigue (Book 2, §§7–8)?[6] Confronted with this aporia, shouldn't we renounce a simple concept of given and distinguish essentially between the phenomenological givenness of the given and the ordinary thematic of the gift?[7] (c) Next, shouldn't we fear some sort of return to "special metaphysics," which givenness would perhaps imply, insofar as it is supposed to imply a transcendental, indeed—*horribile dictu*—"theological" giver.[8] Beyond this superficial polemic, the more essential question is posed about the possibility of deploying givenness solely within the frame of reduced immanence (Book 2). (d) The nature of the third reduction was also investigated: Is it self-evident that it is still enacted within the field of phenomenology? Couldn't it instead subvert phenomenology or leave it behind?[9] I was therefore obliged to try to establish that, far from remaining sunk in the unsayable and irrational, the third reduction permitted one to put on stage phenomena as such, precisely because it led them back to their pure given status, according to radically nonmetaphysical determinations (Book 3). (e) Moreover, the reduction of phenomenality to givenness succeeded in the task of describing certain exceptional phenomena, ones that previous metaphysics and phenomenology had ignored or excluded: the phenomena saturated with intuition, which I call paradoxes (Book 4). (f) Finally, the determination of the phenomenon as given, if it can and must dispense with every giver, nonetheless always comes to a givee. "Who comes after the subject"—I call him "the gifted," with no other *subjectum* besides his capacity to receive and to receive *himself* from what he receives (Book 5).

In what follows, therefore, I have but one theme: if the phenomenon is defined as what *shows itself* in and from itself (Heidegger), instead of as what admits constitution (Husserl), this *self* can be attested only inasmuch as the phenomenon first *gives itself*. Without going back to that through which the phenomenon gives itself, we cannot conceive that it could show itself. And in fact, the thought that does not do justice to the given remains most of the time and first of all powerless to receive a number of phenomena for what they are—givens that show themselves. Also, it excludes from the field of manifestation not only many phenomena, but above all those most endowed with meaning and those that are most powerful. Only a phenomenology of givenness can return to the things themselves because, in order to return to them, it is necessary first to see them, therefore to see them as they come and, in the end, to bear their unpredictable landing.

Two questions still remain to be discussed. (a) I often assume that phenomenology makes an exception to metaphysics. I do not, however, defend this assertion in its entirety, since I emphasize that Husserl upholds Kantian decisions (the conditions for the possibility of phenomenality, the horizon, the constituting function of the I) and similarly that Heidegger upholds subjectivity in Dasein no less than the privilege of the question of Being. It should, therefore, be admitted that phenomenology does not actually overcome metaphysics so much as it opens the official possibility of leaving it to itself. The border between metaphysics and phenomenology runs within phenomenology—as its highest possibility, and I stick with the phenomenological discipline only in search of the way that it opens and, sometimes, closes. But here again, possibility goes farther than actuality; the phenomenological way has not yet reached its endpoint, and I borrow it only with the hope that it will. (b) In describing saturated phenomena or paradoxes (Book 4, §§21–23), I do not hesitate to go so far as the phenomenon of Revelation (§24), namely Christ. Is this a blatant and perfectly unseemly theological turn? Once again, I resist this claim for at least two reasons. (i) Every phenomenon must be describable, and every exclusion must on principle be reversed, in phenomenology as elsewhere, and turned against he who effects it. This was one of the most glaring limits of classical metaphysics from Spinoza to Nietzsche: namely, to have the pretense to forbid phenomenality to what claimed it. For the very concept of Revelation belongs by right to phenomenality, and even to contest it, it is appropriate to see it. (ii) *Here*, I am not broaching revelation in its theological pretension to the truth, something faith alone can dare to do. I am outlining it as a possibility—in fact the ultimate possibility, the paradox of paradoxes—of phenomenality, such that it is carried out in a possible saturated phenomenon. The hypothesis that there was historically no such revelation would change nothing in the phenomenological task of offering an account of the fact, itself incontestable, that it has been thinkable, discussible, and even describable. This description therefore does not make an exception to the principle of the reduction to immanence. Here it is perhaps a case of something like the phenomena that Husserl thought could be described only by imaginative variations—imaginary or not, they appear, and their mere possibility merits analysis and *Sinngebung*. As for the relation that phenomenology, or rather a phenomenology still to be constructed, could maintain with the fact of Revelation, it is not fundamentally different from the relation that philosophy as such maintains with it. And today we are hardly in a position to even pose this question.

What *shows itself* first *gives itself*—this is my one and only theme. I have endeavored to stick to it and orchestrate it the entire length of this work, and I have held no other implicit or esoteric thesis. May I therefore be permitted, so as to avoid any misreadings, to address a supplication to those whom the ancients called "kindly reader": on principle, I mean to say what I try to say and not the opposite of what I have said. Thus when I say that reduced givenness does not demand any giver for its given, I am *not* insinuating that it lays claim to a transcendent giver; when I say that the phenomenology of givenness by definition passes beyond metaphysics, I do *not* say between the lines that this phenomenology restores metaphysics; and finally when I oppose the gifted to transcendental subjectivity, I am *not* suggesting that the "subject" is reborn in givenness.

But such misunderstandings come first from the difficulty intrinsic to the questions being broached and from my own insufficiencies or ignorance. Never so much as on this all too barren and arduous terrain have I been so conscious of this. I cannot do better than this essay, manifestly inadequate to what it is a question of thinking. "E per piú non poter fo quant' io posso—and not being capable of more, I do as much as I can," Bembo said.[10] What is left is to hope that others will go farther. The phenomenality of the given is worth more than what I say about it—and it will make more seen.[11] For what this book succeeds in saying remains far behind what was conceived without being able to formulate it. And what ended up being conceived itself remains well behind what was *seen.*

PARIS, 24 JUNE 1997

Book I

GIVENNESS

§1 THE LAST PRINCIPLE

A Counter-Method

In all science—therefore in metaphysics—it is a question of proving. To prove consists in grounding appearances in order to know with certainty, leading them back to the ground in order to lead them to certainty. But in phenomenology—that is to say, at least in what it intends, in the attempt to think in a nonmetaphysical mode—it is a question of showing. To show implies letting appearances appear in such a way that they accomplish their own apparition, so as to be received exactly as they give themselves.

To show, to let appear, and to accomplish apparition do not imply any privilege of vision. Besides the fact that this so-called privilege often yields in phenomenology to the primacy of touch or hearing, such that it can hardly be invoked without taking sides in a muddled polemic, its disastrous presupposition must be contested. The primacy of one of the senses (vision, but also any other) is important only if perception finally determines appearance, therefore only if appearance itself in the final analysis falls under the jurisdiction of perception—in short, only if appearance refers at the outset to the apparition of the thing itself, where, as in trial by fire, the apparatus of appearance and even of perception is consumed in order to let arise what is at issue. Now, phenomenology has no other goal and no other legitimacy than to attempt to reach the apparition in appearance, therefore to transgress every perceived impression by means of the intentionality of

[margin handwriting: to prove vs. to show]

the thing itself. Even in the vision of mere appearances, what is at issue in phenomenology is no longer exactly what subjectivity apperceives by one or the other of its perceptive tools, but what apparition—through, despite, indeed *without* them—gives of itself and as the thing itself. The distinction between seeing, listening, and feeling (but also tasting and smelling) becomes decisive only when perception is glued to a decidedly subjective determination of its role, as what filters, interprets, and deforms the appearance of the apparition. Inversely, as soon as apparition dominates appearing and revives it, the subjective specifications of appearance by this or that sense are no longer essentially important: whether I see, touch, feel, or hear it, it is always the thing that comes upon me each time in person. And the fact that it comes upon me only in parts and in outline does not stop it from coming to me in the very flesh of its apparition. This very imperfection would not be noticed if it did not already presuppose the apparition in person of the thing, which it limits. The so-called privilege of vision therefore becomes decisive only once we miss the privilege of the apparition of the thing itself at the heart of its (sensible, perceptible, "subjective," etc.) appearance—the sole truly decisive matter. The study of this privilege constitutes the business proper to phenomenology, which admits no other. I will stick strictly to this.

The privilege of appearing in its appearance is also named manifestation—manifestation of the thing starting from itself and as itself, privilege of rendering *itself* manifest, of making *itself* visible, of showing *itself*. This compels me to correct my point of departure: if in the realm of metaphysics it is a question of proving, in the phenomenological realm it is not a question of simply showing (since in this case apparition could still be the object of a gaze, therefore a mere appearance), but rather of letting apparition show *itself* in its appearance according to its appearing. The mere transition from proving to showing therefore does not yet modify the deep status of phenomenality, nor does it assure it its freedom. Moreover, on account of not having perceived this clearly, many phenomenological attempts have simply repeated and corroborated the privilege of (metaphysical) perception and subjectivity over and against manifestation. This first move therefore should be completed by a second: the movement from showing to letting *itself* show, from manifestation to self-manifestation starting from the self of what shows its *self*. But letting apparition show *its self* in the appearance and appearing as its own manifestation—that is not so self-evident. For a fundamental reason: because knowledge always comes from me, manifestation is never evident by itself. Or rather, it is not so self-evident that it can run its own course, coming from itself, through itself, starting from itself, in short, that it can itself manifest its *self*. The initial and final paradox of phenomenology stems precisely from this: that it takes the initiative in losing it. To be sure, like all rigorous science, it decides its own project, its own terrain, and its own method, thus taking the initiative as originally as possible; but, counter to all metaphysics, it has no other ambition than to lose this initiative as quickly and completely as possible, seeing as it claims to connect the apparitions of things in their most initial originarity to the so-to-speak native state of their unconditional manifestation in themselves, therefore starting from themselves. The methodological beginning here establishes only the conditions for its own disappearance in the original manifestation of what shows *itself*. That this reversal must respect precise operations (intentions, fulfillments, reductions, constitutions, appresentations, etc.), according to a rationality of the most strict type, does not weaken this paradox but rather confirms the formal requirement for it.

The difficulty presented by this paradox—without which phenomenology would remain only a new, empty name for a then eternalized metaphysics—has provoked, from its beginning in Husserl, an incessantly reconsidered reconsideration of the theme *method*. To let apparition manifest *itself*, it no doubt seems wise to proceed methodically, and the different senses of the reduction offer the perfect illustration of this task by completely assuming the rational demand for reaching an indubitable basis for knowledge. But the method should not, for all that, secure indubitability in the mode of a possession of objects that are certain because produced according to the a priori conditions for knowledge. It should provoke the indubitability of the apparition of things, without producing the certainty of objects. In contrast to the Cartesian or Kantian method, the phenomenological method, even when it constitutes phenomena, is limited to letting them manifest *themselves*. Constituting does not equal constructing or synthesizing, but rather giving-a-meaning, or more exactly, recognizing the meaning that the phenomenon itself gives from itself and to itself. The method does not run ahead of the phenomenon, by *fore*-seeing it, *pre*-dicting it, and *pro*-ducing it, in order to await it from the outset at the end of the path (*meta-hodos*) onto which it has just barely set forth. From now on, it travels in tandem with the phenomenon, as if protecting it and clearing a path for it by eliminating roadblocks. Dissolving the aporias, it reestablishes the porosity of appearance, if not always the transparency of apparition in it. In any case, this is how the reduction operates par excellence: it suspends "absurd theories," the false realities of the natural attitude, the objective world, etc., in order to let lived experiences bring about as much as possible the appearing of what manifests itself as and through them. Its operation culminates in a clearing away of the obstacles to manifestation.[1] And just as in a lawful state, the public powers must let manifestations happen, opinions be published, referenda be organized—in short, just as they must let transpire what has the right to do so by acting only against actual acts of violence, so too the reduction lets manifest itself what has the right to do so, using its power of suspension only against illegitimate theoretical acts of violence. If one wants to speak of "negative phenomenology," an ambiguous formula to be used only with reticence, it must be understood in terms of the reduction itself.[2] The method does not so much provoke the apparition of what manifests itself as it clears away the obstacles that encircle it and would hide it. The reduction does nothing; it lets manifestation manifest *itself*; it takes the initiative (of considering seriously what is lived by consciousness) only in order to offer it to what manifests *itself.* All the difficulty of the reduction—and the reason it always remains to be done and redone, with neither end nor sufficient success—stems from the swerve it must make, one where it invents itself ("zigzagging" along). The reduction must be done in order to undo it and let it become the apparition of what shows *itself* in it, though finally without it. Or rather, the reduction opens the show of the phenomenon at first like a very present director, so as to then let this show continue as a simple scene where the director is necessary, to be sure, but forgotten and making no difference—with the result that, in the end, the phenomenon so dominates the scene that it is absorbed in it and no longer distinguished from it: self-directing. The reduction is enacted precisely with this turning. Phenomenological method therefore claims to deploy a turn, which goes not simply from proving to showing, but from showing in the way that an *ego* makes an object evident to letting an apparition in an appearance show *itself*: a method of turning that turns against itself and consists in this reversal itself—counter-method.

Question of Principles

In its terrifying simplicity, this turning offers such difficulty that the phenomenological project is forever reconsidering how to formulate it, perhaps without yet having done so completely. This difficulty can be assessed according to the clues provided by the determination of the first principle of phenomenology. And from the beginning, the question of the principle poses a principle question: how to assign a principle to the method or the science (three terms that are synonymous in metaphysics) that takes the initiative to give up the initiative? What type of principle would remain one (indisputable, universal, unconditioned) without contradicting the phenomenological turn itself (without preceding and therefore claiming to produce appearing)? Would it be necessary, therefore, that the very concept of principle suffer—it too and first, as would befit its rank—the phenomenological turn? Would the principle accomplish its primacy only by disappearing before apparition? Without a doubt. But then, should it be determinable by the very thing—the manifestation of what manifests *itself*—that it claims to govern or at least describe? Obviously. In this case, does it always deserve the title "principle"? To be sure, to the (imprecise) extent to which a last and ultimate principle would still remain a principle. But what is to be understood by "last principle"? If it is a question of a principle that is last for us, first in itself, we are back to the beginning aporia (proving extending beyond showing). If it is a question of the last as last (the counter-method), it remains to be understood how this last still remains the first—that is to say, how its primacy can accomplish the turning that orients it to what shows *itself,* starting from no other principle besides itself. The aporia does not concern simply the identity of the ultimate principle of phenomenology, but the possibility and even the appropriateness of formulating one.

If one considers the formulations that could stake a claim to this rank, one must, following Michel Henry,[3] doubt not only their coherence, but above all their access to manifestation. Take the first formulation of a principle: "So much appearing, so much Being."[4] In wanting to reestablish the ontic dignity of appearing, it rehabilitates it to the point of opposing it to Being itself. Husserl thus sanctions a perfectly traditional Platonic opposition, even if he tends, almost like Nietzsche,[5] to reverse it and make it into an equivalence. Appearing thus remains in a typically metaphysical situation. Above all, the primacy thus accorded to appearing, which becomes the sole face of Being, still leaves it entirely undetermined. What does appearing accomplish such that it could, simply when it appears, make Being itself evident? How does it pass beyond the status of mere appearance and become the very manifestation of what is? How could appearing, in this indeterminacy, make what is appear? About this transformation of phenomenality into manifestation, thus about what is essential to the turn, the first principle remains silent. Consequently, it remains phenomenologically insignificant. As for the second formulation of the principle—"To the things themselves!"[6]—it does indeed open the question of appearing, but in such a way that this question is organized by "things" that are supposedly already there, available and accessible if not constituted. No doubt, Husserl insists, these "things" should not be understood empirically, but as "issues" in question (*Sache*). However, even without the phenomenological return to them, wouldn't these "things" remain what they are—precisely what they are without appearing? The primacy of Being over appearing lowers the latter to the metaphysical rank of a mere mode of access, which always shows less than it should since "things" precede it and display themselves without it. Its inadequacy to the phenomenological turn clearly shows. It will be answered that these two principles, though custom attributes them to phenomenology, do not characterize it properly, since it adopts them only while criticizing them and therefore it does not have to assume their insufficiencies. But just what is the criticism that it is supposed to address to them? What other formulation corrects them?

The task now is to examine the third formulation of the principle, in fact the first and only, since Husserl assumes it as such under the unambiguous title "principle of principles"—the genitive here obviously counting as a superlative. It posits—against any "absurd theory" that "*every originarily giving intuition* is *a source of right for cognition*—that *everything* that offers itself *originarily* to us *in intuition* (in its fleshly actuality, so to speak) *must simply be received for what it gives itself*, but without *passing beyond the limits in which it gives itself.*"[7] To be sure, this principle frees phenomenality from the metaphysical requirement of a ground: henceforth, no other right besides intuition is required for a phenomenon to appear. For example, the right to appear no longer depends on a sufficient reason that would assign it to certain "well-grounded" phenomena but refuse it to others.[8] In addition, this principle liberates phenomenality from the frame and the limits of the Kantian analytic by imposing on intuition no conceptual a priori nor even any pure form. Finally, we see that phenomenality finds therein the highest figure of presence, under the heading "fleshly actuality" (*leibhafte Wirklichkeit*), by which it leaves behind once and for all the diminished status of *semi-ens*.[9] But these advances have their price: the intuition justly freed becomes itself the measure of phenomenality. (a) First, because intuition becomes in itself an a priori: according to the "principle of all principles," outside intuition, no givenness. (b) Next, because this principle assumes that sometimes the "source of right" is lacking from what claims to appear; but whence comes it that intuition can be lacking, that the right be missing from the fact? No doubt because the very definition of intuition implies its possible impoverishment. However, there is no analysis that illuminates this possibility or explains in what sense it belongs to the essence of intuition to be potentially lacking. (c) What is more, this possible lack, once admitted, should be pursued, measured, and calibrated. Is it lacking gradually or abruptly? In the former case, where is the limit between sufficient intuition and lacking intuition? In short, what are the degrees of intuition? To these questions "the principle of principles" does not respond, as if it were self-evident that intuition remains univocal and admits neither degrees nor transformations. (d) Above all, intuition remains a limit of phenomenality for another reason, radical otherwise: intuition makes an object seen; the object implies a transcendence with respect to consciousness; therefore intuition "is only a name for this transcendence."[10] Or: intuition always has as its function to fulfill an aim or an intentionality directed at an object; therefore it is organized by objectivity and its ecstatic consciousness. As a result, intuition restricts phenomenality to a limited sense—transcendence, ecstasy, and the intentionality of the object. That this sense of phenomenality is used most often and legitimately does not forbid—even compels—asking if it remains the only possible one, indeed the most decisive one. Does fulfilling intuition applied to an objective intentionality define in general all phenomenality or merely a restricted mode of phenomenality? The intuition of an intentional object no doubt accomplishes a phenomenal manifestation; but despite that, is every manifestation of a phenomenon carried out by the intuition of an objective intention transcendent to consciousness? In short, does the constitution of an intentional object by an intuition fulfilling an objectifying ecstasy exhaust every form of appearing? And even more, we must ask if intuition should be restricted to the limits of intentionality and the object's transcendence, or if it can be understood within the immense possibilities of what shows *itself*? Husserl hesitates here: on the one hand, he seems to claim to liberate appearing (and not only intuition) from every a priori principle; on the other hand, he seems to restrict intuition to the fulfillment of objective intentionality, therefore to limit appearing to it. Intuition finally contradicts phenomenality because it itself remains submitted to the ideal of objectifying representation. (e) This is confirmed by a final twist. The "principle of all principles" comes up before and without the reduction being operative.[11] And yet, without the reduction, no procedure of knowledge deserves the title "phenomenology."

How then could the "principle of all principles" determine for phenomenology its counter-method if it is not articulated in terms of the reduction? And if the giving intuition is not an exception to the reduction, would we have to admit that it provides a tacit presupposition? But then in what way would the reduction remain the inaugural operation for all phenomenological vision? The third formulation of the principle thus does indeed posit appearing as such by assigning it to intuition alone; but intuition fights less for it than against it since it seems to escape the reduction and therefore contradict the appearing that only the latter permits.[12]

So Much Reduction, So Much Givenness

The internal incoherence of the third formulation corroborates what the one-sidedness of the first two already let us suppose: the statements that phenomenology explicitly privileges do not furnish the principle proper to it. Can none be found then? Or would it instead remain implicit? Husserl seems to suggest both at once when he postulates that "one must . . . take phenomena as they give themselves."[13] Would they give themselves, then? And if so, what does it mean phenomenologically that they give themselves? And if they give them*selves*, do they still call for a principle? At the very least, this self-givenness of self would define precisely what, for them, holds the place of principle. To shed light on this hypothesis, or at least to determine the authority and the resources for it, I introduced the fourth formulation of a phenomenological principle: the more reduction, the more givenness.[14] I will justify it in two ways—first textually, then conceptually.

The rule that links reduction and givenness on principle, even if it was not formulated as such until today, is no less observable in the letter of Husserl's text. Better, the first text where the reduction is found also finds it conjoined with givenness. *The Idea of Phenomenology*, the very work which, in 1907, practiced for the first time all the figures of the reduction, is also the work which is most insistent in its privilege of givenness. Let me call to mind several statements that witness this. (a) "It is not the psychological phenomenon in psychological apperception and objectification that is an absolute givenness [*Gegebenheit*], but only the *pure phenomenon*, the reduced [phenomenon; *das Reduzierte*]."[15] What phenomenologically validates a phenomenon as an absolutely given is therefore not its mere appearing but its reduced character: only the reduction grants access to absolute givenness, and it has no other goal but this. (b) "Consequently, the concept of *phenomenological reduction* [*phänomenologischen Reduktion*] acquires a more nar-

row, more profound determination and a clearer meaning: the exclusion of
the transcendent in general as existence to be admitted in addition, that is
to say of all that is not an evident givenness [*evidente Gegebenheit*] in the
authentic sense, an absolute givenness [*absolute Gegebenheit*] to the pure
gaze."[16] The transcendent is thus defined less by its real transcendence than
by whether or not the reduction maintains givenness in it. The criterion of
immanence no longer resides in a real inherence in consciousness along the
lines of a psychological relation, but in evident, pure, and absolute givenness. (c) "It is only through a reduction [*Reduktion*] that we prefer to call
phenomenological reduction [*phänomenologische Reduktion*] that I attain an
absolute givenness [*absolute Gegebenheit*] that no longer owes anything to
transcendence." Transcendencies, "null [and not occurring] for the theory
of knowledge,"[17] are potentially transformed into absolute givennesses only
to the extent that they pass through the reduction to immanence. (d) Still
more clearly, "*The givenness of a reduced phenomenon* [*die Gegebenheit eines
reduzierten Phänomens*] *in general is an absolute and indubitable* [*givenness*]."[18] Between the reduced phenomenon and its indubitability, it falls to
givenness alone to establish the common factor. The connection between
reduction and givenness is therefore established, and firmly so, by Husserl
himself. A phenomenon becomes absolutely given only to the degree that
it was reduced; but the reduction is in turn practiced only phenomenologically—namely, for the sake of giving, thus making the phenomenon appear absolutely.

The connection between reduction and givenness, if it is suggested
by the texts, is corroborated by their concepts. The achievement of the reduction admits as an immediate corollary that givenness be unfurled. The
reduction never reduces except to givenness—reconducts only to it and especially for its benefit. The reduction thus perfectly enacts the two meanings that can be heard in it: first, because the reduction restricts appearing
to what attains real givenness in it; next, because it leads the appearing
whose giving is at issue all the way back to what appears absolutely, the absolute given. The reduction thus operates like a sort of middleman who
leads the visible toward givenness; it leads scattered, potential, confused,
and uncertain visibles (mere appearances, outlines, impressions, vague intuitions, supposed facts, opinions, "absurd theories," etc.) to givenness, according to which it assesses their degree of phenomenality. The reduction
measures the level of givenness in each appearance so as to establish its
right to appear or not. Thus the two operations, reconducting to the con-

scious I and returning to the things themselves, far from being contradictory, mark two versions of the single organization of the reduction by givenness: nothing appears except by giving itself to and in the conscious I, but only what can give itself absolutely to consciousness also succeeds in giving nothing less than what appears in person (*Selbstgegebenheit*). Once again, there is no givenness that does not pass through the filter of a reduction; there is no reduction that does not work toward a givenness.

The more reduction, the more givenness—this principle also allows me to clarify and overcome the aporias that afflict the other three. (a) If one admits, following the last principle, that the phenomenon appears all the more as it gives itself perfectly to be seen and received, but also that it can give *itself* thusly only by giving itself to the conscious I, that is by letting itself be led back to it, which is equivalent to being reduced to it, then apparition gives itself perfectly based solely on the fact that it appears, only insofar as it is *reduced* to its givenness for consciousness.[19] The reduction alone allows for leading back to the instance that receives givenness. Thus the ambiguity of the second principle—"To the things themselves!"—can be removed: returning to the things does not imply any pre-critical realism, but the reduction of the transcendent to lived experiences such as they give themselves to consciousness, therefore such as in them the phenomenon gives itself in person. (b) The reduction, by leading apparition back to the only destination where its appearing can be given, therefore by ordering itself to and by givenness, suspends and brackets all that, in appearance, does not succeed in giving itself, or is merely added to the given as its parasite. The reduction separates what appears from what does not appear, from what renders its apparition deceptive and mimics appearing by fraudulently attaching a fundamental obscurity to it—in short, from what brings into phenomenality that which remains foreign to it—unregulated objectification, "absurd theories." This principle therefore excludes the assumption of any real transcendence and is far from reestablishing any dogmatism. For, the reduction leads appearing to itself only by limiting it strictly to what it gives to be seen. In this way, the ambivalence of the first principle disappears. "So much appearing, so much Being": appearing is equivalent to Being only insofar as this appearing is reduced precisely to itself, thus insofar as, as full and total appearing, it already accomplishes a givenness. (c) Finally, the reduction, by leading apparition back to the conscious I and to the appearing itself, leads it back to its pure given. Now this given is defined without necessarily having recourse to any intermediary whatsoever that would be different from it. In particular, the pure given giving itself depends, once reduced, only on itself. Intuition in particular, thus also the transcendence of intentionality that it fulfills, can sometimes intervene, but it does not define the given; for, certain apparitions are given without objective intentionality,[20] therefore without fulfilling intuition. And even those that pass through these intermediaries are not consummated there. In effect, if intuition deserves a privilege, it owes it not to the ecstasy of intentional fulfillment but to its quality as *giving* intuition. Only holding the place of givenness allows intuition to exercise a regency for the truth. As such, intuition could make nothing visible, perceptible, or even capable of deception, if it did not set itself up by virtue of the givenness it puts into operation. What would an intuition matter to us and what authority would we acknowledge in it, if it *gave* us nothing—be it only the nothing? The limit of the "principle of principles" shows itself here: Just as one has to recognize that intuition as giving plays the role of "source of right" for phenomenality in all the cases where phenomena are subject to ecstasy and transcendence, so too for phenomena which would not be subject to these (if there are any to be found), intuition as such would contribute nothing and givenness could and even should be carried out without intuition, without intentional fulfillment, and therefore without its transcendent ecstasy. Givenness would then pass outside intuition because in such cases the latter would no longer secure the giving function, which is nonetheless indispensable. Givenness therefore is measured only by its own standard, not by that of intuition. The final restriction of the third formulation—"without *passing beyond the limits in which it gives itself*"—in fact admits an ambiguity and a contradiction. An ambiguity because Husserl invokes not the limits of givenness, but those of intuition: apparition should be admitted within the strict limits of its intuition. Whence a contradiction: if intuition suffers limits (and this, according to all of philosophy, is one of its constitutive characteristics), givenness knows none. What gives itself, insofar as given in and through reduced givenness, by definition gives itself absolutely. To give itself admits no compromise, even if in this given one distinguishes degrees and modes: every reduced given is given or not. In contrast to intuition, givenness is not reducible except to itself and is therefore carried out absolutely.[21] Reducing givenness means freeing it from the limits of every other authority, including those of intuition. The fourth formulation is finally established as the principle because it states clearly that givenness is accomplished by the reduction. The essential phenomenological operation of the reduction arrives this time—beyond objectness and beingness—at pure givenness.

"The Stumbling Block"

We can now understand how invoking a principle in phenomenology does not necessarily contradict the phenomenon's right to show *itself* from itself. The principle set up by givenness is precisely that nothing precedes the phenomenon, except its own apparition on its own basis—which amounts to positing that the phenomenon comes forward without any other principle besides itself. In short, the principle, inasmuch as it is a principle of givenness, leaves primacy to the phenomenon—it is therefore not an issue of a first but rather a last principle. Husserl says as much literally: "Absolute givenness is a last [term]—*absolute Gegebenheit ist ein Letztes.*"[22] "Last term" here is not just another way of designating primacy, for the principle of givenness does not intervene before the phenomenon in order to fix a priori the rules and the limits of apparition. It intervenes after the manifestation of appearing, which is displayed freely without any other principle, for the sole purpose of sanctioning a posteriori by reduction what, in appearing, truly deserves the title given phenomenon. Only what is given appears as an authentic phenomenon, and what is given absolutely, as an absolute phenomenon. The principle directs the appearing after the fact, precisely insofar as it lets it appear starting from itself, inasmuch as it observes whether it has given *itself* absolutely—or not. The fourth principle draws its privilege from the fact that it remains ultimate, comes into play only at the last moment, and judges a posteriori—that is to say, from the fact that it is no longer practiced as a principle that produces the phenomenon in advance, but as the rule decreeing that it is necessary to let the phenomenon come forward by itself. Always playing after the fact, the paradoxical principle "So much reduction, so much givenness" does not just free the phenomenon from the three still a priori principles that inflict it with their aporias, does not just contradict the metaphysical definition of all principles in general (and in this sense emancipate phenomenology from the critical project); it above all renounces grounding the phenomenon so as to leave it—finally—the initiative of its apparition starting from itself. From now on, givenness becomes less one phenomenological option among others, which could be accepted or rejected according to one's taste or school of thought, and more the nongrounding yet nonetheless absolute condition of the phenomenon's ascent to its own apparition. One can of course always refuse it;

but this refusal definitively blocks the possibility that the phenomenon might show *itself* starting from itself and as such. Rejecting the principial status of givenness—the principle "So much reduction, so much givenness" —amounts, de facto and de jure, to closing the phenomenological break-through. The decision about givenness is equivalent to a decision about the phenomenality of the phenomenon. The young Heidegger saw this per-fectly, asking: "What does 'given,' *'givenness'* mean—this magic word of phenomenology and the 'stumbling block' for all the others?"[23] For some, the primacy of givenness is a scandal, but in rejecting it prejudicially they close themselves to nothing less than the phenomenality of the phenome-non. For others, what opens access to this same phenomenality of the phe-nomenon remains a "magic" word. The first ridicule the supposed enchant-ment of the second, and all the more so as they remove from it the glory of rationality. The second accentuate the frightful aspects of the first, and all the better as they remove from them the prestige of speculative daring. But it could be that the refusal of the first agrees with the ravishment of the other, fraternal enemies relying on one and the same presupposition—the fact that givenness cannot (or should not) be conceptualized. It is precisely this supposition that I will now set out to challenge: between magic and scandal, another way opens—that givenness rationally articulates the con-cepts that say the phenomenon such as it manifests *itself.*

§2 THE ESSENCE OF THE PHENOMENON

Unevidence

Admitting the phenomenality proper to the phenomenon—its right and its power to show *itself* on its own terms—thus implies understanding it in terms of givenness. Husserl, summing up at the end of his career what was gained in his first "breakthrough work," the *Logical Investigations*, indi-cates exactly what change was demanded of philosophical thought: "It was there [in 1901] that 'evidence' (that dead logical idol) was transformed into a problem for the first time, freed from the privilege accorded scientific ev-idence and broadened to include the universality of original self-givenness [*zur allgemeinen originale Selbstgebung erweiter*]."[24] What broadening is be-ing referred to here? No doubt the broadening of (Kantian) sensible intu-ition to categorical intuition. But Husserl is not concerned solely with the question of intuition here; and for that matter, this broadening itself must be justified. In fact, what is at issue is, more universally, the broadening of evidence to givenness. Broadening or deepening, or—because the "depths" would here seem more disputable than profitable—transformation. Why, that is, does Husserl disqualify evidence as a mere dead idol? Why didn't he instead privilege its use, as well as the whole semantic network that connects it to the gaze, sight, the truth, etc.? Precisely because he redefined it radically —for sight and the gaze would see absolutely nothing if evidence remained a mere subjective impression, an effect of consciousness, in short an idolatrous mirror where the mind refers to itself an impression that impresses only it. For evidence not to close itself up in a simple idol of the gaze and not to remain a dead letter (one that consciousness sends to itself), what is necessary, with an absolute phenomenological necessity, is that evidence give more than a state or lived experience of consciousness, that it carry in its clarity the appearing of a nonconscious, a nonlived, a nonthought. What is needed is that on its screen there be projected and come forward something other than it—the unevident, the phenomenon itself. For this paradox must be admitted: the phenomenon remains, inasmuch as it is an instance exterior to consciousness, completely unevident, since evidence is defined as a mode or state of consciousness alone, independent from and indifferent to a possible transcendence. One cannot, solely on the basis of the criterion of evidence, demarcate solipsistic evidence from a thing's evidence. In order for evidence to decide by itself between a film without depth and the figure of a reality, in short for it to be able to let the phenomenon be seen, or rather, let it appear, a new term has to be introduced—givenness. Evidence sees nothing if givenness does not give it to let appear what does not belong to it, the essential unevidence of appearing as phenomenal appearing. For phenomenology does not begin with appearing or evidence (otherwise it would remain identical to metaphysics), but with the discovery, as difficult as it is stupefying, that the evidence, blind in itself, can become the screen of appearing—the place of givenness. Place of givenness, therefore not its origin but rather its point of arrival: the origin of givenness remains the "self" of the phenomenon, with no other principle or origin besides itself. "Self-givenness, *Selbstgebung*, *donation de soi*" indicates that the phenomenon is given in person, but also and especially that it is given of itself and starting from itself. Only this givenness, having originated in itself, can give the self of the phenomenon and invest evidence with the dignified rank of guardian of phenomenality, uprooting it from its idolatrous death. Of course, this change from dead evidence to evidence charged with givenness is enacted only through the operation of the reduction, but the reduction would not produce any phenomenological advance if it was limited to reducing evidence to the real immanence of lived experiences, however certain they might be. It draws its legitimacy and its fruitfulness only from serving givenness, from which, like evidence (though in an other mode), it receives all. Givenness gives life to the reduction as much as to the evidence, since it alone gives them charge over phenomenality.

The Essential Correlation

As a result, in the entire subsequent development of phenomenology the correlation between reduction and givenness determines the essence of the phenomenon itself. Let me highlight several points. Consider first of all its classic definition by Husserl: "The word 'phenomenon' is ambiguous by virtue of the essential correlation between *appearing* [*Erscheinen*] and *that which appears* [*Erscheinenden*]."[25] This distinction, never subsequently put into question, conveyed by the duality between noesis and noema, will remain until the very end what the *Krisis* calls the fundamental discovery of the relational a priori by the *Logical Investigations*. At stake in the subjective givens are not only these givens themselves in their mere seeming, but above all what they thus give to appear—"this universal a priori of correlation between the object and its modes of givenness [*Gegebenheitsweisen*]."[26] Therefore, if that which appears coincides with the object, the modes of givenness are identified with the appearing—the modes of givenness count as modes of appearing. That is, if the modes of appearing had nothing to do with a givenness, they would of course give nothing, and especially not a thing that appears—dead evidence. It is only insofar as they give that they can, by givenness, let what appears appear. The correlation between appearing and that which appears, therefore the very definition of the phenomenon, rests entirely on givenness. It alone can invest the modes of appearing with a phenomenological dignity sufficient for them to assume the role of apparitions of something that appears, in short, for them to give the appearing object. Similarly, Husserl does not hesitate to think the inner duality of the phenomenon, therefore what appears as well as the appearing, on the basis of givenness alone. For example, with regard to the phenomenon of sonorous perception, one has to admit "within immanence a distinction between *appearing* [*Erscheinung*] and *that which appears* [*Erscheinenden*]. Thus we have two absolute givennesses [*absolute Gegebenheiten*]: the givenness of the appearing [*Gegebenheit des Erscheinens*] and the givenness of the object [*Gegebenheit des Gegenstandes*]."[27] That the two sides of the phenomenon are both deployed in givenness is incessantly emphasized by *The Idea of Phenomenology*: "And the task is just this: within the field of pure evidence or self-givenness [*Selbstgegebenheit*], *to study all forms of givenness* [*Gegebenheitsformen*] *and all correlations,* and to conduct an elucidatory analysis of them all."[28] This must be insisted on: givenness is not multiplied or duplicated. There is not first the givenness of appearing and then that of what appears, or first that of the object and then that of its mode of givenness. In fact, all these mentions of givenness attest that one and only one determination (just givenness), following modalities that are in each case subtly or boldly distinct, renders appearing permeable, as it were, to what appears, or the object porous to its modes of appearing. Givenness does not play only one particular role in the correlation; rather, it invests all the terms because it is one with the correlation itself, whose name it takes and which it alone makes possible. The correlation between the two sides of the phenomenon does not use givenness—it deploys it, accomplishes it, is nothing other than givenness itself.

This is why the metaphysical opposition par excellence, the opposition between essence and existence, is abolished in the face of givenness. While Descartes claimed, in order not to have to define them, that "Nota est omnibus essentiae ab existentia distinctio," Husserl sees in this distinction nothing other than the derivative difference between "two modes of being in two modes of self-givenness [*zwei Modis der Selbstgegebenheit*]."[29] Let us consider the motive for Husserl's advance beyond Descartes. The latter does not define essence and existence, basing his argument instead on their well-known evidence, but he was, in all ways, very much at pains to lead them back to a common concept of being from which he could derive, as from a common source, these two terms; for that matter, he limited himself to positing them together in agreement or opposition. Husserl, by contrast, fearlessly invokes two modes of Being because he can reduce them to two modes of givenness, and therefore finally to givenness itself. Not only does the authority of Husserlian givenness unify what Cartesian evidence juxtaposes, but above all it does so strictly to the degree that it surpasses the concept of being, common or not. This distance from being suggests how much of a divide separates phenomenology from metaphysics. This is why the opposition, also metaphysical, between representation and its object, the "mere thought" and the "actual reality," is absorbed not only in the two sides of the one and only correlation of apparition, but above all in the one and only

givenness that the latter admirably puts into operation: "Even after phenomenological reduction, *apparition* [*Erscheinung*] *and that which appears*
[*Erscheinendes*] *still stand in sharp contrast* [*sich gegenübersetzen*], and this *in
the midst of pure givenness* [*inmitten der reined Gegebenheit*], hence in the
midst of true immanence." If, Husserl adds, "we are taken aback by this,"[30]
this is because we find that we no longer have to choose between the object
(realism) and appearing (phenomenalism), but that one and the other are
inseparably correlated in the one and only givenness, which according to
their distinct roles, makes them possible and actual. This finally is why the
entire phenomenological program amounts to distinguishing within the
one and only givenness given to consciousness the different modes of
givenness of the things themselves: "Everywhere givenness [*Gegebenheit*] is
a givenness [*Gegebenheit*] in a cognitive phenomenon, which is announced
by a simple representation in it or a genuine being, of the real or the ideal,
of the possible or the impossible, in a phenomenon of thought in the broadest sense of the word, and *what is to be sought out in the contemplation of
essences is this correlation that seems so astonishing at first glance.*"[31] The reduction therefore has as its sole objective the reconduction of the whole
phenomenon to givenness, including the (from here on out appearing)
thing itself and no longer just the appearing (which, alone, would be lowered to the level of mere appearance). But how to lead even what appears
back to givenness? How not to remain, according to Husserl's own confession, "overwhelmed" before such an extension of pure immanence and absolute givenness?

The Two Forms of Immanence

Even strengthened by its complex play with the reduction, givenness
could never correlate the two sides of the phenomenon if Husserl had not
taken the final step, one that was no doubt the most decisive—connecting
immanence to intentionality. Taken in its narrow sense, as the self-identity
of consciousness remaining in itself, immanence could forbid not only the
correlation of the two sides of the phenomenon, but above all the givenness of an actual given. Understanding this self-presence as the genuine
identity of a thing with itself would be enough to close all space for what
would not really be the thing or its real contents. Appearing would once
again become mere appearance without gradation, and in the best of cases,
it would claim the privilege of poverty, a privilege that metaphysics used to
accord to the formal sciences, which are supposed to be able to do without

external reality, indeed objective reality—the certainty of logical tautology, the abstract truth of pure forms and categories, materially false ideas, etc. Should this occur, givenness would find itself definitively compromised, since it implies that appearing to consciousness would succeed in staging a "thing," the appearing-thing irreducible to consciousness, which would be given only insofar as it distinguishes itself from consciousness. And if immanence really identified appearing with consciousness alone, it would give only one appearing-thing—consciousness. In short, genuine immanence suspends the correlation of the phenomenon because it first of all obfuscates the connection of givenness with its given. To maintain a thought of phenomenality in terms of givenness, it was therefore necessary that Husserl liberate immanence from any solipsistic drift; by the same token, his effort to remove the contradiction between immanence and phenomenality obviously required that he plumb the depths of givenness.

The decisive operation consists in distinguishing between two types of immanence: "On a closer view, however, *genuine immanence* [*reele Immanenz*] differs from *immanence in the sense of self-givenness as constituted in evidence* [*Evidenz*]."[32] To do away with "the prejudice about immanence as [merely] genuine immanence"[33] (indeed real, if one considers it psychologically) one has to admit an intentional immanence: "It is not merely concerned with the genuinely immanent, but also with what is *immanent in the intentional sense* [*das im intentionalen Sinn Immanente*]. Noetic processes (and this belongs to their essence) have an *intentio*, they intend [*meinen*] something, they are related in this or that way to an object."[34] In this new immanence, consciousness no longer merely receives a new reality genuinely immanent to its own reality (in the sense of the genuine immanence of an image, an affect, a pure sensation remaining like a thing in consciousness taken as a thing). It also does not merely receive in its reality an unreal image (an appearance without correlation with even the lowest level of what appears, an inadequate idea that makes consciousness known and not what is perceived). Along with the appearing lived experience, consciousness receives also and especially what it intends in and through an intrinsic relation, the intentional object. From the outset, the image is governed by the correlational a priori, which gives the lowest level of appearing to and in consciousness only by co-giving in it what appears. Intentionality renders what appears immanent to consciousness, based on the simple fact that appearance (genuinely immanent to be sure) never appears except as always already ordered to its object by intentionality. Immanence, in the realm of intentionality, is in some way inverted (or doubled). The phenomenon taken in its duality remains immanent to consciousness only because intentional consciousness has first become immanent to the appearing object. Appearing becomes immanent only to the extent that consciousness becomes intentionally immanent in what itself appears. In intentional immanence, the givenness of appearance no longer forbids that of what appears because intentionality intends the second and therefore gives it as intended. This is to say that the two sides of the phenomenon arise at one and the same time because the two givennesses are always but one. And this is indeed *the* givenness: that of transcendence in immanence. So long as the two givennesses remain scattered, indeed separate, givenness does not yet intervene with all its profundity. It remains an image that gives only itself and not the object. As for the transcendent object, its nonapparition impedes its givenness. Givenness arises precisely when appearance gives, besides itself (genuine immanence), the object, which without it could never appear even though this object does not amount to it (intentional immanence). Givenness breaks out because the appearing of appearance becomes the apparition *of* what appears—in short, launches what appears onto its own appearing. Givenness gives the intentional object to appear in and as the appearing of the appearance. Appearances no longer mask what appears; they give it its own aspect so that it may appear.

And Husserl at once explicitly draws out the consequences: "The [fact of] relating [intentionally] to something with the form of objectness belongs [to the lived experience], even if this objectness does not in turn belong to it. And the objective [*das Gegenständliche*] can appear, can have a certain givenness [*eine gewisse Gegebenheit*], even though it is not any more real in the noetic phenomenon than it is as a *cogitatio.*"[35] In this "immanence in the intentional sense," we no doubt see what the *Ideas* will call "an *original* transcendence . . . , *a transcendence within immanence*" and what the *Cartesian Meditations* will comment on by saying: "Transcendency in every form is a characteristic of immanent Being, which is constituted within the ego."[36] But this paradoxical formulation would merely name the difficulty without resolving it, if it were not based in the givenness proper to what appears. In fact, what is happening here is a decisive broadening of givenness, such that from now on it will cover the entire field of phenomena, transcendence included, appearing too: "That which is universal is absolutely given [*absolut gegeben*] but is not genuinely immanent." Better, it is "in the genuine [*reellen*] sense . . . transcendent," for the reduction should no longer be understood as "the exclusion of the genuinely transcendent," but solely as the exclusion of existence added in addition, therefore of "everything that is not evident givenness in its true sense, that is not absolute givenness to pure 'seeing.'"[37] Thus transcendence is not left out of the loop as such (the proof: it is still admitted as intentional), but strictly to the degree that it does not satisfy givenness: once again, existence, each time it is not perceived, but not when it is. The reduction reduces everything, except the given; inversely, what it cannot reduce it admits as given. The reduction does not reduce givenness; it leads back to it. Consequently, it succeeds in giving even the transcendent by reducing it to the (nongenuine) immanence of an intentional object. Objects thus appear as such—for "an intentional object is still there, according to the evidence [*evidentermassen da*]," "is given as a being, as a something here and now [*gegeben als ein Seiendes, als ein Dies-da*]"[38]—inasmuch as their appearing no longer represents them (for to be represented is equal to not being there), but *gives* them in person, absolutely: "the things are and are in apparition [*Erscheinung*], and thanks to apparition itself, are given [*gegeben*]."[39]

Givenness thus determines all the levels of phenomenality. Successively, it is put into play in the reduction, which receives its meaning only from it; it establishes the correlation between the two poles of the phenomenon; it broadens immanence to the scope of intentionality; finally and above all, it fixes the sole correct phenomenological status of presence in person for the things themselves: from now on, they are only according to the degree of their absolute intuitive givenness. Givenness therefore determines the essence of the phenomenon (§2), just as it is connected to the reduction when it is a matter of settling its last principle (§1). It is this exceptional role, however, that raises a difficulty: why did Husserl, who never stopped revising the definition and procedures of the reduction, never provide—to my knowledge at least[40]—even the slightest definition of givenness? In this silence about the concept, a silence that contrasts so sharply with the frequency of its occurrences, there is no argument against its principial status. (a) First because, appearances to the contrary notwithstanding, givenness does receive a treatment comparable to that of the reduction. The latter evades all definition in that Husserl never stops revisiting the rules, distinguishing the figures, and refining the demands; in the end, the very excess of definitions winds up forbidding any univocal definition. For givenness, by contrast, the lack of definition results from the fact that it itself defines all other phenomenological acts: the phenomenon, immanence, and intentionality, the "thing itself," the reduction, all come from it or end with it. Givenness plays a role so radical that it reproduces the aporia of Being in metaphysics: to define it, one must presuppose it—here, "the lack of definition is a mark of excellence rather than of defect because it is not due to any obscurity of these things, but rather to their extreme clarity."[41] (b) But this impossibility itself suggests a major clue: the reduction is not defined; it is performed as an act. All the initial phenomenological concepts, for that matter, had at the beginning the status of acts. Consequently, givenness, which the act of reduction makes manifest and by which it is ordered, must also be comprehensible as an act, no doubt the same as that of the reduction, or the recto of a single act whose verso is found in the reduction: the act of reconducting the *ego* to the given as given. That this act is not conceptually defined as a *quid* simply establishes that what is at issue is the concept of an act, and not of a quiddity, an object, or a theory. (c) Whatever the case might be, the lack of a definition of givenness remains patently obvious. Husserl did not conceptually determine givenness, which however determines the reduction (§1) and the phenomenon (§2). He thinks on the basis of givenness, all the while leaving it for the most part unthought. We must admit this fact, less as an objection than as the precise definition of my own work and its justification: givenness remains to be thought explicitly there where Husserl accomplishes it without determining it as such. I do not pretend to begin where Husserl stopped, but simply to think what he accomplished perfectly without entirely saying it.

§3 OBJECTNESS AND BEINGNESS

The Modes of Givenness

It is not so much the case that givenness belongs to phenomenology as it is that phenomenology falls entirely under the jurisdiction of givenness. That is, givenness does not provide phenomenology merely with one concept among others, or even with the privileged act by which it can become itself; rather, it opens the entire field of phenomenality for it. For nothing appears except by giving itself to pure seeing, and therefore the concept of the phenomenon is exactly equal to that of a self-givenness in person. The staging of the phenomenon is played out as the handing over of a gift. When it is a matter of phenomenality, all is decided, in the final analysis, by givenness and on the basis of absolute givenness, "ultimate term."

This rule having been posited, the difficulties begin. For if every phenomenon is given, isn't givenness infinitely diluted, losing in precision (givenness in person, absolute, in the flesh, etc.) what it gains in extension? The enumeration that concludes the essay of 1907 seems to succumb to this danger. Enumerating the *"different modes of givenness in the proper sense,"* it in fact counts nearly all possible phenomena: (a) "the givenness of the *cogitatio*"; (b) "the givenness of the *cogitatio* preserved in a fresh recollection"; (c) "the givenness of the *unity of appearance* enduring in the phenomenal flux"; d) "the givenness of its change"; (e) "the givenness of the *thing* in 'external' perception"; (f) "the givenness of the different forms of imagination and memory"; and, Husserl adds, there is also, "of course," (g) *"logical givenness,"* namely, that of universals, predicates, "etc."; (h) and finally "the givenness of *a nonsense, a contradiction, and a nothing,* etc."[42] Should we be surprised by the breadth of an inventory that includes not only the two poles of the phenomenon (*cogitatio,* "thing"), but also their extreme variations (temporal, imaginative, on the one hand; on the other, logical, to the point of the absurd)? Or rather by the surplus promised by the "etc."[43] and by the highly problematic character of the determination supposed to unify them? To be sure, it is always a matter of leading reduced phenomena to their givenness, but how does givenness give them—what common status, what stable figure, and what common reality does it confer on them if it must cover such a field, one approaching universality?

To this essential interrogation Husserl responds clearly, for once: even if every phenomenon belongs to givenness, "it must not be said that all the givennesses . . . are actual givennesses in the authentic sense" or that *"great difficulties"* might not arise to annul them. Nevertheless, precisely in order to distinguish the types of givenness operative in each case, one must again and always rely "in principle" on givenness, according to the ultimate rule that *"givenness extends just as far as actual evidence."*[44] The "sphere of absolute givenness"[45] therefore admits neither exteriority nor remainder, but itself measures the degrees that calibrate it and is the sole thing that can stigmatize the eventual aberrations in how it is used. Givenness is established as its own criterion as well as that of the nongiven, *index sui non dati.* Givenness repeats the argument of evidence in metaphysics: every criticism of evidence as deprived of criteria (logical, formal) produces and prefers such criteria only because they offer a more secure evidence and strengthen and refine it, far from making an exception to it. As with ferreting out the nongiven, judging the given poor or weak becomes possible only starting from the norm of absolute givenness and within the horizon it opens. And in fact, Husserl's description of essences, idealities, presentifications, nonsense, etc., obey this one single criterion for discriminating them. A perfect example of this prudence can be read in the *Ideen*, when they examine "The Method of Clarification. Giving Consciousness. 'Nearness of Givenness' and 'Remoteness of Givenness.'" Against the background of "an emptiness and vague remoteness," essence appears; grasping it admits "its *degrees of clarity*, as does the single particular floating before us"; if it attains "an *absolute nearness*, so to speak, . . . compared to the series of degrees," then "its givenness [*Gegebenheit*] is absolute, i.e., a *pure* self-givenness [*reine Selbstgegebenheit*] of it itself"; and in this case, it must, as a "*pure* self given [*reine gegebenes Selbst*], *fully and entirely, such as it is in itself*," be opposed to what "would stand merely 'in person' before the gaze and consciousness as 'given' [*als 'gegeben' bewusst*]."[46] Givenness in person can remain a mere consciousness... , without the thing (here an essence) presenting itself absolutely of itself, purely and without reserve. Thinking about... is one mode of givenness; it is another one altogether to find oneself in the presence of—what gives *itself*. Givenness therefore admits degrees, not only for individuals but for essences as well, not only for vague, remote, or poor visions, but for coming forward in person. The whole Husserlian project could even be defined as a classification of the degrees of givenness. The accusation of having left givenness in a univocity so undetermined that it would lower it to the dishonorable rank of a metaphor therefore does not stand.

But this response does not cause the difficulty to dissipate; it signals it. In view of the fact that degrees of clarity are practiced, I can ask once again what givenness accords in terms of status, shape, and reality to the phenomena that give *themselves* in and through it. To give *itself*, what does that give [*qu'est-ce que cela donne*]? To this question, Husserl answered, implicitly at least, though ambiguously: the phenomenon gives itself—also—as a being. Far from this being a later evolution of phenomenology, givenness governs or at least concerns, as early as Husserl, beings, and therefore their beingness. Let me establish this. We have already seen that "the contrast of *existence* and *essence* signifies nothing else than that here two modes of Being [*Seinsweisen*] manifest and differentiate themselves in two modes of givenness in person [*zwei Modis der Selbstgegebenheit*]."[47] In addition to this revival of metaphysical terms, we have already seen that "within the sphere of the phenomenological reduction . . . , things are and are in appearing, and by virtue of appearing itself [are] themselves given [*selbst gegeben*]."[48] In this way, the reduction of the metaphysical categories of being to the modes of givenness is confirmed by the explicit reconduction of the fact of Being to the fact of appearing, and of appearing to the given in person. To be, a being must appear, therefore be given. Whence another passage: *"Every intellectual lived experience and every lived experience in general,* while it is being accomplished, *can become the object of a pure gaze and grasp, and in this gaze is an absolute givenness.* It is given as a being [*gegeben als ein Seiendes*], as a thing here and now, for which it is nonsense to doubt its existence."[49] At issue here is the passage from lived experience and appearing to objectness, for the sake of finally attesting givenness. To give itself appearing must be in the role of object. In both cases, the mode of Being of beings is determined as its mode of apparition—on the basis of givenness. But givenness in turn determines appearing as being (an object). There is more: not only beings, but Being itself—insofar as one can speak in Husserl of such a "Being itself" in its difference thought with respect to beings—is declined in terms of givenness. In this way, the perception of an absolute "here and now" provides "something by which I can measure as by an ultimate standard what Being and Being given [*Sein und Gegebensein*] can mean and here must mean." To be sure, Husserl admits that this equivalence between "Being" and "Being given" can be valid only for "the sort of Being and givenness that is exemplified by a 'here and now,'"[50] thus seeming to doubt that the subsisting presence of a *tode ti* offers the sole, indeed the first meaning of Being. However, even if it is only for this particular case, he nevertheless posits with total clarity the equivalence of Being itself and Being given. These equations cannot be neglected, nor can one consider it an approximation without consequence that beings are, and indeed Being is, determined by givenness. First because the text of 1907 continues to exercise a decisive influence throughout the elaboration of the fundamental concepts of phenomenology. Next because the ontico-ontological scope of givenness is confirmed in the other decisive operation: constitution. That is, Husserl does not hesitate to think it too under the banner of givenness: "And above all, it is not primarily a matter of establishing as given [*gegeben*] certain phenomena, but of making visible the essence of givenness and the self-constitution [*der Gegebenheit und des Selbst-konstituieren*] of different modes of objectness."[51] That constitution belongs to the realm of givenness should, for that matter, hardly be doubted in light of the simple fact that it is defined as a givenness of meaning [*Sinngebung*] as early as 1907 and definitively starting in

1913. It is not self-evident that "every reality should be [a being] by means of a 'givenness of meaning.'"[52] To become a being depends on a meaning assigned by the play of intention and intuition, but this assignation, which is the sole thing to provoke a being endowed with meaning, befalls it only in and through givenness.

The Paradigm of the Object

If Husserl broached the question of Being only confusedly or insufficiently, at least he always envisaged it in terms of the authority that was for him originary: givenness. Submitting all ontology to the reduction is not the same as suppressing the question of Being. That is, since the reduction always leads back in principle solely to givenness, reducing ontology would in the end wind up giving it—in the reduced aspect of a being given.[53] The real difficulty therefore does not reside here, seeing as it appears incontestable that givenness determines the phenomenological meaning that Husserl will maintain for "Being" and "beings." It arises from the twofold lack of precision in which Husserl leaves this determination. The first stems from the fundamental equivalence that being maintains with object: "Immanent or absolute Being and transcendent Being are, of course, both called 'being,' 'object [*Gegenstand*].'" This lack of precision proliferates to the point of incoherence. (i) By what right does one name "Being" what one will also in the same breath call "being," without any sense of something like the ontological difference? (ii) How to identify these two "Beings" under the titles "being" and "object" when one wants by contrast to establish that an "abyss of meaning" separates them? (iii) Above all, how to justify the fact that "being" says nothing other than "object"? The text, of course, proposes an answer: in the second case, it is only a matter of "empty logical categories."[54] But is it permissible in phenomenology to maintain such voids when it is a matter of provoking and considering the phenomenal givennesses of "things themselves"? What obscure authority imposes that all that is and all that gives itself be subsumed under the object and its objectness? Would the answer be that it is a question of "formal ontology . . . which, as we know, is the eidetic science of any object whatsoever"? But by what right do "we know" it, and what is the significance, in the case of the phenomenon, of the "privilege of *primordial objectness* [*Urgegenständlichkeit*]" if not the subsuming of what appears and is given in a category that is not given and does not appear?[55] Will it be argued that this concerns not an authentic phenomenon but rather the empty horizon that accepts all possible phenomena without itself having to appear?[56] For in the end what motivates the phenomenon that appears only insofar as it gives itself to always admit objectness as its originary horizon? Why would this phenomenal horizon not open, starting with, for example, the very givenness that gives appearing to it? What phenomenological privilege should be granted to objectness—which neither gives [itself] nor shows [itself]—when faced with the givenness that gives to show itself? Interpreting beings in terms of objectness should put into question, therefore, not only their beingness, but above all their phenomenality, because it threatens the givenness that renders them both possible.

This leads to the second lack of precision—the one that confuses givenness itself with objectness: "*Set forth [heraustellen] the different modes of givenness in the proper sense [eigentlichen Gegebenheit], that is to say [bzw.] the constitution of the different modes of objectness [Gegenständlichkeit]*."[57] How is this infamous equivalence to be understood? If it was simply a matter of admitting that "what is objective [*das Gegenständliche*] can appear, can have a certain kind of givenness [*Gegebenheit*],"[58] I wouldn't see any difficulty: objectness is, in effect, reduced to givenness through appearing; it indeed ends up at the givenness that renders it possible and defines it as one of its modalities. But for Husserl, it is in fact a question of something else entirely—of measuring givenness by the yardstick of objectness, implicitly assumed as its absolute degree, indeed its standard: "And it is not at all a matter of establishing as givens just any apparitions whatsoever [*Erscheinungen als gegeben*], but of bringing into view the essence of givenness *and* the self-constitution of the different modes of objectness."[59] That the object can also give itself does not imply that the given must always or first of all be objectified. That objectness offers one mode of givenness does not authorize assimilating all modes of givenness to modes of objectness. That givenness offers the ultimate norm of phenomenality, by contrast, excludes on principle that objectness can summarize it, standardize it, or measure it.

Husserl thus blocks his essential victory—that, in and through the reduction, givenness decides phenomenality—by submitting it to the unquestioned paradigm of objectness. Assuming their equivalence, he never questions their essential contrast: a phenomenality of givenness can permit the phenomenon to show *itself* in itself and by itself because it gives *itself*, but a phenomenality of objectness can only constitute the phenomenon on the basis of the *ego* of a consciousness that intends it as its noema. Husserl recoils before his own advance when he restricts givenness to one of the lowest levels of its phenomenological possibilities, the object. What he freed has not freed him. He is frozen before his own breakthrough. Givenness thus remains an opening still unseized.

"Cela donne"—a Breakthrough

To think the phenomenality of Being, therefore Being according to givenness—if this was indeed Husserl's unachieved plan, then Heidegger would never have ceased to be, on this point as on so many others, profoundly Husserlian. From one extreme to the other all along his path of thinking, he poses and maintains the question of Being in the more primordial figure of the "es gibt"—literally of the "cela donne" or "it gives;"[60] but, in the end, he too recoils before the originariness of givenness.

As early as *Sein und Zeit*, where Being should have opened for and onto itself and settled its own horizon (time), it is nevertheless already accompanied and even preceded by the "ça donne" or "it gives." (i) At the outset, it dwells there: "Being lies in the fact that something is and in its Being as it is; in Reality; in presence-at-hand; in subsistence; in validity; in Dasein; in the 'it gives.'"[61] How are we to understand the fact that Being dwells in anything that is not it? If one answers that it is a matter of the ontic deposits where it takes root and opens, one will no doubt be right in the case of all the examples listed here, except for the last, the "it gives," which owes nothing to beings. It is therefore already a question of a nonontic instance rendering Being at the very least accessible. There is no need to recall that in 1927, access to, therefore the possibility of, Being actually resides in Dasein; but it seems helpful to emphasize that Dasein deploys this possibility by exercising and operating a certain givenness. Other texts establish this without ambiguity. (ii) "Only as long as Dasein *is* (that is, only as long as an understanding of Being is ontically possible) does 'it give' Being."[62] Being admits an ontic condition, Dasein, which has to be for Being itself to be—or rather (for Being cannot not be) for Being to come forward in the figure of a givenness. To appear in the mode absolutely proper to it, Being comes forward in an "it gives." (iii) "Only as long as the truth is does 'it give' Being—not beings; and truth *is* only insofar as and as long as Dasein is."[63] With extreme precision, this text unfolds the following sequence: at issue is Being, not beings; therefore the phenomenality of Being cannot be shown in being nor as a being; it is therefore deployed according to the truth that is absolutely its own, a truth that Dasein alone assures, in the role of ontic condition of Being. How is this phenomenality deployed? According to givenness, in and through an "it gives." At the very moment of its still un-contested primacy and transcendence, Being must admit that givenness ac-companies it (at once protecting and spying on it), such that in givenness "it gives" this very Being. It could even be said that the entire Dasein ana-lytic consists only in a staging, thus an "it gives," of Being on the basis of the "complete givenness of Dasein as a whole."[64] Beings are disclosed, but Be-ing "is essentially differentiated from them" by an absolutely unique mode of coming to light.[65] I am advancing the hypothesis that this radically dif-ferent mode of phenomenality is carried out in and through an "it gives." Being, insofar as it differs from beings, appears immediately in terms of givenness. We should not fear overinterpreting metaphors ventured without concepts in *Sein und Zeit*, since Heidegger himself in the end confessed them to have already been decisive: "Passages in *Being and Time* were men-tioned in which 'It gives' was already used without being directly thought in relation to *Ereignis*. These passages appear today as half attempts—attempts to work out the question of Being, attempts to give that question its ade-quate direction. But they themselves remain inadequate."[66] From this 1962 self-interpretation a confirmation and a question must be retained. A con-firmation: at the end of the path that led him from *Sein und Zeit* to *Zeit und Sein*, Heidegger recognizes that the first occurrences of "it gives," there-fore of any givenness whatsoever, foreshadow the final elaboration of this same theme. There is no equivocation in their usage, no rupture. The two meditations, whose titles in chiasmus correspond with one another and cut a single path, confront the same question: givenness, make use of the same paradigm: "it gives." My inquiry can therefore be pursued legitimately. A question remains: in 1962, Heidegger admits that the givenness of 1927 fell short of the advent, the *Ereignis*, and of course, it had not yet been dissolved in it. But is it self-evident that this was a failing? To the contrary, wouldn't the it gives "remain all the more in agreement with givenness as it resists the attraction of every authority, whatever it might *be*?"

The Ereignis, a Recovery

At first glance, *Zeit und Sein* does indeed confirm and radicalize what *Sein und Zeit* put forth: the phenomenality of Being goes hand-in-hand with an originary "cela donne," to the point of passing into it: "We say of beings: they are. With regard to the matter 'Being' and with regard to the matter 'time,' we remain cautious. We do not say: Being is, time is, but rather: it gives [*cela donne*] Being and it gives time. For the moment we have only changed [*geändert*] the idiom with this expression. Instead of saying 'it is,' we say 'it gives.'" But this linguistic turn of phrase indicates more radically a conceptual turn: "Being [itself], presencing [*Anwesen*] is transformed [*verwandelt*]."[67] In what does this decisive change consist? In that Heidegger admits that if only beings are and if Being itself is not, Being can be thought only as it is given—taken in a givenness. In contrast to the Greek beginning where "Being (*einai, eon*) is thought, but not the 'it gives,'" it has to be said that "in the *esti* there is concealed the it gives."[68] To think that "it gives" Being (and time), therefore to transpose Being into the realm of givenness, does not imply an arbitrary act of will. First, because it is necessary to recognize the impossibility of holding Being within the horizon of Being (only beings are, Being *is* not), therefore the obligation of assigning it a new horizon; next, because givenness, from the very first time it is described, allows us to read the most essential trait of Being in its difference from beings, its withdrawal. That is, how are we to understand the claim that "Being withdraws" essentially?[69] According to givenness; for the gift alone has it as proper to it to withdraw itself at the very moment it brings and leaves, gives and abandons [*donne et abandonne*] its given: "A giving [*Geben*] that gives only its given [*Gabe*], but in the giving holds itself back and withdraws [*entzieht*], such a giving we call sending [*Schicken*]." What absolutely must be conceived is that the withdrawal of the giving (gift giving) does not contradict, as if after the fact and from the outside, the leaving that brings the gift given, but rather is one with it: to give the gift, the giving must withdraw "in favor of the gift."[70] The giving (*Geben*) is held back from the gift (*Gabe*), from its visibility and its availability, precisely because in giving it it undoes itself and withdraws from it, therefore turns itself away from the gift and abandons it to itself. By an inescapable consequence, the giving can never appear *with*, or still less *as* the gift given by it, since to give it not only does it leave it behind; it also differs from it. The giving gives the gift fully only by abandoning it decisively—therefore by withdrawing from it. Moreover, the balance, so difficult to maintain, between the ontological difference—at first supposed to help make the "phenomenon of 'Being'" evident[71]—and the history of Being as nihilism (where the ontological difference intervenes as what from the outset remains unthought as such) reaches its highest point solely by reference to the mediation of the "it gives." Actually, the difference does not miss Being, because thought would reach it only in its withdrawal, its absence, and its failure. In contrast, thought has nothing to think beyond this withdrawal, but only this withdrawal itself, as what is proper to Being and its nearest advance. As a result, it is no longer a question of thinking Being directly as such (in the fashion of a being), but rather its withdrawal as such, since this withdrawal is given as Being. The summary diagnosis of nihilism and the first search for the ontological difference can be lumped together into a single misconstrual of the nature of the withdrawal and what identifies it with Being. On the other hand, Heidegger's furthest advance, which overcomes and reconciles the ontological difference and history of nihilism, would reside in the serious consideration not of Being alone (and then inevitably lead back to its metaphysical acceptation), but of the givenness at work in the "it gives." For it alone renders possible, in one fell swoop, the difference of Being and beings and the withdrawal: Being (and time) differs *and* withdraws because it obeys a unique "essential law" unveiled by givenness: "To giving [*Geben*] as sending [*Schicken*] there belongs keeping back . . . for short: withdrawal."[72] Being withdraws from beings because it gives them; all givenness implies that the giving disappear (withdraw) exactly to the degree that the gift appears (advances) precisely because giving demands leaving (it behind). Being advances in its own withdrawal—this paradox is illuminated only in terms of givenness. Givenness alone uncovers beings in (and without) their Being, therefore the ontological difference as well as nihilism.

Would Heidegger have completed the task before which Husserl fled —thinking Being and beings within the horizon of givenness acknowledged as such? To answer, I must first note formally what Heidegger strongly emphasizes: the givenness of the "it gives" can be understood only on the basis of the "enigmatic it."[73] This enigma must be preserved from all metaphysical regression that would interpret the "it" in the sense of an "indeterminate power," one too hastily determined, to the point where it would appear as an ontic agent. And if it nevertheless must be determined, this would be done, at the very least, "in terms of the giving that we have already described," "in the light of the kind of giving that belongs to it."[74] In short, we must "capitalize the 'It'" of "it gives,"[75] so that no proper name might lower the givenness that puts it into operation to the rank of a causation or effectuation by this or that being, privileged or not. The indeterminacy does not save just the enigma; it defends pure givenness. This requirement thus operates a sort of bracketing of all transcendence in the sense that Husserl reduced the grounding God and Heidegger himself proclaimed a methodological "atheism."[76] So that "it gives" truly, the "it" must still be thought in and on the basis of "giving"; therefore, it must remain indeterminate and anonymous as such. Otherwise, it would inevitably turn into a being (indeed the supreme being). The enigma of the anonymous "it" is the only thing to safeguard givenness.

Now, contrary to his declared prudence, Heidegger immediately lifts the anonymity of the "it" and obfuscates the enigma. He violates his own interdiction as soon as he formulates it by baptizing the "it" with the name *Ereignis*: "The It that gives in 'It gives Being,' 'It gives time,' proves to be *Ereignis*," that is, advent. This proof in fact depends on an interpretation, for the "it" does not on its own claim to be an advent, but is overdetermined in this direction. Heidegger admits this explicitly: "The 'It gives' was discussed first with regard to giving then with regard to the It that gives. The It was interpreted as *Ereignis*." But what rule can justify this interpretation? Analogy: just as "the 'It gives' names Being in simple usage more clearly than the mere 'being' which 'is,'" that is to say, just as givenness is substituted for the Being that it brings to light better than it ever could itself—what Heidegger himself just showed—so too does the *Ereignis* also substitute itself for the "it" of the "it gives," therefore also for givenness.[77] This so-called greater light is therefore obscuring. It hides, by the advent of the advent, Being (which remains coherent with the project) as well as givenness (which contradicts the project). Heidegger will admit as much elsewhere: "The gift of presence is the property of the Advent [*Eigentum des Ereignens*]. Being vanishes in the advent [*verschwindet im Ereignis*]."[78] In other words, the first move—reducing presence (Being) to a gift appropriate to givenness—is completed (and also annulled) by a second—abolishing givenness in the advent. Heidegger acknowledges givenness beyond or outside Being[79] only to immediately misconstrue it by supposing that it still only gives (itself) on this side of the *Ereignis* and under its aegis. Givenness to be sure, but only as a brief transition between Being and *Ereignis*, a mere relay, provisional.

This substitution would matter little if it were only verbal. But, as is often the case with words, it concerns what is essential. (i) Doesn't *Ereignis* intervene here exactly as the "indeterminate power" that one must avoid substituting for the "it"? (ii) When Being "disappears in the advent (*Ereignis*), does it sink away in conformity with the phenomenological requirements that permit it to be exposed in the "it gives," or in opposition to them? (iii) Does the recovery of the "it gives" by the *Ereignis*, itself perfectly indefinite and not constitutable, mark a phenomenological advance or, in contrast, a recoil? I think that the irruption of the *Ereignis* tends—without completely succeeding—to hide the fact that givenness, which Heidegger constantly uses to unveil Being, finds itself deserted by it. He certainly does use its properties, but without admitting that they arise from givenness. Above all, this denial frees him from having to think givenness as such. Just one question would be enough to show this: does the "withdrawal" refer, in its full phenomenological meaning, to givenness, to Being, or to the *Ereignis*? If, like Heidegger, one refuses to take sides, would this be from fear of confessing the preeminence of givenness? And why must this be feared? To be sure, Heidegger mobilizes—and more powerfully than any other phenomenologist—certain properties of givenness, but he uses it to the benefit of an undertaking that on principle challenges its phenomenological function as principle. Here, as often, he hides more than he shows—hiding especially that he hides.

Heidegger and Husserl thus proceed in the same way and to the same point. Both in fact have recourse to givenness and espouse its function as ultimate principle—by which they attest it and, at the same time, their respective geniuses. But, one of them, in ending up at objectness, lets givenness escape, while the other, by assigning beingness to the *Ereignis*, abandons it. Both are familiar with givenness without officially recognizing it as such. I ask: on what conditions would it finally become possible to recognize givenness as such? To answer, it helps to return to the ultimate principle—"So much reduction, so much givenness"—which makes an essential connection between the scope of givenness and the radicality of the reduction. If givenness could let itself be covered over by instances which nevertheless remain by right subordinate to it, this no doubt must be attributed to the limits that restrain the corresponding reductions. In short, if objectness or beingness could hide givenness in themselves, this is because their respective reductions are limited to leading back to the object or being, assigning in advance conditions of possibility to the given—nothing gives itself except as object or being—imposing in advance on the phenomenal given that it give itself only according to two particular modes of manifestation. The question of a radical phenomenological givenness can therefore be legitimately posed as that of a pure reduction, one that no uncontested horizon would delimit. Only on this condition would givenness become its own horizon, because it would obey the possibility of determining itself on the basis of itself alone. Then nothing of what appears would appear otherwise than inasmuch as given, for the phenomenon in the mode of object or being can appear only by finding itself more originally given. Objectness and beingness could thus be thought as mere variations, legitimate but limited, quite exactly as horizons, which are outlined by and against the background of givenness. Consequently, from here on out, it is a question of defining givenness in itself and on its own terms.[80]

§4 THE REDUCTION TO THE GIVEN

What Does Not Subsist

Givenness thus goes farther than objectness and Being because it comes from farther away. Extreme figure of phenomenality, givenness precedes or overcomes all other specification of it. But it is not enough just to stigmatize the dissimulation or overlooking of givenness. To justify this criticism, we must ascertain what makes it necessary, and therefore bring it positively to light as such. Givenness can only appear indirectly, in the fold of the given (as objectness in its connection with the object, as Being in the difference from beings). It therefore should be read starting from and on the surface of a given. To reach the phenomenon as given would require reconducting its lived experience of reduced consciousness to an intentional appearing such that nothing other than givenness determines it and, as a result, it appears only as given—without any nongiven residue. Then, on the surface of such a purely given phenomenon givenness itself would appear as a repercussion, seeing as it would stage this phenomenon insofar as given. To identify the intentional correlate of a phenomenon as and with a given without immediately finding oneself on the path toward the object or the being and without borrowing its phenomenality from them—this is how our problem is defined. In short, could we make a purely and strictly given phenomenon appear, one without remainder and that would owe all its phenomenality to givenness? It is not so obvious that we can do so, so heavily weighs the authority of the models *object* and *being,* massively privileged by the metaphysical tradition and provisionally by the current state of phenomenology. As the prolegomena to a more ambitious analysis, I will therefore follow the example of a phenomenon that, in order to appear, stubbornly claims to be at a remove from these two paradigms, one that attempts to show itself even though it escapes objectness and beingness— better: because and to the degree that it slips away from both—namely, the painting. It is by design that I do not take on an overly remarkable phenomenon—man or Dasein, the Other, the sublime, the divine or the supreme being—but a trivial one, at the risk of augmenting the difficulty of my task. My motive is obvious. Since I seek to establish that one phenomenon, indeed all phenomena, even those as ordinary as possible, belong under the jurisdiction of givenness, I should work on an indisputably visible item—the painting. The painting, certainly more visible than a thing of the nonpainted world, since it is arranged explicitly for being brought into visibility, nonetheless remains banal, mediocre, widespread—without the imprecise and solemn pretension of the "work of art," which most often represents only itself. In short, a phenomenon that addresses to your attention nothing if not its visibility (you look at it, you exhibit it in order that it can be looked at), but a visibility that many other phenomena also claim to accomplish, in the same world as that of beings and objects. If this phenomenon, the banal painting, can be led back to the visibility of a purely given given, then all ordinary phenomenality, whose paradigm it would be, could also be reduced to a given. I will therefore stick with the painting, an at once distinguished and banal phenomenon—better: with an ordinary, indeed mediocre, painting. Let us therefore cast our gaze upon a generic, familiar scene, which depicts—for example—a rustic house, a servant at the window, two animals and a man outside beside a table decked with game and produce, indeed "this jug full with milk, this basket full with flowers," all depicted in their colored splendor, according to the somewhat complex play of transparency: a late-afternoon light, warm and omnipresent, bathes all in its downpour. The whole, let us say Dutch from the end of the seventeenth century, comes from the studio of a minor master, no doubt the work of a well-endowed student skilled in copying. In short, nothing but a success, charming but nevertheless limited. Our gaze rests there, with pleasure but without fascination—a painting from long ago, nothing more. The question can therefore be put: what phenomenon is thus given to me; or rather, in what way and to what extent does what appears to me fall within givenness—reduce to a given?

To this question, three answers propose themselves in succession. (a) According to the first, the painting presents itself, that is to say, makes its presence manifest, as subsisting object, within reach of the hand precisely because it stays there, remains and persists in its objective presence (*Vorhandenheit, vorhanden*). But, in fact, subsistence does not do justice to the painting and especially not to its phenomenality. The latter is not or is barely put into play with the former. Consider our painting. It is quite easy to modify what is essential to its subsistence as an object, first by removing or changing the frame, next by taking off the canvas and remounting it on another backing, then by removing the pigments so as to transfer them from one support to another; finally, it will be admitted that precise restorative work could replace these pigments themselves one by one. The painting will thus have changed its subsistence entirely; its subsistence will have been neutralized by the simple fact that each of its elements will have been materially replaced by another. Its general restoration will not have eliminated its subsistence, but will have rendered it unstable, transitory, provisional—paradoxically by prolonging and reinforcing it. The painting, to be sure, subsists in each case, but it subsists only in passing, and the visible in it is not closed up in and as its subsistence but in proportion to the degree to which it is disconnected from it. The painting therefore does not appear inasmuch as it subsists. An obvious counter-example comes from the *ready-made*. It makes visible to the second degree an already visible, constituted object (the toilet, the bottle rack, etc.) according to a new visibility (that of a "work") without in any way modifying its original subsistence. What has been modified? Obviously the way it is staged (whether it concerns a real staging in space or a conceptual hermeneutic of the first subsisting object). For the new visibility does not stem from the subsistence of the materials (already made, prefab in an available object), but from the irreality of the installation, from the pure "making-seen" and "wanting-to-see" that, by definition, pass away and do not subsist. Not only is subsistence not enough to make visible (as in the case of our ordinary painting), but a *ready-made* wins its phenomenality only contrary to its subsisting material, contrary to its first object, strictly to the degree that it reneges and deviates: the visible as a detour from subsistence. But for that matter, doesn't the ordinary painting get its phenomenality from the fact that my gaze knows to see it as such, does not pass it by—pass by its subsistence—without noticing it, therefore from an irreal exchange between the nonobjectivity of its potential visibility and my desire to gaze? Doesn't seeing it consequently imply transgressing what remains in it, no longer seeing it as subsisting in time (witness of past times, vestige come down to us, *monumentum*, etc.), so as to glimpse it as the pure apparition of itself, precisely as a painting, to be contemplated, not just noticed? The first answer must therefore be cast into doubt: the painting (therefore, the phenomenon with ordinary visibility) is not reducible to a subsistence. It is not insofar as it is reduced to objective subsistence that it appears, but despite it.

What Does Not Serve

A second response now arises: the painting, taken in its phenomenality, would be reducible to the manipulable and usable object, to the used or ready-to-hand (*Zuhandenheit, zuhanden*). This sense of phenomenality appears all the more appropriate to the painting as its operation in fact demands that an activity make it work: by manipulating the work, in this case, by moving it so it can be visible, by situating it at the right distance, keeping it under the gaze,[81] by exposing it carefully to the emotions that it can provoke in the spectator, in short by recognizing and admitting that in this or that subsistence already visible of itself (canvas, backing, materials, etc.), there is *also* something else to see besides the subsistent. Seeing the painting demands not only that a painter (or several painters) make the painting, but above all that a spectator (or several of them) be made by it, that he let himself be given over to the intention of the painter and the paint—in a disposition that belongs not so much to a theoretical attitude as to a pragmatics. To see the painting as such (and not as canvas, backing, or surface, etc.) demands deciding to want to see more than the subsisting visible; it therefore demands an act. But this pragmatics does not amount to a manipulation of the ready-to-hand. For manipulation implies that the phenomenon is always operated and intrinsically defined by functional operations within a network of finalities that are themselves directed to the one who, in this case, sees (Dasein the spectator). In the role of manipulated ready-to-hand, the painting could be described as (i) the object of the gaze's aesthetic enjoyment (the pleasurable, according to Kant), which makes it function (manipulates it) by seeing it; or as (ii) the object of a merchant's evaluation, which makes it function (manipulates it) by buying or selling it; finally as (iii) the object of a critical judgment, which makes it function (manipulates it) by submitting it to what are claimed to be formal or scientific standards. These three modes of manipulation, all quite legitimate, nevertheless confirm the limits of applying it to the painting. In each case, it is manipulated inasmuch as it is specified—actually—according to just one criterion: pleasure, value, or doctrine. In each case, it is reduced to one determination, which is enough to reconstruct it in its entirety, but none of these criteria and determinations accord it its fundamental characteristic: namely, the fact that, even though banal, the painting accomplishes itself insofar as it makes itself manifest and it manifests itself starting from itself. The painting escapes the status of the ready-to-hand because in the final analysis it does not serve in any manipulation but appears in, for, and by itself. The ready-to-hand never appears for itself; the painting always does.

Taken as exemplary phenomenon, the painting fundamentally contradicts the phenomenality of the ready-to-hand.[82] Three other arguments confirm this. (i) When Kant defined the beautiful as "the form of the *finality* of an object, insofar as it is perceived in it *without representation of an end*," his thesis is based on the fact that, in the judgment of taste, finality is nothing like an "objective finality, i.e., the relation of the object to a determinate end." This objective finality also does not concern an object known by means of a concept and thus directed to an end distinct from its own definition. Subjective finality, in contrast, is deployed "without any material and concept of that with which it is to agree."[83] This means that the painting is not known conceptually because more radically it obeys a finality for which no concept provides the objective representation. Its finality is not determined by the concept, therefore by an object other than it, because it itself, deploying itself without concept, is no longer determined by objectivity. Finality without end suggests not so much the disappearance of finality (in this case, one would have to say: without finality) as it does a finality without any other end *besides itself*, a finality no longer extroverted toward an other object or an other subject (not even Dasein), but one without an objectifying concept for a phenomenon that is itself nonobjectifiable. The judgment of beauty excepts the painting from the status of the ready-to-hand—from the objective finality of an object ecstatically tending beyond itself toward an external end. The painting, in contrast to the ready-to-hand, therefore refers only to itself. (ii) Whence the second argument. One of the notable characteristics of phenomena classified as ready-to-hand is found, according to a splendid analysis by Heidegger, in the paradox of remaining inapparent as long as they are in use. The tool, the utensil, or the machine go unperceived as long as their proper functioning does not draw our attention to them but directs it through them, as if transparently, toward the ends that they mobilize. In short, as long as they work, we mechanically forget the utility at work in them. It is only when things break down that we are made to notice them, to the point of rendering them insistent by reason of their absence. This is the phenomenality of the ready-to-hand: its visibility increases in inverse proportion to its utility. To appear, the ready-to-hand must no longer function, for usage keeps it in nonmanifestation. And for that matter, we could not live tranquilly in an almost totally mechanical world without the protection of this phenomenological law. Couldn't we conclude from this essential law that every phenomenon of the type of the painting belongs to the ready-to-hand, seeing as, for it too, visibility increases in inverse proportion to its utility? And yet, the contrary is obviously the right conclusion. For, when the ready-to-hand finally appears, it owes this appearance to the deficiency of utility in it—it therefore phenomenalizes itself by a radical contradiction of its definition—whereas if the painting does indeed appear in proportion to its nonutility, it thus accomplishes its most original definition. The ready-to-hand appears only by disappearing as used, therefore by disappearing as such, while the painting appears only as non-used, non-usable, and not even useful, in short, as such. The suspension of functioning, therefore also that of external finality, is something like an exception for the phenomenality of the one, a rule for the phenomenality of the other. The painting always appears as an absolute center, self-referential, immobile; in a word, phenomenologically, it does not move—not even in the case of a "mobile"—because no external, objectifiable, and conceptualizable finality will carry it beyond or outside itself. (iii) Whence a third argument, drawn from the frame that sets the painting apart. What, in the case of the painting, is marked by the frame (materialized in wood or marked by the edge of the canvas)? Framing marks the fact that the visible furnished by the painting no longer belongs to the space of visibility of ready-to-hand and finalized objects, that is to say, to the world of objects subsisting and above all ready-to-hand. Thanks to the frame, protector of extra-territoriality, this caution is tacitly inscribed: "This is not a ready-to-hand"—this colored space is not a collection of colors really available here as an object; it is rather the visibility of what appears without however being objectified. The house with the servant is not here on the wall but, framed, appears here as such, therefore remaining essentially elsewhere—where? No one knows, and it doesn't much matter; what counts is only that it appear in an elsewhere, one that is only defined in opposition to the here, where it appears that the house appears as remaining elsewhere. "Ceci n'est pas une pipe": it is precisely because this colored display makes a pipe visible that there is not one that can be taken in hand—it must be taken only in view. The fruit in the painting is not edible; the nudes in the painting cannot be caressed; the storms and the battles in the painting do not frighten us—because in the frame that signals their un-ready-to-hand unreality, they no longer appear for the sake of..., but rather in order to become visible.[84] The all too common "Untitled" also has this same function: it signals that this visibility, highlighted in its very anonymity, does not furnish any object, any finality, any ready-to-hand. There is no thing or object to recognize in its ins and outs, indeed in its usual ends. There is nothing to see except the seeing itself in its pure and simple arising. Let me conclude: the painting, as phenomenon advancing in its most simple appearing, is nothing like the ready-to-hand.

What Is Not

The final response remains: the phenomenon, in this case the phenomenon of the painting, appears insofar as it is reduced to its beingness, is led back to its character as a being (*ens, Seiendes*). Examining the phenomenality of the "work of art," Heidegger pursued this path as far as possible—to the point where the essence of art is contained in its property of making more manifest the truth of beings: "The nature of art would then be this: the truth of beings setting itself to work."[85] The trouble with this thesis does not lie in the fact, phenomenologically quite hard to contest, that art puts to work the truth of the beings it treats; for this is precisely why we never see beings better than in the irreality of the painting, why princes and principles have always sought to take advantage of this potential to appear better or have always at least indirectly controlled it, and why philosophy has always claimed the right to oversee art as its most essential business. Heidegger here provokes an entirely different question: does putting the truth of beings into operation, which belongs to art *also*, define its *essence*? Does art, considered in a phenomenality so particular that it should be granted the exclusive title of beauty, exhaust its *essence* in the general truth of beings, as a disclosure of beings themselves insofar as they arise neither from the beautiful nor from art? Does art in its essence serve its own mode of phenomenality (beauty), or a phenomenality different from its own: that, universal and indeterminate, of beings, which, for metaphysics as for Heidegger, is named *truth*? Can the phenomenality of beauty be collapsed into the phenomenality of truth as a mere modality of it? Heidegger assumes so unambiguously: "Beauty is a mode according to which the truth deploys itself as unconcealedness."[86] The work manifests itself in terms of its own beauty (therefore its phenomenality) in view of beings, that is to say by organizing itself in terms of an end other than itself—the truth, therefore the phenomenality, of being in general. The (beautiful) work is finally made to work only in view of the manifestation of beingness. Beauty does not work for its own sake but, almost like a ready-to-hand, for the sake of the manifestation of beings. Beauty is therefore accomplished and abolished in the truth. This represents the exact inverse to how I am proceeding: reducing the still problematic and therefore phenomenologically privileged phenomenality of the beautiful to that, more known, of the true, instead of relying on the resources of the phenomenality of the beautiful to accede to a phenomenality not yet won—one no doubt more radical, that of the given. In positing this reduction, doesn't Heidegger confine himself, with ingenious skill to be sure, to repeating the metaphysical theme par excellence: namely, the convertibility of the transcendentals?

That the beautiful first and finally is—this is a claim I will contest. The painting does not appear beautiful as measured by what it is, but without proportion, indeed independently of its beingness. Husserl had already suggested this when he defined the way of appearing of what he called "phenomena invested with spirit." To see a book as a book, for example, therefore to apprehend it as having to be read, I must see it not as thing (what the bibliophile and the illiterate do in barely distinguishable ways), but as meaning: "This is precisely what I am not focused on. I see what is thingly about it insofar as it appears to me, but 'I live in the sense comprehending it.' And while I do so the spiritual unity of the sentence" is what I am dealing with.[87] This can easily be applied to the painting: to see it as a painting, in its own phenomenality of the beautiful, I must of course apprehend it as a thing (subsisting, ready-to-hand), but it is precisely not this that opens it to me as beautiful; it is that I "live" its meaning, namely its beautiful appearing, which has nothing thinglike to it, since it cannot be described as the property of a thing, demonstrated by reasons, or hardly even be said. What is essential—the beautiful appearing—remains unreal, an "I know not what," that I must seek, await, touch, but which is not comprehensible. And for that matter, quite simply, is it? Does it belong to beings if it no longer offers any of the possibilities of knowledge, if it slips away from all the operations by which being is described? It could be that the painting (the "work of art"), far from making the truth of beings work, is emancipated from it—and all the more so as it appears as beautiful. Some clues suggest this but fail to establish it incontestably. (i) The painting (and this counts for everything that falls within the phenomenality of beauty) remains indifferent to its character as thing. Not only because it does not depend on its subsisting in a support (as we have seen), but because it itself supports the proliferation of its supports. That is, the painting, as appearing, remains perfectly indifferent to the ontic conditions of this apparition, since it appears (at least by right, if not also in fact) with the same originarity in its reproductions. The business of infinite reproductions did not begin with the modern procedures of printing, photography, or reproduction; these techniques have done nothing more than secure a greater degree of exactness for a procedure as old as painting and drawing—images of gods, of signs of recognition, icon of the icon not made by the hand of man, proliferating portraits of the glory of the prince, copies of the same painting done ad infinitum in the very studio of the painter, etc. In each case, the power of the original appearing is fully exercised for whoever knows how to see it in conformity with the intentional aim it requires. The painting (the work) remains the same, whether the thinglike support disappears (restoration) or proliferates (reproduction). The question of authenticity can arise only when one stops considering the painting as beautiful, simply put, when one stops seeing it so as to consider it only historically (as a subsisting being) or commercially (as a being ready-to-hand). These two approaches have a certain legitimacy, but they in no way reach the beautiful as such or the originarity of its appearing. (ii) More radically, the painting does not appear because it is, but because it is itself exposed or exhibited. And this process of exhibiting deploys a great phenomenological complexity. No doubt, a painting is exhibited so as to make it accessible to the public, to bring it out of storage or private (and especially privative) collections. This already proves that the reality it has as a being, a reality that can be inventoried (dimensions, date, theme, style, etc.), is not enough for the being to become visible in itself (a remarkable apparition). It needs the possibility of making itself visible, pure relation, taken in an unreal pragmatics. But the access to the painting achieved by the exhibition does not stop there: to hang its canvas on a hook, to "put it there," to attract the buyer, none of this is enough to exhibit the painting. One often risks walking the rooms of a museum and leaving without "having seen anything"; but how can we "see nothing" in an exhibition that we have nevertheless really seen? That does not always or first of all mean that the crowd, distraction, or the mediocrity of the works have diverted our attention from them, but that to see a painting it is not enough to see it—to gather with the sense of sight the information found on a colored being. To this view of a being, what must be added, by degrees or all at once, is the event of its apparition in person (*Selbstgegebenheit*). To the ontic visibility of the painting is added as a super-visibility, ontically indescribable—its upsurge. This exceptional visibility adds nothing real to the ordinary visibility, but it imposes it as such, no longer to my representational sight, but to me, in the flesh, in person, without screen. And each time this event occurs, the initiative always falls to the painting itself, which decides, as a long-closed barrier yields, to let us reach what is all too visible for us to be able to represent it as a mere being. For it is no longer a matter of seeing what is, but of seeing its coming up into visibility—a coming up that has nothing ontic about it. The exhibition should never pretend to exhibit the painting as a being to be made available for desire or information (which would amount to dismissing the painting from its own mode of phenomenality). The exhibition should inversely exhibit the gaze to the painting, which imposes its appearing all the more radically as it presents nothing objectifiable, describable, or beinglike. (iii) The nonontic coming forward of the painting is confirmed by the following property (shared with music): it is not so much a matter of seeing (or hearing) it as it is of re-seeing (or re-hearing) it again and again. This liturgy of re-vision, which compels us to make a trip to re-see this or that canvas (re-visitation), suggests that the painting does not consist in its being (then it would be enough to have seen it just once), but in its mode of appearing (which can be repeated each time in a new way). The painting is still seen in a fitting way as long as a gaze exposes itself to it as to an event that arises anew—it remains seen as long as one tolerates the fact that it happens as an event.[88] Nothing therefore is more threatening to the phenomenality of the painting than the ever more honest and insistent effort not to know it (list, classify, preserve, value, conserve, etc.), but to persuade oneself that by proceeding in this way you will truly arrive at it—while what you have done is simply to substitute for it the ontic support to which it is not reducible, since in the end it *is not*.

The Effect of the Painting

The painting is not a being, any more than it belongs among the subsisting or ready-to-hand objects. It is not, and yet it appears all the more. How are we to justify the paradox of its phenomenality? What then appears in the phenomenon of the painting if neither its subsistence nor its usefulness or beingness reach the phenomenality proper to it? Let us listen to Baudelaire when, all the while doing them homage, he remarks that "the majority of our young colorists lack melody."[89] Why, when colors are at issue, can the absence of melody be something deplorable? What is more normal than that there be such an absence in painting? In fact, it's not about music, but the impossibility of using positive terms and pictorial technique to say what is missing in Baudelaire's eyes, precisely because it does not belong to them—nor to the real visibility of a being in general. It is therefore necessary that he turn to an analogy with sound if he wants to point out a nonpictorial shortcoming (one outside of design, color, or composition) of the painting, inexpressible in terms of real visibility. We can certainly understand that colors "lack melody" because, however skillfully done they might be, they do not "sing"; but in this trivial metaphor, there is much more to be understood: the colors—the painting therefore—do indeed show the things and the beings that they mean to present, but they do not make manifest that which alone would inscribe them in visibility—appearing as such in its arising, the event of the visible happening. We see what the painting shows, what it's about, what we intended to make seen, in short the object and the being; but what is missing is the ascent into visibility itself, the entry of the unseen through the pictorial frame into sight, in short the appearing and its process in the raw.[90] To different degrees but always, the painting (like every phenomenon) does not show any object nor is it presented as a being; rather, it accomplishes an act—it comes forward into visibility.

Can we describe positively what Baudelaire suggests only through its absence? Perhaps we can turn to Cézanne here, whose unsophisticated vitality offers a sure guide. On this issue, he posits a general rule: "The effect constitutes the painting; it unifies and concentrates it," but with the added detail that this effect, in the painting, prolongs or carries out the effect proper to every visible (phenomenon): "Every object . . . is a being endowed with a life of its own and which in consequence has an inevitable effect. Man continually undergoes this psychic influence." It could not be said any better: whether painting or object (in the sense of a phenomenon of the world in general), appearing always has the rank and function not of a representation submitted to the imperial initiative of the gaze of consciousness, but of an event whose happening stems not so much from a form or from real (therefore imitable) colors as from an upsurging, a coming-up, an arising—in short, an effect. "Effect" obviously must be understood here with all its polysemy: effect as the shock that the visible provokes, effect as the emotion that invades the one gazing, effect also as the indescribable combination of the tones and the lines that irreducibly individualize the spectacle. This complexity of mingled effects attests that a meaning—a meaningful effect—autonomous and irreducible, imposes itself, designating the very depths from which the visible surges up, as if from a self—something Cézanne does not hesitate to call the "life" of the visible, wanting as he does to emphasize the self and the quasi interiority ("interior resonance") from which the phenomenon wells up in itself and by itself. But, it will be asked, in this case, what difference remains between the simple object (what I am attempting to overcome) and the painting? Cézanne notes it clearly: "Only the objects that we make a habit of dealing with every day have a totally superficial effect on a man of middling sensibility. Those by contrast that we see for the first time have, unfailingly, a certain effect on us." Between objects and the painting, the difference stems from the strength of the effect produced on the one gazing at them. There, where the object disillusions and "the world is disenchanted,"[91] the painting is "enchanting" because— at least when we let it arise as such, without collapsing it into objectivity— its effect affects us more intensely and more enduringly than any being, ready-to-hand or subsistent. Let me emphasize that Cézanne stands at the other end of the spectrum from Heidegger: it is not that the painting (the "work of art") completes what the object outlines (the phenomenality of beings); rather, the object is judged on the basis of what the painting alone accomplishes (the effect). The painting does not appear as a perfect being, but the object bears a deficit of effect—with regard to the exemplary phenomenality of the painting. What appears of the painting as painting is therefore called the effect. Kandinsky, throughout his definitive meditation on the unreality of art, will pinpoint the paradox precisely through recourse to the effect. Take first a color and a form painted correctly. They deploy, as such, an effect by which "the image lives totally in interiority." This effect is obviously produced physically on the gaze (the white or the yellow, for example, produce a more or less strong effect on the eye according to their intensities, but also according to their form and their environment); but this physical effect nevertheless already attests that a "life" of the visible swells up immediately as from a sensible self. Whence a second effect, or rather a second effect of the first: "This elementary effect provokes a more profound one, which carries with it an emotion of the soul." Here the effect is not limited, as it is in ordinary perception, to affecting the mind by means of physical causes (though it does that also); or rather, the "effect of the object's color, of its form, and the effect proper, independent of the form and the color," transgress the field of things and even that of my flesh "so as to provoke in the soul the vibrations of a pure resonance."[92] In Cartesian terms, one would say that the visible of the painting has for its effect neither a perception (used in reference to physical things) nor an emotion (used in reference to my body), but a passion (used in reference to the soul). The effect makes the soul vibrate with vibrations that evidently represent neither an object nor a being and which cannot themselves be described or represented in the mode of objects or beings. And yet, only this "effect" in the end allows us to define the phenomenality of the painting and therefore, with it, the phenomenality of what shows itself in itself and starting from itself.

Let me return to the mediocre painting that I earlier had my eye on: how can I describe it in its own phenomenality? A generic scene so ordinary, displaying a house, a servant at the window, the animals and a man outside, vegetables and fowl, etc., cannot be analyzed as such. First, because strictly speaking it is impossible to identify it with and by its characteristics as a real being (size, mounting, etc.), which would suit so many other objects—it's not a question of a subsisting being. The same goes for the objects it represents intentionally, objects that can be confused with an infinite number of similar ones on similar canvases. And for that matter, its first function is not to instruct us about these objects; as a painting, it has no utility—it is not a question of a being ready-to-hand. What remains once these two identifications have been reduced? For some element does indeed remain—by which it keeps precisely the rank of a painting. But what do I see when I see with phenomenological rigor? Not the framed canvas, nor the country objects, nor even the organization of the colors and the forms—I see, without any hesitation, the ruddy and ochre flood of the day's last light as it inundates the entire scene. This luminosity itself does not strike me as a fact of color; rather, this fact of color strikes me only in that it makes me undergo a passion: that, in Kandinsky's terms, of ochre tinged with gold—the passion undergone by the soul affected by the profound serenity of the world saved and protected by the last blood of the setting sun. To see the painting, to the point where it is not confused with any other, amounts to seeing it reduced to its effect. The effect of serenity defines the ultimate visibility of this painting—its reduced phenomenality. Its phenomenality is reduced—beyond its beingness, its subsistence, and its utility—to this effect: ochre serenity. Painters look for this phenomenality when, the painting having been completed (or almost so), they wonder to themselves "*ce que cela donne,* what [effect] it gives off." What more does a painting give besides what it shows in showing itself as object and being? Its effect. What more does the painting offer besides its real component parts? Its effect. But this effect is not produced in the mode of an object, nor is it constituted or reconstituted in the mode of beings. It gives itself. The painting (and, in and through it, every other phenomenon in different degrees) is reduced to its ultimate phenomenality insofar as it gives its effect. It appears as given in the effect that it gives. Thus is defined the essential invisibility of the painting,[93] which we can pass by because there is nothing objective or ontic to see in it. In the end, for every reduced being, all that remains is the effect, such that in it the visible is given, is reduced to a given. The painting is not visible; it makes visible. It makes visible in a gesture that remains by definition invisible—the effect, the upsurge, the advance of givenness. To be given requires being reduced—reconducted—to this invisible effect which alone makes visible. Nothing has an effect, except the phenomenon reduced to the given.

The invisibility of what is given by the painting reduced to its effect has nothing contradictory about it. It results simply from the bracketing of all that in this phenomenon does not pertain to pure phenomenality: objectness and beingness. Here we find confirmation for the claim that givenness itself reduces and that the reduction alone permits the given. For the pertinence of invisibility in the painting (the fact that it makes its visibility possible), far from countering, repeats, in a certain sense, the derealization of bracketing in general; it permits the phenomenon to appear precisely inasmuch as it frees it from every thesis in the world. The phenomenon therefore is reduced all the more to its given as it assumes the bracketing of its mundane beingness and reality. It is not surprising therefore that the phenomena most obviously reducible to their givenness are found first in the semantic fields where, by definition, thinglike reality and posited beingness are missing. The painting itself, whose appearing is set apart from what supports it (thing, being) and always claims to be given as pure surface without support (or by absorbing it), lends itself spontaneously to such a reduction to the given. But quite a few other phenomena are also given of themselves as exemplary phenomena without objectness—giving time, giving life, giving one's word—or without beingness—giving death, peace, meaning, etc. For the very way in which they are designated implies a spontaneous reduction of all that could hide the pure phenomenal given. By definition, they give nothing—no object, no being; and for this very reason, they give all the more evidently, clearly, and fundamentally as nothing resists the reduction or hides the pure effect of givenness to which they are reconducted without reserve. The discovery of a new class of phenomena reduced to givenness by themselves calls for two remarks. First of all, it provides a powerful, factual confirmation for my hypothesis of the legitimate possibility of a phenomenality reduced to pure givenness. But it demands establishing that all the different senses of "to give" do indeed come together in a single concept of phenomenological givenness and are not scattered in endless equivocations. I will have to return to this point (II, §§9–11). For now, it is enough to note that the phenomenon, at the very least, *can* be reduced to a pure given, and that it must do so if it is to appear absolutely.

§5 PRIVILEGE OF GIVENNESS

Even Nothing

That the phenomenon can, indeed must, be reduced to a pure given in order to appear absolutely is a proposition that immediately raises two objections, which quickly collapse into just one. (a) Couldn't we imagine that certain phenomena or quasi phenomena that appear in the ranks of common phenomenality and yet play a more important role therein (first of all, death and the nothing) can be described by their radical irreducibility to any givenness, by their very nongivenness? According to this hypothesis, would it be necessary to admit two parallel realms of phenomenality, one reducible to the given, the other not? Could we then maintain the phenomenological universality of givenness? (b) I am claiming that the reduction, whose scope goes all the way to givenness, takes an ultimate step—beyond the reduction to objectness (Husserl) and the reduction to beingness (Heidegger); but what guarantee do we have that this third reduction could not itself fall beneath the authority of another—another reduction, another authority besides the reduction—in short, that the third reduction really is the last? These two questions (universality and primacy) can be joined into one: how do we justify the privilege shown to givenness? I will try to establish that this privilege does not come to it from the outside, therefore in a potentially arbitrary way, but that it belongs to it intrinsically, by definition. Privileges of givenness—as we speak of the privileges of birth. It belongs to givenness to give (itself) without limit or presupposition because it gives (itself)—it alone—without conditions.

Let us consider this piece of evidence at the outset: in whatever way and by whatever means something can relate to us, absolutely nothing is, happens, appears to us, or affects us that is not first, always, and obligatorily accomplished in the mode of a *givenness*. Even the most evident or sensible intuition draws its privilege only from the givenness, sole immediacy, that is accomplished in it; for immediacy amounts to a givenness or remains illusory.[94] No being, no actuality, no appearance, no concept, and no sensation could reach us, or even concern us, if it did not first give [itself] to us. This would be an essential rule: nothing intervenes for or against us that is not first given, here and now. Being, appearing, effecting, or affecting become possible and thinkable only if they happen, before each and every specification of their respective venues, first as pure givennesses. Every fact, every problem, and every consciousness begins with immediate givens, with the immediacy of a given. Nothing arises that is not given.

And even nothing. For, the absence of beings (nothingness), the lack of actuality (possibility), deficiency in appearing (obscurity), as well as powerlessness to affect (the void) must be given—in the mode of lack or of deception—if we are even just to conceive what they take from us and the mere fact that they steal it. This is not a suspension of givenness, but a givenness by denegation. Though denegative,[95] it remains no less an authentic givenness, but it is characterized by its deficiency of content; or rather, it remains a particular givenness, in that it is accomplished by the very absence of given in it. The sole difficulty consists in identifying in each case which paradoxical manner of giving can be at issue in this nongiven; but this evaluation does not officially differ from one that examines the modes of a positive given. In every case, the paradoxical ways of givenness can and therefore must always be described rigorously. (a) In this way, the nothing is given by means of the fundamental mood of anxiety, where the very absence of beings as a whole affects me, and therefore where, at the same time, Being in its difference from beings as a whole ensnares me (Heidegger). The nothing is therefore given quite positively in and through anxiety, and giving the nothingness of beings, it gives no less than Being itself, which transcends beings. This is an eminent occurrence of givenness, to the point that it "discloses *the world as world*."[96] (b) As for possibility, sticking strictly to its metaphysical sense (the opposite of actuality), it is not just given negatively as what existence has not or not yet completed, but above all positively as what does not contradict itself (is not given in order to be amended) in its concept (Leibniz). It therefore gives itself in and through the intuition of essences or categorical intuition. (c) As for the hiddenness of the nonappearing, considered in its three essential meanings, it too is given. Either (i) as the incomprehensible, it gives the positive excess of infinity, according to its own pattern of manifestation (Dionysius, Descartes), or else (ii) in the deficiency of intuition, it gives the simple idea of reason, indeed its ideal according to their unique mode of adequate manifestation (Kant, Husserl); as for (iii) the negative, it can be understood as the operator of dialectical givenness, which puts the concept into motion, to the point of producing it in actuality (Hegel). (d) Finally, the void is given in the deception of anticipated perception or in the frustrated expectation of affection, indeed desire. Every negation and every denegation, every negative, every nothing, and every logical contradiction suppose a givenness, which authorizes us to recognize them and thus do justice to their particularities—in short, a given that permits us at the very least to discuss them.[97]

That their modes of givenness remain complex and paradoxical in no way implies that they make an exception to givenness, but rather marks the extent to which the latter embraces them and makes them possible. We could experience, say, or think nothing of them if we did not first experience them as givennesses possibly without given, therefore as givennesses all the more pure. Hence it is appropriate to follow Husserl when he posits that as with nonbeing (and what follows from it), absurdities (*Widersinn*), like contradictions (*Widerspruch*), fall within givenness.[98] They must be given, in whatever way one likes, for them to appear to us as inferior degrees of rationality, which they actually are. But an important consequence immediately follows. If contradictions and absurdities all fall under givenness, it is hard to see how it could be otherwise for nonmeaning, which is comprehended as such (as noncomprehensible) only insofar as it is in fact given; but then all meaning that is not validated by presence, or all meaning whose intuition—indeed whose concept—is endlessly deferred (differance), would remain in the field of givenness. Since, according to my fundamental thesis, givenness is not equivalent to intuition and does not necessarily require it, the fact that a phenomenon (or a statement) lacks intuition does not prevent it from still appearing as a given, nor does it limit the scope of intuition. Deconstruction, which only considers sensible intuition (for categorical intuition perhaps still resists it), does not broach givenness, which would secure for it any and all pertinence in phenomenology. Deconstruction therefore remains a mode of givenness—to be quite exact that of givenness deferred.[99] It follows finally that one cannot speak, in rigorous terms, of a "nongivenness." When Husserl wants to oppose a contrary to full, originary givenness "in the flesh" (*leibhaft*), he does not have recourse to any sort of "nongivenness" that would limit givenness, but to a *"givenness in the broader sense"* that would confirm its unconditionality. This calls for a two-pronged commentary. (i) This broadened givenness is not to be reproached for not giving, but precisely for giving any and everything whatsoever: "In which it is said, ultimately, concerning everything represented, that it is given in representation (though perhaps in an 'empty manner')."[100] With a term like "representation" (decisive, it is true), we are dealing with an approximation that is satisfactory enough for what we understand by givenness and in no way with a nongivenness. (ii) The distinction is made entirely within the one and only horizon of givenness, which admits no exception. In phenomenological rigor, a nongivenness or a negative givenness remains unthinkable since, to think them, they must first be given to me in order that I might think them as a nongivenness or a negative givenness. If some still use these terms, this can only be due to a certain laxness, or to designate another opposition—for example, one between intuitive and nonintuitive givenness[101]—but it would be appropriate, then, to say so, following Husserl's example. Givenness, *index sui et non dati*, therefore fixes the horizon of the nongiven as much as of the given, precisely because one and the same horizon encircles the given with a ring of nongiven. Givenness opens the unsurpassable space of the given in general. Before whatever might *be* (or even *not* be), the difficulty therefore does not reside in the decision to know if this is indeed a matter of givenness, but simply in deciding its modes.

Death, Too

The following objection will nevertheless be made: even if it precedes all that is or appears, givenness presupposes at least that to which it gives (itself), whatever name one uses to designate it (*ego*, consciousness, subject, Dasein, or "life"). Givenness would thus leave outside its domain that which it affects and which receives it, as its sole nonconstitutable condition. If the event that suppresses every recipient of givenness is named death, it would therefore be necessary to conclude that, in contrast to the nothing, death can suspend givenness and, because it does not fall under its jurisdiction, render it inoperative. However, givenness maintains a much more complex relation with death than can be divined from so weighty an objection. The mere fact that one can, at least in words, "give" and "receive" death already suggests this. What is not—death—could still happen to him who would disappear on account of the fact of his having welcomed this inverted gift (which is not).[102] But isn't this just a word game without conceptual justification? Without a doubt no, if one admits, following Heidegger, that death determines Dasein as the "possibility of impossibility."[103] From this paradox, two arguments follow. (a) Death still remains for us, for us as Dasein, a real possibility, not a nullity. Better, this possibility offers itself as the possibility par excellence because it fixes the event of an ultimate impossibility, one that is absolutely certain though undetermined, indeed one that is all the more certain as it is undetermined. What is more, as death affects, in the role of inescapable possibility, only Dasein, it defines its ownmost possibility—not a worldly being's possibility to be won (or avoided), nor that of the self to be maintained, but the possibility of the transcendence to be accomplished of *this* being, Dasein, in opposition to all the other beings, therefore the transcendence in and through it of Being over being as a whole. Death therefore no longer comes up as a nonevent, which would destroy the conditions of its reception by manifesting itself; for when it happens, I am still there to receive it because it appears well before I disappear; better, it appears as a possibility that is first because last, one that precedes all my actualities, rendering them only possible. The Epicurean paradox does not hold here, which claims that "Death is nothing to us, since when we are death is not [*Hotan men hēmeis ōmen, ho thanatos ou parestin*], and we are no longer when it is [*hotan de ho thanatos parēi, toth' hēmeis ouk esmen*]."[104] For if death does indeed have possibility and actuality as its mode of givenness, the fact that it is not actually present in no way implies that it is not for us, but on the contrary proves that it is indeed for us insofar as not being (actual), insofar as pure possible. The paradox would be valid only if death remained a being, having to be actually in order to be; yet it is not any such being, but rather pure possibility, and it is as such that it exerts itself over us without being or, what amounts to the same thing, does not cease to be for us—at every moment and from every direction. This agrees with what Epicurus says, without fear of contradicting himself: "With regard to all other things, it is possible to find security; but in the case of death, we men all live in a city without walls."[105] A city without walls: this metaphor could just as well define the openness of Dasein as the intentionality of the *I* thrown into the world. For death, as radical possibility, accomplishes nothing less than intentional exposure, thereby opening the world, and therefore finally givenness itself. Death is given and gives me to myself as the possibility par excellence—as a result, Heidegger doesn't describe death, but rather its phenomenological essence, being-toward-death. For Heidegger, it is no longer a question of one event among and after all the others happening to Dasein and, at the same time, putting an end to them. It is a matter of Dasein's original entry into its mode of being of pure possibility without subsistence or usefulness. Therefore, as originary possibility and being-toward-death, death is indeed given to Dasein, not as a final blow, but as a send-off. Death, at least understood as this possibility, is given to Dasein as long as its life—as its life itself, since it too is given only as pure possibility. Far from abolishing the Dasein to which it gives, death gives it its ultimate determination as the being that is toward death. Never does givenness make itself more visible than in such a possibility.

From this refuted criticism, another follows. Even if the possibility of death still remains a possibility, it's a question of the possibility of impossibility. It therefore opens as a possibility only in order to suspend every other possibility. In this sense, it gives nothing but the suspension of every given and in the end nothing, not even that. Givenness therefore encounters its limit. But this second criticism immediately turns against itself. For, if death manifests the suspension of all possibility, it does not give nothing, or little; it gives impossibility, that is to say a phenomenon or a nonphenomenon, a horizonal phenomenon, indeed one of nonhorizon. In short, as the possibility of impossibility, death gives the experience of finitude as an unsurpassable existential determination (of Dasein). For absolute impossibility becomes accessible to us only in the guise of being-toward-death, and the possibility of impossibility would by contrast remain inaccessible as a possibility become actual. This is verified in the case of the death of others [*la mort d'autrui*]: most of the time, it gives me to notice only the factual interruption of life by an accident that is fundamentally without reason, despite all the physical reasons; it strengthens by contrast—in the "they"—the lazy belief that, for those who remain, life continues and death (actual in the case of others) is for me still neither actual nor even possible. Actual death—the death of others—in fact opens no access to their death, closes access to my own possible death. The actual death of others attracts me to the very degree to which it closes the possibility of my death—beneath the same lid as the deceased. Between death (of others) as a mute fact and my death (as possibility of impossibility), what is at stake is not the absence of the recipient of givenness, but the modes of givenness of the *I* transcending its ontic bases—not the deficiency of a worldly actuality, but the free play of a pure possibility. This is no doubt confirmed when, most often without thinking about what we are saying, we invoke death not only as a phenomenon of life, but as a privileged phenomenon—"O Death, where is there one so beautiful!" "fortunate and beneficial death."[106] Here, obviously, we are to understand our own, therefore not yet actual, really impossible death, in short pure possibility. The everyday pathos of death—anxieties, fears, cures, and avoidances—is not fed by actual death, but by its ungraspable, protean, haunting, seductive possibility. In absolute impossibility, which actual death manifests, my death is made all the more accessible as possibility and thus is given without measure. Death—nothing escapes it, but it does not escape givenness, not just because one can "give the gift of death," but above all because it gives itself on its own. Consequently, death does not steal from givenness that which (or he who) could receive it;[107] it inscribes it (or him or her) forever within the horizon of givenness.

The Other Inconcussum

Neither the nothing nor death make an exception to givenness any more than does Being, the phenomenon, the concept, or intuition. It follows that the denial of givenness can be neither thought nor accomplished—since denegation, whatever it denies, implies its own givenness inasmuch as it claims to deny, contest, oppose, in short perform here and now. Since only a given can deny givenness, it confirms it as it contests it. It will therefore be said: let one deny it as much as one wants, one will never bring about that givenness does not give and is not given, since the denegation already gives. Is this a repetition, for the benefit of givenness, of Descartes establishing the *ego sum, ego existo* on the basis of an external deceiver and the internal doubt that claim to deny it? Of course, so patent is the analogy: "In that case I too undoubtedly exist, if he is deceiving me; and let him deceive me as much as he can, he will never bring it about that I am nothing so long as I think that I am something."[108] Just as the *ego* attests (to) itself each time and as long as it thinks—since each time it thinks something (and even something that deceives it), it must first think itself, therefore attest itself—so too does givenness, each time it gives whatever it might be and even when it gives what is not or denies even the least given, first give itself. In this sense, givenness shares with the *ego* the privilege of absolute indubitability: no one can doubt that givenness has always already given for him (if not to him) and gives to him continually, just as every *ego* knows that it is inasmuch as it is thinking and thinking continually. And yet, givenness differs radically from the *ego* with regard to its mode of indubitability. The indubitability of the *ego* stems from the self-possession that assures it a performance of itself (existing) by itself (thinking). Indubitability here equals self-certainty, and this self-certainty equals the possession, indeed the production, of self by self (a *cogitatio [sui]* intrinsically *a se*, if not already *causa sui*).[109] In contrast, givenness gives and gives itself, therefore confirms itself, not because it possesses itself, but because it abandons and abandons itself, does not hold itself back and does not hold back. It makes itself completely in that it unmakes itself by and for the sake of a given; it assures itself of itself by dispossessing itself of itself, by producing an other besides itself in whom it disappears, the given. As a result, givenness remains withdrawn, held in reserve, in the background, dissimulated by its given; it thus never appears as such, therefore especially not as a being, a substance, or a subject, in short never as an *inconcussum quid. Inconcussum* perhaps, but never *quid.* Indubitability pertains not to a being but to a universal act. Can an act pretend to universality? Of course not, as long as by this act we understand a being or something that might *be*; but here we are talking about the givenness of every being and nonbeing, of every phenomenon and every inapparent, of every affection and every affective deception, etc. Should such a universal be understood as a transcendental principle of possibility? Certainly not, because such a principle can impose itself only prior to experience, while givenness is marked only in the very experience of the given, a posteriori more than a priori (see §1). Above all, the transcendental is valid only in relation to a subjectivity, finite and first at the same time. But givenness gives without obligation for such a subject, one that it defines because it is not measured by it, exceeds it, and perhaps, saturates it without measure. Where the transcendental fixes a measure, givenness exceeds immeasurably, such that a possible subject can refer to it only by an essential unmeasuredness. Givenness accomplishes not so much its institution as its destitution; it disconcerts it more than it acts in concert with it. In short, the indubitability of givenness does not mimic that of the *ego*; it inverts it—but without destroying it—by leaving the ego possible as one of its marginal, decentered, impoverished, but legitimate givens. For givenness never destroys, since it gives.

A final remark must now be made. The unconditional indubitability of givenness will become unacceptable if a certain drift is admitted, even tacitly: namely, conceiving it substantially, in whatever manner one likes, with whatever precautions one might take. Since it makes an exception to objectness and beingness (therefore to Being), which come from it without comprehending it or making it comprehensible, if it makes the given appear and sets the stage for the phenomenon—it must therefore be understood as an act. Givenness comes forward and accomplishes, arrives and passes, advances and withdraws, arises and sinks away. It does not subsist, persist, show itself, or make itself seen. It is on the make; it makes the event without itself making up an event. What is more: this act above all should not be understood as a "pure act," a hypostasized actor in a play that it would control and precede. For it is purely and solely a matter of a phenomenological act—in the sense that the reduction, from which givenness cannot be separated since it is the flip side of the coin, has the status of act par excellence for Husserl. Solely on condition of "keeping this concept of act distinguished"[110] will we be able to acknowledge unambiguously the privilege of givenness.

For now, let us stick with this result: denying givenness suffices to confirm it. The privilege of givenness therefore comes to it from its definition. Since givenness always beats a hasty retreat before its given, its very withdrawal confirms it; its absence—not being, object, *I*, or transcendental—attests its activity. It is indeed posited as principle, but on condition that it remain the last.

§6 TO GIVE ITSELF, TO SHOW ITSELF

The Givens

The decision to define phenomenality in terms of givenness falls prey to one last suspicion, seemingly quite formidable: am I not just playing on the ambiguity of a signifier [*givenness* in English, *donation* in French][111] in order to claim to reach a signified that in fact has not been constructed or justified?[112] I would be speaking of *givenness* as a unified concept, while a simple analogy (a paronymy) would enable us to establish a network of terms that remain equivocal (*es gibt, geben, gegeben, Gabe, Gebung, Gegebenheit*, etc.), as would their usage by different authors. *Givenness* would not define a concept and would not even designate a phenomenon but, like an abstract general idea, would unduly fix a confused illusion—an effect of language, therefore without effect. Two arguments can address this objection. (a) First, it's not a matter of exploiting an ambiguity but of honestly observing the fact of it; it would be more arbitrary to deny this patent ambiguity than to admit it as a difficulty still to be illuminated. (b) Next, this ambiguity cannot be sidestepped: *givenness* [*donation*] in fact signifies its act (to give, *donner*), as well as what is at stake (gift, *don*), indeed the actor (giver, *donateur*) and the mode of the accomplished given (given, *donné*, as

characteristic). Therefore, why exclude the possibility that this polysemy results from the fact that a concept organizes them, distinguishes and coordinates these instances with extreme precision? For that matter, if one wanted
to clarify this ambiguity by dividing it into equivocal terms, givenness
would not be clarified—it would be lost, since what is at stake in it resides
in articulating its possible meanings in a single plot. For givenness, as a unified concept, would perhaps not suffer in any way from the play of its sig-
nifiers; it accomplishes itself as a whole therein by thus playing on itself. It
would not suffer from ambiguity if it consisted in the play of its different
and inseparable meanings. The objection therefore does not dissolve the
question of givenness; it poses it. We have to accept it, for in philosophy, if
one can choose questions, one cannot choose adversaries or aporias.

It behooves us to interrogate explicitly the inevitable ambiguity of
givenness [*donation*], so as to articulate the concept of givenness. This difficulty, which arises with the word, should therefore be examined to the letter. We will therefore take as guiding threads, successively, French usage,
then the translation of the German.

In French, *givenness* is *donation*, a word whose usage carries with it an
unavoidable duality, which affects its concept. At first glance, it states what
is found given: the gift made; the supposedly brute and neutral datum of
givenness [*donation*] thus remains only the gift given. The gift then remains as a being that is both subsisting and available, freed from the process that made it possible, actual. Thus givenness [*donation*] does indeed
persist as gift given, but in another sense, it disappears in this given, which
hides in it the giving gift. Why then not content ourselves with nothing
more than this gift given, a pure and simple given, shorn of any trace of its
origin, pure of any relic, cut off from any antecedents? In sticking strictly
to the gift, to the given, to givens, to the datum, wouldn't we liberate ourselves completely from the supposedly dangerous ambiguity of the notion
of givenness [*donation*]? This, however, represents an illusory way out. For
the given, givens, and the datum, even reduced to their brute factuality,
still bear in themselves the ambiguity constitutive of givenness. Let us consider the extreme case of the most neutralized, minimal, empty givens: the
givens in a mathematical problem or a problem of physics. Let us imagine
an appearance without background, established openly and accessible for
each and all, one bearing the mark of the most reduced givenness: that of
the pure object, also named the "subject" of an examination passed out
(given) to candidates in such a way that it is submitted to them unreserv-

edly for the purpose of being solved—in short, the givens of an object submitted to the subject who dissolves it. What is implied by these givens that have been borrowed from the lowest level of givenness? At the very least that a problem has been proposed to someone who can solve it. But how is it proposed? In and through the evidence of the thing-itself in question; but this evidence is in turn imposed in and through the mediation of the one who invented the problem—whether he knows the solution and gives it (the problem Pappus posed to Descartes), knows it and does not give it (the problem Fermat posed to Fermat), or is ignorant of it and seeks it (the problem Fermat poses for us). Ignorance of the solution here defines not simply the problem (still unknown solution), but also the givens (arbitrary choice of premises). Without this ignorance, the givens would no longer be such; they would become mere pieces of information, placed in a series and already intelligible in it. In and through this fundamental ignorance into which they put me, the givens attest that they escape me because they befall me; they therefore prove the movement of givenness that gives them. This positing of the problem such as it proposes its givens to us can be repeated with an even more mundane example. During an academic examination, the givens of the problem have this in particular and evidently as their distinguishing characteristic: it is not I who chose them; or better, there is a problem (therefore the possibility of evaluation or competition) only to the degree that the givens are distributed to or imposed on me, therefore only to the degree that *I* do not give them to *me* myself. Thus not even the givens of a problem maintain a neutrality without ground or withdrawal; they, too, by definition, whether it be through the arbitrary choice of an academic authority who chooses the subject or through ignorance of a question still unbroached, come upon me and impose themselves on me. This movement of imposing itself on me, of arriving upon me from before or in front of me, is just enough to detect a certain givenness. The givens of the problem come from a certain givenness: before their givenness (the distribution of subjects, the publication of the theme of the contest, the scientific diffusion of an aporia or paradox), the givens are still unknown to me, unavailable, unforeseeable—and it is precisely on account of this that they were given. This making the givens available also refers to a certain givenness for another reason: in giving themselves, they not only make themselves accessible; they open a new situation for those who receive them—the examination, where everyone is equal, except for their competence, an arrangement that negates social or natural status—but above all a new temporal sequence—at the moment of the distribution (givenness), time begins again, or rather, in ordinary time, a limit is imposed that marks a new time, that of the ordeal. This time within time, like the social neutralization that makes it possible, designates the givens. But these givens would never arise as such without the arising—givenness. Givenness is not added to the given as an ambiguous background; it simply marks the happening that offers it to itself. On the other hand, if one claimed to take these givens as pure, simple, and brute *facta*, one would be condemned to rendering them unintelligible; no common model would gather them into a coherent whole, no result could confirm their compatibility by deduction. And above all, we would not have any reason to consider these givens the givens *of* a problem—not facts closed on themselves, but pieces of information not yet developed yet nevertheless already intentionally oriented toward results. To work with givens, they must first be read *as* givens, grasped in a coherent (though provisionally unknown) model, which refers to its complete clarification exactly as they first referred to their coming forward. These givens must therefore be accepted *as such*, therefore on the basis of the givenness whence they arise; they must not be closed up in the insignificance of a fact without fabricant. Mathematical givens or the givens of a problem offer a privileged example of the given—a fact that is not self-made.[113] Thus these givens attest givenness by their having been imposed; they also confirm it by their work.[114] Givens and givenness are certainly not identified, but givens without givenness cannot be thought or appear.

The Fold

Givenness is therefore discerned at the very heart of the given, even the most nondescript—the mathematical given or the givens of a problem. Givenness does not colonize from outside the givens of the given; it is inscribed therein as its irreparable character, the articulation of its coming forward, inseparable from its immanence to itself. Even as unabashed a thinker of immanence as Spinoza suggests this compelling character of advent that belongs to the given, which I designate with the name *givenness*. Take an essence explicitly qualified as *given*—a certain necessity follows from it, which necessarily imposes its effects on the mind: "Ex *data* cujusque rei essentia aliquis effectus necessario sequi debet [From any given idea some effect must necessarily follow]."[115] The given is articulated in terms of givenness—its own advent, then the production of the effect—which does not transcend it or overdetermine it from the outside, but simply unfolds the character of given insofar as given. For a necessity to exert itself (for the effect to follow), it is first necessary that the given impose itself (give itself). If Spinoza's necessity does nothing else but deploy in the noetic and corporeal order the infinitely infinite given called substance, which serves as the one and only given of the one and only problem—"Res enim omnes ex *data* natura necessario sequutae sunt [All things have necessarily followed from their given nature]," "Ex *data* perfectissima natura necessario sequutae sunt [They have necessarily followed from a most perfect given nature]"[116]—we must not infer from this any transcendence, any addition of givenness on top of the given; for givenness belongs to the very definition of the given *as* given. It is not Spinoza's supposed immanentism that would keep the given from veering toward transcendence. To the contrary, it is the articulation of the given as such in terms of givenness that safeguards immanence, even in the case of a deduction of the finite modes from the infinite substance. The given, the mathematical givens, the *datum*, is therefore never limited to a neutral, leveled, and closed subsistence. For, from the simple fact of their arising, they already bear the mark of the event by which they are imposed on me. The ambiguity of the given, inseparably fact and means of access to the fact, characterizes them from the outset, and this ambiguity of the given opens directly to givenness. The given is not emancipated from givenness and cannot be. It leads back to it because it comes from it, bears its mark, or rather is identified with it. Every given manifests givenness because the progress of its event unfolds it. Givenness opens as the fold of the given: the gift given *insofar as* it gives itself in terms of its own event. Givenness unfolding itself articulates the gift given (eventually without origin, genealogy, or dependence—it matters little) along the progress of its advent (obscured by the first, or retained, or simply unknowable—it matters little).

By dint of this ambiguity, it is all the more a matter of the essence of givenness. Absent one of these two sides of the fold, the entire question of givenness immediately disappears. This question consists solely in investigating the relation of the gift given with the process of advent. Consequently, the strategy of privileging *what is given* or *the given* so as to avoid having to write *givenness*, in French *donation*, would in the end miss what is at stake; for it is the given itself that bears the fold of givenness [*donation*]. To really dispense with givenness, one would have to demonstrate, following precise phenomenological analyses, that a subsisting phenomenon can appear without bearing any mark of its eventfulness, therefore without any given character that would fold it back into givenness. The alternatives with regard to *givenness*, the French *donation*, are formulated as follows: either every given leads back to givenness [*donation*] according to the unfolding of its fold (its "ambiguity"); or else one renounces givenness in cases where a phenomenon would appear without giving itself, and solely in these cases. But then the burden of proof passes from the first hypothesis—confirmed in the majority of phenomena that give themselves—to the second, which claims to identify phenomena that would not give themselves and would renounce the name given or what is given, all the while appearing. Now, such a hypothesis seems doubly problematic: first, because a phenomenon that does not give itself seems very likely to be a contradiction, or at least an exception; next, because even if one could justify these exceptions phenomenologically, they no doubt would not modify the rule that the phenomenon is implicated in the givenness that delivers it originarily as a given. The initial difficulty is now inverted: it is no longer a question of knowing if one can and should think the phenomenon in terms of givenness, but if one can still think it without givenness. For the alleged ambiguity of givenness would in its very definition end up at the fold of the given.

The Translation

The difficulties of translating the German *Gegebenheit* now take on their real importance.[117] They result from the attempt to transpose into two terms in the target language one term in the original language, at once marking and masking the duality of a single notion: *givenness* in English or in French *la donation* as the fold of the given.[118] Husserl's use of *Gegebenheit* offers an occasion to put to the test my decision to translate this term uniformly by *donation* in French and *givenness* in English and to consider these equivalents as a consistent concept. If one wants to avoid emphasizing, as I have done up until now, the fold of the two possible meanings of *Gegebenheit*—givenness/*donation* as result of givenness (the given) and givenness/*donation* as the process (giving)—wouldn't it be appropriate to distinguish, as an ever insightful translator has proposed, these two meanings by two translations so as to remove all ambiguity? He in fact observes, almost in the same terms as I do, the ambiguity, or better the fold, of the given where givenness opens: "*Gegebenheit*—a term that designates *what* is given as well as the *character* of being given." However, he immediately dismantles the fold by using two heterogeneous translations for one term: "In the first case, I translate as *given*, in the second as *presence*."[119] But, I object, how can the "cases" be distinguished without imposing a necessarily risky or arbitrary interpretation of each occurrence of *Gegebenheit*? It is not at all self-evident that one can divide these occurrences into the given (supposedly neutral) and givenness (character of the given). This is seen in the fact that the French translators have most often chosen to use uniformly either one or the other translation, without pretending to protect the ambivalence —proof of the fact that the choice is not between one or the other translation but between unilaterality (given folded up into itself) and the fold of the given (givenness).[120] There is more: can one legitimately oppose, even out of concern for clarity, presence and givenness, especially when Husserl himself made every effort never to think any presence without a givenness that would grant it to happen as a phenomenon, while in turn he admits some givenness that would not deliver any presence (memory, imagination, appresentation, etc.)? The danger of arbitrariness is so threatening that the translator suspends his distinction on the very page where he had introduced it: "When the text plays on the two meanings at the same time, I have juxtaposed—as here—both translations."[121] This precaution imprudently admits that the two meanings he wanted to keep separate are in fact continually "juxtaposed." It therefore concedes the entirety of my thesis, but does not explain when or how to decide between those cases when this juxtaposition is appropriate and those where it is not. In short, this impracticable combination of "*what* is given" and "the *character* of being given" consecrates the radical inadequacy of any and all division between the sides of the fold formed by the given *as* givenness.

Why then was such a division maintained? There too, for a strictly theoretical reason. Choosing to translate *Gegebenheit* by *given*, or even by a univocal *presence*, has nothing insignificant about it. It implies a conceptual decision with important consequences: separating the given from any relation to the process of givenness and above all to any pole that would possibly give it. In this way, one would succeed, at least on a tangent, in reducing not only givenness to the given, but above all the given to a brute fact, neutralized and leveled off, without the status of gift or the trace left by a process of givenness. The given would then be affiliated with a presence intelligible in and through itself, a subsistence without provenance, pure *Vorhanden* mimicking the *causa sui*—a presence purified of all givenness. But how can we not wonder whether masking the fold of *Gegebenheit* (as much by its being translated without *givenness* as by the concept of a neutral given) does not contradict the whole Husserlian project? Wasn't the essence of what he wanted to do to describe the operations that would permit the different products of objectness to be reconducted to the modes of givenness that alone give them appearing and meaning (*Sinngebung*)? Didn't the phenomenological reduction aim essentially to reconduct the present to the given and the given to its mode of givenness, therefore to unfold it according to givenness? Wouldn't masking or missing the fold of givenness be equivalent to barring access to the very text of Husserl? How to explain the fact that givenness thus risks often finding itself so gravely misunderstood? This is a question of neither a deficiency nor a blindness, but certainly of a conceptual decision, obstinate because often barely conscious—that of avoiding, of enervating, of folding up the fold of givenness. For what reason? For none other than the very difficulty of what I am calling the fold of givenness: such a fold of givenness articulates a process (givenness) with a given; even if the given must by definition give a sense of its donative process and, possibly, what gives it, it can never give them as it gives itself: namely, as a given that is directly visible and present, accessible, indeed available in person. The paradox of givenness stems from this asymmetry of the fold: the given, issued from the process of givenness, appears but leaves concealed givenness itself, which becomes enigmatic. But if it were only a question of seeing already visible phenomena, we would have no need for phenomenology. By contrast, phenomenology earns its legitimacy by finally making visible phenomena that, without it, would remain inaccessible—among which, evidently, the nonevidence of givenness would occupy the front of the line, opening as it does only with the unfolding of the given.

The Phenomenon Gives Itself

In this way, the presumed ambiguity of givenness, the French *donation* (and the German *Gegebenheit*), announces nothing other than its concept—the fold of the given as givenness. It belongs to the phenomenon considered in its essential phenomenality to manifest itself only as given: namely, as keeping the trace, more or less accentuated in each case, of its process of arising into appearing, in short of its givenness. I can therefore legitimately posit that *the phenomenon gives itself*. This formula is important in several ways. (a) It and it alone does justice to the original definition of the phenomenon proposed by Husserl: "The word *phenomenon* is ambiguous in virtue of the essential correlation between appearing [*Erscheinen*] and that which appears [*Erscheinenden*]," a correlation that opens onto "two absolute givennesses [*absolute Gegebenheiten*], the givenness of the appearing and the givenness of the object."[122] There, where givenness as given (appearing) is one with givenness as the arising of what gives itself, it is indeed a matter of the *fold* of givenness. (b) The phenomenon can appear as such, and not as the appearance of something else more essential to it than itself, in short it can appear without the lack implied by an in-itself or the withdrawal implied by a noumenon—and this is indeed the primary goal of phenomenology—only if it pierces through the mirror of representation. Appearing must thus remove itself from (if not always contradict) the imperial rule of the a priori conditions of knowledge by requiring that what appears force its entry onto the scene of the world, advancing in person without a stuntman, double, or any other representative standing in for it. This advance is named, from the point of view of the one who knows, intentionality; from the point of view of the thing-itself, it is called givenness. It can no longer be spoken of in terms of ordinary representation and appearing. In the strict phenomenological sense, the phenomenon is no longer (or not only) visible; it breaks through the frame, is abandoned to the world of which it now makes up a part. It comes forward insofar as it gives itself. Whence this result, which confirms the original formulation: nothing appears in person that does not *give itself*. (c) Reciprocally, it belongs essentially to what gives itself to show itself. That is, if one admits that giving [itself] implies giving to..., and that in phenomenology it is also a matter of giving to be seen by..., how could givenness give a given without making it visible to..., therefore without addressing itself to some instance like a "consciousness"? The arising of the given makes it visible because the movement of appearing ends by bursting on the depthless surface of consciousness like the impact of the gift, which precipitates and bursts there. This projection of the gift onto the conscious screen is enough to provoke appearing. The given is exposed because it explodes. To give itself therefore is equivalent to showing itself. What gives itself *shows itself*. (d) The statement that the phenomenon gives itself echoes Heidegger's classic formulation defining the phenomenon as "what shows itself, *das Sichzeigende.*" What is problematic here resides not in his insistence on the pure and radical phenomenality of the phenomenon (henceforth admitted), but in the discreet lack of precision in the "self" being invoked. What precisely does it mean "to let that which shows itself be seen from itself in the very way in which it shows itself from itself?"[123] This ipseity has nothing in common with that of Dasein, seeing as it counts, officially, for all phenomena, nor is it secured on the basis of these phenomena's modes of

Being, here perfectly undetermined; and it is not self-evident that the privileged investigation into the meaning of the Being of beings would permit us to reach to the "self" of their appearing. Let me suggest that the phenomenality of givenness lets us detect the "self" of the phenomenon, a theme Heidegger uses throughout his work without thinking it. Such a "self" consists in the gap that distinguishes and connects the arising (givenness) to its given. What rises into appearing does so under the pressure of givenness and laden with this move. The appearing of the phenomenon is not imposed in reality because it already has the rank of object or being; rather, it holds these (or other) ranks because its appearing comes forward beneath the authority of a givenness that pulsates and posits in it. To show oneself by oneself demands a "self." It comes only from the givenness that operates the given and that tinges it with a phenomenological mark, the very arising toward visibility. The phenomenon can and must show *itself,* but solely because it gives *itself.*

Showing itself therefore amounts to giving itself. The fold of givenness, in unfolding itself, shows the given that givenness dispenses. For the phenomenon, showing itself is equal to unfolding the fold of givenness in which it arises as a gift. Showing itself and giving itself play in the same field—the fold of givenness, which is unfolded in the given. What remains is to verify in the details of the phenomenon how its phenomenological primacy is carried out.

Book II

THE GIFT

§7 TWO OBJECTIONS

A Revival of Transcendence?

I have granted givenness the right it exercises over the given, or at least I hope to have done so. For it is clear that even if one admits the given as a simple fact without ground or presupposition, one is still much less accepting of the claim that it is articulated in terms of givenness. Avoiding or at the least mitigating the fold of givenness still remains the most common, though most often implicit, conceptual option. Any phenomenology of givenness is likely to face a refusal that is based not on a principle but on a suspicion; it can be tolerated that the phenomenon amounts to a given, but not that this given should refer to givenness, however one defines it. For with givenness, the natural attitude—and it is in fact a question only of the natural attitude —fears the revival of transcendence in its most resolutely metaphysical, if not to say theological, sense. My project therefore cannot shy away from this rebuttal, for even though it is sometimes quite ideological, the rebuttal does proffer a real objection: is the relation of the given to givenness that of cause and effect or principle and consequence? If either were the case, how would the given phenomenon not regress to the dishonorable rank of a mere product? Can the fold of givenness be understood as a phenomenon, or does it boil down to a metaphysical mechanism disqualifiable as such? For the question can be summed up in this simple line of investigation: does the given really demand recourse to givenness in order to appear as such?

The first objection is announced within a theological horizon precisely because it claims to refuse all theological authority. It is based on two suspicions. (a) First of all, givenness would belong within an empty schema because there would be only a very "watered down experience of it," one that would be "attenuated, to the point of annihilating itself," to the point where it becomes a "phenomenology more and more negative."[1] Either givenness has an affinity for the givens that it arranges—and then there is nothing abstract about it, since it gives all that is and appears; or it is envisaged as the pure process of phenomenality itself—and its necessary abstraction responds to that of the reduction or of any first philosophical truth. (b) Inversely, it would fall within a framework that is overburdened with meaning owing to an indiscreet debt to theology, or perhaps only to a "theology that has been made possible (at once prepared and held in reserve)."[2] What is shocking about these approximations is obviously that the criticism ignores the fact that the notion of givenness has no need, since Husserl, of a theological passport to intervene in phenomenology. It is at play there from the outset—officially, permanently, and as if it were at home. But why then attempt to disqualify it by assigning it a theological origin (supposing, of course, that theology implies of itself a disqualification)? Because to contest it on phenomenological grounds alone would prove too delicate, indeed impossible. Whence the effort to assign givenness a pre-phenomenological status by referring it to theology, so as to then interpret it in terms that are as metaphysical and un-Husserlian as imaginable, until one is deluded into believing that the question of givenness repeats the problematic of *metaphysica specialis* and merits this caution: "It should not be forgotten that the *epokhē* equally concerns the positions and propositions of *metaphysica specialis*—the nature of the soul, of the world, and of God."[3] Verdict: not only would givenness fall beneath the blow of the *epokhē*, like all transcendent statements, but it would also be counted among the privileged beings of *metaphysica specialis*—starting with and according to causality and effectivity. What should we keep from this argument?

Itself enacting the regression from phenomenology to metaphysics that it stigmatizes, the objection seems particularly open to contestation on at least three points. (a) Theology, in the sense of revealed theology (*sacra doctrina*), is in no way to be confused with *theologia rationalis*, which belongs to *metaphysica specialis* and arises solely from metaphysics. Rightfully, it should be opposed to it, as the Revelation of the Wisdom of the Word is opposed to the wisdom of the world. As for the claim to have established that givenness in phenomenology makes common cause with a concept of givenness in *re-*

vealed theology (if one indeed can be found there, something that remains to be proven), it should be concluded from this that such givenness would be all the *easier* to distinguish from metaphysics and its causality, as it comes from revealed theology and not philosophy. (b) If no phenomenologist ignores the fact that the reduction brackets transcendence, in all its senses—God too of course[4]—none will ignore the fact that the reduction not only does not suspend givenness but provokes it and makes it increase in direct proportion to the accomplishment of the reduction. There is nothing more absurd than to suppose that givenness can be opposed to the reduction—except to have forcibly assimilated it, as in the previous objection, to *metaphysica specialis.* (c) What remains of this argument without phenomenological validity is its major proposition: all givenness would fall within *metaphysica specialis.* In demonstrating too much, it no longer demonstrates anything, since it would follow that the first theologian of the turn of phenomenology would be Husserl himself (not to mention Heidegger), and that nothing less than the "principle of all principles" (and obviously the *Ereignis*) should be disqualified without even daring to go so far as my own formulation: "So much reduction, so much givenness." To arrive at so strange a result, it is enough to persist in conceiving givenness in phenomenology according to the model of *metaphysica specialis,* therefore in terms of the grounding of common beings on the basis of beings par excellence, therefore in terms of efficient causality. And, in fact, by *metaphysica specialis* is meant nothing other than a rationality that is "supported by any fundamental principle of the justification of the real."[5] This formula (which, for what it's worth, is not historically documented) has no other aim than to devalue givenness to the rank of a principle or a ground come from the world-behind-the-scenes for the purpose of "justifying" the "real" (the given). In this way, to give the given would be equivalent, still and always, to causing it as a mere effect. But who, in phenomenology, has ever held such a position, a position that is too crude to even remain metaphysical? In my own phenomenological work, at least, it has no intelligible meaning whatsoever. (i) First, because the given has no other justification besides its givenness, with or without intuition, besides its own arising, which is one with it. (ii) Next, because givenness is never defined as a principle or ground precisely because it delivers the given from any demand for a cause by letting it deliver itself, give itself. Giving (itself) falls to the given alone, because it falls to it to appear at its own initiative. (iii) Finally, the objection risks interpreting givenness as a "self-sufficiency" and a "self-grounding" on the pretext that pure givenness gives *itself.*[6] It assigns givenness the attributes of the *causa sui*, as if "to give *itself*" could only mean "to produce itself, to be sufficient to itself," in the mode of a cause directed against itself. One thus completely misses the notion that "giving *itself*" is here equal to "letting appear without reserve and in person," to "abandoning itself to sight," in short to the pure appearing of a phenomenon. This criticism, far from abolishing givenness as such, therefore makes its negative manifest in the caricature with which it masks it. It does not so much stigmatize givenness as it opposes to it, term for term, what it alone disqualifies: the *causa sui* and the principle of sufficient reason. This failure makes it all the more urgent that we open the question of givenness in itself, according to its own fold, without undue reference to efficient causality.

At this point, the objection topples. From an obstacle, it becomes an index. That is, if in the wake of meticulous translators (see Book 1, §6), a criticism so well-informed itself produces the misreading that it wants to denounce, this should be attributed not at all to polemics but to a real difficulty: can we use the term *givenness* in phenomenology and think its concept without immediately falling back into the metaphysical model of production, efficiency, and causality? In short, how are we to think givenness in such a way that it accomplishes the pure appearing of the phenomenon arising in person on the basis of nothing other than itself? This will become possible only by introducing a determination of givenness such that it determines all the primal phenomenological acts, and first of all the reduction. This new model of givenness will come from the gift. The first reason in favor of this choice stems, obviously, from the paronymy that joins gift and givenness. And, for that matter, it is surprising that few phenomenologists have tried to establish continuity between *Gegebenheit* and the phenomenon of the gift, so fascinating and inevitable for the analysis of intersubjectivity. Why not suppose that the gift—therefore exchange, the circulation of the given between giver and givee, return and response, loss and gain—can, once purified of its empirical blossoming, provide at least the outline of a noncausal, nonefficient, and finally nonmetaphysical model of givenness? Could one read the phenomenality of givenness according to the clue provided by the gift taken as privileged phenomenon?

Doesn't the Gift Itself Nullify Itself?

It is precisely this question that is addressed in a seminal work on the gift by Jacques Derrida, a work as invaluable on account of what it refuses me as for what it grants me—for the gift gives in many ways, and even when it gives nothing. Derrida begins by laying out the paronymic chain of the gift, according to the treatment its "system" has received from "all the anthropologies, indeed the metaphysics." From the metaphysical point of view—from which it is at once a matter of "departing in a peremptory and distinct fashion"[7]—givenness is articulated in terms of a giver, a gift given, and a givee, which are in principle connected by a reciprocal relation inso-far as gratuity on the part of the giver demands in principle, though tacitly, restitution on the part of the givee. This schema obviously can be traced back to Mauss's famous *Essay on the Gift*, where the gift, in the extreme ex-ample of the excess of potlatch ("total services of an agonistic type"), is still considered within "the system of gifts exchanged." This system implies not only that the giver give, but that he must; not only that the givee receive, but that he must: "The institution of 'total services' does not merely carry with it the obligation to reciprocate presents received. It also supplies two other obligations, just as important: the obligation, on the one hand, to give presents and, on the other, to receive them."[8] This system in fact re-mains thoroughly metaphysical: the giver gives the gift in the role of effi-cient cause, mobilizing a formal and a material cause (in order to define, reify the gift), and pursuing a final cause (the good of the givee and/or the glory of the giver). These four causes enable givenness to satisfy the princi-ple of sufficient reason. Reciprocity repeats this sufficient reason to the point of perfectly applying the principle of identity by bringing the gift back to itself. In this way, Leibniz could define charity in terms that depend on justice; the justness of justice is then erected into the truth of charity, which as such would lack wisdom: "Justice is a charity or habit of loving in conformity with wisdom."[9] One can also understand the apparently ex-treme or aberrant forms of givenness in relation to this model, which is never put in question by their excess. To think givenness would thus always be equivalent to thinking the system of exchange between terms, a system regulated by causality and the principles of metaphysics. *The Essay on the Gift* never treats the gift, only exchange and its system. And, Derrida clearly demonstrates, not only does this model contradict itself in each of its terms, but it voids the gift of all givenness, and its phenomenon vanishes.

First argument: "For there to be a gift there must be no reciprocity."[10] In Mauss's system, it is so blatantly clear that the gift does not contradict exchange that the very title of the *Essay* assimilates them—"*The Gift: The Form and Reason for Exchange in Archaic Societies*,"—as does the title of the introduction: "The Gift, and Especially the Obligation to Return It."[11] It should, however, be obvious that the gift—more exactly, givenness—disappears as soon as reciprocity transforms it into an exchange. To repay or return (a greeting, an invitation, a favor, money) already enters into an economy: the gift is followed by the countergift, the payment of a debt, reimbursement for what has been borrowed. As soon as economy gets hold of givenness, it economizes and givenness falls victim to downsizing. As soon as it is invested in givenness, economy substitutes calculation, interest, utility, indeed equity, etc. No moral considerations need interfere here in a case where it is a matter of making clear the difference between two types of phenomena: if there is givenness, it implies the suspension of exchange; it should therefore also break with the principles of sufficient reason and identity, no less than with the four forms of causality that economy, in its metaphysical regime, follows.

The second argument follows directly from this: "For there to be a gift, *it is necessary* [*il faut*] that the givee not repay, amortize, reimburse, acquit himself, enter into a contract, and that he never have contracted a debt."[12] This refusal to "repay" should not be understood merely as subjective ingratitude—ingratitude comes up only within an already constituted economy of exchange and reciprocity—but as lack of consciousness on the part of the givee, who neither sees nor knows that a gift has befallen him. The givee does not benefit from a gift—understood as pure gratuity—unless he does not immediately interpret it as a gift about to be returned, a debt to be repaid as soon as possible, or an ignominious bankruptcy to be annulled. Moreover, an authentic gift can in fact exceed all knowledge that the givee would have of it, therefore dismiss him from having to offer recognition for a gift that he does not know. In many cases, no doubt the most decisive ones, the gift remains unknown, as with a life given (and perhaps also a death), love (sometimes hatred). The givee does not know and does not have to know what gift befalls him, precisely because a gift can and must surpass every clear consciousness. The nonknowledge of the gift, that is to say, the lack of consideration of the givee in the description of givenness, fulfills at least two irreplaceable functions: it permits the givee to bear its excess—for even an unrecognized gift is still given, and it permits the gift to not depend on the givee, for a mistaken gift is still a gift given perfectly. Givenness therefore demands the bracketing of the givee.

The third argument can now make its appearance: "This forgetting [of the gift] must be radical not only on the part of the givee but first of all, if one can say here first of all, on the part of the giver." In short, the disappearance of the givee implies that of the giver. In effect, the mere consciousness of giving awakens a self-consciousness as giving, therefore "the gratifying image of goodness or generosity, of the giving being who knows itself to be such, recognizes itself in a circular, specular fashion, in a sort of auto-recognition, self-approval, and narcissistic gratitude."[13] Mauss also clearly highlights this trait—without, however, drawing from it the ineluctable consequence: "To give is to manifest one's superiority, to be more, to be higher, *magister*; to accept without repaying or without repaying more is to abase oneself, to become a client or servant, to become small, to drop down [*minister*]."[14] But the best illustration of the giver's narcissistic return to self comes from Descartes, whose *Passions of the Soul* demonstrated—in an absolutely positive sense—that generosity, as self-esteem proportionate to the good use of the self's free will, not only provokes the primary passion of "self-contentment," but repeats in the ethical order the self-certainty first attained by the *ego cogito* in the metaphysical order.[15] To consider oneself a giver, a fortiori a giver unrecognized by the givee, is enough to produce in return a self-consciousness, therefore to establish an economic exchange in self-immanence. In exchange for my unrecognized gift, I receive—from myself?—the certain consciousness of my generosity. In losing it, I give my gift to myself, or rather, I get myself in exchange for my lost gift. The loss becomes the gain par excellence—the best possible outcome, since I in fact win infinitely more than I lost: myself over and against a gift that is worth far less than me. Givenness would thus become thinkable only once liberated from the metaphysical hypothesis par excellence: the preeminence of the transcendental and constitutive *ego*, certain and solid ground—Descartes's *inconcussum quid*, which governs us through and through. As long as the *ego* remains, givenness remains inaccessible; it appears only once the *ego* giver is bracketed.

Finally, a fourth argument puts out of play the given gift itself. This paradox, though extreme, can be maintained if one reconsiders the motive behind the previous suspension of the giver and givee: "The subject and the object are arrested effects of the gift, arrests of the gift."[16] The economic interpretation of givenness as a system of exchange not only freezes giver and givee as parties to commerce, but also submits the exchanged gift to the gaze that they direct toward it, and this exchanging gaze fixes only on an object of exchange. The permanent visibility of the gift, reifying givenness in a subsisting objectness, therefore seals the system of exchange and excludes from it givenness as such. The consequence presents itself straightaway: "*At the very least, the gift as gift* ought *not appear as gift: either to the givee or to the giver.*"[17] It is its very entrance into visibility that objectifies the gift, adapts it to economic exchange, and in the end removes it from givenness. Givenness would therefore remain intact—would appear as givenness—only at the price of the disappearance or nonappearance of the gift given. Such a nonappearing of the gift in no way implies renouncing its phenomenality. First, because only if the gift appeared as an object —and most of the time it seizes appearing for its own advantage—would all phenomenality of givenness have to be renounced. Next, because the reason for such nonappearance is still phenomenological: if the gift becomes a phenomenon of economic exchange, it is frozen in presence in the most metaphysical sense: "If he recognizes it as *gift*, if the gift *appears to him as such*, if the present is present to him *as present*, this simple recognition suffices to annul the gift."[18] What prevents the gift from remaining in givenness and lowers it to the status of an object to be exchanged consists—and this word is appropriate—only in presence, taken as the permanent subsistence of beingness. If presence undoes the present (the gift in terms of givenness), then to reach the present, it would be necessary to remove it from presence. This perfect paradox permeates the fourth argument: "If the present is present to him *as present*, this simple recognition suffices to annul the gift."[19] This result is, strictly speaking, diverting: it makes us turn from the direct path toward givenness, veering from the one that claims to reach it according to the clues provided by the gift. For a twofold aporia closes this path: either the gift presents itself in presence, in which case it disappears from givenness in order to be inscribed in the economic system of exchange, or else the gift does not present itself, but then it no longer appears at all, thereby again closing off all phenomenality of givenness. If it appears in the present, the gift erases givenness by economy; if it does not appear, it closes any and all phenomenality to givenness.

The Gift Closes off Givenness

The two objections that bring us to a standstill can be joined together to designate a single obstacle. The fold of the given with givenness cannot be read on the basis of the gift because the latter does not visibly bear the mark of givenness, but lets it escape and disappear entirely, like water on the sand. Its interpretation does not demand (and does not produce) anything other than two perfectly classical metaphysical concepts: either the gift amounts to the effect of an efficient cause (Janicaud), or else it must disappear pure and simple so as to avoid being frozen in present objectness (Derrida). This dilemma can be narrowed down even more strictly: either the gift is effected and is at once abolished in an object shorn of all givenness, or else it refuses this neutral presence but must disappear. In both cases, the gift does not shed any light on the fold of givenness—worse yet, it serves as an argument against the possibility of ever reaching it. The aporia of the gift engulfs givenness.

§8 THE REDUCTION OF THE GIFT TO GIVENNESS

The Present Without Presence

This is not, however, the obligatory result of such a line of argument. Another reading of the dilemma is still possible. Does the incompatibility between, on the one hand, the gift thought in terms of givenness and, on the other, presence thought in terms of subsistence mean that the gift can neither be thought nor appear, or does it mean that it can do so only by making an exception to the horizon of presence and therefore of appearing? There's no doubt that if appearing always implies being fixed in subsistence, the gift, as soon as it has appeared in its presence, disappears as given, since the given according to givenness is precisely not installed in permanence—gift given as lost and never repaid on the part of the giver, given as never possessed and only conceded by the givee. But in thus disappearing as permanently present, the gift is not lost as given; it loses only the way of being—subsistence, exchange, economy—that contradicts its possibility of giving itself as such. In losing presence, the gift does not lose *itself*; it loses what is not suited to it: returning *to itself*. Or rather, it does indeed *lose* itself, but in the sense that it disentangles itself from itself, abandons itself outside itself—outside of the *self*—in order to be enacted as the loss of self, but not as pure loss. Put yet another way, as pure loss, but as a pure loss that, to give itself, must disappear, one that therefore appears at the price of the pure disappearance of all subsistence in it. This reversal can be said otherwise: if the gift is not present, if it therefore never appears in presence, one can no doubt conclude that it is not; but one can also infer that it neither has to be nor has to subsist in presence in order to give itself. Better, the gift is given strictly to the degree that it renounces Being, that it makes an exception to presence, that it undoes itself from itself by undoing subsistence in presence. The initial paradox—the present (the gift) can be present in presence—is now transformed into another: the present (the gift) is given without presence. The impasse becomes a breakthrough. If one paradox hides another, it owes this to the ambiguity of another name for the gift: the present. For, to present a present is not always, by definition, and in fact hardly ever is, equivalent to producing a presence. The *parousia* certainly governs *presence*, but it does not always control the *present*. The present does not owe everything to presence, and could quite possibly owe it nothing at all. The question of givenness is not closed when presence contradicts the gift; it is, in contrast, opened to the possibility of the present without presence—outside Being.

The fruitfulness of Derrida's analysis is therefore to be measured not only by its intended result, but by the counterinterpretation it can support. With rigor, it ends up at a formulation that will serve as a paradigm for me: "Let us go to the limit: The truth of the gift . . . suffices to annul the gift. The truth of the gift is equivalent to the non-gift or to the non-truth of the gift."[20] How is this knot of negations to be understood?[21] The point is to note a contradiction: the truth is equivalent to the gift but contradicts it as well. That it should contradict the gift is no longer surprising once it is admitted that its being, brought to light in subsisting presence, abolishes the gift. What is more surprising is the possibility that the truth might be suitable to the gift. The most elegant solution would demand distinguishing two senses of the gift—one equivalent, the other contrary to the truth; and Derrida does indeed suggest that the gift doubles itself (or that it can): "There would be, *on the one hand,* the gift that gives something determinate (a given, a present in whatever form it may be, personal or im-personal thing, 'natural' or symbolic thing, thing or sign, nondiscursive or discursive sign, and so forth) and, *on the other hand,* the gift that gives not a given but the *condition* of a present given in general, that gives therefore the element of the given in general." The first sense corresponds exactly to the gift that is annulled by its presence in the economic system of exchange. The second remains: it introduces nothing less than the gift raised to a higher power, on the hither side of (or rather beyond) the gift given, one that gives nothing (no thing), except irreally: "The *condition* of any given in general."[22] It would be carried out par excellence in the cases of "giving time," "giving life," "giving death," etc. Nevertheless, this decisive advance toward new phenomena of givenness could not, in its current state, be enough for my project. First, because it attributes to the new gift the giving of a "condition," that is to say, a typically metaphysical function, that of the ground.[23]

Next, because this modification of the gift (from the "given" to the "condi-tion of the given") is not enough to go back from the gift given to givenness as such (to its fold), nor to liberate givenness from the economic model of exchange. Finally, because duplicating a concept rarely indicates that one has probed its depths, but most often that one is simply juxtaposing the terms of a contradiction.

Economy Economizes on Givenness

At the very least, these two senses let us glimpse a frontier that, when crossed, would open onto a radically other determination of the gift. For if the gift as pure present disappears as soon as it enters into presence, and if presence defines the way of Being of (metaphysical) self-subsistence, then it must be concluded that the gift, if it is ever to be thought as such, must occur outside of presence and outside of self-subsistence. If the truth, in the sense of clear vision into presence, suffices to annul the gift, then the gift will happen only by dispensing with *this* truth. If the subsistence of the gift suffices to annul it in exchange, then the gift will occur only by being delivered from *this* subsistence. If the present as presence suffices to annul the gift, then the gift is accomplished only by being liberated from *this* presence. But, it will be objected, can the gift meet this obligation, or is it just an empty injunction? What can be done if the "conditions of the pos-sibility of the gift . . . designate simultaneously the conditions of impossi-bility of the gift."[24] To address this, it is enough to point out that it already contains its own refutation: to be sure, it establishes the conditions under which what one names a *gift* becomes impossible, but in no way does it es-tablish that what thus becomes impossible still deserves the name *gift*. In identifying the possibility of the gift with its impossibility, this contradic-tion states the essence of nothing at all, therefore not that of any gift what-soever. My response, therefore, is that the conditions of impossibility (or possibility) simply prove that what was studied did *not* deserve the title *gift* and that, if there ever were to be a gift, it would necessarily have other con-ditions of possibility than those of its impossibility. This means positively: the gift can never again be envisaged within the system of exchange, the reciprocity of which connects giver and givee and freezes it in presence. In this so-called economy of the gift, it is literally givenness on which one economizes by totally transforming its gift into a subsisting being present in permanence, endowed with value (use and/or exchange) and finality (utility, prestige, etc.), produced or destroyed by efficiency and calculation, caught in the grips of its causes—in short, into a common being. Such a common being can never appear as a gift, not because the concept of the gift would be contradictory but because this being in no way falls within the phenomenality of the gift. An essay on the gift that believes it can avail itself of an already acquired and self-evident concept of the gift so as to then describe the properties of the gift never reaches anything but a common being—subsisting, in no way given.[25] What's missing from it? A renunciation of the economic horizon of exchange for the sake of interpreting the gift in terms of the horizon of givenness itself. What remains is to describe givenness no longer according to that which it challenges, but as such—if such an *as such* is still suited to it.

Before going further, let me remark on just one point. The two models that it is a question of overcoming, the causal interpretation of givenness and the economic interpretation of the gift, in fact boil down to just one—the standard model. Within its framework, the parties to givenness—the giver and the givee, in the singular or in the plural—who traffic with one another in exchange find themselves already interpreted as causes according to the metaphysical understanding of this concept. The giver produces, like an efficient cause, the gift, which is itself effected and effective; the givee receives the gift as its final cause; finally, the gift as given product calls for a formal cause and a material cause in order to be internally consistent. Since efficiency is dominant among causes, it will also dominate the entire causality of exchange: gratuity, for example, will appear only as a deficiency in efficiency and as an exception to just reciprocity; it matters little whether one praises its disinterestedness or blames it for a shortcoming over which one must triumph. In short, givenness is confined to the region of the efficiency of common beings. But at the same time the economy of efficiency also confirms the gift in its objective status: in order to be exchanged and esteemed, the gift must circulate, all the while remaining equal. It must therefore acquire the consistency of objectness, therefore also its visibility, its permanence, and its availability—in short, the presence that renders it accessible to all the potential partners of economic exchange. Only what does not pass away passes from hand to hand—money, imperishable stone, and earth. Henceforth, having become equally accessible to all those who will put a price on it, the gift becomes indifferent to the terms of its givenness. Stripped of its own secret by its objectness, it condemns the possible secret of the partners who put it in play. Possessed, the gift possesses the actors of the economy—thus, economy leads the present of the gift back to metaphysical presence, while causality confers on exchange the ground for the metaphysical equality between effect and cause.

The standard model of the gift in fact eliminates the gift—at least the gift as complete loss, such that it would imply a break of the circle and a suspension of the gift's return, of the gift in return. If the truth of the gift resides in the payback, the truth lowers it to the status of a loan. Placed in commerce, the gift is already stripped of its poverty; it has exchanged its gratuity for a price. In short, having disappeared as such, it no longer offers any path toward givenness. Thinking the gift in the direction of and on the basis of givenness will require no longer assigning exchange and return as its truth—in short, it will require that its former definition be considered seriously: "Donum proprie est datio irredibilis . . . id est quod non datur intentione retributionis."[26] The gift is not equal to barter, endowment, transfer in general—because it adds a loss, a subtraction. It gives (itself) without a return on the investment, without awards received in return. The gift appears when it begins to be lost, and it is lost so long as it continues to be recovered. Gratuity does not suffice to define it: first, because it still has parallels to venality (transfer of property, paid for or not), therefore also because it deploys itself within exchange (gratuity for some, not for others). This again provides only a clue to an otherwise radical determination—giving itself without interest, therefore without motive, on the basis of itself and by itself. The gift arises from itself without being inscribed in the economic circle where exchange would in advance orient it, prompt it, and consume it. The singular appearing of the gift must therefore be described such as it shows itself of itself insofar as it gives (itself).

The Triple Epokhē

Where can it be found if it is never retrieved anywhere? How to reach it? If economy always economizes on the gift, if cause merely causes givenness to disappear, the gift will appear in itself only by undoing itself from economy, and givenness only by liberating itself from causality. We must therefore cease and desist from any and all interpretation of givenness that proceeds according to the clues laid out by the gift considered within exchange, seeing as the gift itself obeys, in the natural attitude, determinations that contradict givenness. Inversely, it seems wise to think the gift with a view toward givenness, for the sake of emancipating the latter from its causal determination. But how to reduce the gift to givenness and givenness to itself without falling either into tautology (isn't the gift equivalent to givenness?) or contradiction (doesn't givenness necessarily imply some transcendence from one term to another?)? But this very question points the way toward the solution: if there must be a reduction, this can only happen, even in the case of the gift and givenness, in the way that the reduction is always enacted in phenomenology—by the bracketing of transcendencies, whatever they might be. Reducing the gift to givenness and givenness to itself then means: thinking the gift as gift while abstracting from all transcendence, whatever it might be. Reducing the gift to givenness and givenness to itself therefore means: thinking the gift while abstracting from the threefold transcendence that affected it heretofore—by the successive bracketing of the transcendence of the givee, the transcendence of the giver, and finally the transcendence of the object exchanged. If the *epokhē* succeeds in treating the gift, it will be enacted by liberating the gift from the terms of exchange and from objective status, both transcendent. Thus it will reconduct the gift to givenness pure and simple, at least if such givenness can occur.

In such an operation, the reduction of the gift to givenness and of givenness to itself would be accomplished not *despite* the threefold objection made by Derrida, but indeed *thanks to it*. In effect, the so-called "conditions for the impossibility of the gift" (no givee, no giver, no given object) would become precisely the conditions for the possibility of its reduction to and for pure givenness by a triple *epokhē* of the transcendent conditions of economic exchange. The objection itself would open onto the response: the gift is reduced to givenness and givenness to itself once the givee, the giver, and the objectivity of the gift are bracketed, thereby detaching the gift from economy and manifesting it according to givenness purified of all cause. Reducing the gift to itself, that is to say, to givenness, and givenness to itself implies no longer thinking the gift within an exchange where, as a present object, it would pass indifferently between the giver and the givee, but as a pure given. Can such a reduction actually be accomplished? Can one think the gift as gift without necessarily inscribing it in terms of exchange? Once liberated from its transcendent conditions, is givenness still identifiable; doesn't it vanish in a cloud of smoke, the last breath of a fading concept, of an excessive paradox, of an all-too-pure experience? But must I say again that paradox and abstraction are at least as characteristic of the normal state of philosophical evidence as is the ease of common sense?

To respond, I will try and sketch this threefold *epokhē*. When a gift is given, therefore when givenness is accomplished, what in fact is given to me? In other words, in order to speak of a gift, what lived experiences (*Erlebnissen*) are required? It is of course necessary to make a distinction between the lived experiences of the gift affecting a consciousness playing the role of giver and those affecting a consciousness playing the role of givee. It must also be admitted that the bracketing of the two extremes poses a difficulty far removed from that raised by the bracketing of the gift given. The given object, if it happens to be reduced, would indeed be reduced— but for which consciousness? Obviously for either that of the giver or that of the givee, for they alone can accomplish a reduction and receive a phenomenological given since they alone take on the function of a "consciousness." Consequently, even if one and the other could in fact fall simultaneously beneath the blow of the reduction, this reduction would demand —for it to be accomplished—that at least one of the two make an exception to the reduction in the role of its quasi "consciousness." In short, even if the giver and the givee could, de facto, be reduced simultaneously, the reduction would demand, de jure, that one of the two (in alternation and without definitive privilege) remain in the position of the transcendental I. Consequently, the given object could find itself reduced in relation to both "consciousnesses" (givee, giver), but neither of them could be reduced without the other securing for it the function of transcendental I. Between the gift, on the one hand, and the giver and the givee, on the other, there results an inevitable imbalance—but perhaps also a movement.[27] The status of what assumes, in an alternating fashion, the role of "consciousness" will be treated more explicitly later.

§9 THE BRACKETING OF THE GIVEE

The Anonymous

It is a question of bracketing the givee. Can we do so without also suspending the entire process of the gift? Certainly. Not only does the bracketing of the givee not invalidate the givenness of the gift, but it characterizes it intrinsically: without this suspension of the givee, the very possibility of *giving* the gift would become problematic.

The gift does not tolerate, it requires, the bracketing of the givee; it would disappear purely and simply if the givee remained always visible, accessible, present. That is, if the givee preceded the gift—in expectation of receiving it, or even by asking for it—and if it subsisted after it, appropriating it and enjoying it, the gift would suffer a double disqualification. (i) The givee could claim to be not only one of its actors but one of its causes: the efficient cause, by possibly having prompted it through supplication, indeed threats; the final cause, too, by having justly deserved it through its misery or its deeds. In both cases, the gift would have excellent motives underlying it. What would be so surprising in this case, seeing as it had, in its receiver, so potent a cause? The gift would be summed up as a simple effect, once again absorbed in a common metaphysical schema. (ii) There is more: if the givee remains after the accomplishment of the gift, always there in front of its benefactor, how are we to avoid the fact that, however gratuitous this gift in principle might have been, it becomes almost impossible not to repay it? Even mere recognition can function as a price to be paid in return, sometimes a burden more difficult to discharge than its weight in gold. Consequently, the gift would immediately regress to the status, however honorable, of an exchange, where reciprocity (real or wished-for) would reestablish pure commerce. The receiver of the gift, if he remains visible and accessible, can therefore disqualify all its givenness; his mere presence makes it possible to appoint him as cause and to inscribe the gift within an economy. No doubt it is just a possibility, but this—even without an actual demand for repayment—is enough to set a price, an intention, an exchange value for the so-called gift. In the gaze of the givee, humiliated or moved, the giver sees his gift disappear in a mere investment with interest, a payment in arrears; he wins recognition—but of a debt. The giver is paid with the indebted recognition of the givee. The gift never took place.

On the other hand, it takes place when what could be called a law of *non*return liberates the gift initially given from all repercussions, redirection, retribution, repartee, etc. The gift, to be given, must be lost and remain lost without return. In this way alone does it break with exchange, where one gives only to have it repaid (with a marginal profit). It is not simply a matter of gratuity—gratuity does not exclude exchange or reciprocity; it can merely accomplish these without financial mediation, and as a result, one can rightly imagine economies of gratuity. Beyond gratuity, it is a question of the pure and simple loss involved in giving with abandon. This should not be confused with spending wildly, which can do nothing more than serve the interests of the spender. Hence the paradox: the gift must be lost for me, but not for everybody. It's necessary that an Other[28] receive it and definitively deprive me of it. It's also necessary that this other not pay me back, not only that he not want to (psychologically) but that he cannot (on principle) thus reinscribe the gift, me, and himself in economic exchange. Paradox therefore: the gift demands a givee who does indeed receive it, but without being able to repay it. This situation belongs to the essence of givenness: one must always give at least *as if* the givee never had to repay, simply did not intervene, except in the instant of the givenness that puts him in play, except to swallow the gift and thus to validate (consecrate) it as a gift given. In short, it becomes possible for the gift to be given only on the formal condition of bracketing the givee. But doesn't this phenomenological situation, already quite complex in itself, quickly show itself even less likely to be put into practice as it concerns, precisely, a practice? Can we seriously imagine a gift given to someone such that he could, on principle, never repay it? Wouldn't this exercise demand a lack of consciousness or a devotion that would in fact disqualify the practice of the gift?

The case is quite the opposite, and the bracketing of the givee in fact allows not only for the gift to be seen, but for it to be seen that we practice it. The first figure of the gift given to a reduced givee is found in the most basic, because most spectacular, form of altruism: the campaign to raise money for a humanitarian cause, for what the *media* regularly propose to the generous emotions of the public, consenting or not—in short, *solidarity* with your fellow man. In this case, there is indeed a givee who receives: the charitable or, according to lay terminology, "humanitarian," organization. This real givee receives without return, but most often I, as giver, do not know the exact amount of the sum finally collected, nor what it is used for, not its result; it is, for me, bracketed. To be sure, an imaginary givee will be added: a face, deeply troubled and deeply troubling, but carefully chosen for its seductiveness, that of someone gravely ill, starving to death, or leprous, etc. This givee will never repay anything: first because he perhaps does not exist (the photograph chosen does not belong to the real population at issue) or does not exist any longer (he will die before the end of the campaign); next because our geographic and cultural separation, my being quick to forget, and his complete ignorance of me and the other givers prevent him from doing so. He is therefore, for me, bracketed. In fact, even the real givee—the organization, the United Way—remains obscure, like every anonymous society—which is, as a result, all the more obliged to have recourse to borrowed faces, which are familiar and sometimes real (moral authorities, televised silhouettes, etc.), since these faces confer upon it the face that they themselves cannot have. The givee is thus actually bracketed: strictly speaking, I do not know to whom I give, though I do know who takes possession of what I give.[29] This is an example of a spontaneous and trivial situation where the transcendence of the givee is reduced. However, it cannot be denied that "the gifts pour forth from everywhere," that these campaigns succeed even (or especially) in unfavorable economic periods. It cannot be denied either that these gifts essentially remain gifts, withdrawn from economic exchange, at least from the point of view of their givers. If they can be reinterpreted economically, that happens only later, with their being made to operate on the earth, where markets, costs, interests, and politics naturally come first; but for the giver, during the time of the gift (the collection campaign), it's not about expecting a return or an exchange; it's about a gift given with abandon. The paradox of bracketing the givee here finds its first validation—neither rare nor lofty, but ordinary, even trivial. With this validation, one essential consequence also appears: the gift can be given—here out of concern for efficacy—*without regard for the face of the Other*; and if one admits that ethics is governed by the silent injunction of the face of the Other, by definition transcendent because Other, then it must be concluded that the gift does not fall strictly within ethics. Phenomenologically, the problematic of the fold of givenness unfurls in terms of the gift showing itself insofar as giving itself, without yet having to take into account the more complex and therefore derivative question of the ethics revealed in the face. The givenness of the gift does not depend on ethics, but inversely, ethics no doubt supposes the givenness of the gift.

The Enemy

This first validation is not enough, however. It can be objected that the givee still has the power potentially, if not actually, to repay the gift. According to the evidence, this possibility remains open. Consequently, I must advance a second confirmation, in which return is, on principle, excluded even though the gift was given without return, and accordingly, the givee is found to be reduced absolutely. This givee incapable of reciprocity is named *the enemy*. This incapacity does not belong to him by accident, but rather defines him: to act as an enemy means never to repay the gift, to repay the gift only by striking back. But how to give to the enemy, seeing as not only does he not repay, but he does not accept (and does not accept obligation)? Here is where the injunction to love thine enemies intervenes. It can seem at first glance quite plainly impossible to put into practice,[30] a mere pedagogical means to suggest the logic of "love thy neighbor"; and yet love for a neighbor, even a lovable, indeed a loving one, already sets a task so difficult—well beyond mere reciprocal sociality—that the love of one's enemies seems well-nigh impossible. Nevertheless, for a phenomenology of the gift, it is not. If one restricts the sense of *to love* to "to give" in a privileged sense, this gift conforms to itself (therefore to givenness) only insofar as it does not give way to exchange, where reciprocity would annul gratuity. The gift demands, in order to give *itself*—therefore to let it make its own decision about itself—giving without return or response. The givee must not be able to repay, or at least the hope that he can or should must not intervene when the gift gives *itself*. Such a givee, identifiable as the receiver of a gift who is absolutely incapable of repaying it, is named the *enemy*: he who does not love in return and therefore allows for loving gratuitously, in pure loss and with abandon. To give to your enemy is to give in vain, for nothing, without reason; it is therefore to give pure and simple, in the raw—but it is precisely then that the gift is given without confusion or any strings attached. It is *given* and not exchanged, seeing as it loses *itself*. If the gift does not die, it is not given absolutely, therefore is not manifest as such. The gift owes its loss to the enemy. Only the enemy makes the gift possible; he makes the gift evident by denying it reciprocity—in contrast to the friend, who involuntarily lowers the gift to the level of a loan with interest. The enemy thus becomes the ally of the gift, and the friend its adversary. The enemy alone, who is the figure for the givee in the realm of the reduction, the denegating givee, receives the gift without repaying it—but by the same token, admits it as such, a gift according to givenness, without any commerce.[31] This psychological paradox answers a phenomenological necessity: the reduction of the gift demands bracketing the givee and reduces his transcendence to my lived experience of an enemy.

The Ingrate

No doubt it will again be objected: this bracketing of the givee, itself required by the reduction of the gift, in fact renders the gift impossible; for if the givee (the enemy) does not repay the gift, he does so not in order to preserve it from exchange but because he denies it as gift—by refusing it, either through contempt and disgust or through violent possession. But does a gift denied, not accepted or not recognized, still remain a gift in the full sense of the word? In short, doesn't the enemy, in the very moment when he makes the gift manifest, disqualify it?

To answer this objection, what must be done is to establish that a gift refused still remains a gift in the full sense of the word,[32] therefore that the bracketing of the givee is not only necessary (as we just saw) but also possible. Let us suppose a gift refused (seen, but rejected or taken by force) or even purely ignored (not even noticed, forgotten, silenced)—what remains of it? What remains is the gift, inasmuch as now given without return, without even the slightest chance of a countergift. Henceforth, the gift, lost between its two poles, remains in a state of abandon, with or without its objective support. It was abandoned by its giver, then by its (non)givee, but in this abandon, it remains clear that the gift was well and truly given, and given in a complete loss, since in fact it is rediscovered as lost. It is rediscovered lost—no paradox here, for literally it is rediscovered insofar as it is discovered (as) lost. In this abandon it appears incontestably as an accomplished gift; there remains only this: this gift accomplishes *itself* unrepentantly, since it persists in giving itself even without recognition or reception. That a gift once given is rediscovered abandoned does not abolish its givenness, but to the contrary, confirms it—no reciprocity, not even that of a confession, will disturb its clear distress. Moreover, the abandon to which the gift submits also indicates that it surpasses not only all return, but above all any acceptance cut to its measure: having to bear its arrival and its grandeur is enough to discourage even the best-intentioned givees. The givee is absent not by anonymity or by hatred or ignorance, but because, weighing the burden of the gift, he flees it, overwhelmed. There is no dearth of cases where this excess makes it nearly impossible not only to accept it, but even to recognize it, indeed just to admit it. As a result, in the situation of the abandoned gift, the bracketing of the givee is enacted in a third figure: the figure of his absence—*the ingrate*. No longer as he who would repay the gift at the risk of lowering it to the level of exchange (humanitarianism) nor as he who would deny it (the enemy) but simply as he who does not bear it, does not want to and in any case cannot repay it (the ingrate). The ingrate is defined first not by a negative will or his impotence to repay good with good, but by his incapacity, impatience, and exasperation simply in receiving it. He refuses the charge not only of acquitting himself of this debt (which would remain within exchange), but of ever having incurred one—of ever having been offered a gift. He suffers from the very principle that a gift affects him by befalling him. He does not refuse this or that gift with or without this or that objective support; he refuses indebtedness pure and simple—or rather the admission of it. In a stubborn struggle against the evidence of the gift already given and without his consent, the ingrate has the pretense to maintain that his consent alone decides the gifts given to him. He sticks strictly to the base principle that "I don't owe anything to anyone," but this baseness applies, without assessing its significance, the metaphysical principle of self-identity, which is simply shaped to fit the case of the gift reduced to givenness. The ingrate misses the gift because he does not want to admit the upsurge by which this gift itself decides on its own to lose itself without return and, consequently, to break self-identity. But at the same time, the ingrate manifests, *a contrario* and in all its purity, the gift reduced to givenness, since he proves that this gift is perfectly accomplished without the givee's consent. The ingrate lays bare the pure immanence of the gift. He is a figure of the reduced givee, absolutely governed by the pure givenness of the gift.

The Eschatological and the Universal

These three bracketings achieve the same end—reducing a transcendence of the givee—though they rest on three irreconcilable postures of this givee: anonymity, hostility, ingratitude. But this incompatibility arises only from a strictly psychological description of the givee by an empirical consciousness (in this case that of the giver). It in no way belongs to the phenomenological operation of reducing the givee to his or their lived experiences in transcendental consciousness. If the proliferation of figures of the givee does not weaken the one and only reduction—and this is indeed the case—it must be concluded that their psychological incoherence has not influenced the transcendental status of the pure reduction, in short, that the separation of phenomenology and psychology has been respected.

It remains the case, however, that these three postures of the givee offer the strange peculiarity that they privilege only absent receivers or those who deny the gift, therefore that they reduce only gifts that have not been received or accepted (it is not a matter of repaying). Is it possible to carry out the bracketing of the givee only in cases of gifts aborted by absent givees or destroyers—as if to make the gift manifest it was necessary to suspend its ontic accomplishment? It would be a strange illustration of givenness that would impose its erasure! Whether this bracketing can also be accomplished in the case of a givee who truly receives the gift is a question that therefore must now be examined. There is no cause to doubt that a positive response can be furnished. I will set it out in two examples. (a) The first comes from the phenomenological interpretation of an eschatological parable. When Christ—as he himself teaches—returns at the end of time, he will separate the just from the wicked according to the gifts they will have made or not made on this earth—therefore by himself assuming the position of the universal givee. But the elect as well as the reprobate will be surprised never to have seen, encountered, or identified as starving, thirsty, with neither hearth nor home, naked, sick, and enslaved the givee that they will or will not have fed, given to drink, sheltered, clothed, cared for, and visited. Among the potential givers, no one will ever have seen the givee—here, Christ: "Then they will answer him: 'Lord, when did we see you?'"[33] They will have given (or not) without even seeing the givee par excellence. This invisibility marks, once again and indisputably, a bracketing of the givee—as in the three previous figures; but this time, the givee does not refuse the gift. Quite the contrary, since he judges the giver according to this gift (or lack thereof). Simply put, the givee accepts, receives, but slips away, disappears likes a thief—done deal, gift received. In short, interpreted phenomenologically, the givee in the parable brackets himself, really and in advance. From this situation—gift accepted, givee unknown—what results? Far from blocking the gift or weakening it, invisibility reinforces the givee by universalizing him: every man could have been and can still become the face of the givee precisely because the latter knew how to make himself invisible—"In truth, I say to you as you did to the least of my brethren, so will you have done to me."[34] It is beneficial to us that he depart, for the impossibility of empirically identifying the givee par excellence, Christ, allows his role to proliferate: the absent but still to come givee opens the universal place of his own face to every human face. His eschatological delay institutes his absent face as the universal scene where the gift can come into play (accepting it, refusing it, passing it by in silence) in every other human face, repeated indefinitely. The withdrawal of Christ permits "the least of [his] brethren" to come forward and expose himself to the gift as a face of the givee. His return will not abolish the role of the givee played by the infinite number of the humble (therefore by all), but will reveal this: in receiving (or refusing), nobody was just defending his own interests in economic exchange; rather, everyone, in these gifts, was in fact playing nothing less than a part in the trinitarian plot of God with himself. Therefore the bracketing of the givee no longer implies the refusal of the gift (not accepted, mistaken, ignored), but rather provokes the universalization of the givee.

This first example would be enough to confirm our thesis. However, even though its interpretation is phenomenological, its theological origin could be troubling to the scrupulous. It therefore seems wise to repeat it in a second example. (b) A contemporary and verifiable case of a gift accepted in such a way that the givee can never repay it, to the point that it becomes invisible therein, is witnessed in devotion to a community. The "gift of self" for the nation (death for the fatherland, etc.), for humanity, for a chosen fraternal order, and finally for the children cannot really be repaid (even if one claims symbolically the opposite). What is given—time, energy, life—will never be returned to the giver, since he gives *himself* and since this *self* that he loses cannot be given back to him by anyone. The gift really offered and accepted is, however, addressed to givees who are bracketed—absent. Absent first because no individual can be set up as universal givee when the gift is addressed to a community; no one can say thank you for the sacrifice of a soldier, just as no one can be held responsible in a case of collective guilt. But there is more: the givees are absent because they can accept the gift only for the sake of transmitting it not back toward the giver, but toward givees still to come. The acceptance of the gift does not consist in ratifying it by sending it back upstream (toward the giver), but in repeating it by sending it downstream (toward a givee yet to come). This situation is called tradition—a forever future givee. The student correctly receives the gift of knowledge that his master abandons to him not by celebrating his memory, but by himself becoming the giver of a new knowledge. This law of the gift without givee counts for every gift to a community, as is put perfectly by Claudel: "The Love of the Father / Does not call for a return; it does not participate in a contract. . . . What he gave cannot be repaid."[35] The giver gives to a givee who is ignorant of him and of whom he is ignorant, or to one who cannot even conceive what is given, or to one who is yet to come. And yet the gift is given, accepted, or refused, according to the precept of common morality that "a good deed is never wasted." This certainly does not mean that every gift, even abandoned, would end up reinscribed within the economy of exchange and rewarded (experience proves the contrary), but that without any other legatee, thrown into pure loss for the sake of someone absent and unknown at the instant of the gift, every gift in the end finds this givee; only at the end, because it finds a truly unforeseen givee only with an obligatory delay. And it is precisely this double lack of presence (delay, unforeseeability) which attests that the givee, absent at the origin, was not the origin of the gift, that he therefore never, in the case of the first gift, could have decided matters, promised its reward, or delivered it into the economy of exchange—in short, that the bracketing of the givee has been accomplished. Thus universalized by the absence of the givee, or rather by his withdrawal—which makes a place for universalizing the function of the givee—the gift, accepted but free of any givee, achieves its perfect figure: it is given without distinguishing among persons, in complete indifference to the worthiness or unworthiness of the givee, in complete ignorance of any possible reciprocity.

It will therefore be concluded that the givee can and must be bracketed. For the givee situated according to the natural attitude in the world-region ("partner of exchange," "economic agent," etc.) is substituted, in the realm of the reduction, the lived experiences immanent to consciousness (that of the giver): the givee as faceless ("humanitarianism"), as the enemy, the ingrate, the absent yet to come. These lived experiences remain immanent since they all describe the suspension of the givee according to the natural attitude. They are enough to describe a gift that conforms to givenness although, or because, freed from a transcendent givee. Absent the givee, the gift can no longer appear except to the giver, who becomes, from now on, its receiver. On one condition, however: the giver, who (within economy) should have produced the gift in terms of efficiency, must (in the realm of the reduction) receive its modes as so many lived experiences of his consciousness; it falls to the giver to become the phenomenological witness of the gift without givee. Hence this paradox: the giver who with respect to its reality is the supposed producer of the gift, with respect to its phenomenality receives this gift in so many lived experiences. The giver then plays—phenomenologically and not in terms of natural attitude—the role of a givee: it is to him that the gift is given to appear. Thus, even without givee, the gift is accomplished; for it is enough that it give *itself* for it to show *itself.*

§10 THE BRACKETING OF THE GIVER

Inheritance

Can the giver be bracketed? And can we do so without suspending the gift? Most certainly, for not only does bracketing the giver not invalidate the givenness of the gift, but it is obligatory in the definition of givenness. Without this suspension of the giver, the possibility of giving the gift would be compromised, indeed forbidden. Without this bracketing of the giver, who would remain visible, available, and permanent, the gift would disappear as such (according to the fold of givenness). To establish this, let us carry out this short-circuiting. Take a gift, any gift, consider it in such a way that its giver remains absent—either unknown in reality or actually undecidable—in short, let us imagine it as something like an anonymous gift whose giver is lacking. Does this gift still remain a gift?

Consider the first case, the most simple one, where the giver is empirically absent. To the question "Who did that to me, or perhaps gave that to me?" the only response is complete silence, as if it were a matter of interrogating a wrongdoer who willfully conceals himself. The giver flees what he is responsible for as if he felt guilty, hunted down and hidden. Let us set aside for a moment the hypothesis that would falter before the factuality of the gift (we will broach it soon enough) and stick with the obvious absence of the giver of a gift declared as such. Let us consider, for example, the case of an inheritance. Me—in the position of givee—I am going to receive; much or little, naturally or legally, it doesn't matter, seeing as the gift is accomplished anyway, as is proven by the fact that I should (and could) pay taxes and fees in proportion to the gift received. These taxes and fees constitute returns, counterbenefits—I repay partially in an economic exchange what befell me as a gift; but I do not, however, repay the one who gave me the gift (whoever he might be or not be). Rather, I repay the State and the lawyers who gave me nothing and yet take their cut—the cut that I owe them (according to social economy) even though it is not for them (according to the gift). I repay someone who gave me nothing. To the one who gave to me, on the other hand, I repay nothing because I owe nothing and because the gift requires, for me to receive it, that I not attempt to repay it. I do not repay the one who gave to me because I obviously cannot. (a) First, because the giver is no longer alive and, physically, is forever lacking to the call; he has lost the status of a subsisting (animate) thing among the other subsisting (animate or not) things in the world and for the natural attitude. He no longer belongs to the terms of exchange. (b) Next, because in the case of an inheritance, the impossibility of repaying the gift stems from the fact that the deceased legator no longer can, as such, at least in bodily reality, receive anything: a prize, recognition, love. He no longer perceives or grasps anything, in the twofold sense of theoretically knowing (through sensation) and militarily receiving (taking possession by distribution). Nothing ready-to-hand any longer remains to him; he himself uses nothing, nor is he used by anything. He no longer falls within readiness-to-hand. His death therefore prevents reception. (c) Finally, especially because the absent giver had the very intention that I not repay him, since in bequeathing his good to me, he wished only to oblige me without return; better, he meant that his good should remain in the very degree to which it would become forever mine. I can therefore do justice to his gift only by not paying it back. I can accede to his—last—will only by keeping for myself as a gift what is not mine but comes down to me. The economy of exchange is thus suspended perfectly. The gift can appear, precisely because what gives is lacking.

A variation on the first figure is seen when the giver remains simply unknown without dying. The case, so ordinary in novels[36] and so rare in reality, of an inheritance or endowment from an unknown giver hardly modifies the situation. The impossibility of repaying, when one is indebted to an identifiable deceased, is not noticeably increased in the case of the anonymous (living) giver. For death itself, if it sometimes extinguishes the surname, always removes the name (the Christian name, the one that counts since it individualizes in the name of a saint). If the surname survives, it is precisely through the gift of the giver who relinquishes it for the sake of his descendents and therefore no longer bears it as his own proper name; the surname thus becomes anonymous, taken up in an inheritance. As for the name, the little of it that survives depends on the memory and the piety of the living; its anonymity progresses with the extinction of its recognition—quickly, that is. The dead share the same anonymity as the unknown giver. In the end, the dead are all unknown—or almost unknown. This variation therefore does not call into question the paradox that the dead giver causes to appear: absence (nothingness, disappearance, death) gives, not like one among many possible givers, but par excellence. For if the actuality of a last will and testament takes effect only with the fact of the death of the willer and testator, then strictly speaking, what decides inheritance is not the will of the giver but his decease. Here disappearance itself gives: the gift from this absent, unknown, inaccessible giver par excellence appears as a gift, no doubt as a good deed; and insofar as I acknowledge myself as its givee, I should indeed take note of the fact that I am in a position where repaying the gift is on principle impossible for me, whatever my intention might be, even and especially if it is my best. There is nothing to say or do. I benefit from the gift and cannot repay it. It therefore remains for me to accept it without any more thank-you's. Far from compromising the evidence of givenness, this impossibility marks the fact that the gift gives *itself* in a complete loss without any return or commerce as soon as the destination of such return or commerce (the giver taken as second givee) is missing. It is precisely a question of a gift, in no wise of a loan or future repayment, because the gift has burnt up its giver (as one burns bridges) and abandoned itself without reserve or withdrawal. In fact, by disappearing and being missing, the giver, far from failing, fulfills his function all the better in absentia. He truly gives a gift, whose given character can never be contested, since no return can (through lack of a destination) reduce givenness to the rank of a commercial transaction. The giver acts perfectly because he disappears perfectly.

Un-consciousness

Moreover—and this is the second figure of this reduction—the giver's obscurity (anonymity, death) in the eyes of the public, in particular of the givee, merely reproduces a more original obscurity—his own obscurity to himself. The giver is in effect the first to be unaware. When he truly gives, gives without reserve, or "gives it his all" (as the popular expression has it)— he never knows what he does. Obviously he knows what he does insofar as he remains closest to himself and self-affected, but this immediate self-consciousness is still ignorant of the effect that it produces on a possible givee. Such an effect (the effect that this makes), public or private, can be detected only from the outside, by an other with a decidedly irreducible point of view and affective tonality. The giver is not self-conscious: he is not inhibited by seeing the gaze of others upon himself. By contrast, he often suffers the violence of a gap between what he experiences of himself in himself and the effect whose image he receives. This effect constitutes the last form of the gift (as we saw).[37] Consequently, if the effect remains inaccessible to its giver, it must be inferred that the latter does not know the effect, therefore that the effect has no need of the giver in order to be given. There is no dearth of examples of this figure: the athlete, the artist, and the lover—each in his own way gives pleasure to a givee other than himself, the performance and the victory, the aesthetic effect, erotic pleasure; but in each case, he is unaware of this pleasure. There is a possibility that he knows—but this is already a lot; and often he has to be told, provided confirmation, indeed lied to about if, when, and just how far he has gone. He will never know the nature, depth, or especially taste of this pleasure. What are they made of, how are they to be known or understood, how did it feel?—strictly speaking, he does not know and will never be able to. As regards their most proper and difficult gifts, these givers (and they are the givers par excellence) are ignorant of the effect they have on the other, givee.[38] In fact, the giver receives his consciousness of having given, therefore his self-consciousness, from the uncontrollable witness of the givee. He himself, in withdrawing from the gift that he gives, in return confirms that the gift does not require him and is deployed perfectly in his absence.

In this sense, the gods give (in principle at least) without jealousy, *aphthnoi*, because they give without knowing it; they give and don't want to know about it. Hence, the essential law of givenness: to give, it is necessary not to know oneself if one gives. In other words, "When you give alms, let your left hand be ignorant of what your right hand does."[39] The giver does not know if he gives, and he especially does not want to know if any possible givee knows that he gives because he himself does not want to know this. He gives neither for the sake of knowing it, nor making it known, nor making himself visible—but for the sake of giving, nothing more and nothing less. If the gift is given absolutely only in a complete loss, accomplishing the gift in effect requires positively the loss of the giver. Not only that the giver irrevocably lose what he gives, but that he also lose his own recognition of it, therefore the very possibility of recognition. The ontic loss of self, sacrifice, then becomes a mere consequence of this self-forgetting of the giver. The bracketing of the giver thus offers the paradox that accomplishes the absent initiating I of givenness, which turns out to be inversely proportional to self-identity in the sense of a self-certainty obtained through self-consciousness. The giver gives all the more perfectly as he renounces the self's return to identity with itself, that is to say, as he renounces not only self-consciousness—*cogitatio sui*—but the *cogitatio* itself, in that, fundamentally, it leads that which it cognizes—(and whatever it cognizes) back to the self. Givenness, by contrast, fundamentally never gives anything other than what the withdrawal of the giver finally abandons of itself; for as intimate as the gift may be to the giver, he will never return to it. The *ego is* inasmuch as it returns identically to itself; the giver *is not* (lacks, disappears, remains unknown, anonymous) insofar as he gives (*himself*).

Indebtedness

But there is more—the third figure of the bracketing of the giver—now that the impossibility of reaching the giver (an impossibility even for himself) creates, in principle, the impossibility of repaying him for the gift, therefore simply of repaying. Independent of the contradiction between givenness and the effort to repay the gift (return to exchange), the

vanishing of the inaccessible giver suppresses from the outset and definitively all partners to exchange, therefore all accounts to be credited in return. I cannot repay, for there is no longer anyone whom I could repay. At
once, it also becomes clear that the givee is entirely reduced to givenness in
a precise figure: since he can no longer repay anything to anybody, the
givee must himself acknowledge himself as definitively in debt, therefore as
intrinsically givee. The title givee will never be done away with since the
debt will never be repaid, not for lack of good will or a shortage of means,
but from lack of a creditor.[40] The debt is not added to an already constituted consciousness assured of other objects, one which would be originally
certain of itself. It is in recognizing its debt that the givee's consciousness
becomes self-consciousness, because the debt itself precedes all consciousness of it and defines its self. The self as such, the self of consciousness, receives *itself* at the outset as a gift (given) without giver (giving). The debt
gives rise to the self such as it discovers itself already there, that is to say
factual and therefore strictly given. The consciousness of owing (oneself)
to the missing giver makes the self, the debt, and the consciousness of all
these coincide. The givee is found to be originally insolvent in and through
the recognition of the irreparable anteriority of the debt to all response—
the anteriority of the gift of self given to the self over and above the self itself. The debt therefore designates not so much an act or a situation of the
self as its state and its definition—possibly its way to be.[41] This function of
the debt is again named differance: the absence of the giver[42] precedes all
that he (or she) gives in such a way that the gift already bears as a shadow,
in arising into visibility, the mark of its belatedness in relation to what
gives it but is lacking from the outset: the giver. Differance therefore passes
from the giver to the gift given, then from the gift given to the givee. What
is therefore lacking to the givee, as a lack in his self-consciousness, is the
giver—or rather the giver in the gift, the fold of givenness. For the giver,
insofar as he conforms to givenness, is lacking at the origin. Each and everyone is originally lacking. Consequently, it is necessary that the consciousness of receiving the gift also experience this differance with respect to the
giver as a differance with respect to itself—since the obligation prompted
by a gift given (the consciousness of debt) is definitively delayed behind the
givenness that put this consciousness in an indebted state. All recognition
of debt, therefore all recognition regarding the absent giver, thus, far from
eliminating, confirms differance. But such a differance, if it makes itself felt
with debt, ultimately manifests givenness itself.

Recognition

The impossibility of reaching the giver thus opens the royal road to reducing the gift to itself—that is to say, to givenness, whose fold then appears. The interdiction placed on the transcendence of the giver fully brings to light the phenomenological function of the (reduced) givee. But if the giver is lacking, the givee is charged with the full burden of givenness. As the only place where the lived experiences of the gift are given, it falls to him to constitute this gift as an official phenomenon, in other words, to respond to two questions. (a) The first is put this way: "Is there in general a gift?" Confronted by a gift without giver, with an anonymous or unknown giver, what then obliges me or even authorizes me to speak of a gift? No particular ontic sign (otherwise the gift would confess its giver). The sole clue is found in the supposed intention for the gift. It would not be just a chance occurrence if this service, this tool, this money, came to me, since my need and its crisis demanded that I take advantage of them without delay. These arrive in the nick of time, at the right moment, save me just when I need it. The criteria for interpreting events as a gift still stand. The gift character therefore comes from the suitability of what arises, or more exactly, from my admission of their suitability, from their recognition as given to me without me. Even supposing that they are only fortunate chance occurrences (but there too, indisputable indications are always lacking), interpreting them as gifts would still depend more on my confession of a deficiency or lack—which, *a contrario*, is confirmed by my right to ingratitude. No evidence can annihilate it, and I can always interpret a gift, even a considerable, blatant one declared as such, as an implicit exchange, a demand to repay, an attack on my independence, etc. I can always deny the gift as gift, thus confirming that the gift is recognized first in the recognition I have of it. Identifying the gift as a gift falls more to the givee who admits it than to the giver (reduced anyway). And if I most certainly do not produce the gift in the natural attitude (where the transcendent giver is in play), I institute it in the realm of the reduction (with reduced giver). But if there is recognition, how is it accomplished? By the admission that the arising of the gift does not belong to me—no more than it belongs, as to its cause, to the givee. Since it gives *itself*, the gift appears as gift to the givee only if the last mentioned is indeed recognized as last, or at least as second—as who receives, incurs a debt, owes something to he knows not whom or what. This recognition of debt, contrary to appearances, is no small matter. At issue is what phenomenologically and morally is the hardest ordeal: to succeed in making an exception to the principle, "I don't owe anything to anybody." To suspend this principle is equivalent to nothing less than renouncing the self's equality with itself, therefore to renouncing the model par excellence of subjectivity and also, at the same time, to suspending the principle of identity that metaphysically underlies it.[43] (b) The second question asks: "Is there a giver to recognize?" For, once the gift is admitted and the hypothesis of a chance occurrence dispelled, it remains to be decided whether or not a giver must be admitted. Does this gift refer to a giver or not—for gifts without any sender happen sometimes, or at least they appear to ("gift of nature," "gifts from heaven")? If there is a giver, which being is it? For the fact that the giver is lacking does not suppress the question, but rather opens wide the space for a response, since no authority weighs on it any longer. By its very absence, the giver gives to the givee, besides the gift, the decision to identify who gives. He abandons to him the determination of his own existence; better, he hands his fate over to the prestige that the given gift possesses in the eyes of the givee himself. In contrast to the recognition of the gift as gift, which the givee can accomplish by knowing the gift (at least partially), the givee's decision about the lacking giver demands recognition without cognition. It would be necessary to dismiss this requirement as perfectly meaningless if it concerned nonknowledge of an object or a being; however, the gift (possibly a being or object) can be cognized, and it should be recognized (as gift) on the basis of its being cognized. Wholly other, recognition without cognition concerns access to the giver (no doubt a personal Other) in the gift without giver, to the lacking (reduced) giver of a known gift. At issue is an absolutely specific separation, where nonknowledge is less a handicap than a special way of access. If the giver could be known in the way in which the gift is known, he would become a given gift, but would not appear as giver.[44] To cross this divide, to recognize the giver without cognizing him, demands more than mere recognition (of the known gift)—only love could risk it. It is precisely because the giver withdraws (reduction) that the givee could risk loving him (or not). In having recourse to this concept, which is so difficult to use, we decisively transgress the economic interpretation of the gift in order to admit the dimensions of givenness that, through the bracketing of the giver, the gift reaches.

It will therefore be concluded that the giver can and must be bracketed since a gift is still accomplished without him. For the giver situated according to the natural attitude within the world-region ("origin," "principle," "cause," "father," etc.) is substituted, in the realm of the reduction, the lived experiences immanent to the consciousness of the givee, allowing the phenomenon of the gift to be seen: the giver as the deceased in inheritance, as the giver without consciousness of giving, and finally as irreducible debt. These three lived experiences belong to immanence and owe nothing to transcendence—from which the natural giver was reduced. Phenomenological consciousness requires nothing more to describe a gift that conforms to givenness—a givenness now pure since purged of any transcendent giver. But as it is here the giver who is lacking, the description of the phenomenon of the gift can be constituted only on the basis of the givee, holding the role of pure phenomenological consciousness. The givee receives the charge of constituting the gift, which suits the essence of the gift: first of all to be received as a given for consciousness. Hence it follows that the paradox of the preceding reduction (the supposed producer of the gift with respect to reality receives it with respect to phenomenality) disappears. The phenomenological reduction of the giver coincides exactly with the essential character of the gift—that it is to be received by the givee to whom it appears. Thus even without giver, the gift is accomplished, for it is enough that it show *itself* for it to give *itself* to the givee.

§11 THE BRACKETING OF THE GIFT

The Gift Without Object

The previous two bracketings leave nothing in play but the gift—free now, both from the givee and the giver. Since neither givee nor giver is in charge of its being effected (in the realm of the reduction, each, even the giver, receives it as a phenomenon that is triggered and comes forward without him), the gift depends only on itself to give *itself*. It imposes itself alternatively in the lived experiences of the givee or the giver, but without ever resulting from their crossed causalities; in short, it does not depend on their efficiency. One will object, however, with the authority of common sense, that whatever reduction has been enacted, one bit of residual evidence cannot be put in question: a gift, even if it gives *itself*, is found to be given only in being transferred as a being, an object, or a good from a giver to a givee; and if sometimes one or the other of these two terms happens to be missing (by admitting the reductions undertaken), this is precisely because the transfer persists, which calls for a fixed point—the gift as the neutral and permanent third which passes without harm from one to the other.

Therefore there cannot be a bracketing of the gift given, and the reduction would come to a standstill with it. Faced with this objection, it is necessary to reverse the argument: are we obliged to forbid the bracketing of the given gift because it has to be conceived only as a being, an object, a neutral third; or inversely, is the given gift conceived in this objective mode only because its bracketing was not seriously undertaken or even glimpsed? Inversely, could the given gift, once apprehended in the realm of the reduction, be conceived in another mode besides that of a being or an object, transferred and neutralized? How does the gift give itself? When it gives itself, obviously. But precisely what does it mean for the gift to give *itself*? Here there is a radical difference between the consideration of the gift giving itself according to the natural attitude and its consideration in the realm of the reduction. In the first case, the gift would give itself when the transfer of a being or an object is effected from the giver to the givee, this neutral third remaining unchanged in the course of its transfer. In the second case, would the gift consist in the transfer of a being? Most certainly not. First, because transfer does not always have to assume the status of ceding ownership of a good (it can be a loan, an usufruct, rights to usage, etc.); it could even not involve the least juridical status (concerning a private agreement, a tacit accord, etc.). For that matter, in and of itself, such regulation would be enough to threaten the very status of the gift by leading it back, under the justice of the law, to that of exchange.

But the gift is to be distinguished from the transfer of an object or a being for another, more radical reason: the gift is often not associated with even the lowest level of object. When it is a matter of making a promise or reconciliation (or a break), or enacting a friendship or a love (or hatred), the indisputable gift is not identified with an object or with its transfer; it is accomplished solely on the occasion of its own happening, indeed without object and transfer. In the case of a blessing or a curse, like that which Harpagon "gives" to his son,[45] strictly speaking no thing, nothing real is denied; and this, by the way, is the reason why the gift of the curse can, in turn, be so forcefully resisted; but the material consequences of the curse, as serious as they might be (loss of inheritance), are less than its immaterial effects (loss of filiation, of identity, etc.). Now this nothing—no thing or object—does not, however, block the gift from being carried out fully, as gift of the curse, all the more comprehensive and decisive as it is perfectly symbolic—unreal. Far from being confused with the gift, the object either disappears from the game or is reduced to merely an extra, interchangeable, and optional support (souvenir, keepsake, or wage, etc.), in short, to a mere index of what's really at stake in the gift, much more precious and serious than the object that conventionally represents it. In fact, the more the gift delivers a considerable, indeed immeasurable, largesse, the less it succeeds in becoming visible as an objective thing—or rather, the less the object that makes it visible corresponds to the phenomenal accomplishment of the gift. (a) The gift of *power* offers a clear example of this. To hand power to an heir or the next elected official never equals handing to him power itself as such, since power does not consist in an object or even in a sum of objects, but in a new and absolutely unique relation to each and every one of the uncountable and unmeasurable objects and beings. This relation, strictly speaking nothing objective or like a being, cannot itself be transferred or handed over. Consequently, the gift of power is consummated in a handing over of mere signs of power: the *pallium*, the crown, the Cross, the keys, or the confidential code to the nuclear arsenal, etc., and these signs do not confer (do not give) power; they merely symbolize it, which is enough. Remaining just objects, the signs—even of power— cannot give more that what they themselves have and are. Therefore, the signs of power do not give power. Moreover, the mystery of power stems precisely from the fact that the gap between its signs and its effectivity rests solely on this nameless and unreal authority, which can be called prestige or glory. That is, power is not given with objects because—giving a new relation to a sum of objects—it is not an object or in the mode of objects, but appears in the mode of the unreal. To give power is never equivalent to transmitting one or several objects, but rather to giving, on the occasion of an object transmitted (symbol), the unobjectifiable gift of rule over objects. (b) A second example can be added: to give *in person to the Other*. This gift—whose gravity is too costly for us to contest—obviously does not coincide with the transfer of ownership of some object. The proof of this is that the offering of my body to the Other for his enjoyment—shared life or marriage as the enjoyment of the sexual properties of an Other[46]—is annulled as a gift of self as soon as this transfer becomes either an appropriation by the Other or the price for exchange. Appropriation and exchange interpret my body as the object that, by right, it never is. The transfer of my body annuls the gift in a commerce and forbids the gift of it in favor of an object. To offer my body to the Other therefore does not, of itself, allow for giving myself to him. The objectification of my body disqualifies it as gift. The more I deliver my body in exchange for reciprocity (reimbursement, economy), the less I give it: my body is offered, my heart guarded—it does not give itself (Arletty). The gift does not consist in an object—because it does not at all consist. Consequently, to make the unobjectifiable gift visible, one has recourse to strictly incidental objects. The wedding ring (band of a supposed bond) attests that the Other has given himself, through the bracketing of the giver, to me in giving me this object, and reciprocally; but the two gifts (the ring and the Other) never coincide, for this ring obviously does not of itself accomplish the gift made by the Other, because it is not worth enough to pay in return my own engagement (as if this ring of gold counted for my life, my consent, my own abandon) or to confirm what the Other gave to me in giving himself in person. By contrast, the ring attests the gift that I became in receiving (that of) the Other precisely because in reality it is *not* equal to it, but offers the symbolic index of this gift, without common measure with what is nevertheless shown in it. (c) Hence a third example: to give one's *word*. What do we give when we give our word? Evidently, we do not give an object; we do not even promise a being. And yet, we truly give an observable, tangible gift that affects: that of suppressing lies, removing doubt as to the sincerity of our behavior—in short, that of giving confidence. That is, the gift of the word, precisely because it does not coincide with any particular object, succeeds in radically modifying the status of each of the objects I deal with—things (pieces of property, decisions, conduct) will be set forth in conformity with my word. To give my word does not amount to making my statements adequate to the things (theoretical truth), but rather the things adequate to what I promise to a certain Other (practical truthfulness). The truthfulness thus provoked can be extended to every being or object because it is not identified with any of them and operates on their status, not their contents. The unreality of the word given is also confirmed by its particular temporality: to give one's word of course implies holding to it, but I hold to it only if I hold to it all the way until the moment fixed by the engagement. This delay can remain finite (in a business, political, or other similar engagement); however, in the strong sense of the word given, the delay goes all the way to the end of life: the lover can only give his word forever, for life. Consequently, the word given is not yet accomplished during the entire time of the delay, unrealized as long as it accomplishes what it promised. It is realized in each instant by being realized without end, therefore before the end. Not one of its accidental objects at any moment coincides with its objective—to remain faithful to what was said. The word given is therefore not only given in the future; rather, it is accomplished according to the future, with the status of a strict possibility that neither can nor should be effected in an object or a being. It is indeed a question of a gift—the truthfulness of a word energizing the intersubjective relation—which governs objects and beings, but of a gift that itself is not given as an object or a being.[47]

In this way, the gift can, at the very least, sometimes not coincide with the object it puts into operation. Better, it must be suggested as a fundamental rule that the more considerable a gift appears, the less it is realized as an object and by means of a transfer of property. Only simplistic gifts, and the poorest ones, coincide perfectly with the transfer of an object; it is not even self-evident that all commercial transactions (excluded from strict givenness) can be exhausted in this simple transfer. Or: the more the gift is radicalized, the more the object is reduced to the abstract role of support, occasion, symbol. Reciprocally, the gifts that give the most and most decisively give *nothing*—no thing, no object; not because they deceive expectation, but because what they give belongs neither to reality nor to objectness and can thus surpass all expectation, indeed fulfill a desire. In the realm of the reduction, the gift is accomplished all the better when it is not reified in an object.

Givability

But if the gift, from the giver's point of view, does not coincide with any object, by what is it recognized? To respond, let me try and consider as strictly as possible how the object could possibly become the object of a gift, or rather (since it is only a matter of an incidental object), how the gift is decided. It is a fact worth noting that the gift is not accomplished at the moment when the giver transmits, transfers, or transports the possible object to the givee. Most of the time, this act already results from a decision that is immaterial but the only one to attest it (as the lowering of prices comes after the counsel that decides them). When is the gift decided—that there is giving, giving this, to this one, for such and such a reason or, more often, for what absence of reason, etc.? All the reasons, all the circumstances, and all the passions in the world cannot provoke the gift necessarily—except by making it necessary, therefore annulling it as gift. The calculation of the best is opposed to the good of the gift in that it submits it, though at the limit, to the principle of sufficient reason. The freedom of the gift implies that the decision to give it obeys only the logic of givenness, therefore its gratuity without return. But how can the decision to give respect this requirement? When the giver considers on his own, for the first time, this gift (indeed this object incidental to the gift) as a possible gift, or more exactly, as givable.[48] And if the gift (indeed its incidental object) becomes givable, it does not owe this to any real predicate added on, as if a new determination had been added to those that already characterize it. The object remains the same, whether it is givable or not, indifferent to its possibility of becoming gift. But to the degree that givability strikes it or not, its modality, its aspect, in short its phenomenality will be modified. At least for one of the gazes directed to it—specifically that of the future giver—what to the others is still a good to be appropriated as before-being-possessed appears to him as before-being-given. Between that which is turning givable and the gaze that receives it as to give, the relation is not immersed in subjectivity (for the gaze does not provoke the givable) nor in reality (for givability is not summed up in a real predicate). The relation of givenness summons them with the same name. It lays hold of both the one and the other with a single authority, that of the mode of appearing that belongs to what shows itself as givable for the one who sees it as about to be given. This equal relation, which governs the two terms of the appearing, constitutes precisely pure givenness in one of its essential phenomenological functions. It arises from time to time, unforeseeable and silent, stopping this one single gaze, from among a crowd of others that do nothing but possess and trade, before a particular good upon which it imposes—at least to *this* gaze—that it give it. Hence, in a flash givenness opens a new horizon of visibility, yielding to "the joy beneath my heart, this thing in us that gives."[49] Thus givability defines the lived experience for the giver of the reduced gift. The gift is given as such, in pure immanence, and without objective transcendence, when the potential giver feels the burden of givability.

Thus the gift does not consist in a transferred object, but in its *givability*. By *givability*, I mean a determination of the gift given as well as of the giver. (a) Givability characterizes certain phenomena in certain circumstances of appearing not as a passive potential (this phenomenon susceptible, by its value and its availability, to being chosen from among other comparable ones to become the gift), but as a positive potentiality: this phenomenon appears in such a way that it demands, of itself, passing to the state of gift, of giving *itself*. Givability does not merely permit the gift to give itself; it demands it—the gift as (the) about-to-be-given. Paradoxically, it is the demand for givenness exerted by the givable that makes the gift, and not the giver who yields to it (or not). (b) Reciprocally, givability is exerted over the giver in the way we have just seen. The potential gift appears to the giver as about to be abandoned, released, lost. Little by little, it appears either as a stranger's goods, or as imperceptibly optional, or as the means of access to the Other, etc., until the moment arrives when the I finds itself irreparably in the situation of giving, in the posture of a giver. This assault of givability on the I increases in direct proportion to the rise of the same givability in the aspect of the phenomenon in question. In the end, givability invades the phenomenon to the point that the I admits that the principle "I don't owe anything to anyone" can, here at least, suffer an exception. The gift begins and, in fact, is achieved as soon as the giver imagines that he owes something—a gift without thing—to someone, therefore when he recognizes himself not only in the situation of a givee but also first as a debtor. The gift arises when the potential giver suspects that another gift (received but not yet perceived) preceded him, one for which he owes something, which he ought to repay, to which he ought to respond. To be sure, the gift resides in the decision to give made by the potential giver, but the latter can decide only insofar as he yields to givability, that is to say, recognizes that an other gift already obliged him. It will therefore be concluded that in the realm of the reduction, the lived experience where the gift is given consists in the decision of the gift—the giver's decision to give the gift, but especially that of givability deciding the giver to give. In deciding the giver to give it, the gift gives *itself* of itself.

Acceptability

Is this paradox confirmed when, in order to define the lived experience that corresponds to the gift in the realm of reduction, we shift from the perspective of the giver to that of the givee? What does it mean for the givee to receive a gift thus reduced? Is it to transfer an object from the ownership of the Other to his own? No doubt it is not. First, because such a transfer no longer concerns the gift, but exchange and its economy, where it signals buying and selling; in short, it falls within the realm of commerce. Next because, here as already from the perspective of the giver, a number of gifts are carried out without any transfer of property, because their reality does not reside in an object. As we saw, to receive from the Other life, time, death, confidence, his word, his love, or his friendship is never spoken of or accomplished in terms of property (no more than in terms of dispossession). That is, every object is absent here, except the possible incidental objects (symbols, etc.). Above all, the act of receiving a gift consists neither in the transfer of property nor in the object received (for the obvious reason), but in the acceptance, or rather the *acceptability*, of this gift. Two circumstances show this clearly, the gift *ignored* and the gift *refused.* (a) Let us suppose a perfect gift in its reality (as an object, a being)—a real object intentionally proposed by an identifiable and rational giver. Though proposed according to the rules, it happens that this gift cannot be carried out as a perfect gift, and this is for no real reason, since it isn't lacking any thinglike determination. For this to be so, it is enough that nobody (no potential givee) know or want to recognize it as a gift, that we ignore it purely and simply and let it pass without seeing a gift—that is to say, a gift to receive. Letting pass without asking or taking anything, therefore finally without seeing anything phenomenal in the instance of givenness—this was Perceval's attitude when the procession of the Grail unfurled before his eyes: "The young man who arrived there that night saw this marvel, but refrained from asking how this thing had happened. . . . He feared that, had he asked, it would have been thought impolite; and so he did not enquire."[50] Later, the event of the adventure will reveal that the refusal to ask, that is to say, the refusal to see a gift to be received as such, resulted first from some bad advice (a knight should not speak inconsiderately), but above all from a repressed evil deed (to have abandoned his mother, who died of it): "It was through having received that sin that you came to ask nothing about the lance or the grail, as a result of which you suffered many misfortunes."[51] What then was missing from the Grail that Perceval did not receive it as the gift par excellence? Nothing real. It was missing an unreal determination—its acceptance, its reception, or more precisely, that an initially neutral witness (the spectator disengaged from the procession) should decide that this incidental object (the Grail) shows itself only to be given, so that it can be received as the gift of Christ. The gift lacked merely Perceval's gaze for it to be seen as a gift and find a givee. The decision to receive the gift in the role of its givee implies no real effort and yet costs much. It is in effect a matter of receiving an (incidental) object no longer as due or paid for, but as a gift, by definition undue. At least at first, receiving an undue gift imposes the humiliation of owing something to someone—to the gift, which gives alms of itself, one must in turn give this other alms, acceptance. The gift appears, within the immanence of the I in the situation of givee, through the lived experience of the humiliation connected with its reception. Once the transcendence of its object is bracketed, the

gift is reduced—to the lived experience of the one who is to receive it—
and might not be. This is its acceptability.

Let us next suppose (b) this gift really accomplished and in addition
recognized as a gift given to a potential givee. It can still, without losing any
of its real perfection, fail to be accomplished as a gift. For this, it is enough
that the potential and nonetheless confessed givee refuse it. Either through
contempt ("too little") or mistrust ("et dona ferentes") or pure malice ("that
would be all too pleasurable").[52] What is missing from this gift that it is
barred from being deployed? Evidently nothing real, since all the difficulty
comes from the fact that one has already made available everything that, in
the gift, has thing-status, without the gift truly giving itself. The Greeks'
present was indeed brought forward; its materiality (it is fashioned of wood,
is tall) and its availability (it is hollow, mobile) cannot be disputed; Berenice
no doubt loves Titus, who does not repay her well. The lack is not owing to
anything real that is already perfectly acquired. What's lacking is only its
pure and simple acceptance: that the Trojans indeed want the horse from
the Greeks, that Titus indeed wants Berenice—only the acquiescence is
lacking, the decision to receive: "Do not give a heart I may not receive."[53]
The gift is perfectly accomplished when I—the givee—resolve myself to receive it. Its performance stems more from my decision to accept it than
from the availability of its incidental object. There is more: this decision is
one that I suffer as much as I make, since it depends first on the mode of the
gift's appearing. To the extent that it shows itself more or less what has to be
given (and to me), I acquiesce (or not) to receiving it. Its phenomenal allure
alone renders it more or less acceptable to me (that is to say, suitable, appropriate, attractive, seductive). The debate does not take place between my
neutral free will and the neutral object, but between my gaze seeing the phenomenon given and the receivability of its appearing. My possible desire or
raw need changes nothing, for they are still addressed to the appearing of
the gift such that it can be received, accepted (or not). The gift, in effect, has
to be accepted and, for that very reason, can often see itself impugned, ignored, condemned. The phenomenality of the gift plays itself out, among
other characteristics, in its acceptability. But the acceptability of the gift is
further specified as its receivability. In bureaucratic language, the receivability of an application, a judicial action, an appeal, or a request for clemency
—in short, of a demand—designates its conformity with a collection of
laws or regulations, therefore its being taken into consideration. A gift, like
a lament, demands that someone receive it; it pleads for its receivability,

with all the glamour of its appearing before a tribunal that weighs it and compares it with its own laws—the givee. The gift shows itself (phenomenally) in such a way that it wins (or imposes) its receivability in a givee—it shows itself so as to give itself.

To Decide on the Gift

It will inevitably be objected that the gift reduced to receivability does not coincide with the gift previously reduced to givability. In other words, that the character of "deciding" (on the gift) cannot have the same meaning when it is a matter of deciding to give the gift, as in the case of the giver, as it does when it is a matter of deciding to receive it, as is the case for the givee. That is, givability is a lived experience referred to a phenomenon, while acceptability consists, at best, in a decision of the will, without phenomenal content. This objection in fact rests on an apparently obvious presupposition: there is nothing easier to conceive than the possibility of receiving (for who does not wish spontaneously to receive?), while givability by contrast remains problematic, and therefore can be subject to analysis (for who would wish spontaneously to give?). Now these evidences from the natural attitude must be strongly contested: the concept of the decision to receive (acceptability, receivability) in fact remains essentially aporetic. (a) First of all, because to receive implies to receive what was not expected, to be exposed to the unforeseeable contingency of an event, which arises at its own command. To accept the gift in its status of appearing implies, we will see, a phenomenality of the unforeseeable. Better, what is peculiar to a gift is often that—to use the ordinary expression—"it is not a present." The gift gives what one does not wish for, indeed what one fears. Since it is first given starting from itself, it happens more often as an accident than as good fortune. Nessus's tunic also arrived as a gift. Acceptability therefore implies being exposed to the pure contingency of the event, to its unforeseeability, to its unavailability. It always imposes an ordeal and the appropriate lived experiences (submission, fear, lack of knowledge, etc.). (b) Next, because to decide to receive, one needs much more than desiring to possess and watching one's own interests. It is even necessary, in many cases, to bracket them, since receivability demands renouncing autarchy in that it rests on the principle "I don't owe anything to anyone." Just as we saw above that givability (as one of the lived experiences of the reduced gift) required suspending this principle of self-identity, we also observe that acceptability (inasmuch as it is another lived experience of the reduced gift) demands the same bracketing. To receive the gift implies recognizing that one owes something—(the gift) to something—sometimes the giver. To decide to receive a gift therefore demands accepting, with and for the gift, owing something to...; in short, it demands receiving at the same time as this gift the knowledge and the acknowledgement of a debt. The gratuity of the gift is paid for with recognition—of the gift and its very gratuity. To decide to receive the gift is equivalent to deciding to become the one obliged by the gift. The decision between the potential givee and the gift is therefore not so much one that the givee exercises over the gift as one that the gift exercises over the givee. It is necessary that the gift, by its attractiveness and the glamour of its phenomenality, decide that the givee accepts it; that is to say, it leads him to sacrifice his autarchy in order to receive it. In the final analysis, the gift itself decides its acceptance by deciding (for) its givee. The gift shows *itself* so as to give *itself* and to give its reception.

It will therefore be concluded that, in the realm of the reduction, the lived experience where the gift gives itself also consists in its acceptability. But this acceptability depends, as with givability, on a decision—that of receiving or giving the gift. To decide on this double decision certainly falls to the givee and the giver, but always starting from the reduced phenomenon, to the extent that the gift gives *itself* of itself under the aspect of the lived experiences of givability and acceptability. The gift reduced to givenness gives *itself* to consciousness as what gives *itself* of itself, as much from the perspective of the giver as from that of the givee. This first determination has nothing paradoxical, nor even tautological, about it. It indicates that the gift demands only that one give oneself over to it, by giving it or receiving it only insofar as it gives *itself* first. However, this gift appears fully only from the moment that its protagonists give themselves over to it—recognize it in the occasion of a being, an object, indeed the absence of beings and objects. To thus recognize the gift implies a strict and particular phenomenological gaze: that which, faced with the fact, sees it as a gift. It is, if one wants, a matter of hermeneutics, but of a hermeneutic that does not so much give a meaning as receive it and then understand a gift. Less a gift of meaning than a meaning of the gift; coming from the gift, it sees the fact as a gift because it envisages it on the basis of givenness. For if the gift *itself* decides, it decides in terms of the power of givenness, which weighs equally on the giver and the givee. The insistent power of givenness makes the gift decide *itself* as gift through the twofold consent of the givee and the giver, less actors of the gift than acted by givenness.

As a result, the gift, reduced as what decides *itself* (as receivable and givable), gets its character "given" from givenness, that is to say from itself. The gift is given intrinsically to give *itself.*

§12 INTRINSIC GIVENNESS

The Reduced Gift

The bracketing of the gift in its three dimensions has permitted us to make evident a reduced gift.

This result allows us first of all to define the properly phenomenological sense of the gift—namely, that it owes nothing to any anthropological or sociological model. Not that they must be disqualified or even corrected; as with its formal critique (Derrida), the attempt at an "essay on the gift" (Mauss) remains fully legitimate, and I have not failed to find in it an indispensable basis. But this basis only allowed me to depart from it, as a hurdler endeavors to move away from his point of impact. For it is enough to observe and admit that these essays and this critique don't concern the gift and define (or challenge) only exchange. The gift is twice opposed to exchange. (a) It excludes the reciprocity that the other demands. It is accomplished perfectly with the disappearance of one of its extremes (giver or givee), without which the other would become obsolete. The gift does not consist in a real (ontic or objective) transfer even if it possibly tolerates some incidental objective support, while the other has no other function but to make a thing pass from one owner to another. Here the gift contradicts exchange as economic; far from the economic model of the essays on the "gift" opening a path toward the gift conforming to givenness, this model marks the first, if not principal, obstacle to the gift. To be sure, to win the figure of the gift, we must take our direction from givenness, and not from economic exchange between real terms; but above all, it must be admitted that the gift, of itself, never permits access to givenness, which by contrast it masks. Hence, all the objections that could be addressed to givenness on the basis of insufficiencies or contradictions in the gift, such as the essays on the "gift" understand it, become obsolete. For me, it is not a matter of understanding givenness in terms of the gift, but of radically redefining the gift (Book 2) in terms of givenness (Book 1). This has been attempted. (b) The second opposition stems from the very method of phenomenology. While the gift according to exchange is stymied in the natural attitude, the gift in terms of givenness arises in the realm of the reduction. For, if the nonintervention of either of the two extremes, or substituting for the object of the gift its receivability or its givability, makes progress toward gratuity (as is the case), they owe this, more essentially, to the reduction that makes them possible. It alone brackets the reciprocity of exchange because it shows that the gift is still enacted without one of its extremes. It alone also suspends the transfer of the gift by proving that it is not identified with an object or a being. The difference between the two senses of the gift (in terms of economy or in terms of givenness) depends, in the final analysis, on the difference between the natural attitude and the phenomenological act. Thus I have been able to answer the second objection: it did not demonstrate the impossibility of the gift, but merely an impossibility that befits exchange, still leaving to be thought the possibility proper to the gift. To reach the latter, it was therefore necessary to break with the economy of exchange (and the natural attitude) through recourse to bracketing. This has also been attempted.

This finally phenomenological sense of the gift according to givenness also permits me to dismiss the first of the two objections (§7). It criticizes givenness, therefore also the gift (both the one and the other left indeterminate), for being based on an efficient cause that would produce the gift, thereby considered a being or an object—this cause evidently attesting to a transcendence, in the sense of both phenomenology and theology. But if one passes from the gift according to the natural attitude to the gift in the realm of the reduction, none of the transcendent terms, posited as indispensable by the thesis of the world, any longer offers even the least bit of usefulness or legitimacy. The gift is given, even and especially if one of the two extremes of the exchange is reduced for the other (playing the role of the *I*), even and especially if the gift loses all ontic or objective support. In short, the gift is accomplished all the better according to givenness as the reduction delivers it from the transcendencies that hid it. The reconduction of the gift to givenness goes hand-in-hand with the reduction of transcendencies, those of objectness as much as those of theology—or at least, of what one claims by this name, for thinking the gift in terms of a transcendent efficient cause defines not revealed theology but, in the best of cases, the rational theology of *metaphysica specialis*. Revealed theology could, on the other hand, be defined as a thought of the gift without reciprocity because without transcendent condition external to it (§7).[54] I cannot, however, evoke it here—first, out of respect for the distinction of disciplines and the fact that I stick strictly to philosophy, and above all, because to unravel this thought of the gift as such, it would be necessary to engage in an examination of trinitarian theology, outside the scope of phenomenology as well as of metaphysics. Let me note at least two weighty differences. (i) If in the Trinity as in the reduced gift, three terms are at play, in the Trinity each of these three (Father, Son, Spirit) fulfills in its own way all three functions (giver, givee, givability/receivability). Thus the pattern of givenness reaches a degree of sophistication not matched by the reduced gift, which would be much more trivial. (ii) While the gift according to givenness ends up, in principle, at the equivalence of what gives *itself* and what shows *itself* (§6), the trinitarian gifts are given in such a way that, for us at least, they never show *themselves* without remainder—by which they transgress the phenomenological field. The triple reduction of the gift and its reconduction to givenness exclude on principle the possibility that even the least bit of transcendence could subsist—especially transcendence in a theological (or supposedly theological) sense.

Pure Immanence

The exclusion of exchange and the reduction of transcendencies finally define the gift as purely immanent. Givenness characterizes it intrinsically, no longer extrinsically. What remains, therefore, is to describe the givenness intrinsic to the immanent gift. This being done, we will observe a decisive point: the way in which the gift gives itself coincides exactly with the way in which the phenomenon shows itself. What is accomplished as reduced gift is also described as constituted phenomenon. Let us recall what is acquired by means of the reduction. (a) One of the two extremes of exchange is bracketed; therefore, exchange disappears with its conditions of possibility. It is now a question of a gift conforming to givenness (outside economy); but it will also be a matter of an immanent phenomenality, without transcendence outside consciousness. The gift will now manifest itself of itself, without depending on an efficient cause (giver) or a final cause (givee). (b) When one of the extremes falls beneath the blow of the reduction, what status do the rest take on? In terms of givenness, the response goes without saying: the giver, even without givee, is still enough to perform a gift that conforms with givenness, since he abandons without return his lost gift. Reciprocally, a givee, even without giver, can still carry out a gift according to givenness, since he abandons himself unreservedly to the arising gift. In fact, both the one and the other separately succeed in suspending the principle that forbids the gift ("I don't owe anything to anyone"), thus manifesting givenness all the better. From the point of view of phenomenality, the solution is also clearly imposed: the remaining term assumes the function of the transcendental I such that it receives (undergoes) the given lived experiences and constitutes them as full phenomena, without leaving the intentional immanence of consciousness.[55] Thus, when the givee brackets the giver as transcending his consciousness-region, it still undergoes the reduced gift in the lived experience of receivability and, on the basis of this given, constitutes a phenomenon of complete givenness (inheritance, unconsciousness, debt; §9). When the giver suspends the transcendence of a givee, he still receives the reduced gift of a lived experience of givability and on this basis can constitute a complete phenomenon of givenness (enemy, ingrate, absent, etc.; §10). The remaining interlocutor of the reduced gift plays the role of the consciousness-region in the manifestation of the reduced phenomenon. (c) There is more: the gift itself can, in this analysis, attain the status of a gift given and finally extricate itself from the model of exchange only insofar as it removes the impediment of an objectness or beingness to be transferred. But it succeeds in doing this (according to givenness) only because (according to the reduction) it brackets the transcendence of the exchanged object and thereby lays bare the two (reduced) lived experiences of receivability and givability. With each of them, the corresponding consciousness (that of the remaining givee or that of the remaining giver) can constitute (reconstitute, rather) the entire phenomenon of the gift, this time deployed solely insofar as it appears (§11). Of course, this constitution presupposes that the agent playing the role of the I exerts, each time, over and through its lived experiences, an intentionality; but every intentionality, even insofar as it is intentionality of the thing itself, still remains immanent. (ii) If it is freely admitted that the extreme term remaining each time (givee or giver) assumes the role of consciousness-region, and that consciousness-region is by definition identified with pure immanence, one will have to conclude that the remaining term—the fixed point of the gift—itself remains perfectly immanent. From now on, the three terms of the gift are practiced in terms of givenness only by submitting to the reduction. They become pertinent, with regard to givenness, only to the degree that they are immanent according to the reduction. Showing *itself* (immanence, reduction) is equivalent, once again, to giving *itself* (without exchange). And reciprocally, what gives *itself* without return or exchange arrives in the end at this unreserved abandon, the visibility of the phenomenon that gives *itself*.

The character "given" in the phenomenon can now be sketched more precisely. No more than the gift consists in an object of exchange does the phenomenon reside in an object or being in transcendence. If this were the case, both could circulate, move about, and return without modification or alteration. The beginnings of a description in terms of givability/receivability (which belong to it par excellence) establish well enough that this is not how it goes. In each case, the gift appears and the phenomenon gives itself in a new and incomplete mode, to be taken up again and again. The gift and the phenomenon in effect come forward according to an axis (intentional perhaps)—the path and meaning of their arising, at the level where the givenness of meaning that will constitute them must be accomplished. They therefore come forward with respect to an axis according to which their lived experiences deploy themselves, and it is along this line that consciousness must seek to align itself if it wants to receive the gift and the phenomenon as lived experiences. It is necessary to align oneself along the coming forward, to await the phenomenon there where (and as) it gives itself, or the gift there where (and as) it shows itself. It is not a question of a fixed point or perspective (where the I, immobile, fixes what it sees), but of a point of arrival, of encounter, a target, where what arrives from above is exposed and received. The visible arrives to the I as a gift and, reciprocally, because the phenomenon arises, offers itself, rises toward itself—and takes form in it. I will call this identification of the phenomenon that gives *itself* and the gift that shows *itself anamorphosis* (§13).

The phenomenon's taking form in its gift is deployed according to the axis of the visible and its intentionality. It therefore accomplishes immanence, rather than threatening it. More generally, givenness does not cut through the gift transitively; it stays there permanently. It belongs to the fold of givenness to organize the gift, and to manifestation to unfold it. Givenness is discovered as the instance par excellence of immanence. It is therefore no longer, as in metaphysics, the cause that would remain immanent to its effects (supposing that this proposition could ever really be thought without contradiction), but givenness that remains *immanens, non vero transiens* in the gifts.[56]

From the Gift to the Given Phenomenon

I can finally respond to one last objection. Haven't I tried to demonstrate too much by treating, on the one hand, the fold of givenness in general as universal phenomenality (Book 1) and, on the other, the gift in particular as regional question of exchange (Book 2)? Shouldn't I choose between two equivocal conclusions? Either I mean: the gift gives itself to its givee starting from its reduced giver (or reciprocally); in this case, the gift would give itself *inasmuch as gift*, phenomenality in general remaining intact. Or else I mean: the gift gives itself by virtue of phenomenological givenness, according to the absolute immanence of the phenomenon reduced to consciousness; in this case, the gift gives itself *inasmuch as phenomenon and like every other phenomenon*, and its gift character does not matter. In the first case, the question concerns only the doctrine of givenness; in the second, it concerns phenomenology as a whole, but without a necessary connection with the gift. In stating that the gift gives *itself*, without choosing between the two senses, wouldn't I once again have fallen victim to "the ambiguity of the notion *givenness*"? Unless, quite to the contrary, the error consists precisely in denouncing an equivocality where conceptual analysis compels us to recognize a single concept, perfectly univocal—givenness. Givenness determines the gift as much as and in the same sense as the phenomenon because the phenomenon shows *itself* as such and on its own basis only insofar as it gives *itself* (§6). As for the analytic of the gift in terms of exchange, it has been of service only in reaching, by inversion and rupture, a model of the gift conforming to givenness; but this corrected gift has immediately taken a place in the fold of givenness in general, such as it governs phenomena universally. The gift as gift, in appearing as such outside exchange, immediately played the role of one phenomenon among others, though one privileged to attest the fold of givenness. The gift uprooted from exchange serves, with neither equivocality nor ambiguity, as privileged phenomenon in the attempt to win access to givenness and the fold, according to which it organizes every phenomenon as a gift giving itself. To win access to the fold of givenness (Book 1), I retrospectively followed a privileged phenomenon, the gift of the giver and the givee (Book 2). For all that, its privilege does not consist in overdetermining givenness with equivocalness, but solely in leading to it and, once the fold of givenness has been attained, in inscribing and absorbing itself therein, like every other phenomenon. The difficulty does not stem from the equivocalness and the supposed gap between the gift and givenness; it consists rather in laying bare the characteristics of given, by which each phenomenon would clearly attest that it is unfolded starting from the fold of givenness—showing *itself* inasmuch as it gives itself.

Book III

THE GIVEN I: DETERMINATIONS

§13 ANAMORPHOSIS

Intrinsically Given

The determinations of givenness—first as such, then in its conversation with the gift—confirm that it is fundamentally equivalent to phenomenality (what appears gives *itself*, what gives *itself* appears or, better, shows *itself* [§§6 and 12]) by assigning the gift the immanent and intrinsic characteristic of givenness. It follows that every phenomenon falls within the given, to the point that the terms could trade places. "Given phenomenon" sounds like a pleonasm, and the same goes for "phenomenal given." Whoever wants to make an objection would have to—even before demonstrating the argument that led to it—point out just one phenomenon that is not given or one gift that does not appear. The equivalence of showing itself and giving itself is not an opinion, option, wish, or even a doctrine— but something theoretically compulsory, or rather, dare it be said, a given. Phenomenology agrees with empiricism in privileging recourse to the fact, even if it stands apart from it in refusing to limit the facts solely to empirical sensibility.[1]

This empiricalness of the given phenomenon can be described only if three requirements are respected. (a) First of all, it is necessary that givenness, therefore in fact the reduced lived experiences of givability and acceptability, allow the phenomenon to be described *intrinsically* as purely and strictly given. This implies that the description never, as regards the giver, has recourse to an efficient cause and, at the same time, a transcendent givee;[2] the characteristics of the coming forward must always remain immanent to the consciousness that we have of the phenomenon. We must therefore renounce relying on any and all relation, even an intersubjective or ethical one, at least as long as its transcendence has not been reduced or rendered compatible with intentional immanence. Mere recourse to the Other is not enough to determine as a gift what changes hands from him to me (or inversely); nothing forbids this gift from still functioning in the mode of economy. By contrast, most of the time, the intervention of the Other blocks the givenness of the gift by collapsing it into a transcendent relation and disqualifying its intrinsic character as given. (b) Next, it is necessary that givenness characterize entirely, solely on the basis of the lived experiences of givability and acceptability, the phenomenon as *irrevocably* given. This means that the phenomenon finds in givenness not a mere entry into phenomenality, but the entire mode of this phenomenality. It is not a question of a propaedeutic procedure, such that certain phenomena would come forward by means of givenness but would then detach themselves from it in a resolute and merry widowhood; nor is it a matter of one among other means of access to visibility, in the fashion of an efficiency that leaves no trace in its effects and abandons them to neutral subsistence (equivocal and transitive causality). Immanent givenness remains within what it gives, therefore determines it forever. The phenomenon must therefore be described as still given well beyond its arising into appearing. In each moment, it will appear as given—having been able not to be, trembling so to speak with a phenomenality come from elsewhere. At no moment does the given phenomenon wash its hands of givenness so as to close itself off in a subsistence shorn of all beginning, of temporal alteration, of the mark of its event. It could even be that only the perspective of givenness permits truly distinguishing between subsistence and usability (therefore exchange), precisely because it distinguishes these two modes of Being not only from another mode of Being (that of Dasein), but above all from every mode of *Being*. Givenness succeeds in doing this only to the degree that it gives without having to be and therefore can even give Being. (c) Finally, it is necessary that givenness, using the lived experiences of givability and acceptability, be able to determine the given phenomenon *radically*. In order to avoid having givenness characterize it only extrinsically and provisionally, it is appropriate that givenness determine it also as such: phenomenon insofar as given, appearing insofar as determined by givenness. This "insofar as" should be understood in all its radicality: it is not a matter of interpreting an already accessible phenomenon as additionally given, thus leaving open the hypothesis that it could also appear without givenness. It is rather a matter of interpreting the phenomenon as such in the very degree to which it is interpreted as given. "Phenomenon insofar as given" counts as a pleonasm and an equality in which it falls to the second term (given) to decide the first (phenomenon). This is the case with Aristotle's *ē̄* (*qua*): the project of considering beings insofar as beings would most certainly be meaningless if beings were already accessible before it. It must be emphasized that only the operation of the *ē̄* provokes the appearing as that of a being because, without it, no being would ever be offered for consideration. For it is not only the second "being" that results from the *ē̄*, but also the first. Without this *ē̄*, this "insofar as," no being would be available to see as a being; there would be only the living or the mineral, lines or surfaces, men or gods—in short, beings already specified for other sciences. With this "insofar as," Aristotle lets appear beings, therefore phenomena, which without it would remain completely invisible. It does not add an additional characteristic to what would lack it (since "being" is the poorest determination) but, by contrast, suspends derivative characteristics for the purpose of staging the intrinsic, definitive, and constitutive characteristic of all that which at first glance (that is to say, to the gaze of the sciences as well as opinion) has neither need nor reason to be determined as being. This operation can already be understood as a type of reduction, no doubt phenomenological, but belonging to a phenomenology that is from the outset oriented toward and limited by beingness.[3] Now, I'd like to suggest that the reduction operated by givenness is also carried out thanks to a comparable "insofar as." In this case, it is a question of making the given appear as integrally phenomenal and, in turn, the phenomenon as integrally given—the phenomenon insofar as given, the given insofar as phenomenon. But here, the "insofar as" no longer reconducts the phenomenon to beingness; it reduces it to the status *given*. Respect for this triple requirement can help us avoid regressing out of phenomenology to the hither side of the reduced gift. And yet, at this point, I have established the equivalence between the given and the phenomenon still only *logikōs*, formally, in terms of the requirements of givenness in general. It still remains for me to establish that, as such and in its most proper determination, the phenomenon shows itself insofar as given and the given gives itself insofar as shown [*en tant que montré*]—literally a freak show set loose [*un monstre délivré*]. The analysis of givenness has already established the following: first, that the transcendent relations of exchange and commerce, such as they stage the gift and abolish it in metaphysical economy, should fall beneath the blow of the reduction; next, that the gift thus reduced, far from disappearing, finally appears as such. From now on, since no transcendent condition any longer blocks the gift, its character of *given* becomes immanent to it; every reduced phenomenon can also be called given since this givenness falls to the given insofar as it is considered in its reduced immanence. Once again, it is necessary to describe positively the immanence intrinsic to the given in terms of its character of givenness.

As constitution is equivalent to a givenness of meaning (*Sinngebung*), it is a question of *giving* it intrinsically the meaning *given*. This task offers a clear difficulty: givenness had been compelled to reduce the transcendent relations of exchange (§8). To constitute the given intrinsically, it is now necessary to contradict nothing less than the classic definition of the gift as "what we have from elsewhere, *quod aliunde tenemus.*"[4] This definition imposes a very specific dilemma. On one hand, to have the gift from "elsewhere" is enough to announce its transcendence, seeing as this determination implies that the same fact could count either as a gift or a possession depending on whether or not it comes from its (causal) relation to an "elsewhere" (the gift remains essentially relational and relative, extrinsic, therefore transcendent). On the other hand, this "elsewhere" nevertheless also belongs legitimately to the gift, seeing as it attests its facticity such as it imposes on me the receiving or giving of it and whereby it slips from my grasp by assigning the gift to another instance besides my possession. How to overcome this dilemma? A single, paradoxical path lies open: attempting to conceive even this "having from elsewhere, *aliunde habere*" as a determination intrinsic to the given phenomenon, that is to say, determining it in a strictly phenomenological mode ("elsewhere" as a character of the mode of appearing) and no longer a metaphysical one ("elsewhere" as the indication of causal dependence). The arising into appearing of what gives itself in appearing always bears the mark of an ascent to the visible; this ascent, as free and autonomous coming forward, is, with effort, detected in this mark on account of its arising from an "elsewhere." But this "elsewhere" does not necessarily indicate an origin, cause, or agent of exchange since it can always—we saw in §§9–10—make itself felt without pointing to one of them and since, inversely, they can come to present themselves only on the basis of an after-the-fact interpretation of the "elsewhere" as a transcendence. By itself, to appear starting from "elsewhere" is not enough to disqualify the immanence of givenness to the given; by contrast, it highlights the intrinsic character of what gives *itself* to us without depending on or referring to us, indeed by coming upon us despite us. The "elsewhere" thus indicates the first radical property of the given phenomenon—giving itself, showing itself: that of accomplishing itself independently of our exchange, our efficiency, and our foresight, therefore weighing on that which it comes upon. Here (in the realm of the reduction), this weight of the arising come from "elsewhere" betrays no transcendence, but rather attests the irreducible makeup of the self of what shows *itself* in that it gives *itself*. Phenomenologically, this "elsewhere" and the *self* reinforce each other, while in the natural attitude they contradict one another.

Anamorphosis

That the phenomenon accedes to its visibility only by way of a givenness; that in order to rise into appearing it must cross a distance (an "elsewhere") that separates it and therefore must (sur)render itself there (in the sense of abandoning and moving itself); that this arising is unfolded according to an immanent axis with which the I must fall into alignment if it is to receive an appearing—all that defines one of the essential characteristics of the given phenomenon, its anamorphosis.[5] Though here it is not a matter of pictorial procedures, these can help us clarify by analogy the phenomenological sense that I am imposing on this term. This procedure involves first presenting to the uncurious gaze of the viewer a surface entirely covered with colored pigments but apparently void of any recognizable form whatsoever, then moving this gaze to a precise (and unique) point from which it will see the de-formed surface trans-form itself in one fell swoop into a magnificent new form. This aesthetic situation offers analogies that can be useful in determining the phenomenon that shows itself only insofar as it gives itself. (a) Every visible (but likewise everything perceived, with whatever sense)[6] by definition appears. It therefore has a form, as vague and unformed as it might be, but this appearing is not yet equal to a figure of apparition. That is, if form indicates only a momentarily isolatable portion on the indistinct surface of things, it neither distinguishes nor separates this phenomenon from that other. In the following instant, the form will deform itself and re-form itself into another; in short, it will let the phenomenon it supervises dissolve without having ever brought it into appearing. The phenomenon therefore succeeds in appearing only by passing from a first form—unformed—to a second form, which informs it as such because it fixes a figure of apparition for it. This second-level form does not merely make the phenomenon visible; above all, it distinguishes the phenomenon from others by detaching it from them as if from the depths. The second-level form refers the first-level forms to the depths of the visible and tears its phenomenon from there as from a mere background. The second form marks the first arrival of the phenomenon in its appearing. Form of arrival, the *ana*-morphosis of the phenomenon insofar as it is given, thus designates its property of *rising* from the first to the second form—of passing from that which goes its own way (for a vague, unfocused gaze) to that which comes in its own way (of what shows *itself*). Or rather: from the depths of the self of the phenomenon. (b) But these two forms would not follow one another if they were not essentially different from one another. The first in fact offers no identifiable figure, lays bare the appearing of no phenomenon, and therefore exercises no authority over the gaze: blank, expressionless. This amorphous form offers itself to no particular view, neither as an object resisting it nor in capitulation. The case is quite different for the second form, the form of arrival. To accede to it, not only must a gaze know how to become curious, available, and enacted, but above all it must know how to submit to the demands of the figure to be seen: find the unique point of view from which the second level form will appear, therefore make numerous and frequently fruitless attempts, above all admit that it would be necessary to alter one's position (either in space or in thought), change one's point of view—in short, renounce organizing visibility on the basis of free choice or the proper site of a disengaged spectator, in favor of letting visibility be dictated by the phenomenon itself, in itself. Set in its terminal form, the phenomenon no longer appears as soon as I open my eyes to it, like an object summoned to the gaze that produces it; rather, it arises when my gaze has satisfied the demands of the perspective, therefore of the appearing, proper to what shows itself starting from itself. Ana-*morphosis* indicates that the phenomenon takes *form* starting from itself. In this way, we better understand that the phenomenon can come at once from "elsewhere" and from itself. It comes from its own depths to its own form, according to a phenomenological distance that remains strictly internal. The phenomenon always comes from "elsewhere" since it appears as giving itself; but because it gives itself of itself, this "elsewhere" remains intrinsic to it. From here on out, the task will be to describe the different characteristics of the given phenomenon according to its essential determination by and as anamorphosis—ascent to visibility that remains internal, since in this way it is only itself that it gives to be seen of itself.

Contingencies

A phenomenon appears to me. This apparition, accomplished right before my very eyes, is not contested. First, because it is a question of an appearing—which, as such, has only to appear to accomplish itself perfectly. Next, because it arises in visibility. The appearing can therefore appear only de facto, according to what I will call, following Husserl, a contingency: "Individual Being of every sort is, quite universally speaking, *'contingent' [zufällig]*."[7] What does such a contingency mean? Before meaning the mere opposite of the necessary, contingent says what touches me, what reaches me and therefore arrives to me (according to the Latin) or (according to the German) what "falls like that," therefore "falls upon me from above." The phenomenon appears to the degree to which first it goes, pushes, and extends as far as me (it becomes contiguous with me; it enters into contact with me) so as to then affect me (act on me, modify me). No phenomenon can appear without coming upon me, arriving to me, affecting me as an event that modifies my field (of vision, of knowledge, of life, it matters little here). It takes place, picks a date, takes its time to take form (anamorphosis); there is no neutral phenomenon, always already there, inoffensive and submissive. It makes a difference solely by its coming up. To see it, it must first be endured, borne, suffered. I will describe this contingency in three figures: the phenomenon either arrives to me, comes upon me,[8] or finally imposes itself (and imposes on me)—thus is accomplished its singular contingency, *contingit.*

The contingency of the phenomenon is felt (a) first in that it *arrives to me* insofar as I am knowing, so that I might know it. It arrives in the mode of what becomes indubitable in the very measure to which it proposes itself, posits itself, therefore gives itself. For the phenomenon does not arrive directly as an object, but first as a lived experience of consciousness. All that consciousness undergoes and lives remains immanent to it; therefore, every lived experience is identified with consciousness and becomes as indubitable to it as it is to itself. The arrival of the lived experience makes the phenomenon possible, but at the same time it also attests contingency. The contingency of the phenomenon, however, implies no uncertainty of the lived experience; to the contrary, the fact that the lived experience arrives to and over consciousness so as to really occupy its flux indicates only an indubitability in fact, of the very fact that the lived experience arrives incessantly. Descartes, too, concedes this indubitability in fact of the lived experience, even the sensible lived experience, on condition that it is taken as such: "The intellect can never be deceived by any experience, provided that it intuits it in a fashion exactly corresponding to the way in which it possesses the object, either within itself or in the imagination."[9] As immediate and indubitable lived experience, the phenomenon arrives according to an essential contingency. But it also arrives as intentional object of lived experiences, this time in a wholly other sense: the object at which intentionality aims does not give itself so long as its signification is not adequately fulfilled, but such a fulfillment remains, for a worldly phenomenon at least, thoroughly problematic. The paradigm for this impossibility is seen in even the most simple intentional object (the cube, the table, the inkpot, etc.), whose geometric faces we never, by an essential impossibility, perceive all at once. The instantaneous summation of all its aspects remains impossible to effect by perception; the first object already eludes the grasp. This impossibility stems from the pure form of space, but above all from the phenomenological law of which this form offers only a particular instance. For the intentional object, fulfillment arrives only by a succession of adumbrations, all partial and to be completed indefinitely. This succession is deployed *a parte mentis* in the flux of lived experiences parading in (or over) consciousness, a flux that, by definition, never ceases to arrive and never arrives at cessation. The intentional object "tree," but also that of "triangle," etc., can be fulfilled only by an indefinite intuition, for which each conscious lived experience offers an expected but insufficient moment. The objects "tree" or "triangle" therefore admit, for their fulfillment, a flux of lived experiences that sketch as it were their immanent history. The distinction between natural, obviously temporal, objects and theoretical objects (objects of mathematics or logic, essences, etc.) that could pretend to eternity ("eternal truths") is not pertinent here. Contingency does not characterize first this or that object of the theoretical attitude; it likewise does not depend on the stronger subsisting character (*vorhanden*) of some with regard to others. Rather, it is accomplished in the theoretical attitude itself, where objects arrive in phenomenality only according to the flux of the lived experiences that suggest them. Their supposed permanent subsistence (*Vorhandenheit*) in theory forever attests phenomenologically to an insurmountable contingency, based on the very fact that they arrive to me in a flux of consciousness. The theoretical attitude itself confirms contingency. In this way, phenomena, as lived experiences as much as intentional objects, arrive according to their essential contingency.

This contingency is unfolded next (b) to the extent that every phenomenon *comes upon me* as practitioner, in praxis. The gap between the mere "to arrive" and "to come upon" resides first in the status of the recipient. To be sure, in the theoretical attitude, there is an *I/me* to whom it arrives; but this *I* still remains a disengaged spectator, officially if not factually, unscathed by what arrived to it with an eye only toward knowledge—knowing phenomena to be seen (heard, touched, sensed), nothing else. Phenomena arrive here like the news arrives in and through the media: in each instant that they appear, they have already disappeared; one must therefore come to know them before they disappear and before they are lost for knowledge. They arrive, but without leaving a trace. This is no longer the case when one passes from the mere arrival to the coming upon me. We speak of a phenomenon having come upon me when, without me (and not a mere *I*)—or, more radically, without my being implicated and practically involved—the phenomenon itself cannot show itself or give itself as such. This type of phenomenon comes upon itself (appears) only to the degree that it comes upon *me*—that is, to the degree that it no longer arrives to me merely as a spectator (not even a transcendental spectator), but rather employs me as an associated actor. In this situation, the functions of user, receiver, destination, givee—in short, all the modes of its coming upon me—belong also and first of all intrinsically to its mode of givenness. This unique contingency of coming upon is deployed broadly as soon as, instead of considering just subsisting objects within the scope of the theoretical gaze (*vorhanden*), one considers the things available for use, that is to say, the things that demand that I take them in hand (*zuhanden*)—the phenomena of equipment. Take the example closest to hand, that of the computer I am using. As an available object, it can certainly arrive as a knowable object. An electrical engineer, indeed a technician, can, if not disassemble, transform, and reassemble it materially, at least read and understand perfectly the technical manuals, the diagrams showing wiring and microprocessors, run all the programs, indeed create new ones, etc. It still remains that this computer will truly appear as such—as equipment—only once it functions, and it will function only once a hand, as inexperienced as it might be, even one with no other guide besides first-order knowledge (hearsay or trial-and-error), turns it on, taps on a key, fiddles with the keyboard. To carry out so simple a gesture, it is in fact necessary to accept the risk of making all sorts of false maneuvers, including even those most harmful for the equipment and above all those most harmful to the user: the humiliating retraining in writing. This training (my own, which tames my hands, exasperates my patience, and burdens my memory—which in short occupies me) is not added on optionally and externally to the computer, but belongs to it obligatorily so that it might appear as the equipment it must be. The computer truly appears only in proportion to the training to which I consent. Without this gesture, not only will it never come up that I one day succeed, finally and according to the procedures, in writing more quickly than before (if not better), in recording and printing (if not thinking) more, but above all the computer will never appear. From functioning equipment, it will regress to the ignominious rank of subsisting without being used. The computer therefore accedes to its phenomenality only if it makes a request of me, mobilizes me, makes me contribute—comes upon me. That I lend myself to its playing defines the no longer theoretical but practical condition for the appearing of equipment. These phenomena are given only if I let them come upon *me*, and this double movement designates a new figure of contingency: the interaction of my being at stake with the being on stage of the phenomenon. Objects with the mode of Being of technology generalize this figure of contingency by doubling, paradoxically, the contingency of the theoretical object (arriving to me) with the contingency of the practical object, more exactly, of the equipment to be put to work, to be made to function (come upon me). These pieces of equipment come up in their ownmost and full phenomenality ("it works") only on condition that they are tended to by a consciousness well-versed in them (theoretically, the "expert," the technician) and especially one who knows his way around them and gives himself over to them unreservedly (practically, the "professional" permanently available on the hotline). What is called technological progress imposes on its beneficiaries, before any concrete result, a permanent formation. This banal observation, however, masks and detects two decisive points. First, technological apparatus depend so essentially on their users for their "functioning" that they also depend on them more radically for their appearing, such that a second contingency affects them: that of putting their phenomenality into practice. Next, the smooth regularity of objects, whose increasing (or at least proclaimed) self-regulation claims to imitate the eternity of the world and abolish all contingency, in fact requires ever more controls, competence, and investment on the part of their user—the result being that they arrive only through him and therefore exactly to the degree that they happen to him.[10] Equipment, which is employed to deny all contingency in its results and products, does so only by placing even greater demands on its users, that is to say, by contingency in the phenomenological sense. Or rather: the more the phenomenality of equipment belongs to the mode of Being of technology, the more it depends on the coming upon that hands them over to an *I* in order to appear, and the more it illustrates it. Thus is defined the second figure of contingency, this time according to phenomenology— coming upon me.

A third still remains: (c) the contingency of what *imposes itself on me*. For some phenomena appear, ones that I most certainly can know (first contingency), indeed use (second contingency), but that surpass these two modes of phenomenality. Let us consider some. The tree before me casts its solitary shadow in a meadow (or a desert: you must at least once have *seen* a tree in a desert). I have no need of identifying the species (subsistence) or of ascertaining its value on the market for wood (usability) to hurry without delay beneath the branches that embrace me and shield me from the sun. It is the tree that imposes itself on me since it appears to me as what shelters me, opens as a world. A car passes. I have no need of knowing its technical characteristics or what model it is, nor of using it (driving it or repairing it) to rush toward it crying out "Taxi!" or jump aside while cursing the brute who was about to run me down. That is, it appears to me immediately as that on which I depend in order to transport myself in space or dispatch myself to another world, in both cases embracing me as what imposes itself on me. More so than the phenomenon of dwelling or habitation (already illustrated and henceforth agreed upon), we can also consider the phenomenon that perhaps most contradicts the phenomenality of habitation: that is, the monstrous commercial city, almost unlimited and without form, oozing its own vulgarity, awash in items for sale. I obviously do not know its dimensions or residents, nor the shipyards, shareholders, bottom line, or financial results. I do not always know how to use it—to use its cards, its credits, or even its opportunities. I almost never know in advance what I may happen to buy, and sometimes, when leaving, I am still unaware of what I have acquired; but these unknowns and these impotencies in no way forbid me from being swallowed up in its submerging bustle— quite the contrary, this is where its morbid fascination resides. I am never lost so long as I resist letting myself drop out of the buying, not so much of real (subsisting or usable) objects as of reified images, endlessly arising before my inert sight and resulting in my ensnarement and impoverishment.

In short, they all impose themselves on me. Consider finally the television screen. I do not even have to move forward to see it or gaze at it, for it has always already been turned on in advance such that it is what attracts me, holds me back, and more or less regards me. Bracketing exceptions, I fix my gaze on it not in order to know anything whatsoever (even the news is reducible to a pure pleasure) or to associate myself with a community (excepting the interactivity of games or the passionate intersubjectivity of sports), but literally to distract myself. Distract? It cannot be said any better: divert my attention from the transcendent world of things, help me be carried outside myself (diversion), bury me in pure appearance, which is enough of an imposition on me to annul all intentionality, indeed all self-consciousness. The television screen distracts (displaces) me from myself to it; it imposes itself on me, a mere surface but nevertheless more inside me than myself. These phenomena (and numerous others) share one exceptional property: I no longer remain simply outside them, as if faced with what is an object to me, at the distance of intentionality and manipulation; rather, they happen to me or arrive over me like what successively shelters me, embraces me, and distracts me—in short, imposes on me. I can enter and yield to them or withdraw and exit them; but in all cases I must inhabit them or (what amounts to the same thing) be exiled. On principle, I must habituate myself to them. I call these phenomena *habitual phenomena*. Habit does not mean that they function longer than the others (some of them are signaled by their brevity and incessant changing), but essentially that we must habituate ourselves to them. Habituating ourselves to them sometimes implies taking the time to accustom *ourselves* to them (thus renouncing having ourselves make *them*) [*de nous y faire (donc de renoncer* les *faire)*][11] and always finding the right attitude, the correct disposition, the *hexis* or the *habitus* that helps resist them, behave in relation to them, use them, eventually understand them. When habitual phenomena are at issue, the question therefore consists only in knowing and being able to inhabit them. But inhabiting them calls less for building and thinking than for habituating oneself, and habituating oneself depends on a certain gaze or appearing. Thus, other phenomena appear to me according to the contingency of what imposes itself on me.

These three characteristics (arriving, for the known and subsistent object; coming upon me, for manipulable equipment; imposing itself on me, for habitual phenomena) define, schematically at least, the contingency of what appears insofar as it touches me. To appear by touching me defines anamorphosis. The phenomenon crosses the distance that leads it (*ana-*) to assume form (-*morphōsis*), according to an immanent axis, which in each case summons an *I/me*, according to diverse modalities (arrival, happening, imposing), to a precise phenomenological point. This being brought into line aligns me in a direction rigorously determined by the anamorphosis of the phenomenon, in no wise by the subject's choice, but which in contrast submits the subject to its appearing. If I do not find myself exactly at the point designated by the anamorphosis of the phenomenon, I simply will not see it—at least as such, as it is given. Anamorphosis therefore attests that the phenomenon is given. It *gives* itself because it crosses its phenomenological distance by arising from its nonseen into its final visibility, in a thrust that I have to receive, therefore contain, eventually fend off as a violence. It gives *itself* since anamorphosis (in arriving at, happening to, and imposing itself on) attests that it possesses phenomenality's center of gravity, since it imposes its constraints on the *I/me*. In this way, anamorphosis in its threefold figure marks the first determination of the phenomenon according to givenness: it appears given by itself.

§14 UNPREDICTABLE LANDING

From One Contingency to the Other

This interpretation of contingency as anamorphosis could be surprising: doesn't it go without saying that contingency is defined first as the property of what is not necessary, and not by the three declensions of "what touches me" (*contingit*)? But how could the metaphysical opposition between contingency and necessity remain pertinent as such in phenomenology? In fact, it shows itself to be inadequate, indeed erroneous. First, inadequate. Take the very example that Aristotle chooses to articulate these two modalities: that a naval battle happens tomorrow is not necessary, but contingent; that a naval battle does not happen tomorrow is also not necessary, but contingent; but it is necessary that tomorrow a naval battle either happens or does not happen. What remains is that—a point Aristotle does not develop explicitly—the very contingency of the alternative (either a naval battle or not) will be necessary only "tomorrow."[12] This implies that the necessity (embracing the contingency of the alternative) is inscribed in the temporality of the future, therefore that it depends on an event, therefore that it will appear necessary only after the fact, therefore that it falls into the realm of what arrives—which means that it is inscribed within a higher contingency including the two terms of the first alternative. Aristotle thus admits that the necessary alternative between contingency and necessity is itself still temporalized, and thus falls into the realm of an event, in short, that it arrives according to a more original contingency. This more original contingency corresponds precisely to what I just laid bare—what arrives, happens to me, imposes itself on me. Erroneous: understanding contingency by simple opposition to necessity is also erroneous because it hides its essential phenomenological character—that the phenomenon arises and touches me (*contingit*). The contingency of phenomena is summed up not in that some of them can arrive without necessity or foresight anticipating them, but in that all arrive. It must be taken into account that the reputedly necessary phenomena are distinguished from the contingent ones by the fact that they arrive *more* often, regularly, and by design than do the contingent ones—in short, according to my determination of contingency, the metaphysically necessary phenomena appear phenomenologically more contingent than the metaphysically contingent ones because they arrive more radically.

To arrive must here be understood in the most literal sense: not of a continuous and uniform arrival, delivering identical and foreseeable items, but of discontinuous, unforeseen, and entirely dissimilar arrivals. Sometimes phenomena arrive, sometimes they do not, and each time, differently. They differ by not resembling one another; they differ especially by delaying (or accelerating) their arisings. Rather than of arrivals, we must therefore speak of the unpredictable landings[13] of phenomena, according to discontinuous rhythms, in fits and starts, unexpectedly, by surprise, detached each from the other, in bursts, aleatory. They make us wait, desire them, before seeing them.[14] In these mountings of visibility (as one speaks of mounting vigor, fever, desire, or anger), we—the *I/me*—no longer decide the visibility of the phenomenon. Our initiative is limited to remaining ready to receive the shock of its anamorphosis, ready to take a beating from its unpredictable landing. This powerlessness to stage the phenomenon, which compels us to await it and be vigilant, can be understood as our abandoning the decisive role in appearing to the phenomenon itself. Not that synthesis or constitution must be renounced, but it must be admitted that they come after the unpredictable landing and anamorphosis, without perception having any possibility of anticipating them. At best, constitution re-constitutes, synthesis re-covers, they never institute. To be sure, even if the phenomenon comprehends and precedes us by its unpredictable landing, through thought we comprehend and constitute it; but we can comprehend it only insofar as in advance it arrives to me, happens to me, and imposes itself on me, following the free contingency of its own arising. The original contingency of the phenomenon is accomplished by its unpredictable landing; every phenomenon, even the apparently most subsistent one, exercises by itself the initiative of making itself visible. Thus is confirmed one of the characteristics of the reduced gift: givability, the intrinsic property of giving *itself* by itself and on the basis of itself alone. Whence the putting into operation of its other intrinsic property: if, from the depths of the unseen, it can impose (itself) on me (by) its contingency, it owes this to its receivability—to its characteristic of being able by itself to make itself accepted. Unpredictable landing, as purely phenomenological acceptation of contingency, therefore follows, in two ways, from the reduction of the phenomenon to the given.

However, the contingency thus redefined (such that it is opposed to its metaphysical sense) suffers an objection that is crucial from the perspective of a phenomenology of givenness: it remains an extrinsic determination of the phenomenon, contrary to its intrinsic reduction to givenness. In effect, this second-order contingency overcomes the ordinary alternative (between the necessary and the non-necessary) only by relying on an unpredictable landing upon . . . , therefore by relying on the relation of the given phenomenon to an *I*. Shouldn't it rather be attributed to the *I*? For, to recall some traits, the lived experience arrives only as my lived experience, the fulfillment of the intentional object arrives only because it is successive in the flux of my consciousness, equipment happens only insofar as the training in its use is temporalized according to my mode of Being, the habit imposes itself only to the extent that I must inhabit certain phenomena. In short, contingency would not determine phenomena according to their givenness so much as it would their different relationships to my finitude. Spinoza had pointed this out: "A thing is termed 'contingent' for no other reason than in relation to [*nisi respectu*] the deficiency of our knowledge."[15] Consequently, the same phenomenon, having been contingent, could become necessary to the extent that it is referred extrinsically to a perfectly rational subjectivity: "It is of the nature of reason to contemplate things not insofar as they are contingent, but insofar as they are necessary."[16] This objection, however authoritative it might be, is not coherent, even sticking strictly to the terrain it chooses. First, unjustifiably, it leads contingency back to a difference from necessity. Next, it assimilates this difference between ontic modalities to the difference between finite and infinite knowledge, without discussing it. Finally, it attempts to annul the ontic difference by the tangential assimilation of two realms of knowledge. Now, not only does such a reduction remain at best programmatic (for Spinoza) or problematic (according to Leibniz), but above all, even if it is admitted, it is of no concern whatsoever in the real exercise of knowledge while we reside, until proof of the contrary, in the realm of finitude (as specified by Descartes, Kant, Heidegger). Henceforth, *for us*, extrinsic or not, the contingency of what touches me remains necessary with an essential necessity: *for us*, every phenomenon appears as if the contingency of its appearing characterized it intrinsically. For the rest—of what importance to us is angelic or divine understanding?[17] But above all this objection of extrinsicity claims to annul contingency only by interpreting it arbitrarily as noetic; it can disqualify it as a relation only by presupposing precisely that it concerns only knowledge. And yet this presupposition does not hold. Even in the epistemological order where subsisting beings reign, we have seen that these still arrive (lived experiences, flux of consciousness, and adumbrations) and confirm a contingency already in the theoretical attitude. Besides the arrival, we saw two other figures of contingency—coming upon me (equipment), imposing themselves on me (habits)—that overcome the theoretical attitude. Even supposing there is a sense in claiming complete knowledge of the computer or television screen, this still would not dismiss us from training or habit. Contingency is not reducible to the uncertainty of knowledge; it is therefore not summed up by an extrinsic relation of the known to the knower. The phenomenon does not arrive (contingency) because it changes (epistemologically); it changes because it rises into the visible, through anamorphosis and unpredictable landing.

Two Validations

And yet, to assure the validity of a contingency intrinsic to the given phenomenon, it is not enough to impugn the objected contingency with respect to knowledge; it is still necessary to describe it positively. The difficulty here resides in the fact that we cannot avoid opposing, in conformity with metaphysical usage, contingency and necessity, while—and this should be shown—contingency taken in its triple phenomenological sense not only does not exclude necessity, but recovers and confirms it. A first way to think this compatibility was opened by an illuminating paradox from Thomas Aquinas: the contingency of the created world does not contradict its possible eternity. This amounts to positing, according to our thematic, that the contingency of the world, like the phenomenon of the totality of phenomena, determines them always and forever, and therefore intrinsically. Before explaining this, let me note two preliminaries. We will admit, as a *lectio difficilior*, the hypothesis, highly debatable today, that the world admits neither beginning nor end in time; we will note especially that the world here puts into operation, in the role of the phenomenon of the totality of phenomena, the three types of contingency—what arrives for knowledge, what comes upon me for the purpose of being used, and above all what imposes its habit on me. What goes for such a total phenomenon therefore also goes for singular phenomena. Take the question: "Could something that is made have existed forever?"[18] It is equivalent to this one: "Are the following ideas contradictory: to be created by God according to a thing's entire substance and to lack a temporal beginning?"[19] The solution then consists in dissociating causality and temporality. The world can remain eternal and in this sense necessary, even though it would depend on a cause and, in this sense, be contingent. In effect, certain causes are accomplished instantaneously (*subito*), therefore without duration, that is to say, in full compatibility with eternity. This instantaneous causality does not arise solely in the case of the world, but is also clearly seen "from induction, based on all instantaneous changes, such as illumination and the like."[20] Thus illuminated light (*lumen*) shines simultaneously with the sun (*lux*) without claiming independence from it; on the contrary, this simultaneity supposes a sudden, instantaneous, permanent dependence. Thus the trace of the man walking, whose imprint is impressed in the dust simultaneously with his step, does not depend on it any the less, but rather all the more. Consequently, what is in the mode of the creature—that is to say, the totality of beings (the world), as eternal as it might possibly appear—depends for its Being on an instance (here named cause) other than itself. In itself, though it exists and might possibly be eternal, it does not remain any the less a strict nothing, instantaneously (*subito*) dependent on a being making it be: "A creature does not have existence except from another; regarded as left simply to itself, it is nothing; prior to its existence, therefore, nothing is its natural lot . . . its nature is such that it would be nothing if it were left to itself."[21] This establishes, in the figure of paradox, a contingency that is no longer epistemological and transitory, but ontic and "eternal"—I would say, more precisely, intrinsic: the nothing intrinsically determines the beings of the world, though they be, or rather precisely because they are in their own mode. The creature remains *in se* a nothing, though indisputably, indeed for eternity, it is. Reciprocally, the

Being that makes it remain, perhaps eternally, happens to it only *ab alio*.[22] The thing is, insofar as it is, other than itself—intrinsically marked with the extrinsic, necessarily affected with non-necessity.[23]

This validation, it must be agreed, is still burdened by a weighty ambiguity: it is deployed in a horizon that is largely metaphysical (within it, contingency is always defined in terms of necessity and causality) and theological (contingency defines created being). However compelling this analysis might be, this necessary contingency is not yet suited to the methodological requirements of phenomenology. The objection is less burdensome than it might at first seem, for Husserl himself repeated this analysis of the contingency of the world in a strictly phenomenological mode without referring to causality, eternity, or necessity. "Let us note here what follows: every fact, and therefore also the fact of the world as fact, is, as is generally admitted, *contingent*. This means that if it is in general, it could also be otherwise and perhaps even not be." Able to be and also able not to be: doesn't that define contingency in the current, "generally admitted" meaning of the term? Not at all, because in contrast to ordinary contingency, phenomenological contingency (unpredictable landing) is posited together with givenness in person: "*While I am perceiving* the world and experiencing it in general and while I am perceiving it as perfectly as possible, *while* I am conscious of it with irrefutable certainty as given in person [*als selbstgegeben*], as [a world] whose existence I simply cannot doubt, it nevertheless has a constant *contingency of knowledge* [*Erkenntniskontingenz*] and this in the sense that this *self-givenness in the flesh, on principle, never excludes its nonbeing* [*diese leibhafte Selbstgegebenheit ihr Nichtsein prinzipielle nie ausschliesst*]."[24] This contingency does not stop with the certainty of the givenness in person of the phenomenon of the world. In contrast to ordinary contingency (which in proportion to the degree it constructs the fact, causally reconducts it to its necessity) it even persists "during"[25] the occurrence of givenness in person; it remains "compatible"[26] with it. Why don't these determinations contradict themselves? Because they engage, on the one hand, the empirical certainty of the given in person, which according to experience, arrives to me and never ceases to confirm itself by a new arrival, and on the other, a transcendental possibility: that what arrives could arrive otherwise than it has until now arrived, could no longer arrive or arrive by contradicting its previous befalling. In accordance with what I had laid out as the first figure of contingency (theoretical), arrival, the givenness of a phenomenon, and of the phenomenon of the world par excellence, is deployed according to an indefinite series of adumbrations and therefore requires an intentional confirmation, always to be resumed, of the lived experiences. There is no end to the advance of this flux, which approaches validation only asymptotically. It is, therefore, on principle proper to it that it potentially not be subject to confirmation, seeing as, in fact, its confirmation depends on an essentially incomplete flux. The fulfillment of the perception of the world remains an idea, not a fact: "Its givenness is subordinated to the idea of an always possible perfection, of an always possible correction." Hence a first figure of transcendental contingency: "Doesn't the possibility remain open, and *constantly* [*ständig*] open, that this structure of unity (which is itself only an empirical presumption) will dissolve, that experience will no longer unfold in the mode of a progressive correction, nor of a progressive continuity of entirely comprehensive corrections?"[27] It must be emphasized that doubt does not bear on the given insofar as the given arrives in experience; nothing contests this fact. But this fact is overshadowed by another instance: neither an argument in favor of doubt, nor an uncertainty of the lived experience, but a pure and simple possibility—"the possibility of the nonbeing of the experienced, despite and during the experience itself."[28] This contingency does not depend on an empirical uncertainty, relative to some founding instance, but on a transcendental possibility, always at work because intrinsically implied in the certainty of the given. The given remains a lived experience, whose correlation with the appearing can never be guaranteed in the natural attitude. The correlational a priori that connects the two sides of the phenomenon can always, at least once, be absent. Hence the second figure of phenomenological contingency, which connects it to the reduction: "According to eidetic law, it is the case that *the existence of things* (in the experience flowing coherently and pursuing its coherent flux in the present) *is never required as necessary by its own givenness* [*durch die Gegebenheit*], but [as] always in a certain manner *contingent* [*zufällige*]."[29] Givenness, as indubitable as it might be, never assures the given an absolute necessity—the given insofar as given is still contingent, arrives. The absolute primacy of givenness is therefore never equivalent to necessary existence—because the given has no need of it nor even the least bit of interest in it. That in the end this contingency intrinsically determines every phenomenon and therefore the phenomenon of the world in general is confirmed by nothing more than the opposition that, faced with the "*positing of the world, which is a 'contingent'*" world, enacts the mere "*positing of my pure I.*" Only the I of the consciousness-region makes an exception to contingency, since its pure immanence exempts it from the correlational a priori. Thus is confirmed the claim that the contingency of the given phenomenon recovers, by another path, the inseparable plot where reduction and givenness are woven together.

Unpredictable Landing

Thus not only do the creation (contingency) and eternity (necessity) of the world not contradict one another, but givenness (necessity) "on principle never excludes" the possibility that this given might not be (contingency). To do justice to these paradoxes, the phenomenon must therefore be defined in this way: that which, inasmuch as given, always appears as, each time, having been able not to appear. What remains to be understood is how the two terms of the metaphysical pair necessity ("always") / contingency ("each time") can be taken up in a single and new, phenomenologically superior contingency.

Let us return to the attempt at a definition. The phenomenon necessarily shows itself as what, in each instant, could have not shown itself (contingency, non-necessity). In other words, it shows itself necessarily as non-necessity of showing itself. This juxtaposition of contrary modalities loses its strangeness, however, as soon as one considers it in terms of its determination as given. For if, on the one hand, the phenomenon appears (shows itself) insofar as it gives itself (§§6, 12), and if, on the other, this givenness can only come upon (§13), then the given should show itself in an *unpredictable landing*. Now, the unpredictable landing does indeed institute a sort of superior, because strictly phenomenological, contingency: the phenomenon always appears by arising (it arrives to me, happens to me, and imposes itself on me). Its anamorphosis (§13), which aligns me along the line of its appearing, confirms the claim that the initiative falls to the phenomenon. Therefore, it appears all the better and more powerfully as it shows *itself* starting from itself, that is to say, from the unfolding of givenness—in short, as it gives *itself*. Unpredictable landing—not the uniform arrival, but the unforeseen, spastic, and discontinuous arising of appearing—in the end emphasizes that the given gives *itself*. But, quite obviously, such an unpredictable landing of the appearing that arises necessarily implies what, in metaphysical terms, is called a contingency—that the phenomenon appear, here and now, not before or after, undoubtedly never again in this way, undoubtedly for the first time, always depends on the fait accompli of a given. This being so, its unpredictable landing does not weaken the phenomenon but attests the arising proper to it, in short, its determination as given. Unpredictable landing unfolds givenness by delivering the ineluctability of the arising and, inseparably, its unforeseeable and unproducible initiative. In effect, givenness accomplishes its primacy in that it lets the given vibrate with an essential remainder that it neither can nor should ever erase, since it belongs to it intrinsically in the role of showing *itself*, of giving *itself*. In drawing on this *self* of the phenomenon insofar as given, we recover the type of perseity that we had accorded to it on the basis of its determination by anamorphosis (§13); but we can also confirm it directly by considering that the unpredictable landing secures, each time, the final individuation of the given. That is, arriving as a *self* that cannot be predicted or produced, in conformity with its arising, the given takes a position temporally. This temporal determination is not added to its definition, supposedly complete without it; rather, it determines it in an irreplaceable way. For the same phenomenon given in another moment, therefore to other interlocutors and with other interferences, will definitely not remain the same. The given remains the same only for the moment of its happening; this moment is therefore not added to its definition—it enacts it. In any moment, no other moment coinhabits this single moment. Hence, the ultimate instance of individuation for this phenomenon (with and beyond the network of other phenomena and interlocutors that mutually define it) resides in the singular, irreplaceable, and unrepeatable moment that temporalizes its arising. Fixing this moment falls to the unpredictable landing.

§15 THE FAIT ACCOMPLI

The Factum par Excellence

The contingency of the given phenomenon is therefore not felt, as metaphysics believes, in the mere non-necessity of its presence, but rather is accomplished by the very fact of arriving to me, of coming upon and imposing itself on me. The unpredictable landing, as it breaks with all continuous flux, is marked as a fact—either it happens in fact, or not, but always in fact. It should be emphasized that Husserl had from the beginning linked his phenomenological reinterpretation of contingency to the instance of the *fact*: "Let us here note what follows: every fact, and therefore also the fact of the world as fact is, as is generally admitted, *contingent*. This means that if it is in general, it could also be otherwise and perhaps even not be." No doubt, there remains an ambiguity: is this contingency a matter of the fact of the world or of "every fact?" Husserl does not decide: "If and to what degree this actually counts for *every* fact is not important to us here." That is, wanting to reach the reduction in its universality, he could only privilege the fact *of the* world, universal fact. It remains, however, that he leaves open the hypothesis that "a contingency of an entirely new type" also characterizes "every" fact *in* the world, therefore every phenomenon: "The sense of this contingency, which is called facticity."[30] The arising of the given phenomenon (*contingit*) would here find its meaning in the facticity of a fact (*factum*) that would give itself by appearing in the mode of facticity. How are we to understand this transition?

The task before us, then, is to justify phenomenologically the hypothesis of an essential connection between contingency (unpredictable landing) and facticity in the given. Consider the phenomenon that is characterized by a contingency in "an entirely new mode."[31] This contingency does not stem from its epistemological uncertainty, since the latter can vary by degrees and approach certainty, even in the case of irregular phenomena. Rather, it stems from the fact that the phenomenon should first be produced and manifest, in fact, if a certain knowledge of it is to become possible. The fact-characteristic, in short, facticity, marks "the entirely new type" of phenomenological contingency: no longer the non-necessity of the knowledge of the object, but the enactment of what gives itself. And by the way, it was thus that the phenomenon of the world could appear at once as eternal (Thomas Aquinas) or certain (Husserl) and contingent—because phenomenological contingency stems from the fact of the phenomenon giving itself and not from the modality of the representations describing it. To appear always demands, for the phenomenon in general, finally coming to the fact of arising and arising in fact. What is the import of this fact? What arrives to me in fact can be known de facto only once it has already arisen, arrived. For, what arrives in fact is not produced in effect, nor as an effect. Let this be noted: the effect presupposes, by terminological rigor, one or several causes or reasons that precede it and permit it to be seen in advance; the fact, on the other hand, precisely insofar as it arises in fact, annuls the legitimacy of asking for its cause. First of all, because its cause or causes are unimportant, seeing as it is already found there, in fact. Next, because if the inquiry into its cause or causes ever becomes possible, this will only happen after the fact, by relying on the fact that it already arrived in fact. Without this fact, the search for causes will be senseless and there will never be an opportunity for it.[32] In this way, the unpredictable landing in fact of the given phenomenon in some way dismisses it from its past; it renders inessential, aleatory, indeed useless, the investigation into the causal process supposed to have provoked it—a phenomenon without genealogy. It also frees it in some way from its future since, even if this given fact should subsequently be undone, nothing can later make it so that the fact did not give itself as it manifested itself—what's done is done and every undoing to come can only confirm that this was done [*ce qui est fait est fait et toutes défaites à venir ne pourront que confirmer que cela fut fait*]—violence of the fait accompli. Facticity says its fact to the given phenomenon, which is done irrevocably.[33] It therefore does not intervene as a substitute for effectivity, simply appropriated to the given phenomenon, seeing as it radically contradicts the temporality of the effect produced. Here the fait accompli is excepted from the past of its possible causes (reconstituted, at best, after the fact) and also from the future of its (unforeseeable) persistence. It is focused on the presence of a moment that is described by what metaphysics names at once "contingency" and "necessity." It resides obstinately in its fact, established forever or just about, essentially undecided—in short, organized by the unfolding of the given. Facticity does not replace effectivity in the given; it annuls it and frees its phenomenon.

One should then apply to every given phenomenon the character of a fact that Schelling describes so perfectly with regard to just one (Revelation): "About this event, nothing more can be affirmed but that it occurred, it took place; it is, so to speak, the primordial fact (the beginning of history), the *factum*, the happening par excellence. It is, in consideration of human consciousness, the first thing that took place in general, the primordial event, the irrefutable fact that, once overcome, cannot be revived any more than rendered a nonhappening."[34] Related to the given phenomenon, this passage could be analyzed in this way: (i) For every fact (as for the given phenomenon), one cannot affirm anything before having acknowledged that it took place, that it occurred, that it in fact appeared; (ii) in each case, this fact is absolutely first, originary (without cause) and without precedent (individualized) such that it can possibly (but not always) inaugurate what could be temporalized in a history; (iii) for the phenomenological consciousness, which arises continuously from the fact of the originary impression, the fact of the phenomenon is given in each instant and retentionally as irrevocable, always already and definitively overcome, such that, even once it has descended from retention to the depths of memory, it will never be able not to have arisen as originary impression. The given phenomenon therefore arrives to me in fact, that is to say, in the role of originary fact, par excellence and irrevocable.

It is important to see that the factic characteristics of what comes upon me do not concern only phenomena marked with empiricity (as, here, the world or mythology), but also universal and pure statements. Kant provided the most perfect example of this by recognizing the facticity of what, in his eyes, is most distinct from every phenomenon: namely, an idea of reason. The difficulty of the moral law resides in the fact that it consists only in an idea of reason, universal and without intuitive fulfillment, as such powerless to contest sensible and pathological movements. The moral law is nevertheless imposed as an unconditional imperative—thanks to the feeling of respect; but for all that, it comes upon consciousness in the form of a fact: "The consciousness of this fundamental law may be called a fact [*Faktum*] of reason since one cannot ferret it out from antecedent data of reason, such as the consciousness of freedom (for this is not antecedently given [*nicht vorher gegeben*]) and since it imposes itself upon [*für sich selbst uns aufdringt*] us as a synthetic proposition a priori based on no pure or empirical intuition."[35] On the occasion of defining the moral law, and even though from his point of view it was no longer a question of phenomenality, Kant in reality is very much to the point in describing what I understand as the facticity of the given phenomenon. Reason can be "grounded" as practical neither by discursive deduction (in this case it would no longer be originary, and for that matter rationality does not establish any fact) nor by empirical intuition (which cannot ground a law) nor by pure intuition (no intellectual intuition is available to us). How then does it impose itself, seeing as "it imposes itself on us . . . as originally giving the law [*sich als ursprünglich gesetzgebend . . . ankündigt*]"? It is imposed inasmuch as, in distinction from the consciousness of freedom, which is not "first given," it "is given as a fact of pure reason, a fact of which we are a priori conscious [*als ein Faktum . . . gegeben*]."[36] But again, how can the given, without any ground, be imposed originarily? Precisely insofar as a given that announces itself, imposes itself, and arrives to me (unpredictable landing) in the style of a fact—a fact of reason. Pure reason becomes a fact in order to become practical. Thus it gives itself as, in principle (according to Kant at least), only sensible phenomena should give themselves—and better than them, since a priori. By assuming the traits of facticity pointed out by Schelling, it will therefore be said that (i) the absence of "ground" does not shake the moral law, but by contrast permits it to take on the status *given*, a given that arrives to me and arrives to me as a fact; (ii) a fact that is all the more originary as nothing has made it possible, nor paved the way for it, nor grounded it; a fact that is all the more irreducible as it does violence even to the sensibility by the respect that it inspires; (iii) a fact that is finally all the more irrevocable as even transgressing the categorical imperative confirms this fact of reason. As a result, "a fact in which pure reason proves [and attests] itself in a practical act [*sich . . . bei uns in der Tat praktisch beweist*]" comes upon moral consciousness.[37] Pure reason thus succeeds, in contrast to the Kantian doctrine but in conformity with the thing itself, in reaching the facticity of a phenomenality of the given.

A Restricted Facticity?

This result is not enough, however, to justify extending facticity to all phenomena. Two arguments oppose it. (a) We just followed three authorities: Husserl thinks facticity in terms of the fact of the world; Kant, in terms of the fact of reason given to the moral subject; and Schelling, in terms of the fact of revelation (and of mythology). Together they trace a figure of facticity whose very coherence provokes a difficulty. For this triad could easily be read as a barely displaced repetition of the three disciplines of special metaphysics—facticity according to *cosmologia rationalis*, then according to *psychologia rationalis*, and finally according to *theologia rationalis*. Even if this is only a distant or forced analogy, it would feed a twofold suspicion. (i) Facticity would always remain special—specified only in the phenomenon par excellence—far from determining phenomenality as such without exception. (ii) This delay to the universalization of facticity could stem from its pure and simple confusion with the brute fact; for we have perhaps not yet established sufficiently if and to what point it is essentially distinct from the brute fact. It is not enough to admit the fact as a fact, even given, to define facticity as such, still less to universalize it.

This objection is reinforced by a second: (b) The insistence with which Heidegger emphasized that facticity falls among the existentiales; it characterizes only Dasein, is read only off of it, suits only it. On the one hand, facticity falls properly to Dasein. Only "Dasein exists factically [*faktisch*]"; it "always exists factically [*faktisch*]" since "existing is always factical. Existentiality is essentially determined by facticity."[38] If facticity determines existence and is attached to it, and if moreover existence properly defines Dasein, facticity can obviously concern only Dasein. But on the other hand, to respect this exclusive attribution, facticity should itself be thought on the basis of Dasein's own mode of Being, such that it is not collapsed into the brute fact, which suits the phenomenality of ordinary beings: "*Facticity is not the factuality of the* factum brutum [*Tatsächlichkeit des factum brutum*] *of something present-at-hand* [*Vorhanden*], *but a characteristic of Dasein's Being—one that has been taken up into existence, even if proximally it has been thrust aside.* The 'that-it-is' [*das Dass*] of facticity never becomes something that we can come across by beholding it."[39] Facticity belongs to the way of Being proper to Dasein, existence, such that it is essentially opposed to the two other ways of Being of beings: presence-at-hand (*Vorhandenheit*) and readiness-to-hand (*Zuhandenheit*). To be factically, it is first necessary, therefore, to be in the mode of existence, in the role of Dasein; like existence (concern or anxiety), this cannot be made accessible to the gaze, which fixes beings in terms of their factuality. Facticity withdraws in direct proportion to the visibility of the brute fact. The divide runs so deep that nothing less than the most originary outlines of the ontological difference are at issue: "Dasein's facticity is essentially distinct [*sich unterscheidet*] from the factuality [*Tatsächlichkeit*] of something present-at-hand"; or: "The 'factuality' [*Tatsächlichkeit*] of the fact of one's own Dasein is fundamentally quite different [*grundverschiedenen*] ontologically from the factual occurrence of some kind of mineral, for example. Whenever Dasein is, it is as a Fact, and the factuality of such a fact is what we will call Dasein's '*facticity*.'"[40] From these unequivocal declarations, it must be concluded that facticity is applied to Dasein alone and is inscribed in its foreshadowing of the ontological difference—and, consequently, that it cannot be universalized as a determination of phenomenality in general as it pertains to all phenomena, even ordinary ones.

This clear-cut conclusion hardly stands up to examination, however, even when following the argument literally. That is, the very passage that emphasizes the difference between the facticity proper to Dasein and the simple factuality of a rock clearly marks, though not without confessing a "problem," that Dasein is exposed by the very fact of its own facticity to the encounter with beings, which are not of its mode of Being. "The concept of 'facticity' implies that an entity 'within-the-world' has Being-in-the-world in such a way that it can understand itself as bound up in its 'destiny' with the Being of those entities that it encounters within its own world."[41] In other words, facticity, by virtue of its defining Dasein alone, and being defined in terms of it, bears Dasein's characteristics—and first of all that of being-in-the-world. Now Being-in-the-world is not equivalent only or first to Being on the inside of the world (for how not to be and where to be, if not in the world?), but rather implies—for Dasein too, ontically in the world like every being—ontological openness in such a way as to make a (whole) world of the other beings that, only then, can be encountered in it. Only the intentional comportment of opening, by which Dasein becomes the fact of the world, allows phenomena to come into this world for Dasein. Phenomena are encountered only in the encounter with Dasein.[42] If the facticity of Dasein is defined as "Being-already-in," then it opens a world for beings, which can thus come to meet Dasein, who first brings about the encounter. The phenomenon always stays, by itself, a mere encountered phenomenon, met only by virtue of the more essential encounter in which Dasein first exposes itself to the phenomenon. Henceforth, the unshakeable correspondence between the openness of Dasein bringing about the encounter and the unpredictable landing of the encountered phenomenon means that the facticity proper to Dasein is first exposed as such in the encounter with phenomena that are *not* of its mode of Being. Far from restricting Dasein to a monadic singularity and narrowing it down even more, facticity deploys its intentionality and encounter in the direction of phenomena, which in fact arise only in dependence on its factuality. Precisely because facticity characterizes Dasein properly, it also determines phenomena within the world. To be sure, this factuality of beings is never confused with the facticity of Dasein, but it becomes possible in and through it. The facticity of Dasein thus makes each phenomenon accessible in its fait accompli. The ordinary phenomenon accomplishes its fact through and in the shadow of Dasein's facticity.

If only Dasein's facticity opens the fait accompli of the phenomenon in general, what remains is for me to describe how facticity brings about the encounter with a fait accompli. Facticity arranges the meeting in that it does not merely posit me in fact (as suits every other being), but posits that I am in fact for a fact, one that will be *accompli* precisely because I factically expose myself to it in advance, one for which I am always "already-in."[43] The already resolute expectation of the fact to come or implication in the *fait* already *accompli* refers in the same breath to this unique belatedness of facticity, where the fact is always already done, the cards already dealt. Consider the moment when an accident arrives to me, really arrives, when I "see" it coming. In fact, it has already arrived since I already can no longer remove myself from it; its future is immediately reduced to a future anterior (or rather, an irreality of the present). It immediately becomes too late to see it coming in the future, or even in the present. From the get-go, it's already done, I'm done and done for. Consequently, when confronted with this phenomenon (at the moment of skidding, losing my wits, receiving the blow, etc.), I never act as if I saw it objectively. I never saw anything. In this arising occurrence, it is no longer a matter of knowing, describing, as only a third person could see what arrives. But here, a third party is no longer found. I cannot ask anybody, "Please, take my place for a moment"—not only because *mon semblable, mon frère* will have no desire to take upon himself the danger that assaults me, but above all because, as much as he might like to, he cannot do so by definition; he would have to be located exactly where I am and at the precise moment when the accident occurs in order to suffer the fait accompli. In these times and in this world, there is a place for just one, me, and if I wanted to soothe an other, I could no more put myself in his place than he could take my own here and now. Thus, for the phenomenon—the danger, whose fact is accomplished [*dont le fait s'accomplit*]—to appear, much more is needed than to see it as its substitutable vis-à-vis. This phenomenon must be taken for itself. Or, as we say without thinking when we feel the blow arrive and understand instinctually that I am no longer the spectator but the target: "This time, my time has come, it's my turn, my number has been called."[44] Facticity does not consist in my being reducible to the factuality of a fact, but in exposing me to the fact, which can thus be accomplished only by weighing on me, no longer as a detached observer but as an engaged actor—or better, a critical patient into whom the fact has crashed in being visibly accomplished. The phenomenon can accomplish its appearing only by finding a foothold on a screen— therefore, by weighing on it. Its fait accompli arrives to me from above; it is a fact made *for* me, not *by* me, but at my expense. It is a fact made on my account; by it, I am made. Along the same lines, intentionality is inverted: I become the objective of the object. My facticity no doubt designates me as something done and to do..., however, not in such a way that I accomplish these deeds and would be accomplished therein ("I'm a self-made man"), but inversely, in such a way that the phenomenon itself accomplishes them and accomplishes itself therein as a fact. Facticity comes to me only insofar as it exposes me to the phenomenon's fait accompli: I do not make it by the fact of me, confronting the fait accompli; I let (myself) be made, I let it make me.... The colloquial French phrase "*je me suis fait,*" considered with all its possible verbal complements, unambiguously marks this sort of middle voice, where I am neither the author nor the spectator of the phenomenon, but where my encounter with it, exposed without flight, leaves it the power to say its fact to me and appear in its fait accompli. By understanding the facticity of Dasein in the middle voice, as what "happens [*se fait*]..." and "happens to [*se fait à*]..." more than as a fact making itself, I obtain two decisive results. (a) I maintain the irreducibility of facticity to the factuality of the brute fact, and I understand why the latter depends on the former, far from making it a part of it. (b) I can posit that, in bringing about the encounter, facticity brings it about that phenomena are encountered, and therefore it also determines, in a gradation, all phenomena—precisely because they give themselves.

A Broadened Facticity

This statement of a facticity broadened to include the phenomena themselves finds confirmation in each of the three modes of Being of beings. (a) In the field of Dasein itself, and therefore in relation to its way of Being, I just described the fait accompli of the accident. I could without difficulty decline it in terms of connected phenomena, such as sorrow, desire, joy, etc. (b) In the field of usable beings (*zuhanden*), taken and carried in hand, as they are by definition encountered in the world, it goes without saying that they are put into operation on the basis of Dasein's facticity; but, far from my facticity (therefore its referential system of finalities) determining the factuality of equipment, it is equipment that imposes on me one or several of its finalities, according to which I must organize myself in such a way that it thereby exercises its fait accompli over me. Consider, for example, the tool, in the strict sense of the being that ontically reifies a finality. It cannot be asserted that I set a finality for it, since every finality I assign to it should, in a more or less narrow way, apply the finality, or one of the finalities, that it ontically enacts. No doubt, a wrench or a screwdriver can serve as lever or hammer, but aside from the fact that their performance will be mediocre, they are no doubt first directed by their own finalities (grasping, twisting, screwing, unscrewing, etc.), whose evident ease of use nearly obliges me. The tool appears as what gives itself by, at the same time, setting possibilities; it determines them as so many open (or closed) possibilities for me, in fact. Its availability for use can no longer be confused with brute factuality. The tool imposes itself as a fait accompli because it imposes its possibilities on me as my own. Also, it is given according to its fait accompli only by determining facticity. Curiously, for that matter, the more equipment in general remains undetermined in its finalities, the more it weighs on my possibilities. For example, in the case of the tool to which one must apprentice oneself:[45] because I am still unaware of its reified finalities, I must suspend my own; because I am not aware of "how it works," I must suspend every intention to avail myself of it, the time to "make myself accustomed to it." Thus, when something breaks, the tool is given all the more as a fait accompli as it becomes incapable of assuming the finalities that it nevertheless reifies (Heidegger). Above all, the breakdown interrupts the submission of the tool to my finality and subordinates me to its own—precisely insofar as the absence of its finalities makes them manifest and manifestly irreducible to me. The same holds when we substitute for the manufactured tool (reifying a finality by design) the undetermined tool, the one that no finality specifies, that is "of no use"—a stone, a piece of wood, a sheet of paper. I will avail myself of them as of a tool though they are not tools. I will try to submit them to one or another of my finalities, but since they cannot as such serve them adequately, I will have to tinker with the finalities and capacities of these ill-equipped tools. It is therefore their limits (fragility, the wrong size, irregularity, etc.), by which they can *not* play the part of tools, that decides my own ends (revised downward according to unforeseen occurrences). Their nonsuitableness establishes these nontools as the norm for the possibility of my finalities. Equipment deploys its facticity in and through the fait accompli in the very measure to which it remains absolutely insufficient. The fait accompli of the usable being therefore falls under my facticity.

Is the same true for (c) the simply subsisting being (*vorhanden*)? Simple with respect to the theoretical attitude whose permanent and, in principle, unchanging object it becomes, it still seems foreign to the fait accompli. This indifference, upon more careful examination, seems highly debatable. Take the case of physical beings: however subsisting they might be, or rather precisely because they subsist, they are officially temporalized. They end by passing away exactly as they begin by arising. Each makes itself and unmakes itself. It therefore accomplishes itself as a fact—slow, almost sempiternal if one will, but as a fact having to undo itself. It will be objected that the beings that subsist without material support (mathematical, logical idealities or essences) are not temporalized, therefore that they do not fall within the fait accompli, according to a classic metaphysical division of phenomena (Plato, Aristotle, Descartes, Kant). This second argument for denying facticity to subsistent beings is fragile, for at least three reasons. No doubt, one can speak rigorously of a nontemporality of ideals and consider them unchangeable. The fact remains that none of them has ever been known except by this or that, that is to say, in a time, a place, and precise circumstances. The ideals can indeed, if one sticks just to the ideal, remain for eternity, but in fact their apparition (their invention or discovery first by just one, then their adoption by several) is always inscribed in a time and place, each time accomplished in fact. Ideality does not perhaps possess facticity, but its appearance does. For me, who learns them from a master or rediscovers them in pure reason, the ideals impose themselves in precise times and places as facts that are accomplished for, before, and without me. There was a place and a day when I thought I understood for the first time the *cogito*, integral calculus, the fall of bodies, etc. (not to mention the sciences of fact). With each apprenticeship, the ideal instructs me more than I construct it, opens for me new possibilities (impossible without it), in short, appears to me in the mode of the fact accomplished (fait accompli) over me. With an eye toward radicalizing the moment of apprenticeship to the point of bracketing it, Descartes postulated the creation of the eternal truths, in order to demonstrate the fait accompli of even subsistent idealities. At first glance, the formula appears obviously contradictory: eternal, therefore necessary, how could these truths admit being created and inscribed in contingency? But necessity itself can (metaphysically) result from an act that establishes them: "And even if God has willed that some truths should be necessary, this does not mean that he willed them necessarily; for it is one thing to will that they be necessary and quite another to will this necessarily, or to be necessitated to will it." The necessity of the truths (ideals) itself results from a "will," therefore from an act of establishment— a *fait* always already *accompli* precedes it. The fact character that the truth takes on certainly results from its necessity, but this necessity depends extrinsically on the fact that establishes it. What Descartes here names "God" has as its sole function to accomplish in fact the (necessary) fait accompli of the truths: "Quia voluit tres angulos trianguli necessario aequales esse duobus rectis, idcirco *jam* hoc verum est et fieri aliter non potest [Because he willed that the three angles of a triangle should necessarily equal two right angles, this is *now* [*jam*] true and cannot be otherwise]."[46] The necessary equality becomes true and unchangeable only in a given time (*jam*), therefore, once a fact is accomplished [*donc une fois un fait accompli*]. In this way, independent of all learning, the mathematical ideals are considered in the fact of their having been established as necessary. This establishment, far from weakening their subsistence, is the only thing that can establish it, so much does the facticity of the fait accompli determine originarily the phenomenon in general. And here it is a matter of the fait accompli par excellence because it bears on the beings that are in principle the most irreducible to facticity—subsistent, without materiality, without sensible intuition, possibly without real phenomenality.[47]

For me, here, the task is to establish the intrinsic character of the givenness of the given phenomenon. I relied first on contingency, redefined as anamorphosis (§12), then its unpredictable landing (§14), both of which impose themselves on me and summon me. Pushing the analysis as far as the fait accompli, I reach a new characteristic of the phenomenon inasmuch as given: after its perseity and its individuation, it appears as a fait accompli before which we are always found "already in" it—preceded, determined, "facts." The phenomenality of all beings, namely insofar as given, factically imposes their finalities on me or possibly posits them together with my own: my resolutions result essentially from what the phenomena give me. The fait accompli produces neither chance nor necessity; it opens the possible by giving it. "A throw of the dice/will never/even when launched in eternal circumstances/abolish/chance."[48] This strange passage obviously gives rise to a line of questioning: doesn't the roll of the dice, precisely, give birth to chance, far from abolishing it? But it must be understood in a wholly other fashion: the die, in being cast, in its falling and its incidence, decides to fall on one side or another. If it serves chance before being thrown, it settles it and therefore abolishes it as soon as it is thrown since, at the moment of being thrown, it has always already accomplished the fact. The die, in actually coming into play, makes chance pass to the rank of fait accompli. The die transforms chance into necessity in the very measure to which it is accomplished as a fact. The die makes and unmakes in the same fact—chance—and is accomplished by this very unmaking. But what the die in fact factically provokes, as irrevocably factual as it might be, does not remain absolutely eternal, since the realized fact enacts only one of the sides of the die, one of chance's possibles, and without giving its reason. The fait accompli thus always remains such that it cannot not be what it is, but such that it could be wholly other than what it is. The coincidence between necessity by fact and contingency by right determines the chance not abolished by the fait accompli—the interlacing of *this* contingency and *this* fait accompli intrinsically characterizes the phenomenon according to givenness.

§16 THE INCIDENT

Coming Without Nothing

Considered according to its fait accompli, the given phenomenon arrives—crashes even—over consciousness, which receives it. It appears properly only at the moment when it explodes on the screen. Before this explosion, it simply did not appear. It was still an unseen, still unaccomplished. Its phenomenal accomplishment therefore comes up only at term —once anamorphosis has been deployed (§13), once its unpredictable landing has touched down (§14), in short, once the ascent to the visible has been completed. As it is accomplished only with the end and the fact, the given phenomenon must therefore fall on and arrive to consciousness in order to come to itself. Following the path toward its final appearing, it is defined by its obscure movements and appears only when it finishes, by falling upon what receives and then sees it. This process of the phenomenon authorizes me to think it as the incident. By incident, dictionary usage means a—small —event that comes up. This could not be put better, on condition of understanding it as literally as possible: what comes upon me in such a way that it consists of nothing other than this first and last coming upon, without existing or making itself visible prior to this. Before the incident explodes on the screen of lived experiences and pierces through its unseen, it as yet shows nothing. Its final moment, that of the fait accompli (§15), coincides with its first moment, that of the explosion coming forward (§16). The incident resides entirely in the fact of its initiating accomplishment, without any background, foresight, or forewarning, reduced to its fact.

Aristotle, in defining the *sumbebēkos*, had already, to an extent still to be determined, laid bare certain characteristics of the incident. Let us consider them. (i) The *sumbebēkos* comes forward, arrives, goes (*bainō*) just as the incident falls, crashes, and happens. Both appear only at the terminal point of a process in a fact that cannot be induced, deduced, or foreseen, but whose accomplishment must be awaited. (ii) This arrival is accomplished without any preliminary, warning, or preparation; for the *sumbebēkos* happens without "definite cause" (*oude aition hōrismenon*) to the point of appearing "indeterminate," *aoriston*. While I qualify this indeterminacy in a more phenomenological mode as the explosion without preliminary of the incident, wanting thereby to mark the positive character of an arising without genealogy, metaphysical language can only point to it as a deficiency—absence of cause. However, even this roundabout approach lets us see just how far the freedom of the incident goes: it "attaches to something and can be truly asserted of it"—at issue therefore is neither an appearance nor an illusion or error—but it comes not from a cause, "nor does it happen of necessity or usually." How to admit the possibility of a phenomenon that arises without necessity, without even an at least probable (*ut plurimum*) regularity? To describe this unconditioned occurrence, shouldn't we rather have recourse to the concept of a pure form, an entirely free visibility, a "vague" phenomenality? Aristotle, radically metaphysical in this, chooses the opposite hypothesis: the appearing without preliminary, because without cause or rule, should still be explained (justified, if not rendered intelligible); its explanation will assign it precisely to what most obviously contradicts its mode of appearing since, by definition, it ignores the *eidos* and never appears—the *hulē*. This is what should nevertheless explain the free appearing of the incident as "cause that makes it possible that the accident appear otherwise, other than what usually is."[49] One sees here what distinguishes metaphysics and phenomenology: the first devalues phenomenality, even indisputable and overabundant phenomenality (like the incident), because it is free of a cause, the operator of objectifying intelligibility; in short, it disqualifies the phenomenon in the name of an instance without relation to appearing. On the other hand, the latter accepts all phenomenality, provided only that it appear, without reason or objectness. (iii) This refusal to grant the incident the right to appear provokes a major contradiction in Aristotle's thought. On the one hand, the incident is denied all access to theory (*oudemia esti peri autōi theōria*) to the point that there remains for it "neither a definition nor a property nor a genre."[50] But, at the same time as he decrees the theoretical nullity of the incident in principle, Aristotle employs all his speculative energy to reestablish a positive doctrine of it—the accident by itself, potential passing into act, the composite of form and matter, etc. In a word, the accident escapes science in principle, but the real sciences that would neglect it remain sterile (mathematics, physics, biology, ethics, indeed the theory of forms engaged in materiality). The accident, or more exactly the incident, therefore gives rise to an obvious dilemma: noetically, the incident remains impractical, degree almost zero (just above the *hulē*) of knowledge, but it nevertheless offers a privileged figure (the only real one) of phenomenality, since it gives *itself* without preliminary, presupposition, or foresight. This situation, which is, it seems to me, unavoidable, at the same time designates it as a paradigm of being given: its coming upon (unpredictable landing, anamorphosis, fait accompli) is carried out without cause, without form, without necessity—in short, with nothing but it alone. "Coming upon" here takes on an almost privative sense, as if one could read it (obviously contrary to the letter) "*a*(d)-venue," coming with nothing besides itself, besides the self of what shows itself by being given.

For this privation, whose phenomenal privilege he does not recognize, Aristotle has described three figures. In the first—finding a treasure chest while digging in the garden—the incident is added on to something, in a place and a moment, but without any *dioti* saying why they are such, why that falls here and now and not otherwise. Purely fortuitous, the incident gets the unpredictability of its landing from the gap between its fact, really accomplished, and its *aition*, still indefinite. Must it be seen as a lack of "cause," or rather as an excess of phenomenality over and above any "why"? Aristotle opts for the first hypothesis, while in phenomenology the latter is incumbent.[51] In the second figure—arriving in Aegina, taken by pirates or by storms, when one wanted to go there freely or else reach Piraeus—men and the elements (the aptly named "fortunes of the sea") provide a most real and sufficient cause. The divide of incidence is not cut directly between the fait accompli and its missing *aition*; it is, by contrast, found in the flaw that turns each party from their own intentions (the pirates from ransoming, the sea from letting float, the traveler from coming to Aegina or Piraeus), each party from itself. The intention is accomplished (or not), but not as itself, only as other than itself, *oukh hēi auto all'hēi heteron*.[52] If I arrive at Aegina (where I want to go), but as a prisoner, or adrift on the currents of the sea, my intention is realized in fact, but contrary to itself; and if the pirates carry me prisoner to Aegina, they realize my intention (but reroute it; for I wanted Aegina, not kidnapping) in realizing their own intention (but rerouted; for they intended to find their resting place in Aegina, not my destination); and the rerouting would be still more clear if my intention was to go not to Aegina, but Piraeus. In all these cases, the cause (the intentions, etc.) is not missing; a hijacking simply separates it from itself. It no longer comes up except as foreign to itself, other than itself, *hēi heteron*, contradicting itself, even suspending the principle of contradiction.[53] Incidence could in this case alone be understood as a coincidence: with, or in the place of, what must (should) arrive, there arrives also (*etiam*)[54] what falls contrary to all expectation: I wanted to see Piraeus, Aegina was seen. The incident comes up with and on the occasion of what should arrive (or should have arrived), in full knowledge of the cause, incidentally, most intimately and by digging a divide at the heart of its coming forward. Co-incident, it is detached from what it marks most intimately. It goes with (*sum-bebēkos*) the regulated coming up, but less as a travelling companion than as, in a mixed lot, "what goes along with," the supplement or the scrap.[55] The incident stands apart from itself (becomes other than itself), in order better to contradict the intention, foresight, and causal regulation of phenomenality.

"Adveniens extra"

The third figure of the incident is surprising, so much does it contradict the ordinary understanding of accidentality, and yet it nevertheless definitively brings to light the incident as such. Let us consider the example proposed: for a triangle to have the sum of its angles equal two right angles. Between the property and the triangle, the relation remains one of belonging by itself, *kath' auto*, and to be sure, a simple proof always and necessarily deduces from the figure of any constructed triangle, through the principles of parallel lines and the equality of opposite angles, that the sum of its angles equals 180°. Aristotle even concedes that these types of knowing "admit being eternal, *aidia*" But since this concerns a self-evident, repeatable, mathematical (immaterial), and even eternal truth—in short, one that satisfies the strictest epistemic requirements—by what right is it still considered an incident, one whose everyday characteristics (materiality, chance, unintelligibility, etc.) it contradicts? A single response remains possible: the incident is not defined first, indeed not at all, by these already subsidiary traits, but rather by another characteristic, which sometimes renders them possible but precedes them and dispenses with them. This fundamental character of the incident, Aristotle determines with an all the more admirable precision as it undermines his previous analyses. Bearing the name *incidents* are those phenomena that "belong by themselves [*kath' auto*] to each thing, but are not in the beingness of that thing [*mē en tēi ousiāi onta*]"[56] Not to be in the *ousia*—essence as substance, in short, beingness according to Being—defines the incident. Here a point essential to the phenomenality of the given phenomenon is at stake. As if in passing, Aristotle concedes the point that for me is capital: the horizon of beingness does not succeed in doing justice to the given insofar as it shows *itself.*

What follows is a strange and radical turnabout. Since *ousia* does not allow for a definition of the incident, it's better to define the incident alone by excluding *ousia* from the definition. Now, from the perspective of a phenomenality of what is given, the incident is not so much added accidentally to *ousia* as inversely *ousia* can, in the best of cases, coincide (from the outside and not without a gap) with the incident such as it shows *itself* from itself, without it, and solely on the basis of its befalling. This could be confirmed by following the Aristotelian theory of the accident and material substances,[57] and above all by remembering Maimonides' doctrine concerning Being as accident, which does not beat around the bush in developing the opening conceded by Aristotle: "It is known that Being is an accident [*'arid*] coming in addition to a being. For this reason, it is something superadded to the quiddity of the being in question." Or, according to Avicenna: "Thus in a certain way substance is accidental to the nature [*accidentatis naturae*] of its subject because it is Being and added to the nature of being [*adjuncta naturae entis*]."[58] As is often the case, it falls to Thomas Aquinas to set the strictest formulation of this thesis. He begins by repeating Avicenna, relying simply on the accidentality of Being to beings: "Creation, taken passively, is thus a certain accident in nature;"[59] but he goes further when, plumbing the depths of the accident, he finds a coming upon that carries well beyond the accident insofar as, metaphysically, it is opposed to essence. For if on one hand, "Everything that does not belong to the concept of an essence or quiddity comes to it from outside [*adveniens extra*]," and if on the other, "Being [*être*] is other than essence," then it must be inferred that *esse* itself comes upon from the outside, *adveniens ad extra*, as an incident for all that does not have Being and essence coincide within it, as God alone can do.[60] *Esse*, not on the hither side of essence like the accident but beyond it, nevertheless happens to it as an incident, as *the* incident par excellence. This strange pronouncement is set forth in two paradoxes. (i) No doubt, it reinforces the thesis of the real co-positing of Being and essence in the created;[61] but it would not do so if it did not first assume unreservedly that created essence can be conceived without Being—without the potential to be, but also without the obligation to be, in short without Being. The coming upon of Being implies nothing less than this prior absence of Being considered essentially. The incident, to show itself, no more has to be than it has to designate its causes. Through this absence of essence, therefore of Being, Being can subsequently come upon as from the outside. *Adveniens extra* itself implicitly requires the possibility of an appearing without Being. It is therefore fitting to think the incident that remains outside essence as nonessence, indeed nonbeing. Aristotle himself suggested as much, provided at least that this doubtful reflection is admitted literally: "It seems that the incident [*sum-*

bebēkos] is something close to nonbeing [*enggus tou mē ontos*]."[62] Almost nothing certainly, but on that account accomplishing in an exemplary way phenomenality in general. (ii) But when it concerns the pure individual, such as when it happens as incident, without essence or remainder, and yet is nevertheless in the mode of finite being, how are we to connect its quasi non-Being to this Being? Answer: Being can rejoin it only by coming up for it incidentally, *adveniens extra*. Being itself is enacted, therefore, at least for the created and the finite, according to the figure of the incident. An extraordinary conclusion! First, because the incident, which had on principle been pushed to the margins of the ontic domain by degrading all its essential dignity, rediscovers its license to be, though without *ousia*. Next, because this Being without *ousia* is recognized in fact, without receiving any explanation or official rehabilitation. Are the incident by itself and the quasi non-Being equivalent to a disguised essence or a contradiction in terms? This dilemma—and others—can obviously find a solution only in passing from metaphysics to a radical phenomenology. Finally and above all, as soon as it imposes its figure on Being itself (it too *adveniens*), the incident becomes the ultimate norm for the entire field, whose margins alone it was supposed to occupy. Being should henceforth be thought according to the determinations of the incident, far from the incident being ontically devalued into a marginal accident. The exception becomes the rule—no one understood this better than Thomas Aquinas.

What Affects Us

Thus, and despite appearances, even in metaphysics, the incident (or the accident, the attribute, etc.) is not always limited to the role of product derived from *ousia* (essence, subsistence, etc.). Descartes's thesis about substance provides a privileged example of this. At first, he affirms the absolute primacy of *ousia* (whose role is here played by *substantia*) because it alone subsists by itself. *Ousia* therefore precedes its attributes, accidents, and modes that it disqualifies and also requalifies on the basis of its own excellence. That is, from the ontic (therefore metaphysical) perspective, *substantia* dominates the incident. Another perspective remains possible, however: the knowledge of this same *substantia*. At once, the question becomes quasi-phenomenological and asks how it is still possible to know and reach substance—in short, how it appears to us. Descartes, scrupulously faithful to the thing itself, answers without hesitating that at the outset we cannot observe a substance solely from the fact that it is an existing thing because that alone does not affect us: "Verumtamen non potest substantia primum animadverti ex hoc solo quod sit res existens, quia hoc solum per se nos non afficit."[63] Bare existence, even if it can claim an absolute ontic primacy, displays a radical phenomenological shortcoming—that of not affecting us. To affect, *affecter*—a wise term: it *does* [*fait*] nothing to us because it does not come *upon* [*ad*vient] us (*ad-ficit, ad-facio*).[64] No unpredictable landing or fait accompli opens its anamorphosis. Since it does not come upon or even arrive (still less impose itself), it does not succeed in being given; it therefore does not show itself. In short, shut up in its reserve, substance (*substantia, ousia*) is absolutely not phenomenalized; there is no phenomenon of it. This result, seemingly excessive, will nevertheless receive ample confirmation in all of Descartes's successors—directly with Berkeley's immaterialism and the thing-itself in Kant, indirectly with the unicity of substance in Spinoza and the absence of an idea of God in Malebranche's occasionalism, indeed in Leibniz's arranging of all substances on the cognitive paradigm. It will nevertheless be objected that in the end Descartes admits a knowledge of substances, one that he will sometimes even abuse (when he believes he has proven the existence of material substances). To be sure, he reestablishes the possibility of knowing substance, but never its possibility of appearing. In effect, substance is known indirectly, through the mediation of attributes (incidents), which alone are perceived as being present here: "Aliquod attributum adesse percipiamus," we perceive as manifest given only an attribute, indeed several. Substance, on the other hand, never receives anything but an *adesse* derived (*etiam*) on the basis of the sole original and perfect *adesse*, that of the accident: "Aliquam rem existentem sive substantiam . . . etiam adesse."[65] If the attributes exist in and through substance, substance is known only through the attributes. This reversal attests a clear conflict between the ontic requirement and a quasi-phenomenological claim. Descartes accords it, furtively but indisputably, citizenship therein, for example when he summons together a plurality of attributes (*varia attributa*) simply to secure the mediated manifestation of substance, "ad manifestandam substantiam."[66] Here it is indeed a matter of phenomenality, and even of the phenomenality of what, in itself, remains nonmanifest—which defines precisely the task proper to phenomenology. And phenomenality, even that (derivative, *etiam*) of substance, is in play in the attributes, accidents, and modes which all fall under the incident. The standard model of the phenomenon (the incident) is therefore not posited over and above the standard model of metaphysical beingness (substance), but is opposed to it or subordinates it. Substance appears —if it appears—only last, by owing all its belated visibility to its incidents, "next to nothing." It can show itself only by latching on to their manifestations, which alone are full, by coming incidentally to add itself thereto, "adveniens ad extra." If we must still speak of an accident in phenomenology, we would have to conclude that substance shows itself only as accident of the accident—as second-order incident. Thus is confirmed the paradox noted, thanks to Aristotle and Thomas Aquinas. Thus especially is confirmed my fundamental thesis: only the incident shows itself because it alone gives itself—what shows *itself* gives *itself.*

The phenomenological primacy of the incident over form, cause, or essence could obviously be confirmed in many other cases. A particle can arrive (to me) without its mass or spatio-temporal coordinates being simultaneously definable. A painting can happen to me without form, simply by the impact of a single color. And when the face of the Other imposes itself on me, no substance or depth intervenes, only the intentionality on the surface of its gaze. Always, the incident dispenses with any and all depth, any and all background, but thus arises only more keenly. I will not develop these cases here because this is not the place to do so and because others, more competent than myself, could do it better. What I nevertheless still can do is emphasize the determination of the given phenomenon that the incident delivers. Consisting in its pure arising, in the fact of its bursting forth, the incident remains unforeseeable, exceeds all antecedent, and rests on no *ousia.* As a consequence, it remains unconstructable, unconstitutable, and therefore unavailable. Even once its fact is accomplished, its fait accompli, even after the fact, a posteriori, it still keeps the indetermination of what, in itself, could still give us to see or divine other suggestions, other characteristics or properties. Here a remark from Descartes concerning the "full and perfect conception of things . . . which includes all that there is intelligible in them" must be taken into consideration. He admits that this obviously escapes us in the case of "the infinite," but also that we do not attain it in the case of "anything else, however small it may be."[67] Every phenomenon, insofar as given, in effect keeps something like a surplus over and above what receives it. As fully delivered as it might be, its exile from *ousia* and the shortage of cause leave it finally not equal to adequate knowledge. But this inequality does not mean a defect of thought so much as an excess of the thinkable. Be it only by its irreducible unpredictable landing, the given always shows itself too broadly for the scope of our grasp. The limit of knowledge stems first of all from its ineradicable belatedness to the event of what shows *itself.*

§17 THE EVENT

Without Definite Reason

The phenomenon, insofar as given, rises to the visible by itself, according to its anamorphosis (§13), is individuated in its unpredictable landing (§14), is imposed irrevocably by its fait accompli (§15), and resists complete construction by arising as a pure incident (§16). It is clear that all these determinations are organized around the original equivalence between showing itself and giving itself (§§12–13). Because it shows itself only inasmuch as it gives itself, the phenomenon appears to the degree that it arises, ascends, arrives, comes forward, imposes itself, is accomplished factically and bursts forth—in short, it presses urgently on the gaze more than the gaze presses toward it. The gaze receives its impression from the phenomenon before any attempt at constituting it. Indeed, to this point, my analysis has aimed at nothing if not to describe how and how far, in the appearing, the initiative belongs in principle to the phenomenon, not the gaze.

One last point remains: if appearing implies showing *itself,* as showing *itself* implies giving *itself,* both imply a *self* of the phenomenon.[68] Such a *self,* supposing it could be reached, would in no way be equivalent to the *in itself* of the object or the thing. That is, both are defined by the constitution (possible or impossible, it matters little) exerted over them by the I held to be original. Here, in contrast, the issue is the anamorphosis and unpredictable landing of the phenomenon, such that it appears starting from its own depths and from depths that burst forth only on the surface, without background (§16). Therefore, the *self* of what shows *itself* and gives *itself* can never be verified through inference or constitution, which would collapse it equally into the *in-itself* of the object (or the thing without phenomenality). But it could be through the impression, or rather through the pressure that it exerts over the gaze (and, of course, over the other modes of perception). This pressure bears down in such a manner that it makes us feel not only its weight, but also the fact that we cannot in any way master it, that it imposes itself without our having it available to us—we do not trigger it any more than we suspend it. The *self* of the phenomenon is marked in its determination as event. It comes, does its thing, and leaves on its own; showing *itself*, it also shows the *self* that takes (or removes) the initiative of giving *itself*. The event, I can wait for it (though most often, it surprises me), I can remember it (or forget it), but I cannot make it, produce it, or provoke it. Let us describe the event, where the phenomenon gives *itself*, to the point of showing itself *itself*.

The reason for this phenomenological unavailability stems, we have seen, from its absence of definite reason—*oude aition hōrismenon*. The extraordinary import of this thesis still remains to be assessed. For if the incident, in the role of mere (metaphysical) accident, already suspends the principle of contradiction[69] considered in and with all its phenomenological importance, it also suspends the principle of reason. Let it not be objected, from a metaphysical point of view, that the given phenomenon should then renounce all intelligibility—without cause, without reason, therefore also irrational, absurd. For, even in metaphysics, there are two ways, not just one, of not subscribing to the principle of reason: of course, that of the accident, chance, or matter (first or else *insignata*)—noncausability by defect, lacking the potential to be inscribed in a succession of causes/effects ruled by a law, incapacity for repetition, deficiency of foreseeability, unintelligibility by obscurity; but there is yet another, that of God—uncausability by excess, infinite essence, who is excepted from every univocal relation with his always finite effects, a fortiori with the least antecedent, unrepeatability of the unique, unavailability of the unforeseeable because invisible, incomprehensibility by surplus, even of qualifications, therefore of evidence. These two senses of uncausability are named, traditionally, Being by *itself*, *a se* negatively (accident) or positively (God). What to keep, for the phenomenology of the given, of such a metaphysical distinction? Do we want to claim for the *self* of what shows *itself* the *self* of the positive *a se*, to identify the given phenomenon with the "God" of metaphysics? This project would obviously be meaningless. It is rather a matter of posing two questions. (i) Can the model of the noncause or quasi (non-)cause (*causa sui*) that was elaborated by the medievals and Descartes, respectively, be of any help in putting us on the trail of a positive interpretation of the uncausability of the event of the given phenomenon? For we cannot set aside, by a refusal that would itself also be without reason, the astonishing isomorphism of the uncausable God (removed by excess from the causal relation) and the phenomenon without cause (unavailable to the causal relation). At least formally, both the one and the other benefit from the same and extraordinary privilege of not having to respond to the question that enjoins all other beings to offer a reason for their existence and their appearance. (ii) Which leads to the second question: if the given phenomenon (therefore the totality of phenomenality) makes an exception to causality, and if "God" (the principle, or whatever one would like to name it, therefore the origin of the totality) is also excepted from causality, what remains as its field of application, over what kingdom reigns that which claims this exception— the universal title of "great metaphysical principle" of sufficient reason before being offered to reason? Obviously, this principle administers to objects and the way they follow one another according to laws that are at once presupposed and confirmed. But just how far does the domain of objects extend? Can objectness characterize, therefore rationalize, the entire field of phenomenality? By contrast, haven't we already established (§§4–5) that neither objectness nor beingness exhaust phenomenality and that the phenomenon shows itself first insofar as it is given, before possibly being qualified as a being or as an object? Don't we merely recover, for the ultimate determination of the given phenomenon confronted with causality, the clear rupture that we had confirmed during the inquiry into givenness? Henceforth, the determination of the given phenomenon as event without cause or reason will be seriously justified (and assessed) only by putting into question the principle of causality—and by giving it again its legitimate, limited role.

In metaphysics, cause does not exist merely as one categorical function among others; it is set up as the universal category for all beings. Thus for Suarez: "There is no being that is not an effect or a cause"; for Pascal: "All things caused and causing"; or for Kant: "Everything of which experience teaches that it happens [*geschieht*] must have a cause."[70] But the universality of causality could still seem purely constative, as if in fact beings, things, and events were inscribed in a network of causes and effects. Quite obviously, it is no such thing—it is not a question of empirical observation, but a transcendental principle. Establishing one of the categories into such a principle is accomplished only at the end of a long history, whose complexity need not be retraced here. Let it suffice to note that Descartes incontestably played a decisive role in it; it falls to him to have posited, as first of the "axioms or common notions," that "concerning every existing thing it is possible to ask what is the cause of its existence. This question may even be asked concerning God." Why is it permissible to ask this, seeing as, for example, God does not in the strict sense need one? Because it is a question of a transcendental principle, or in Descartes's language, of an

edict, indeed a *diktat*: "The light of nature does dictate [*dictat*] that if anything exists it is always permissible [*liceat*] to ask why it exists; that is, we
may inquire [*inquirere*] into its efficient cause, or, if it does not have one,
we may demand [*postulare*] why it does not need one."[71] The edict of reason decrees (*dictat*) therefore that it is permissible (*liceat*) either to inquire
into the antecedent cause for every existence duly observed or, if this existence pleads for an exemption from cause (in reality, only in the case of
God), to call for (*postulare*) the reason behind this exemption. It is appropriate here to emphasize the status of principle, imposed by the authority
of the will to truth, indeed by its violence, of what will become the principle of sufficient reason. *Principle* here implies that the experimental, or
rather phenomenological, confirmation of its requirements is still to come.
What phenomena admit without exception or equivocation one or several
causes, thereby lending themselves to letting their existence or their given
be interpreted as effects? It seems clear that God escapes from this demand, while objects—on first analysis at least—submit to it without reserve or remainder. I suggest that phenomena as such, namely as given, not
only do not satisfy this demand, but far from paying for their refusal with
their unintelligibility, appear and let themselves be understood all the better as they slip from the sway of cause and the status of effect. The less they
let themselves be inscribed in causality, the more they show themselves and
render themselves intelligible as such. Such phenomena are named events
—seeing as the characteristic of eventness gathers together all those previously recognized in the given phenomenon.

Negentropies

Let us consider the principle of causality such as Descartes introduces
it for the first time in the order of reasons—without proof, by virtue of a
supposedly incontestable evidence: "Now it is manifest by the natural light
that there must be at least as much [*tantumdem ad minimum*] reality in the
efficient and total cause as in the effect of that cause. For where, I ask, could
the effect get its reality from, if not from the cause? And how could the
cause give it to the effect unless it possessed it?"[72] I myself ask: is it self-
evident, for a phenomenological gaze, that the Being or reality of the effect
always remains on this side, that is, at best equal to that of the cause, therefore that the cause always possesses "at least as much" as the effect? This ontic equality (or rather this superiority) of the cause in fact has nothing
"manifest" about it; the "natural light" could by contrast admit that the ef-

fect contains at least as much, if not sometimes more, Being or reality than the cause. Let me sketch two arguments in favor of this reversal. A classic, but pertinent, objection can be put forward first: efficiency alone never suffices to make the entire effect; it only produces it; for it to happen, it must be posited along with a form (formula, plan, industrial design, etc.) and an end (a use, a need, or a "niche" in a market, etc.). At the outset, efficiency cannot equal the reality of the effect. There is more: even conceding the restriction of all causality to efficiency alone (set up as total and unique cause), it can never be demonstrated that the effect results from just one efficient cause. The one that triggers its apparition could simply be the one that ends a process which also mobilizes other efficiencies: the technician, the machine, the motive force, the transport, etc., converge in a proliferating, indeed equivocal and indistinct, efficiency. Above all, when efficiency, even supposedly known, triggers the apparition of its effect, other factors, provisionally negligible or unknown, of an indeterminate number but always required, can also interfere. In particular, the privilege brutally accorded to efficiency (here called total—sole sufficient) hides the residual function of the final cause, the material cause—not only the material (which can still on principle be perfectly known), but the indeterminate factor (*hulē*), the work that can make the material play, deforms it in opposition to the form and admits conforming only to a final deformity. Now, this play of the material can never be eliminated or foreseen. Even the most highly effective production techniques remain slave to the material's actual performance (its resistance, etc.), but above all to its ineliminable materiality (scraps, recycling, pollution). The effect pollutes, wears out, and weighs down. This second effect of the effect, though the cause makes it, is not foreseen or made expressly by the cause, which never absorbs it. Nevertheless, to understand the effect, it must be understood with its induced, secondary and still to come, unforeseeable effects. The cause does not know all that it does in producing what it does only in part. It produces the effect without seeing that the effect makes an effect that escapes it, ever since the origin of the causal process. In short, the effect contains always as much, often more, reality (possibly dangerous or negative) as the cause. This is the first mark of negentropy in the event.

There is another. The Cartesian relation compares the reality of the effect to that of the cause and concludes their equality (=) or the inferiority (<) of the former to the latter. Now, such a quantitative comparison between two terms obviously supposes that they can be arranged together and at the same time in two extremes of an inequality—in short, that they remain stable, contemporaries, both the one and the other in the present. According to the evidence, however, this is a fiction, no doubt one that is epistemologically acceptable by convention, but one that has no phenomenological justification. (i) In the natural attitude, it is proper to the effect to come after the cause; for even if in any given moment (the "shock") they are contemporaries, it should be conceded that one begins after the other, sometimes when the other ceases. We therefore cannot, with any rigor, compare them in a stable relation, unless by abstracting from temporal succession and the variations it implies. The effect does not follow the cause after a more or less brief encounter—it replaces it as soon as it arises and disqualifies it while confirming it. (ii) From the perspective of the reduction, one sees in addition that the effect is radically given in the causal relation as a phenomenon that begins, arises, shows itself, while the cause at best persists in its appearing, but most often suspends it. The relation therefore cannot be described as if it were deployed spatially (since it flows in time), nor can it be reversed at will to meet the needs of a comparison (since the effect has the peculiar characteristic of arising, the cause of persisting or ceasing). In the relation, the effect therefore shows a massive privilege over the cause: its phenomenality begins with the effect; it continues or finishes its own. Even in the (hypothetical) case of equal "reality" between them, the effect still marks its decisive phenomenological superiority—it alone arrives, comes upon, imposes itself. It alone initiates a new anamorphosis according to a new unpredictable landing. In short, in the effect alone is an incident added to phenomenality. This preeminence of the effect is also confirmed in terms of time. Even if, at the initial moment of efficiency (admitting the pertinence of "moment" and "efficiency" when it is a matter of phenomenality), cause and effect must be simultaneous as soon as the fact of the effect is accomplished, the effect occupies the present and suppresses the cause, which endures as is or ceases. Let me here dispel a possible misreading: cause and effect do not differ in terms of their persistence in the present, since the cause can sometimes persist in presence as long as its effect, indeed longer. But the temporal privilege of the effect does not stem from its presence in the present (persistence, subsistence); it stems from the fact that the effect uses this present in presence to arise, to appear, in short to give *itself* to and in the present. For the effect, it is not a matter of making its debut in persistence in presence, but of showing its advent there for the first time. The effect alone is in effect in the present, for it alone makes an event therein, while the cause, at best, persists in presence. Consequently, the effect, as event, belongs within phenomenality, but the cause, like persistence in presence, belongs to (metaphysical) ontology. Whence a second mark of the negentropy of the event.

First the Effect

Although I have reversed the hierarchy of cause and effect so that one is referred to metaphysics, the other to phenomenology, I have not yet pushed the paradox to its conclusion. For as I had redefined substance as accident of the accident (§16), I should also construe the cause as effect of the effect—of the effect understood in terms of the event. Barring this reversal, access to the event in its phenomenological specificity is obscured, indeed closed off. In taking the event as the product of a cause, one confuses it with a simple fact, added afterwards to others: the "events" of the day, the month, the year, which one actualizes on the stage of actuality and which therefore are not put into operation by themselves. Or else, it is distinguished as an image among other products, one that is simply more visible. Whence the turn of phrase "event-making"—a formulation that is perfectly contradictory since the event makes *itself* as it gives itself and shows itself. On the other hand, if we stick strictly to the event taken as the arising of a phenomenon, it becomes possible to think its multiple specificity. (a) The event *precedes its cause* (or its causes). The temporal privilege of the effect—it alone arises to and in the present, gives *itself*—implies that all knowledge begins by the event of the effect; for without the effect, there would be neither meaning nor necessity to inquiring after any cause whatsoever. But this search also supposes that the event, having once come forward without any condition other than its own unpredictable landing, is after the fact reread in the figure of an effect—the result being that only this interpretation of the event as an effect establishes its relation to a supposed cause. This chiasmus was observed perfectly by Descartes: if causes "explain" effects, "it is the causes that are proved by the effects." On the one hand, causes offer reasons for effects, but solely in terms of intelligibility. Provided they make up clear and distinct objects, they can be constructed according to all the hypotheses; causes therefore serve the purely epistemological function of subsequently producing the evidence for the effects. They remain "suppositions" (possibly conjectural or chosen from equivalent hypotheses). On the other hand, the effects, no doubt awaiting evidence and epistemologically dependent on causes, keep the notable ontic privilege of being and being "quite certain."[73] The effect alone imposes itself with certainty; consequently, one rests on it in order to "deduce," after the fact, the cause, whose function consists less in producing it than in understanding it. Kant too marks a similar reversal. The objective causal relation does not correspond to the subjective apprehension of the succession of the manifold in apprehension; it begins only when "in conformity with such a rule" (the principle of the second analogy of experience), I act in such a way that "the given-event [*die Begebenheit*], as the conditioned, thus affords reliable evidence of some condition, and this condition is what determines [*bestimmt*] the given-event."[74] Here again, the cause subsumes in its concept an already given phenomenon, an event (in fact collapsed into the effect) that, according to experience, in fact precedes it. The cause remains an effect of meaning, assigned to the effect by the will to know, or rather, imposed on the event to compensate for its exorbitant privilege—namely its arising as being, its having come forward as phenomenon—with an epistemological dependence. The cause does not merely come after the effect so as to secure its belated and hypothetical commentary, but above all to mitigate or deny it the status of event—the *self* of the given phenomenon.

One could nevertheless make the following objection: if this reversal of the causal relation in favor of the effect could perhaps count as a scientific explanation, it is forbidden by technological production. To produce a product, one must know its cause completely before and in order to produce its effect. It has therefore already been tested on the consumers and verified on the calculators; it has even been reified before production is initiated (in the precise sense of "industrialization"). How better to know what, prior to the product in the chain of production, precedes it and effects it? But this objection again confirms my analysis. For what permits qualifying a cause ("qualifying" a machine, an engine, an airplane, etc.) as cause, therefore listing it before the regular and sure production of its effects (the "product," thing or services, it matters little), if not its performances or its results, in short the observation that "it works" and that each time it continues to "work," that is to say, to arrive, arise, produce *itself*—in short, the event? In the apparent continuity of the chain of production, it is in fact only a matter of a succession of discontinuous events that are no doubt alike in a number of ways but unalike in all the others according to their *hulē*, and especially according to time. And also, how does one see that "it works," that one has indeed reached "total quality," that objectives are being met, except by observing results a posteriori, through cost analysis and statistics, by drawing lessons from experience, therefore by studying the effects or more exactly what can be interpreted as effects in the each time irreducible events? Industrial production therefore does not contravene the phenomenological reversal, but confirms it. The "good" product is such not on account of its causes (its definition, its properties, etc.), but on account of its effects (its efficiency, its sales, etc.). Only the result counts—the effect decides itself.

Overcoming Measure

I can now pass to the second causal characteristic of the event. (b) Inasmuch as it is a given phenomenon, *the event does not have an adequate cause* and cannot have one. Only in this way can it advance on the wings of a dove: unforeseen, unusual, unexpected, unheard of, and unseen. The upstream inquiry aiming at a cause can be deployed only on a twofold condition, or if one prefers, within a twofold limit. A cause (explanation, hypothesis, theory, ideology, etc.) must first be able to set forth the conceptual power required to offer a reason, at least provisionally but also globally, for the effect. The effect therefore should not "exceed the understanding" and its concepts. Next, the event must be interpretable as an effect; that is to say, it must remain (in principle, in rational experience, if not really) repeatable, constitutable, definable. To make (a) good effect or good impression (susceptible of cause), the event should therefore not have too much effect, not "overcome measure." Now, it happens that the event—precisely because it arises in an unpredictable landing—overcomes measure and the understanding, and therefore is excepted from all adequate cause.[75]

Let me illustrate the claim that the event dismisses all cause in two—apparently quite different—cases. (i) For the historian, "The more the event is fraught with consequences, the less it is possible to think it in terms of its causes" (F. Furet).[76] It's not a matter of there being a shortage of causes, which would remain unknown because the information, inquiries, and particular studies would be lacking. Quite to the contrary, the information—here concerning what triggered the First World War—is overabundant. The event, already considered in technology's mode of Being, benefits, in the scholarship of all the modern languages, from all imaginable information: geographic documentation, demographic statistics, economics, ideological and scientific production, state of civil and military technologies, investigations by the press, etc.—and the imagination stops conceiving more often than the banks of data accumulating. Troops of archivists and the curious have elaborated this information; squads of researchers have treated it and organized it into objects; generations of historians have interpreted it in terms of so many causes and systems of possible and often probable causes. In effect, in the case at hand, we have an overabundance of available causes, all of which are sufficient: expansionist rivalries in Europe, imperialist confrontations in the colonies, economic competition for basic resources and access to waterways, demographic pressures, territorial claims linked to the principle of nationalities, bellicose and revolutionary ideologies, finally all the forms of development or all the forms of crisis, including the anecdotal psychology of the players, even the least among them (Princip or Villain), etc. All these causes, in one way or another, competed; all are widely documented for us. The event therefore accepts all the causalities one would assign to it. But it is precisely this overabundance that forbids assigning it a cause, and even forbids understanding it through a combination of causes. In effect, what qualifies it as event stems from the fact that these causes themselves all result from an arising with which they are incommensurable. We pursue them because the event happens by itself, far from its happening as a consequence of what they teach us. Its irrepressible bursting into the tranquil air of popular enthusiasm in the summer of 1914 does not arise from its causes to come, but from itself, from its unpredictable landing and its incident. Only this fait accompli, individuated by its irrevocable perseity, prompts the inquiry into causes and crystallizes the whole phenomenal field on its basis. Profoundly struck by the precursors of this very event, the Great War that would dislocate him, Péguy describes this perseity of the event as such: "Nothing is more mysterious . . . than these points of profound conversion, these overturnings, these renewals, these profound new beginnings. This is the very secret of the event"—this is the interaction and unanalyzable intrigue of infinitely converging causes. However, their overabundance paradoxically lets the event's absolute independence from any cause appear: "But when there is nothing more that one could start from, one feels that one is in the midst of the event itself and its aging. / Nothing any longer pretties up and disguises its aging and this irreversible stream."[77] The event, looked at in the eye of its storm, arises and accomplishes itself when nothing more comes to pass—nothing identifiable by or identifiable with one or several causes—or rather, when the thing itself, after the fashion of an avalanche, a landslide, a burst of thunder, collapses by *itself*, puts *itself* into motion, decides for itself and by itself, without cause or reason besides its declared *self*. Only in this way can a singular event possess both the modalities of necessity—everything is articulated and organized necessarily around this event, once its irrevocable fact is accomplished—and of contingency (nothing could foresee its incident or its unpredictable landing). In metaphysics, this would be a contradiction; in phenomenology, not at all, since the event sustains its causes exactly in the measure to which it makes an exception to causality, offers a reason for it, insofar as it gives itself its own (sole) reason.[78]

It may be objected that this concerns a historical event, therefore one that is complex, collective, heterogeneous, one that by definition no construction, however complete it might be, could pretend to objectify, and that accordingly the confusion of causes does not imply their suspension, still less causal exception. (ii) Let me therefore consider an event that is excessively individual and focused. "At the very instant when the warm liquid, and the crumbs with it, touched my palate, a shudder ran through my whole body, and I stopped, intent upon the extraordinary happening going its own way inside me. An exquisite pleasure had invaded my senses, but individual, detached, *with no suggestion of its cause.* And at once the vicissitudes of life had become indifferent to me, its disasters innocuous, its brevity illusory—this new sensation having had on me the effect which love has of filling me with a precious essence; or rather, this essence was not in me; it was myself."[79] Here there is indeed an event, determined as given phenomenon. An anamorphosis first aligns the "me" along the axis of the visible's ascent ("the extraordinary happening going its own way inside me") to the point of identifying one with the other ("it was myself"). An unpredictable landing occurs "at the very instant," discontinuous and unique, which could come only toward "me." The fait accompli is marked in that the pleasure "had at once," therefore always already irrevocably "invaded." The incident is spotted in that what appears "goes its own way," since it happens outside the norm—"extraordinary," therefore nonconstitutable. These determinations of the given phenomenon are summed up finally in this phrase, which properly defines the event: "with no suggestion of its cause." As if by chance, but by design, the writer says what phenomenology thinks. An event—this pleasure—therefore arises determined as given phenomenon, consequently without cause. But what precisely does it mean here to appear without cause? Let us follow the guiding light of our perplexity. We are surprised first that a phenomenon or rather a mere lived experience, barely intentional and absolutely immanent to consciousness ("was myself"), can remain unexplained by a cause. Isn't every feeling and

every "passion" defined in principle by its cause (Descartes)? But this is precisely not a matter of a passion produced by an object or its representation—no idea of an object (and especially not the perfectly arbitrary, though
agreeable, sensation of cake) precedes the event, which arises without preliminary: pleasure without cause, pure given. Hence the second surprise:
the event imposes itself on *me* ("a shudder ran through my whole body,"
"filling *me*") to the point that far from trying to submit it to some antecedent, I can only consider it as showing *itself* on its own ("intent upon
the extraordinary happening going its own way inside me") by itself. Better, renouncing the assignation of this *self* to a cause other than it, I can
only let myself be assigned to it, to the point of receiving a new "essence"
from it. The event thus attests its nonconstitutability by constituting me,
myself, its effect. Whence the third surprise: the event that comes forward
with this pleasure is not summed up in it. At issue is the remembrance of
the narrator's entire past, not only a reactivation of his memory (secondary
retention), but the return of the living present in and through present retention of a past that, at the moment it was lived, was not even remembered or perceived. The event announced by this pleasure provokes, immeasurably beyond, the arising of a world, the world. The event prompts
not only the memory of an individual (the narrator), nor just the work in
which this past would again become a living present (*Remembrance of Things
Past*), but precisely the total world of history: the event of the summer of
1914, which will end up in the disastrous alteration of Europe as well as the
transformation of Mme Verdurin into the Duchess of Guermantes. For, the
narrator's pleasure, "with no suggestion of its cause," belongs to the same
exact event as the one that the historian cannot "think on the basis of its
causes." The most global event joins the most intimate event; they are collapsed into each other and, in both cases, described by the same determinations. "The rose is without why," but also the event. For that matter, the
rose, when it opens, arises like an event, just as the event blossoms—when
it is ripe.

Three Notae: Unrepeatable, Excessive, Possible

From the emancipation of the event from cause, there follow its other
characteristics, its *notae*. (a) *Unrepeatability*. If it comes from itself and without precedent, the event of unknown cause remains a found event, absolutely unique. Even on the hypothesis (in fact meaningless) that the *hulē*
would make a difference, the temporal gap of arising would defer the events

so that they differ without confusion: the same event in two different times would differ from itself. And reciprocally, two absolutely similar (a hypothesis that the *hulē* renders absurd) and supposedly perfectly contemporary events would differ in terms of the exteriority of the space that their incommensurable contexts would impose on them. Investigating the criteria that permit identifying or individualizing events has hardly any meaning: they are individualized by their very event. And finding these criteria in the causes comes only from a misreading: the event is individualized only by its irreducibility to the cause.[80] Each event, absolutely individualized, arrives only once (*hapax*) and once and for all (*ephapax*), without sufficient antecedents, without remainder, without return. The nonrepeatability of the event thus takes up in two senses the other determinations of the given phenomenon. In the sense of uniqueness, it takes up individuation by unpredictable landing (§14) and nonconstitutability according to incident (§16). In the sense of temporality, it takes up anamorphosis (§13) and the irrevocability of the fait accompli (§15). (b) *Excessiveness*. Obviously, one cannot deny that prior to each event, there are antecedents, and innumerable ones at that—antecedents in general, which arrive before it or pre-exist it, but also antecedents that offer similarities, distant or precise, precedents ("there are precedents"). But one can speak of event only to the degree that it exceeds these precedents ("I've never seen such a thing"). The more the excess is noted, the more the event imposes. The level of eventness—if one can speak thus—is measured by the amount of the phenomenon's excess over its antecedents. The definition of existence as ex-sistence, outside of causes, says this in a metaphysical way: *to exist* means, for a being, to posit itself at a distance from the causes that produced its existence. In a phenomenological mode, one says: the event happens only by ex-isting outside its causes, antecedents, or precedents—that is to say, by exceeding them to the point of leaving them. This excessiveness—indeed, this ex-ceeding that posits outside of... —guarantees that one can never produce the event. It makes itself and, so long as it has not come up on its own, it is not made, nothing is made. And when it finally gives *itself*, one understands precisely that it alone could show *itself* and that "it had to happen." The strangeness of what most often seems banal must be measured here: the unpredictable landing of each phenomenon, therefore, in the first place, the excessiveness of each event *adds* to the visibility and phenomenality of the world; for phenomena that intervene only once and for all, each new arising accelerates the cumulative effect of all. What is valid for painting—it increases the sum of available visibility through the unseen's anamorphosis in the painting—is valid all the more for worldly phenomena. From surplus to surplus, the finitude of the world shelters and concentrates an indefinite, nonconstitutable, saturating phenomenality. Phenomena, in the measure to which they are given, devise a limitless manifestation—undefine the world in the twofold sense of rendering it nonfinite and forbidding it any definition. (c) *Possibility*. Since it exceeds the preceding situation, the event not only is not inscribed therein, but in establishing itself, redefines a partially or entirely different situation. Essentially, because it never restarts, the event begins a new series, in which it reorganizes the old phenomena—not without violence, but by the right that events have to open horizons. The possibility that it accomplishes, therefore, has nothing in common with the possibility that metaphysics defines. In the ordinary sense, we mean by *possibility* that whose concept includes not a contradiction but a real essence, or the essence of a thinkable thing. In more technological terms, we declare possible the object that is thoroughly calculated and studied, for which, in addition, "feasibility" studies guarantee that it can be produced at an industrial cost compatible with prevailing market conditions. *Possibility* here means a thorough intelligibility, a sufficient foreseeability, and a calculation—to reach actuality, all that is lacking is the transition to production. In this way, we come upon the metaphysical definition of existence as a mere complement of essence.[81] Reciprocally, possibility (essence) could be defined as an existence already absolutely conceived but simply awaiting actualization. It is self-evident that the possibility of the event is described in a mode that is in principle distinct from this metaphysical sense. To confirm this, we need only take stock of some of its determinations as given phenomenon. It happens "outside of essence," therefore by lifting the principle of contradiction (§16), but also "without the idea of its cause," by suspending the principle of sufficient reason (§17). These two particularities imply therefore that the essence of the event is, from a metaphysical point of view, impossible, just like its actualization. But how can it be denied, seeing as before its *fait* is *accompli* (§15), the event remains perfectly unforeseeable, unthinkable, therefore strictly speaking impossible? Doesn't the incident (§16) consist precisely in imposing in the phenomenality of things what remains nevertheless "outside essence"? Isn't the excessiveness of the event recognized by the fact that it renders actual what, before the fait accompli (§14), was not only nonexistent but not even thinkable? There is therefore a contradiction of the possibility of the event by that of metaphysics. From the metaphysical point of view, the possibility of the event can be defined as follows: the event passes directly from impossibility (in the concept, according to essence) to the fait accompli (holding the place of existence and the effect) without passing through phenomenological possibility. But the event can be described from its own point of view: possibility is first exercised not in relation to an essence in order to foresee an actuality, but, in an exactly inverse sense, by an ascent toward form that delivers an unpredictable landing and provokes a fait accompli, in the end freeing the incident "outside essence." While metaphysical possibility actualizes nothing that it has not foreseen, the possibility of the phenomenon, beginning with the fait accompli, always gives more than the gaze has foreseen. This excess, for a gaze resistant to anamorphosis, can indeed sink into impossibility. But for whoever exposes himself to what shows *itself* insofar as it gives *itself,* this impossibility designates the very possibility of the phenomenon.

§18 THE BEING GIVEN

Return to Givenness

I took as my project to confirm the equivalence of showing *itself* and giving *itself,* according to the last principle—that the phenomenon shows itself only insofar as it gives itself (§§1, 6, and 12). This confirmation required that I fix determinations that would eventually permit translating phenomenality into the terms of givenness—in other words, reducing the phenomenon to the given or giving a phenomenon reduced to givenness. At the end of this path (Book 3), what remains is for me to verify whether or not the determinations thus laid out do indeed lead phenomenality back to givenness and whether they do indeed secure the mediation of the one for the other, as in the schema concept and intuition. I will therefore try to make the determinations of the given phenomenon (Book 3) correspond as closely as possible to the characteristics of the givenness of the gift (Book 2).

The determination of the phenomenon by anamorphosis (§13) indicates that it arises from an invisible to a visible form according to a precise axis of visibility, in such a way that the only one who can apprehend it is the one who puts himself at the precise point on the line where the coming forward imposes itself. One must expose oneself to the phenomenon to receive its form—as one receives a blow, a shock, or an emotion. We can thus easily see that anamorphosis determines the phenomenon in terms of its final arrival and describes it inasmuch as received, therefore from the point of view of the givee. It thus repeats, in the lexicon of manifestation (showing itself), the bracketing of the giver in the lexicon of givenness (§13). The determination of the phenomenon as an event (§17) indicates that this same arising is accomplished without cause, that is to say, without dependence on any other term, according to an inaugural, absolute, and new possibility, origin without origin. As nothing precedes it that could account for it, nothing can recall its beginning; it thus gives itself without recall, irrevocably. We see immediately that the event determines the phenomenon according as its beginning has come upon me and describes it as giving itself, therefore from the point of view of the giver. Determination by the event thus reproduces in the register of phenomenality the bracketing of the givee in that of givenness (§9). The determination of the phenomenon as unpredictable landing (§14) lays bare the *self* of its arising and its unforeseeable initiative, in such a way that it succeeds in showing itself only with the halting steps of an essential contingency. We can therefore admit that unpredictable landing determines the phenomenon in that it arrives to me by affecting me; that is to say, we can describe it inasmuch as it is a gift to receive, according to receivability. Consequently, as unpredictable landing describes the receivability of the phenomenon without ever being obliged to constitute it as an object or a being, it transposes into the field of phenomenality what the reduction of the gift had first indicated in the field of givenness (§11). The determination of the phenomenon as incident (§16) confirms that of the unpredictable landing and refers in the same way to givenness. In effect, the incident appears at the outset as an already reduced phenomenon, since in it transcendent cause, theory, and essence have already been bracketed. By definition, the incident is reduced to its own appearances, suspends all objectness or beingness, and therefore remains in its own pure lived experiences such as they can be received only in consciousness. Consequently, the incident repeats in the style of phenomenality the pure receivability of the reduced gift such as givenness had previously recognized it (§11). Let us consider finally the determination of the phenomenon under the heading "fait accompli" (§15). It makes me undergo it as weighing down on me, rendering itself apparent by itself and at my expense, to the point of redirecting intentionality so that it goes from it toward me. The phenomenon not only shows *itself* insofar as it makes *itself*, but it has always already taken the initiative of making *itself* seen, and I always observe it with an insurmountable delay. The fait accompli has always annulled, therefore bracketed, the probable transcendent conditions set for phenomenal arising. Therefore it is reduced to its pure initiative of appearing. In this way it transposes into terms of phenomenality (showing *itself*) what the reduction of the gift to its own givability (giving *itself*) had previously outlined in terms of givenness (§11). The conclusion is obvious: the determinations of the given phenomenon (Book 3) can all be transposed, term for term, into the characteristics of the reduced gift (Book 2), and vice versa. This twofold correspondence certainly offers acceptable support for the respective analyses of the reduced gift and of the given phenomenon; but more especially, they confirm apodictically the differentiated equivalence of what shows *itself* and what gives *itself*. Givenness and phenomenality each unfold from the other, the one for the other.

Given—Intrinsically, Irrevocably

Another requirement still must be secured. At the moment of beginning to lay bare the determinations of the given phenomenon, I had fixed three requirements: that they be intrinsic, irrevocable, and radical.[82] How do they stand at the end? Intrinsic, these determinations are so because the given phenomenon was described not merely without recourse to a cause, real essence, or constituting *I*, but by bracketing them explicitly. In each case, the phenomenon gives *itself* to appear on its own basis, its fait accompli, without the transcendence of an object or a being ever being produced, and without the *I* passing beyond its transcendental role as a mere screen for lived experiences—and for intentional lived experiences, often experienced through counter-intentionality. At no moment was it necessary, when describing the given phenomenon, to have recourse to situations of intersubjective or ethical relations. The description was always able to stick strictly to intentional immanence. These intrinsic determinations of the given phenomenon therefore guarantee the immanence of its character *given*. Irrevocable, these determinations always appear so: the character of *given* that they lay out affects the phenomenon not provisionally but definitively. First, because two of these determinations, those of the fait accompli (§15) and the event (§17), consist literally in irrevocability and—closely connected to it—nonrepeatability. Next, because I laid them out by means of a reduction, to be transcribed in terms either of givenness or of phenomenality. For perseity, individuation, unconstitutability, and of course irrevocability or irrepeatability could not be discovered in the natural attitude, where the phenomenon seems obligatorily alienated, indiscernible, exhaustively constitutable, reproducible, and repeatable, like an object submitted to causality; but since passing to the reduction is always definitive, if the determinations of the given phenomenon appear only in the realm of the reduction, then the latter must be considered as irrevocable as the former. The given phenomenon—given inasmuch as reduced—always keeps the marks of its givenness, since they come to it from its reduction, therefore from its appearing. The given phenomenon therefore trembles permanently with a phenomenality that comes to it—intrinsically—from elsewhere, *aliunde.*

Radically Given? The Question of the Being Given

The third requirement raises a greater difficulty. It demands that the determinations of the given phenomenon be radical—by which it is meant that the phenomenon appears inasmuch as given, without any other gap between it and its givenness other than its fold, even more radically than beings are only insofar as being or than objects to be known as objected. For this radicality to hold, not only must some phenomena unfold as given phenomena and some givens open up as phenomena, but all phenomena, simply insofar as they appear, must always at the outset be identified as given phenomena. But can I and should I claim to have "made all things givable"?[83] At the point where we are, this question still remains undecidable. On the one hand, one can hold that the phenomenon, insofar as given (accorded strictly to givenness), occupies only a region of phenomenality, one whose borders are still to be tested, but which in any case is distinguished from other regions. Which ones? They have already been identified, since the third reduction—the one in view of the given phenomenon and in terms of givenness (§4)—is won by repressing and surpassing the reduction to objects according to the theoretical attitude, as much as the reduction to being according to the ontological difference (§3). What is more, the two determinations of the given phenomenon, by anamorphosis (§13) and by the fait accompli (§15), also respect this hierarchy. They begin with the object and the being so as to overcome them in the given as such. From this, it could be concluded that the phenomenality of givenness simply rules a new region, that of the given phenomena, leaving intact (only bypassed) the region of objective phenomena (for the most part opened by Husserl) and the region of being phenomena (for the most part conquered by Heidegger). It should then be conceded that these two phenomenalities remain foreign to the fold of givenness. On the other hand, one can legitimately hold that the fold of givenness extends to all regions of phenomenality. (i) The first argument in favor of this thesis stems from the possibility of applying even to the object the determinations of the given phenomenon. The subsisting object already arrives to me in anamorphosis; the object to handle and manipulate (equipment) comes upon me (§13). The fait accompli exercises itself even with the permanent objects ("eternal truths") of the theoretical attitude. Therefore, by right, one cannot set aside the pertinence of givenness to describing the phenomenality of other objects. (ii) The second argument takes its stand on the possibility of reinterpreting in toto the phenomenon as being according to givenness. I name it, in anticipation of analyses to come, *the being given*. Let me merely indicate the decisive point: the popular expression "being given (that)" marks clearly enough that a state or a being of things (a state of beings) happens as a fait accompli (§15). In conceptualizing this expression, it will be said that the being given would permit overdetermining the categories of worldly being, indeed certain existentials of Dasein, on the basis of the ultimate determination of the given phenomenon, the event. For example, we have already seen several categories of being that are radically redefined once applied to the given phenomenon: contingency and necessity (§§14–15), accident and substance (§16), cause and effect (§17), for instance, are inverted and reconfigured on the basis of givenness. It could also be that anticipatory resoluteness not only tolerates but is obliged to be read as a privileged case of the event, therefore according to givenness. For without cause, without motive, without object, transcending every being and every essence ("nothing"), but essentially temporalized toward the future, it defines the possibility of all possibles. Just how far can one push the extension of the being given, therefore the recovery of the phenomenality of beings in their Being by givenness? We have seen that Husserl had already understood objective phenomena on the basis of givenness and that Heidegger had, at least provisionally, reconsidered the phenomenality of beings in terms of givenness (§3). The fact that they recoiled, in different ways, before the full development of this possibility does not disqualify it, but makes it all the more legitimate.

In this new direction, a final argument can be advanced. (iii) Between the given phenomenon and the other realms of phenomenality, we have until now, implicitly at least, admitted a relation of exclusion or juxtaposition, on the model of the regional carving up promoted by Husserl with his "uncrossable difference" between the world-region and the consciousness-region and by Heidegger with his "ontological difference" between the modes of

Being of worldly beings and Dasein. Couldn't we imagine, by contrast, that givenness admits variation by degrees? On this hypothesis, the determinations of the given phenomenon, while remaining originary and definitively acquired, would modulate with variable intensity. As a result, thresholds of phenomenality in terms of givenness would define discontinuous strata of phenomena, which would then be distinguished by their level of givenness and no longer by their belonging to a region. It would thus be necessary to pass from the determinations of the given (Book 3) to its degrees (Book 4) in order to finally do justice to the phenomenality of givenness. We could then broach two questions still held in suspense: the relation of intuition to givenness, last seen as one of exclusive conflict (§§1 and 5), and the privilege of certain given phenomena over others, until now rightly avoided in the name of the reduction (§7).

For if all that gives *itself* shows *itself,* all does not give *itself* in the same way.

Book IV

THE GIVEN II: DEGREES

§19 THE HORIZON AND THE I

Phenomenality and Possibility

The equivalence that I established and then confirmed between givenness and phenomenality therefore raises a major difficulty. Must it be understood in such a way that only some phenomena, privileged in an as yet undetermined sense, illustrate givenness within what should be named a regional phenomenality—that of the given phenomenon? Let me note that even mere regionality would deserve serious attention, seeing as it would demand the admission that, in certain cases at least, to give oneself and to show oneself amount to the same ascent to the visible, to the same anamorphosis (§§6 and 12). But another interpretation can also be advanced, one in which the equivalence between the phenomenon and the given would no longer suffer any exception. As the fundamental determination of phenomenality (governing all those taken into account in Book 3), givenness would organize phenomenality universally and without exception. But within the hypothesis of such a univocity, how are we to understand the fundamental differences that continue to distinguish the different types of phenomena? How are we to claim that objects all show themselves given in the same mode, be they mathematic idealities, logical utterances, or material things? Or that givenness determines phenomena of the objective type in the same way as it defines those that belong under beingness (and possibly a nonobjectifiable being)? Among beings, doesn't givenness differ radically depending on whether it concerns beings that are subsistent (*vorhanden*), useful (*zuhanden*), or in the mode of Being of Dasein? Above all, what are we to say about those phenomena that belong directly to givenness, without passing through the mediation of objectness or beingness (as, for example, the painting)?[1] I have doubtless already suggested an answer, first when I posited the privilege that admits no exception, givenness (§5), next when I indicated that even logical idealities and the mathematical "eternal truths" belong to the given taken in its fait accompli (§15). But these arguments still remain partial, and therefore are not enough to pin down the possible limits of the being given, as well as the phenomenon given. Above all, they do not yet enable me to indicate the differences between phenomena solely in terms of the criterion of givenness. For givenness still needs to be refined, its details specified, its potential released. It is fitting therefore to return to the initial line of questioning: according to what modes and degrees is phenomenality exercised in terms of givenness, that is to say, to what extent does givenness render phenomenality possible?

But this question as to the possibility of the phenomenon as given is not separate from another. If, as we have seen, metaphysical possibility amounts to passing from impossibility (in essence or concept) to the fait accompli (existence) without doing justice to possibility in the strictest procedural sense (§17), then it should be inferred either that the real possibility of the phenomenon escapes its metaphysical determination or that metaphysics assures this possibility only in a radically insufficient mode—that is to say, by submitting it to a more essential impossibility. Phenomenality would never become possible except on the basis of a more originary impossibility; the phenomenon could of course sometimes appear there, but with an always deferred possibility. If metaphysics always imposes a limit to the possibility of the phenomenon, it will be at the precise point of this limit that we could test *a contrario* the possibility for a phenomenality of givenness to pass beyond impossibility (or not) and deploy itself as such. Degrees of phenomenality would then be thinkable and could be determined according as givenness reaches beyond or falls short of its metaphysical limits; we could therefore also decide if givenness encompasses all phenomenality or if the metaphysical limits of the latter are enough to regionalize it. I will therefore try to verify (or disprove) the determination of all phenomena by givenness by following the clue provided by the possibility or impossibility of phenomenality in metaphysics.

I will rely, obviously, on Kant. He states the metaphysical definition of possibility in this way: "That which agrees with [*übereinkommt*] the formal conditions of experience, that is, with the conditions of intuition and of concepts, is possible." What is astonishing here resides in the close connection that Kant establishes between possibility and phenomenality; that is, among these conditions, intuition comes up—which indicates that experience has the form of a phenomenality, that experience has a form ("formal conditions") precisely because it experiences sensible forms of apparition. Here possibility depends on phenomenality. Should it be concluded from this that the phenomenon imposes its possibility, instead of submitting to its conditions? In no way, because the possible does not agree with the object of experience, but with its "formal conditions." Possibility does not follow from the phenomenon but, by contrast, from the conditions posited for every phenomenon. A formal requirement is therefore exerted not on behalf of but over and against possibility, as Kant indicates shortly thereafter: "The postulate of the possibility of things requires [*fordert*] that the concept of the things should agree with the formal conditions of an experience in general." Clearly the possibility of the phenomenon results not from its own phenomenality, but from an authority that is marginal, other, if not external: that of the conditions of experience for and by the subject. The phenomenon's access to its own manifestation should be submitted to the requirement of possibility, but this possibility itself depends on other conditions besides its own—the "formal conditions of experience," forms arising before the very form (*eidos*) of the phenomenon. How, in the final analysis, to fix these "formal conditions," this original form determining phenomenality and possibility together? Kant indicates an answer indirectly, but unambiguously, in emphasizing that "the categories of modality . . . express only the relation to the faculty of knowledge."[2] The formal conditions of knowledge are here articulated directly in terms of the power of knowledge, not the phenomenon's power of appearing. This is to say that intuition and the concept determine in advance the possibility of appearing for every phenomenon. The possibility—therefore also and especially the impossibility—of a phenomenon is decreed according to the "power of knowledge," therefore the play of intuition and the concept in a finite mind. Possible is any phenomenon that agrees with the finitude of the power of knowledge and its requirements.

Kant here only confirms a decision already made by Leibniz. To be sure, one thinks phenomenal possibility on the basis of a finite mind, the other on the basis of an infinite (or tangentially indefinite) mind; but both the one and the other end up at the same conditioned possibility of the phenomenon. That is, metaphysics obeys the "great principle . . . which holds that nothing takes place without sufficient reason, that is to say that nothing happens without its being possible for one who has enough knowledge of things to give a reason sufficient to determine why it is thus and not otherwise."[3] Thus nothing "occurs," "arrives," in short appears, without attesting that it is "possible." This possibility is equivalent, in turn, to the possibility of knowing the sufficient reason of such an apparition. As with Kant, the right to appear—the possibility of a phenomenon—is played out for Leibniz in the power of knowledge putting into operation the sufficiency of reason, which, whatever it might be, precedes what it renders possible. Since the "power of knowledge" will establish the conditions for possibility, sufficient reason is enough to render possible what, without it, would remain impossible. This dependence is marked with particular clarity in the case of the sensible. To be sure, "sensible things" appear and do indeed deserve the title "phenomena," but they owe it to another "reason," different from their apparition, which alone is sufficient to qualify this appearance as a phenomenon: "The truth about sensible things consists only in the linking together of phenomena . . . (for which there must be a reason)."[4] When, among the beings that he recognizes as permanent ("Creatura permanens absoluta"), Leibniz opposes the full and complete being ("Unum per se, Ens plenum/ Substantia/Modificatio") to the diminished being that he assimilates to the phenomenon ("Unum per aggregationem. Semiens, phaenomenon"),[5] we must avoid the misreading that imagines that the phenomenon has the rank of a being halfway or a half-being because it suffers from an insufficiency of reason. To the contrary, precisely because it benefits from a perfectly sufficient reason, the phenomenon regresses to the rank of being halfway. It is precisely as "phaenomena bene fondata,"[6] that phenomena confess to being founded, therefore conditioned, by a solely sufficient reason and that they themselves do not suffice to secure themselves. If reason can ground phenomena, this is first because it must save them; but it would not have to do so if it did not judge in advance that left to themselves these phenomena would be lost. In short, sufficient reason saves only what it has already considered as lost. It is therefore not enough that the apparition actually appear for its possibility to be justified. It still must have recourse to reason, which —all the while dispensing with its own having to appear—renders the actuality of the apparition possible because it renders this possibility intelligible. The phenomenon attests its lack of reason when and because it receives its reason from reason. For it thus appears only in the role of conditional phenomenon, having appeared on condition—on the condition of what does not appear. In the metaphysical realm, the possibility of appearing never belongs to what appears, nor its phenomenality to the phenomenon.

It will perhaps be objected—with Schopenhauer, however occupied he was with establishing the contrary[7]—that the *Critique* never relies on the principle of sufficient reason and therefore could not impose it on phenomenality. Literally fair, this argument nevertheless hides what is essential. For, when Kant states the two supreme principles of judgments, he first recovers the principle of contradiction in order that he might secure the supreme principle of analytic judgments. Therefore, when he formulates the supreme principle of synthetic judgments, he puts forth a statement that, without being reduced to Leibniz's *reddenda ratio*, nevertheless repeats it, since it holds its place: "The conditions of the possibility of experience are *at the same time* [*zugleich*] the conditions of the possibility of the objects of experience."[8] And, in fact, conditions can only *ground* [*condere*], as a principle alone grounds, while a *Bedingung* precedes and produces transitively [*be-*] the thing [*Ding*] in play. The conditions—grounds—of experience therefore ground the objects experienced, that is to say, make them experienceable. The conditions offer a reason for the possibility of experiencing an object; the conditions offer a reason for possibility; possibility remains beneath the sway of sufficient reason. What possibility is at issue here? That of the objects of experience. What then does experience experience? Obviously objects having the status of phenomena and whose entire experience consists in their appearing. As a result, the condition that offers a reason for possibility also offers a reason for the appearing of phenomena. They therefore appear only on condition—on condition of the conditions of experience. Kant prolongs, by displacing, the conditional phenomenality instituted by Leibniz. Even more, he radicalizes it. For in the place where Leibniz assigned the principle of sufficient reason to "the ultimate reason of things . . . what we call God,"[9] Kant attributes it to transcendental apperception, therefore to finitude: "The supreme principle of the same possibility [of sensibility], in its relation to understanding, is that all the manifold of intuition should be subject to conditions of the original synthetic unity of apperception." Phenomenality therefore no longer draws its possibility directly from the phenomena themselves, but receives it as if from the exterior by two supreme principles: first strictly in the measure that they "are given," then insofar as they "must allow of being combined in one consciousness."[10] Given, but to a consciousness; combined, but by a consciousness: phenomena appear only on condition, alienated by an imposed phenomenality.

From the "Supreme Principle" to the "Principle of All Principles"

From this alienated phenomenality, phenomenology escapes—or tries to escape—at one fell swoop when it opposes to the principle of sufficient reason as well as to the supreme principle of possibility the "principle of all principles," a principle that (in principle) broadens unconditionally the heretofore conditional phenomenality. The "principle of all principles" posits in effect that "every originarily giving intuition [*Anschauung*] is a source of right for knowledge, that everything that offers itself originarily to us in 'intuition' [*Intuition*] is to be taken simply as it gives itself, but also only within the boundaries in which it gives itself there."[11] This is not the place to assess once again the decisive importance of this principle nor its function within the whole of the other principles of phenomenology.[12] It will suffice to highlight three of its characteristics.

According to the first, intuition no longer operates solely as a source of the fact of the phenomenon, one that guarantees its brute actuality without yet grounding it in reason, but as a source of right, justificatory of itself. Intuition is itself attested by itself without the background of a reason still to be offered. Thus the phenomenon according to Husserl answers in advance to the phenomenon according to Heidegger—what shows itself on the basis of itself. This is clear: what shows itself on the basis of itself as pure apparition of self without remainder, and not of an other than self that does not appear (a reason). To justify its right to appear, intuition is enough for the phenomenon, without any other reason; it is enough for it to be given in and through intuition—according to a principle of sufficient intuition. But intuition becomes sufficient only inasmuch as it operates without background, "originarily," says Husserl. Now, it operates originarily, without any presupposition, only inasmuch as it provides originary givens, therefore as it (itself) gives (itself) originarily. Intuition is justified rightfully only by laying claim to the unconditional origin. But can it justify this claim without going so far as to mimic the reason that suffices for offering (*reddendae rationis*), that is to say, by offering itself, therefore by giving itself in person? Only givenness suggests that the phenomenon guarantees at one stroke its visibility and the official right of this visibility, its apparition and the reason for this apparition. We must, however, still test whether or not the "principle of all principles" ensures such a right of appearing for all phenomena and does indeed open for them an absolutely unconditioned possibility, or if it renders them possible only according to some condition. Now it happens that the giving intuition does not yet authorize an absolutely unconditioned apparition, nor therefore the freedom of the phenomenon giving itself on its own basis. Not only because intuition as such might already limit phenomenality, but also because it remains framed, inasmuch as it is intuition, by two conditions of possibility, themselves nonintuitive yet nevertheless assigned to every phenomenon. That is, the second and third characteristics of the "principle of all principles" contradict the first as a condition and a limit that undermine the claim to absolute possibility opened by giving intuition.

The Horizon

Let us consider next a second characteristic of the "principle": intuition justifies every phenomenon, "but also only [*aber auch nur*] within the boundaries in which" it gives itself. This suggests a limitation, a restriction that attests a twofold finitude of the giving authority, intuition. First, a factual restriction: intuition admits "boundaries [*Schranken*]." These boundaries, in whatever way one understands them (since Husserl hardly specifies), indicate that all cannot be perfectly given. From the outset, intuition obeys a logic of penury, is stigmatized by a threatening insufficiency. We will have to question the status and presuppositions of this de facto shortcoming (§20). But there is more: this restriction can already claim a limitation de jure. Every intuition, in order to give within certain de facto "boundaries," must first be inscribed de jure within the "limits" (*Grenze*) of a horizon, just as no intentional aim at an object, signification, or essence can be carried out outside a horizon. Husserl indicates this point by an argument that is all the more powerful as it is paradoxical. Considering what he nevertheless names the "limitlessness [*Grenzenlosigkeit*] of the immanent intuitions going from the fixed lived experience to the new lived experiences that form its horizon, from its fixing to those of its horizons, etc.," he admits that every lived experience is forever referred to new, still unknown lived experiences and therefore to a horizon of novelties that are irreducible because always renewed. The function of the horizon cannot be underestimated. In effect, when it is a question of seeing an object, transcendent by definition, I cannot apprehend it all at one fell swoop. The sides of the cube are six in number, but no one has ever perceived in lived experience more than three sides together. We therefore must, by moving the observer or the object, add new lived experiences for each of the missing sides; however, this movement carries with it the disappearance of the previous ones. The organization of all the successive lived experiences around one single object implies that the known (the immanent lived experiences already recorded) remain not only in memory, but be co-posited within the same horizon as what still remains unknown (the lived experiences yet to come), for the sake of a single intended transcendent object. It is therefore necessary that the irrepressible novelty of the flux of lived experiences, therefore of intuition, remain, de jure, always included within an already defined horizon where lived experiences not yet given could simply be united with the lived experiences already given (or already past and confided to memory) in one and the same objective intention: "A lived experience that has become an object for a gaze of the I, which therefore has the mode of the gazed-upon, has its horizon of unregarded lived experiences [*seinen Horizont nichterblickster Erlebnisse*]." Or: "A thing is necessarily given in mere 'modes of appearance' where we find necessarily a *core* composed of what is 'actually figured,' surrounded by a horizon of inauthentic 'co-givenness' and of more or less vague *indeterminateness*."[13] Within the horizon, the unknown refers in advance to the known, because it welcomes and fixes it: "Anything unknown is a horizon of something known."[14] The horizon—etymologically speaking, delimitation—exerts itself over experience even there where only unregarded lived experiences are any longer found, that is to say, there where experience has not yet taken place: "On principle, there always subsists a horizon of determinable indeterminateness [*bestimmtbarer Unbestimmtheit*] as far as we advance in experience, as large as the *continuum* of present perceptions of the same thing might be."[15] The exterior of experience is not equivalent to an experience of the exterior because the horizon in advance takes possession of the unknown, the unexperienced, and the not gazed upon, by supposing them to be always already compatible, compressible, and homogenous with the already experienced, already gazed upon, and already interiorized by intuition. The intention always anticipates what it has not yet seen, the result being that the unseen has, from the start, the rank of a pre-seen, a merely belated visible, without fundamentally irreducible novelty, in short a pre-visible. The horizon therefore does not so much surround the visible with an *aura* of the nonvisible as it assigns in advance this nonvisible to this or that focal point (object) inscribed in the already seen. Here one can only take note of a fundamental ambiguity. With this horizon of the unseen as essentially pre-seen and pre-visible, are we just talking about the mere recognition that every lived experience resides in the flux of consciousness, and is therefore oriented in advance toward other lived experiences still to arise, in accordance with the aim at one and the same intentional object.[16] Or rather is it a matter of the anticipated submission of unseen, nonlived experiences to a horizon that in advance includes their intuition within a limit—be it the flux of consciousness—without the possibility of opening the phenomenal unforeseen beyond the intentional pole of an object foreseen and expected? Along these lines, shouldn't we ask if "the principle of all principles" does not presuppose at least one condition for givenness: the horizon itself, which designates the object of all givenness? There is more: doesn't the very necessity of a horizon result from the assimilation of givenness to intuition? That is, through a succession of lived experiences, intuition proceeds to fulfill its intentional aim at an object; it therefore stakes out a horizon within which it can retain (remember) them, compose them, and anticipate them around a noematic core; in short, only the flux of intuitions requires the permanence of an objective pole and its delimitation in advance within a horizon. Phenomenality is here grasped and included in advance within a horizon of appearing always already seen, or at least visible—openness would be equivalent to a visual prison, a panopticon broadened to the dimensions of the world, a panorama without exterior, forbidding all genuinely new arising. Henceforth, in the inverse hypothesis, according to which givenness would not tie its fate to intuition, should it still admit limitation, de facto and de jure, by a horizon? Shouldn't we imagine freeing givenness from the prior limit of a horizon of phenomenality?[17]

The I

As for the third characteristic of the "principle of all principles," it is found in the claim that every intuition presents what appears only by giving it "to us." This turn of phrase has nothing trivial or redundant about it. First of all because it betrays a classic ambiguity of transcendental phenomenology: the givenness of the phenomenon on its own basis to an I can always veer toward a constitution of the phenomenon by and on the basis of the I. Metaphysical (in fact, Cartesian) egology is a paradigm that always haunts the I, even reduced, even phenomenological; for, according to it, the notion of constitution would drift away from meaning the acknowledgment of a meaning that the phenomenon would first have given itself [*Sinngebung*] toward a mere synthesis by consciousness of its lived experiences according to an intention aiming at an object. Next, even if one does not overvalue this threat, the reference of intuitive givenness to the I does not remove another difficulty. If givenness does fill its originary and justificatory function, even more so than the "principle of principles" will admit (a principle that ignores the reduction and subordinates givenness to intuition), what hierarchy does it maintain with the I? What it gives has, inasmuch as given, neither the possibility nor especially the need to justify itself before the tribunal of the transcendental I. In effect, givenness precedes every other instance (including and above all the I), and it therefore falls to givenness to judge, according to the criterion of the given, the theoretical validity of all that claims to appear. If the I still laid claim to the role of judge (and constitutor) of phenomenality, what other criterion could it use to secure its claim besides givenness itself? To avail itself of a criterion all its own, it would have to conserve its transcendental posture, which alone is equal to the task of fixing forms and concepts a priori, thereby determining phenomenality in advance according to conditions of experience; but as soon as the reduction has suspended these a priori and givenness is accomplished without reserve or limits, the I must renounce every claim to the synthesis of objects or the judgment of phenomenality. In the realm of givenness, it no longer decides the phenomenon, but receives it; or else, from "master and possessor" of the phenomenon, it becomes its receiver. Does this radically new posture of the figure and the function of the I receive the elaboration that the primacy of givenness would demand for it? According to the evidence, "the principle of principles" does not even try to outline it. We can even suspect that Husserl never puts into question some of the most characteristic aspects of the transcendentality of the I, at the risk of compromising his advances, however decisive, toward pure givenness. That is, the concept of horizon maintains a direct relation with such an I, since the lived experiences, considered in their "now," form an "*originary horizon* [*Originaritätshorizont*] *of the pure I*, its total originary *Now* of consciousness."[18] The ultimate (because temporal) horizon of lived experiences is therefore, for Husserl, one with the I. There is no better way to emphasize the equivalence of the second and third characteristics of the "principle of all principles," presupposing that every givenness must admit the I as transcendental and as horizon. Based on this, how can we not try to define the I without recourse to transcendentality or the exercise of the a priori, but solely on the basis of its function as beneficiary of the phenomenon such as it gives itself on the basis of itself and itself alone? What would become of the subject if he were determined only according to givenness (Book 5)?

More generally, what would happen, as regards phenomenality, if a givenness was accomplished without the limit (the principle of a horizon) or condition (the transcendental I) still imposed on it by the intuition of the "principle of principles"? How are we to conceive a givenness that is finally absolutely unconditioned (without the limits of a horizon) and absolutely irreducible (to a constituting I)? Can we imagine phenomena such that they would invert limit (by exceeding the horizon, instead of being inscribed within it) and condition (by reconducting the I to itself, instead of being reduced to it)? To declare at the outset that this hypothesis is impossible would immediately betray a phenomenological contradiction, seeing as phenomenology is defined and deployed according to the guiding thread of possibility. I will therefore assume the hypothesis of such phenomena, which, at least as imaginative variations, would permit us to go to the limit in determining phenomenality and experiencing afresh what possibility means or can give. Limits of course remain on principle indestructible and no doubt indispensable. It does not follow, however, that what contradicts them cannot still be deployed paradoxically as a phenomenon. Quite to the contrary, certain phenomena could appear only by playing at the limits of phenomenality—indeed by making sport of them.

§20 INTUITION AS SHORTAGE

The Duality of the Phenomenon

Evoking the possibility of a phenomenon that is unconditioned (by its horizon) and irreducible (to an I), that is to say, a phenomenon par excellence, demands first that such a possibility truly open, without being debased to illusory possibility, through a passage beyond undue limit, which would simply destroy phenomenality in general—in short that such an unconditioned and irreducible phenomenon not lead to "telling stories." To establish this guarantee, I will have to finish by describing such a phenomenon directly (§§21–22), but I will do this at first only indirectly, by destroying the ordinary definition of the phenomenon such as it reigns in metaphysics according to Kant, as well as in phenomenology according to Husserl (§20). In this way, I will attempt to decide if this definition—which submits every phenomenon to a horizon of apparition and a constituting I—opens the field of phenomenality or instead confirms its essential closure. In other words, I will try to specify what decision limits the phenomenon in its common definition so that I can then lay bare what possibility would, by contrast, remain open to an unconditioned and irreducible acceptation of phenomenality.

Husserl will maintain throughout his career a definition of the phenomenon that is determined by its fundamental duality: "The word 'phenomenon' is ambiguous in virtue of the essential correlation between the appearing and what appears."[19] This correlation is orchestrated in several different pairs—intention/intuition, signification/fulfillment, noesis/noema, etc.; it serves to better determine the phenomenon as what appears in correlation with apparition. This is why the highest manifestation of any phenomenon whatsoever, therefore the highest phenomenality, is accomplished in the perfect adequation between these two terms, when subjective appearing is equal to what appears objectively:

And so also, *eo ipso*, the ideal of every fulfillment, and therefore of a *significative* fulfillment, is sketched for us; the *intellectus* is in this case the thought-intention, the intention of meaning. And the *adaequatio* is realized when the objectness meant is in the strict sense *given* in our intuition, and given precisely as it is thought and named. No thought-intention could fail of its fulfillment, of its last fulfillment, in fact, insofar as the fulfilling medium of intuition has itself lost all implication of unsatisfied intention.[20]

Not only does adequation here, as in metaphysics, suffice to define the truth; it above all remains a limit, exceptional, case: "the ideal of ultimate fulfillment."[21] This privileged case of perception is equivalent to what Husserl names, in a Cartesian fashion, evidence; or more exactly, the objective truth is subjectively accomplished by evidence considered as the experience of adequation made by consciousness. Now this ideal of evidence, supposedly designating the maximum and extreme ambition for the truth, nevertheless claims, with strange modesty, only an "adequation," a mere equality. This paradigm of ideal equality weighs so heavily that Husserl multiplies it into no less than four figures: (a) "the full agreement between the meant and the given as such [*Uebereinstimmung zwischen Gemeintem und Gegebenem*]"; (b) "the idea of the absolute adequation [*Adäquation*]" between the ideal essence and the empirically contingent act of evidence; (c) the "ideal fulfillment for an intention"; (d) and, finally, "the truth as rightness [*Rechtigkeit*] of our intention."[22] What is surprising here is not found so much in this insistent multiplication as in the fact that adequation, to which the ambition for truth is already limited, is in addition a pure ideal—"the ideal of an ultimate fulfillment," "the ideally fulfilled perception," the object of an "idea of absolute adequation as such.[23] How can these terms not be understood in a Kantian fashion? In this context, since the idea remains a concept of reason such that its object can never be given by intuition, the ideal (like the object of the idea) should therefore never give itself.[24] If adequation, which subjectively provokes objective evidence, still remains for Husserl (as for Kant) a mere "ideal," it must be inferred that adequation can never be realized, or at least only rarely. But, with this, wouldn't it also be truth that becomes attenuated or inaccessible? This danger marks an aporia, which in turn raises questions concerning the decisions that made it inevitable. Why should adequate evidence remain mostly a limit, indeed an excluded case? Why does the equality between noesis and noema, essence and fulfillment, intention and intuition, appear inaccessible—or almost so—at the very moment when the dignity of the truth is (perhaps wrongly) vested in it? Why does Husserl compromise the return to the things themselves by stamping evidence and truth with the mark of ideality?

Answer: because the equality that Husserl officially maintains between intuition and intention in fact remains inaccessible to him. Intuition is (almost) always (partially) lacking to intention, as fulfillment is lacking to signification. In other words, intention and signification surpass intuition and fulfillment. "A surplus in meaning [*ein Ueberschuss in der Bedeutung*] remains" because in principle "the realm of meaning is much wider than that of intuition."[25] Intuition remains essentially deficient, poor, needful, indigent—*penia*.[26] Adequation between intuition and intention therefore becomes a mere limit, an ideal habitually evoked by default. It should not be objected that evidence is commonly achieved in mathematics and formal logic; for this fact, far from weakening the deficiency of evidence, confirms it. In effect, the ideal of adequation is realized precisely in only those domains where the significative intention claims, in order to accomplish itself in a phenomenon, only a formal intuition (space in mathematics), a categorical intuition (logical beings), indeed no intuition at all (empty tautology). Mathematics and logic, precisely because they deal only with an ideal object—that is to say, strictly speaking, an object that has to just barely give itself in order to appear perfectly, in short, a minuscule or degree zero of phenomenality—reach adequate evidence by default, an evidence that claims only an empty or poor intuition. Adequation is easily realized in this case because it concerns phenomena with no, or only very weak, intuitive requirements. In this way, even if the ideal of evidence is sometimes realized in phenomena that are poor enough for one to quickly reach sufficient intuition, it is not at all self-evident that this minimalist certainty can serve as a paradigm for phenomenality as a whole, nor that it is worth the phenomenological price one pays for it. In any case, if evidence is realized only for poor phenomena, when full phenomena are at issue—when, that is, it is an issue of the apparition of the "things themselves" fully given by intuition—adequation will once again become an ideal, that is to say, an event imperfectly given, by at least a partial shortage of intuition. The equality officially required between intuition and intention will be absent there —owing to intuition. The senses deceive, not with a provisional or accidental deception, but with an ineluctable powerlessness: even an indefinite sum of intuitioned adumbrations will never fulfill the lowest level of intentionality aiming at real objects. When a thing is at issue, intention always exceeds its intuitive givenness, which has to be completed by appresentation.[27] What keeps phenomenology from letting phenomena appear unreservedly is therefore, first of all, the fundamental deficit of intuition that it assigns to them—without appeal or recourse. But the phenomenological "breakthrough" only postulates this intuitive shortage as a consequence of metaphysical decisions made by Kant—in short, Husserl here suffers the outcome of decisions made by Kant.

For it is first Kant who, always defining truth by *adaequatio*,[28] inferred from this the parallel between intuition and the concept, supposedly playing a role tangentially equal in the production of objectivity.

Without sensibility no object would be given, without understanding no object would be thought. Thoughts without content are empty, intuitions without concepts are blind. It is therefore just as necessary to make our concepts sensible, that is, to add the object to them in intuition, as to make our intuitions intelligible, that is, to bring them under concepts. These two powers or capacities cannot exchange their functions. The understanding can intuit nothing, the senses can think nothing.[29]

In principle, the phenomenon, therefore the real object, appears strictly to the extent that intuition and the concept are not only synthesized, but find a balance in this synthesis. *Adaequatio*—therefore the truth—would thus rest on the equality of the concept with the intuition. Kant, however, is the first to disqualify this parallelism; for if the concept corresponds with intuition, it nevertheless depends on it radically. If the concept thinks, it is in effect limited to making intelligible after the fact and derivatively what intuition principally and originarily alone can give: "Our knowledge springs from two fundamental sources of the mind. . . . Through the first [receptivity] an object is *given* [*gegeben*] to us, through the second [the spontaneity of concepts] the object is *thought*."[30] To be sure, intuition without concept is as blind as the concept without intuition is empty; but blindness counts more here than vacuity: even blind, intuition still gives, while the concept, even if it alone can make the given seen, remains as such perfectly empty, therefore quite incapable of seeing anything whatsoever. Intuition without concept, though still blind, nevertheless gives material to an object, while the concept without intuition, though not blind, sees nothing, since nothing has yet been given to it to see. In the kingdom of the phenomenon, the concept is not king, but rather the intuition which alone has the privilege of giving: "The object cannot be given to a concept otherwise than in intuition [*nicht anders gegeben werden, als in der Anschauung*]"; for "the category is a mere function of thought, through which no object is given to me, and by which I merely think that which may be given in intuition [*nur was in der Anschauung gegeben werden mag*]"; or again: "The intuitions, through which objects can be given to us [*uns Gegenstände gegeben werden können*], constitute the field, or the complete object of possible experience." In this way, intuition does not offer a mere parallel or complement to the concept; it secures its condition of possibility—its very possibility: "Intuitions in general, through which objects can be given to us [*gegeben werden können*] constitute the field or the global object of possible experience [*möglicher Erfahrung*]."[31] The phenomenon is thought with the concept; but to be thought, it must first be given, and it is given only in and through intuition. The staging in intuition conditions conceptual objectification. As unique and prior giver, intuition breaks the parallelism with the concept in its own favor. From here on out, the extension of intuition fixes that of phenomenal givenness. The phenomenality of givenness is indexed to intuition.

Lack and Nothingness

We should therefore expect that Kant would dedicate himself to thinking this unheard-of privilege of givenness—to securing nothing less than the bishopric of givenness. And yet in a stupefying reversal, he emphasizes this privilege of intuition only in order to better stigmatize its deficiency. For if only intuition gives objects, there falls to human finitude only a decidedly finite intuition, in this case a sensible intuition. Consequently, not only all the objects that demand an indefinite intuitive fulfillment, but also all those that probably necessitate a nonsensible (intellectual) intuition, are barred from appearing. Phenomenality remains limited by the lack of what makes it partially possible—intuition. What gives (intuition insofar as sensible) is but one with what is lacking (intuition insofar as intellectual or indefinite). What gives is lacking. The very thing that is lacking is precisely the only thing that could and should give. Intuition determines phenomenality as much by what it refuses it as by what it gives it. "Thought is the act which relates given intuition [*gegebene Anschauung*] to an object. If the mode of this intuition is not in any way given [*auf keinerlei Weise gegeben*], the object is merely transcendental, and the concept of understanding has only transcendental employment."[32] Thinking is more than knowing objects given by intuition, renouncing all those that no intuition will ever give, considering the immense cenotaph of phenomena that never appeared and never will appear, in short, taking the measure of intuition's lack. Intuition, which alone gives, is essentially lacking. A paradox follows: from here on out, the more phenomena give themselves in sensibility, the larger grows the silent crowd of those that cannot and should not claim to give themselves. The more intuition gives in terms of the sensible, the more it attests its deficiency in bringing about the appearing of the phenomenal possible—held to be impossible. The finitude of intuition betrays its problematic character with the—"necessary," Kant admits—permanence of the idea. The idea, although—or rather because—it is a "concept of reason to which no corresponding object can be given in sense experience," nevertheless always remains *visable*, if not visible in the sensible apparitions from which it is excluded.[33] "Absent from every bouquet," the flower of thought calls sensible flowers to the "glory of long desire"[34] and survives them. Likewise, the idea, in aiming *outside* the conditions fixed for phenomenality, marks its limits all the more. In the quasi-ghostlike mode of a nonobject, the idea accuses the limits of an intuition that can no longer give it. By not becoming sensible, therefore, the idea not only attests its own failing, but stigmatizes the failing of sensible intuition in general.

The phenomenon is therefore characterized, according to Husserl and Kant, by its lack of intuition, which gives it only by limiting it. Two observations confirm the radicality of this decision. (a) One would be the investigation of the privilege that theories of knowledge (from Plato to Descartes,[35] from Kant to Husserl) have almost always accorded to logical and mathematical phenomena. They are set up as models for all the others on account of their certainty, while they are distinguished from the others by their shortage of intuition, the poverty of their givenness, indeed the unreality of their objects. It is not self-evident that this marginal poverty can serve as a paradigm for the whole of phenomenality, nor that the certainty it assures is worth the price paid for it. To organize all of phenomenality around the essentially marginal case of phenomena poor in, indeed barren of, intuition blocks access not only to the ideas of reason and the extreme cases of givenness, but first of all to certain common-law phenomena—the beings of nature, the living in general, the historical event, the face of the Other in particular (§23). In fact, according to this choice, none of the real phenomena with which we traffic daily and obligatorily can be analyzed adequately, and what is more, they are barely even granted the right to appear. Metaphysics thus confirms its nihilism by organizing itself around the paradigm of phenomena that do *not* appear, or appear just a bit, and by ignoring the paradigm of those that appear sufficiently to lay claim to the rank of official things. It contests them in the very degree to which they demand appearing.

Moreover (b), Kant himself, going almost to the point of provocation, explicitly established that intuition is indeed operative in the realm of lack by trying to define the meaning of nothingness on the basis of intuition—as if it was first with essentially deficient, though giving, intuition that shortage in all its dimensions could be defined. The lexicon for the four senses of nothingness is in effect a review of the four modes of deficiency of intuition. (i) Consider first nothingness as *ens rationis*. It is defined as "the object of a concept to which there corresponds no intuition that could be given [*keine anzugebende Anschauung*]." Limited to the sensible, intuition produces nothingness in and through its incapacity to give intuition corresponding to a rational being. (ii) Take next nothingness as *nihil privativum*. It is defined as "the concept of the lack of an object," that is to say, as a double lack of intuition: first as a concept, therefore as what, by definition, lacks intuition; next as the concept representing the very lack of intuition, sole giver of objects. A double lack of intuition produces a second nothingness. (iii) Consider nothingness as *nihil imaginativum*. This sense is paradoxically significant. In principle, the imagined should extricate itself from nothingness since a minimum of intuition (precisely the imagined) would seem to give a minimum being. And yet Kant does not even accord this positivity to intuition; he accords it only a "mere form of intuition" and reduces it again to an "empty intuition." It will be observed that "empty" characterizes the concept and that intuition no longer even has the right to its "blind" solitude—so true is it that here the form of intuition is assimi-

lated to the empty form of the concept. The form of intuition is thus reduced to a third nothingness. (iv) Finally there remains nothingness as *nihil negativum*. As "empty object without concept," it would seem to have
to be defined by the deficiency of the concept and not of intuition, left for
once free from accusation. Similarly, this nothingness defined as "the object
of a concept that contradicts itself" would seem to admit a purely logical
and no longer intuitive explanation. And yet, strangely enough, this is not
the case. Kant puts forward an example—a rectilinear figure with two sides
—whose contradiction is conceived only in space, therefore again in intuition. For that matter, he specified previously, "There is no contradiction in
the concept of a figure which is enclosed within two straight lines, since the
concept of two straight lines and of their coming together contains no
negation of a figure. The impossibility arises not from the concept in itself,
but in connection with its construction in space."[36] The concept is lacking
because the object contradicts itself, but this contradiction is not logical. It
results from the conditions of experience, here from the requirements for
construction in space. It is therefore a contradiction from the perspective of
intuition, more exactly from the perspective of the finitude of this intuition. Nothingness is said in many ways, like Being for that matter; but this
polysemy is entirely organized on the basis of intuition, precisely because
the latter is thought in terms of its different lacks, as first of all finite, therefore also lacking. Its deficiency characterizes intuition essentially enough
that nothingness itself might be modulated in its voids.

Excess

I had been asking how the phenomenon is defined when a phenomenology (Husserl) and a metaphysics (Kant) agree to determine it within a
horizon and according to an I. Its definition as conditioned and reducible
is accomplished by a de-finition: phenomena are given in and through an
intuition, but this intuition remains finite—either as sensible (Kant) or as
lacking or ideal (Husserl). On principle, phenomena no longer appear except with a deficit of intuition, therefore a shortage of givenness. This radical lack has nothing accidental about it. It results from a phenomenological (or rather, non-phenomenological) necessity. For, in order that every
phenomenon might be inscribed within a horizon (find its condition of
possibility therein), this horizon must be delimited (such is its definition),
and therefore the phenomenon must remain finite. And for a phenomenon
to be reducible to an obviously finite I constituting it, it must be reduced

to the status of finite objectivity. And therefore the two finitudes of the horizon and the I come together in the finitude of intuition itself. Phenomena are characterized by the finitude of givenness in them, which alone allows (and imposes) that they enter a constitutional horizon and admit being led back to an I. But inversely, one could also conclude from this equivalence that unconditioned and irreducible phenomena (if there are any) would become thinkable and possible only if a finally nonfinite intuition could secure their givenness. At this point in the analysis, only one question remains: must the common definition of phenomenon be reversed? To the limited possibility of phenomenality, shouldn't we—in certain cases still to be defined—oppose a finally unconditionally possible phenomenality, whose scope would not be the result of the finitude of the conditions of experience? To the phenomenon supposedly poor in intuition, can't we oppose a phenomenon saturated with intuition?[37] To the phenomenon characterized most often by lack or poverty of intuition (a deception of the intentional aim), indeed, exceptionally, by the mere equality of intuition and intention, why wouldn't there correspond the possibility of a phenomenon where intuition would give *more, indeed immeasurably more,* than the intention would ever have aimed at or foreseen?

This is not a gratuitous or arbitrary hypothesis. First, because it results directly, with a slight correction, from the common definition of the phenomenon (Kant, Husserl)—a definition that puts two terms (intuition and concept/signification) into relation with only two forms of their possible relationship (absence of intuition and adequation), ignoring the third (surplus of intuition and/or lack of signification), which these terms nevertheless imply and designate; for, the hypothesis of a saturated phenomenon does nothing more than turn against itself one of the possibilities of the common definition of the phenomenon. Next, because it is Kant himself—the thinker of the intuitive shortage of the common phenomenon—who had a foretaste of what I call a saturated phenomenon. That is, the doctrine of the idea admits at least two types. If "an idea of reason can never become a cognition because it contains a concept (of the supersensible) for which no suitable intuition can ever be given"—phenomenon not only poor, but deprived of all intuition—it nevertheless offers only one of the types of the idea. The idea is defined as the representation of an object according to a principle, such that it can never become knowledge. In this way, corresponding to the idea of reason—representation according to the understanding—is the "aesthetic idea": representation according to intuition. It too can never become knowledge, but for a contrary reason: "Because it is an intuition (of the imagination) for which a concept can never be found adequate."[38] Inadequation always threatens phenomenality and suspends it, but it is no longer a question of the nonadequation of (lacking) intuition leaving a (given) concept empty. It is inversely a question of a deficiency of the (lacking) concept, which leaves the (superabundantly given) intuition blind. As a result, it is the concept that is deficient, no longer intuition. Kant highlights this unambiguously: in the case of the aesthetic idea, "the representation of the imagination . . . occasions much thinking [*viel zu denken veranlasst*] though without it being possible for any determinate thought, i.e., concept, to be adequate to it [*adäquat sein kann*]." The excess of intuition over every concept also makes it such that "no language fully attains or makes intelligible" the aesthetic idea;[39] in short, it prevents the aesthetic idea from making an object visible. It is important to insist on this: the failure to produce the object does not result from a shortage of givenness (as for the ideas of reason), but well and truly from an excess of intuition, therefore from an excess of givenness —"occasions much thinking [*viel zu denken veranlasst*]." Excess of givenness, that is, and not only of intuition, since according to Kant (and, for the most part, Husserl) intuition always gives—in it and in it alone, it is a matter of giving what shows itself. Kant formulates this excess of givenness in a rare term: the aesthetic idea, which defines an "inexponible [*inexponible*] representation of the imagination." This can be understood as follows: because it gives "much," the aesthetic idea gives intuitively more than any concept can expose. To expose here equals disposing of (or organizing) the intuitive given according to rules. The impossibility of the concept arranging this disposition comes from the fact that the intuitive superabundance no longer succeeds in exposing itself in a priori rules, whatever they might be, but rather submerges them. Intuition is no longer exposed in the concept; it saturates it and renders it overexposed—invisible, unreadable not by lack, but indeed by an excess of light. That this very excess should forbid the aesthetic idea from organizing its intuition within the limits of a concept and therefore from giving a definite object to be seen does not however disqualify it, seeing as, acknowledged in the end for what it is, this "inexponible representation" plays perfectly "in its free play."[40] And this play plays the sublime. The difficulty consists solely in trying to understand (and not repeat) what phenomenological possibility is put into operation when the surplus of giving intuition begins thus to play freely.

The path to follow now opens more clearly. I must develop as far as possible the less common hypothesis glimpsed by Kant himself—and against him. In other words, I must describe the characteristics of a phenomenon that, in contrast to the majority of phenomena, poor in intuition or defined by the ideal adequation of intuition to intention, would receive a surplus of intuition, therefore of givenness, over and above intention, the concept, and the intended. Let me remark that it is not a question of privileging intuition as such, but of following in it (indeed eventually without or against it) givenness in its widest possible scope; moreover, when intuition is considered strictly on the basis of givenness, whose rule it most often secures, it could indeed take on new shapes, at once paradoxical and more powerful. Let me also remark that such a saturated phenomenon will no doubt no longer constitute an object (at least in the Kantian sense), for it is not self-evident that objectivity has enough authority to impose its norm on the phenomenon. What shows itself gives itself before being objectified, and it would never even become an object if it was not first given, be it only in a basic and humble way. We must therefore follow as far as possible the hypothesis of a phenomenon saturated with intuition. It demands our attention because it designates a possibility of the phenomenon in general, and in phenomenology, even the least possibility obliges.

§21 SKETCH OF THE SATURATED PHENOMENON: THE HORIZON

According to Quantity—Invisable

I will sketch a description of the saturated phenomenon by following the lead of the categories of the understanding defined by Kant. But the saturated phenomenon exceeds these categories (as well as principles), since in it intuition passes beyond the concept. I will therefore follow them by inverting them. The saturated phenomenon will be described as *invisable*[41] according to quantity, unbearable according to quality, absolute according to relation, irregardable[42] according to modality. The three first characteristics put into question the ordinary sense of horizon (§21); the last, the transcendental sense of the I (§22).

First, the saturated phenomenon *cannot be aimed at* [*ne peut se viser*]. This impossibility stems from its essentially unforeseeable character [*son caractère essentiellement imprévisible*]. To be sure, its giving intuition ensures it a quantity, but such that it cannot be foreseen. This determination can be made clearer by inverting the function of the axioms of the intuition. According to Kant, quantity (extensive magnitude) is declined by composition of the whole in terms of its parts. This "successive synthesis" allows for the representation of the whole to be reconstituted according to the representation of the sum of its parts. In effect, the magnitude of a *quantum* implies nothing more than the summation of the *quanta* that make it up. From this homogeneity another property follows: a quantified phenomenon is "(fore-)seen in advance [*schon . . . angeschaut*] as an aggregate (sum of the parts given in advance) [*vorher gegebener*]."[43] This sort of phenomenon would always be foreseeable, literally seen before being seen in person or seen by procuration, on the basis of another besides itself—more precisely, on the basis of the supposedly finite number of its parts and the supposedly finite magnitude of each among them. Now these properties are precisely the ones that become untenable when the saturated phenomenon is at issue. That is, since the intuition that gives it is not limited by its possible concept, its excess can neither be divided nor adequately put together again by virtue of a finite magnitude homogeneous with finite parts. It could not be measured in terms of its parts, since the saturating intuition surpasses limitlessly the sum of the parts by continually adding to them. Such a phenomenon, which is always exceeded by the intuition that saturates it, should rather be called incommensurable, not measurable (immense), unmeasured. This lack of measure, however, does not always or even first of all operate in terms of the enormity of a limitless quantity; it is most often marked by the simple impossibility of our applying a successive synthesis to it, permitting an aggregate to be foreseen on the basis of the finite sum of its finite parts. As the saturated phenomenon passes beyond all summation of its parts—which often cannot be enumerated anyway—the successive synthesis must be abandoned in favor of what I will call an instantaneous synthesis whose representation precedes and surpasses that of the eventual components, instead of resulting from it according to foresight.

A privileged example is found in amazement. According to Descartes, this passion affects us even before we know the thing, or rather precisely because we know it only partially: "Only the side of the object originally presented [is] perceived, and hence [it is] impossible for a more detailed knowledge of the object to be acquired."[44] The "object" offers us only one "side" (we could also say only one *Abschattung*) and yet is, at the same time, imposed on us with a power such that we are submerged by what shows itself, most likely to the point of fascination. And yet the "successive synthesis" has been suspended ever since its initial term; another synthesis, instantaneous and irreducible to the sum of its possible parts, is being carried out. Every phenomenon that produces amazement is imposed on the gaze in the very measure (more exactly, in the excess of measure) to which it does not result from any foreseeable summation of partial quantities. The synthesis takes place without complete knowledge of the object, therefore without *our* synthesis. It is thus freed from the objectness that we would impose on it so that it might impose on us its own synthesis, accomplished before we could reconstitute it (a passive synthesis, therefore). Its coming forward precedes our apprehension, rather than resulting from it. The phenomenon's anticipating what we foresee of it is out of keeping: it comes before our gaze at it, it comes early, before us. We do not foresee it; it foresees us. As a result, it is amazing because it arises without measure in common with the phenomena that precede it but cannot announce or explain it—for, according to Spinoza, "Nullam cum reliquis habet connexionem [It has no connection with any others]."[45] Disconnected from the rest of the phenomena and from their already known concepts, it imposes itself without precedents, parts, or sum.

Another privileged example comes from cubist painting, which is built around the observation that in fact and on principle the phenomena to be seen go beyond the foreseen sum of their parts—their adumbrations and their aspects. In other words, for cubist painting, to see the phenomena, one must unfold appearing in an ever finite number of facets, which (as in the basic case of the cube for Husserl) continually proliferate and accumulate. The objects that are supposedly the most simple—violin on a stool, with newspaper and vase—in fact always give more to see, and from afar, more than we can think. What we perceive by momentary intuitions and what we conceptually think of these moments remain incommensurably poorer than what we really have to see there. The concepts, by which we know what there is to see so well that we no longer take the time or the trouble to go and truly see, serve only to sum them up, simplify them for us, so as to mask their exuberant splendor. Most of the time, we want to get an idea of things without having any intention of seeing them, so that we can handle them easily, like equipment. If we were to forget their concepts, we would see that there are so many things to see—so many things to see in this old violin on the simple stool, a rumpled newspaper and sad little vase. If only we could let all the facets of each of them appear (distinguished by the variegated plays of color they offer to the light, which modify it so), all the perspectives on each object aligned with the other such that by moving ourselves around them (anamorphosis) we can actually aim at them, and not only the real perspectives but also and especially the unreal ones such as we could imagine and even see them if we could pair the opposite side of one (for example the violin case) with the obverse of the other (for example the newspaper title), the left of the one above (the vase) with the right of the other (the feet of the stool, below), the floor with the ceiling, etc. For all their combinations are by right visible, even though our vision—therefore our intentions and our intuitions—attains only an improbably small number of them. The cubist painter knows this, he who no longer wants to bring into visibility what just anyone—forewarned, busy, practical-minded—sees, excluding all that he does not know in advance, therefore does not recognize, as well as all that does not serve a purpose and therefore is not interesting. The cubist painter wants rather to bring into visibility what could be visible if we tried every intention, every combination of intentions, and even all those that are forbidden to us in the finitude of common intuition, but which we could try to divine. The cubist happily exhausts himself in the endless race toward the impossible and ever elusive summation of the visible bursting—for the visible bursts, if one lets it arise in appearing, like a wave crashes with exploding fireworks of water drops, each different in form and color, in time and space, in trajectory and how they glimmer. More radical than the impressionist, who means only to show all that he experiences exactly, the cubist tries, sometimes successfully, to let appear what he could not actually see, but whose least possibility he stubbornly lets ascend into the visible.

In this way, the saturated phenomenon could not be foreseen, for at least two phenomenological reasons. (a) First, because the intuition, which continually saturates it, forbids it from distinguishing and adding up a finite number of finite parts, thereby annulling all possibility of foreseeing the phenomenon before it gives itself in person. (b) Next, because the saturated phenomenon most often imposes itself thanks to amazement, in which all the intuitive givenness is accomplished by the fact that its possible parts are not counted up, therefore also not foreseen.

According to Quality—Unbearable

Secondly, the saturated phenomenon *cannot be borne.* According to Kant, quality (intensive magnitudes) allows intuition to fix a degree of reality for the object by limiting it, eventually to the point of negation. Each phenomenon would admit a degree of intuition, and this is what perception can always anticipate. The foresight at work in extensive magnitude is found again in the anticipation of intensive magnitude. An essential difference separates them, however: anticipation operates no longer in a successive synthesis of the homogeneous, but in a perception of the heterogeneous, in which each degree is demarcated by a dissolution of continuity with the preceding, therefore by an absolutely singular novelty. However, because he privileges the case of the poor phenomenon, Kant analyzes this heterogeneity only in terms of the most simple cases—the first degrees starting from zero, the imperceptible perceptions, etc. This is to say that he approaches intensity only by strangely privileging phenomena of the weakest intensity, precisely where intensity is lacking, to the paradoxical point of basing it on the very absence of intensity, negation: "A magnitude which is apprehended only as unity, and in which multiplicity can be represented only through approximation to negation=o, I entitle an *intensive* magnitude."[46] Intensity is defined starting from its degree zero. There is no better way of saying that the absolute and unquestioned dominance of the paradigm of a poor phenomenon, indeed one empty of intuition, definitively blocks, in metaphysics at least, every advance toward the liberated phenomenality of givenness. From this perspective, one might not even suspect the opposite case of a saturated phenomenon, in which intuition gives reality (first category of quality) to the phenomenon without any negation (second category) and, of course, without collapsing into limitation (third category). For the intuition saturating a phenomenon attains an intensive magnitude without measure, or common measure, such that starting with a certain degree, the intensity of the real intuition passes beyond all the conceptual anticipations of perception. Before this excess, not only can perception no longer anticipate what it will receive from intuition; it also can no longer bear its most elevated degrees. For intuition, supposedly "blind" in the realm of poor or common phenomena, turns out, in a radical phenomenology, to be blinding. The gaze cannot any longer sustain a light that bedazzles and burns. The intensive magnitude of intuition, when it goes so far as to give a saturated phenomenon, cannot be borne by the gaze, just as this gaze could not foresee its extensive magnitude.

When the gaze cannot bear what it sees, it suffers bedazzlement. For not bearing is not simply equivalent to not seeing: one must first perceive, if not clearly see, in order to undergo what one cannot bear. It concerns a visible that our gaze cannot sustain. This visible is undergone as unbearable by the gaze, because it fills it without measure, after the fashion of the idol. The gaze no longer keeps anything in reserve from free vision; the visible invades all its intended angles; it accomplishes *adaequatio*—it fills. But the filling goes by itself beyond itself; it goes to the brink, too far. Thus the glory of the visible weighs down with all it has, that is to say it weighs too much. What is here weighty to the point of making one suffer is named neither unhappiness, nor pain, nor lack, but indeed success—glory, joy: "O/Triumph!/ What Glory! What human heart would be so strong to bear/That?"[47] Intuition gives too intensely for the gaze to have enough heart to truly see what it cannot conceive, only barely receive, or sometimes even confront. This blindness stems from the intensity of intuition and not from its quantity, as is indicated by blindness before spectacles in which intuition remains quantitatively ordinary, indeed weak, but of extraordinary intensity. Oedipus blinds himself on account of having seen his transgression; he is therefore bedazzled by a quasi-moral intensity of intuition. Whoever finds himself smitten by love owes it, most often, only to the silence of a gaze that no one saw except for him. And He Whom no one can see without dying blinds first with his holiness, even if his coming is announced in a mere gust of wind. Because the saturated phenomenon cannot be borne, on account of the excess of intuition in it, by any gaze cut to its measure ("objectively"), it is perceived ("subjectively") by the gaze only in the negative mode of an impossible perception—of bedazzlement. Plato too has described this perfectly in connection with the prisoner of the Cave: "Let one untie him and force him suddenly to turn around [*anistanai*] . . . and to lift his gaze toward the light [*pros to phōs anablepein*], he would suffer in doing all that, and because of the bedazzlements, he would not have the strength to see face on [*dia tas marmarugas adunatai kathoran*] that of which he previously saw the shadows." It is indeed a question of "suffering" by seeing the full light and of fleeing it by turning away toward "the things that one can look at [*ha dunatai kathoran*]." What keeps one from seeing are precisely "the eyes filled with splendor."[48] This bedazzlement, moreover, is valid for intelligible intuition as well as sensible intuition. First, because in the final analysis, the allegory of the Cave concerns the epistemological obstacles to intelligibility, for which the sensible scene offers an explicit figure; next, because the idea of the Good, also and especially, is offered as "difficult to see [*mogis horasthai*]," not by defect, seeing as it presents "the most visible of beings," but indeed by excess because "the soul is incapable of seeing anything . . . saturated by an extremely brilliant bedazzlement [*hupo lamproteron marmarugēs empe-*

plēstai]."[49] In all these cases, what forbids seeing comes from the excess of the light's intensity, be it sensible or intelligible.

The painter too produces saturation in terms of quality, for he always, indeed first, paints light. But most of the time, he paints it as we see it—always already spread over the things that it makes evident, therefore invisible and, as such, withdrawn from the painting that it opens. Even when Claude (Lorrain) divides his canvas—*The Embarkation of Saint Ursula* or *Dido Building Carthage*—with a blood-red ray of light from the dying sun, he is interested, as much as in this light itself, in registering the subtly shaded effects on the buildings, the boats, and the people who, as if seated on either side waiting to welcome it, end up confiscating it and distracting our attention from it. But when Turner consciously takes up the same theme with the same organization—for example in *The Decline of the Carthaginian Empire*—his essential task is to bring the sun itself to the center of the painting. Or more exactly, so that its light might appear truly as such, not only does he cover the other protagonists in a paradoxical darkness to the point of diluting them; he even ceases to show the sun's flux (*lumen*) directly—which the gaze cannot bear any more than death—in order to "render" only its bedazzling fulguration (*lux*). An unbearable circle diffusing a fiery whiteness, where nothing can any longer be distinguished or staged. To show the sun in effect demands showing what cannot be designated as a thing and what has as its own peculiarity to forbid showing not only anything else, but also itself. This is why in the Venetian canvases (for example, *Venice with Salute*), Turner no longer lets even the slightest flicker of a cupola show through, so much does the unmoving brilliance of the light, saturating the canvas without rest, ravage with whiteness every possible countryside and nullify every project to make even the least *veduta*; nor does he let even the least silhouette subsist, and the church is swallowed in a hazy dark stain, glazed under the deluge of light, like a small remainder of scattered ashes. Thus, the eye experiences only its powerlessness to see anything, except the bursting that submerges it—almost metallic and vibrating[50]—which blinds it. Thus appears the excess of intensive magnitude in the pure and simple impossibility of even maintaining it within the horizon of the visible.

Bedazzlement thus becomes a characteristic that can be universalized to every form of the intuition of an intensity surpassing the degree that a gaze can sustain. No doubt this degree varies with the scope of each gaze (which I have not calibrated here), but the aim always ends up reaching its fulfillment. Now this is not just some exceptional case, which I merely mention as a matter of interest while discussing the poor phenomenon, supposedly more frequent and therefore approximately normative. To the contrary, it is a question of an essential determination of the phenomenon, one that two lines of argument make inevitable. (a) The Kantian description of intensive magnitudes, however original and to the point, massively privileges the degree zero in order to maintain a resounding silence about the notion most characteristic of intensive magnitude—the maximum. For even if it cannot be defined universally, for each gaze and in each case, there is always a maximum, a threshold of tolerance beyond which what is seen is no longer constituted as an object within a finite horizon. Bedazzlement begins when perception crosses its tolerable maximum. The description of intensive magnitudes should therefore prioritize the consideration of their most elevated degrees, therefore the maximum signaled by the bedazzlements. (b) The intolerable, as before with unforeseeability, designates a mode of intuitive givenness that is not only less rare than hasty examination might suspect, but especially one that is decisive for a real recognition of finitude. Finitude is proven and experienced not so much because the given falls short before our gaze as, above all, because this gaze can sometimes no longer measure the range of the given. Or inversely, measuring itself against it, the gaze undergoes it, sometimes in the suffering of an essential passivity, as having no measure in common with it. Finitude is disclosed more in the encounter with the saturated phenomenon than with the poor phenomenon.

Without Relation—Absolute

Neither *visable* according to quantity nor bearable according to quality, the saturated phenomenon appears *absolute* according to relation, which means it evades any analogy of experience.

Kant defines the principle of such analogies in this way: "Experience is possible only through the representation of a necessary connection of perceptions." Mere apprehension through empirical intuition cannot ensure this necessary connection; it will have to produce itself at once through concepts and in time. For "since time, however, cannot itself be perceived, the determination of the existence of objects in time can take place only through their relation in time in general, and therefore only through concepts that connect them a priori."[51] This connection permits three relations: inherence of accident in substance, causality between cause and effect, commonality among several substances. But Kant establishes them only by employing three presuppositions, the contestation of which will again allow me to describe *a contrario* the saturated phenomenon. (a) First presupposition: in all its occurrences, a phenomenon can manifest itself only by respecting the unity of experience, that is to say, by taking place in a network as tightly bound as possible by lines of inherence, causality, and commonality that assign to it, in the hollows as it were, a site. This is a strict obligation: "In the original apperception, the manifold must [*soll*] be unified in terms of its relation in time."[52] In this way, a phenomenon would appear only in a site predetermined by a system of coordinates, itself governed by the principle of the unity of experience. But another interrogation insinuates itself here: *Must* every phenomenon, without exception, respect the unity of experience? Is it legitimate to rule out the possibility that a phenomenon might impose itself on perception without assigning it either a substance in which it resides like an accident or a cause from which it results as an effect, or even less an interactive *commercium* where it is relativized? And for that matter, it is not self-evident that the phenomena that really arise—in contrast to the phenomena that are poor in intuition, or even deprived of intuition—can at first and most often be perceived according to such analogies of perception. It could be quite the opposite— that they happen without being inscribed, at least at first, in the relational network that assures experience its unity, and that they matter precisely because one could not assign them any substratum, any cause, or any commerce. To be sure, after a moment's consideration, the majority can be reconducted, at least approximately, to the analogies of perception. But those, not so rare, that do not lend themselves to this henceforth assume the character and the dignity of event. Event, or unforeseeable phenomenon (in terms of the past), not exhaustively comprehensible (in terms of the present), not reproducible (in terms of the future), in short, absolute, unique, coming forward (§17). It will therefore be said: pure event. As a result, the analogies of experience concern only a fringe of phenomenality—phenomena of the type of objects constituted by the sciences, poor in intuition, foreseeable, exhaustively knowable, reproducible—while other levels (and first of all historical phenomena) would make an exception.

The second presupposition (b) concerns the very elaboration of the procedure that allows us to secure temporal and conceptual necessity, therefore the unity of experience. Kant presupposes that this unity should always be accomplished by recourse to an analogy. For "all empirical time-determinations must [*müssen*] stand under rules of universal time-determination.

The analogies of experience . . . must [*müssen*] be rules of this description."[53] In short, it falls to the analogies of experience and to them alone to actually exercise the regulation of experience by necessity, therefore to assure its unity. At the precise moment of defining these analogies, Kant himself recognizes the fragility of their phenomenological power. That is, in mathematics, the analogy remains quantitative, such that by calculation it provides the fourth term and truly constructs it; thus the equality of two relations of magnitude is "always constitutive" of the object and actually maintains it in a unified experience; but, Kant specifies,

In philosophy the analogy is not the equality of two *quantitative* but of two *qualitative* relations; and from three given members we can obtain a priori knowledge only of the relation to a fourth, not of the fourth member itself. . . . An analogy of experience is, therefore, only a rule according to which a unity of experience may arise from [*entspringen soll*] perception. It does not tell us how mere perception of empirical intuition in general itself comes about. It is not a principle *constitutive* of the objects, that is, of the appearances [phenomena], but only *regulative*.[54]

Clearly, when it is a question of what I have called poor (here mathematical) phenomena, intuition (here the intuition of pure space) succeeds neither in saturating nor in contradicting the pre-established unity and necessity of experience. In this case and in this case alone, the analogy remains quantitative and constitutive—in short, there is an analogy of experience provided that the phenomenon remains poor. But, by Kant's own admission, as soon as we pass to physics (without yet speaking of a saturated phenomenon), the analogy ceases to be capable of regulating anything, except qualitatively. If A is cause of effect B, then D will be in the position (quality) of effect vis-à-vis C without our being able to identify what D is or will be, and without our being able to construct it (by lack of pure intuition) or constitute it. Kant's predicament culminates with this strange use, in the analytic of principles, of principles whose usage remains purely "regulative," which can be understood in only one sense: the analogies of experience do not really constitute their objects, but state the subjective needs of the understanding. Let us suppose for a moment that the analogies of perception, thus reduced to a mere regulative use, should have to treat a saturated phenomenon. The latter already passes beyond the categories of quantity (unforeseeable) and quality (unbearable); it also already gives itself as a pure event. As a result, how could an analogy—above all one that is merely regulative—assign to it, especially with necessity and a priori, a point whose coordinates would be fixed by inherence, causality, and commonality? This phenomenon will by contrast evade relations because it will not maintain any measure in common with these terms; it would be free of them as from all other a priori determinations of experience that might claim to impose itself on the phenomenon. In this sense, I will speak of an absolute phenomenon: disconnected from all analogy with any object of experience whatsoever.

Without Analogy

Accordingly, the third Kantian presupposition becomes questionable. (c) The unity of experience is deployed against the background of time, since "all phenomena are in time."[55] Thus, Kant posits not only time as the final horizon of phenomena, but above all the horizon in general as the condition for the appearing of these phenomena, which it at once welcomes and restricts. This means that before any phenomenal breakthrough toward visibility, the horizon awaits in advance, first; and it means that each phenomenon, in appearing, is in fact constrained to actualize a portion of this horizon, which otherwise remains transparent or empty. When a question sometimes arises about this, it bears on the identity of this horizon (time, Being, *Ereignis*, indeed ethics or the good, etc.). This should not, however, hide another question, one more simple and more radical: could certain phenomena exceed their horizon?

This does not mean dispensing with a horizon altogether, since this would no doubt forbid any and all manifestation; it means using the horizon in another way so as to be free of its delimiting anteriority, which can only enter into conflict with a phenomenon's claim to absolute appearing. Let us suppose a saturated phenomenon, one that wins its absolute character by being emancipated from analogies with experience—what horizon can it still acknowledge? Two phenomenological situations must be distinguished here. (i) Either the phenomenon receives an intuition that exceeds the frame set by the concept and signification that aim at and foresee it. In this intuition, there no longer remains even the slightest halo of the not yet known surrounding the noematic core of the known. The concept or signification of the object coincides exactly with the limits of its horizon, without a significant reserve as yet unfulfilled. Intuition not only attains adequation with signification, but fills it, as well as its entire horizon. Thus is realized the first figure of saturation: intuition, by dint of pressure, attains the common limits of the concept and horizon; it does not cross them, however, and running up against them, it reverberates, returns toward the finite field, blurs it, and renders it in the end invisible by excess—bedazzlement. In this first case, saturation is again accomplished within the horizon, but against it. Fulfilling its horizon, the saturated phenomenon is no longer constituted as object and withdraws behind the bedazzlement it provokes.[56] (ii) Or, having attained the limits of its concept or signification as far as *adaequatio*, then having fulfilled all its horizon and even the halo of the not yet known, the phenomenon saturated with intuition can—in contrast with the preceding case—pass beyond all horizonal delimitation. This situation does not imply doing away with the horizon altogether, but articulating several together in order to welcome one and the same saturated phenomenon. It is a matter of reading this phenomenon, which exceeds all norms in its essentially distinct, indeed opposed, horizons, for which perhaps only an indefinite summation will permit accommodating the excess of what shows itself. Let me emphasize that this hypothesis has nothing strange or uncommon about it, even in rigorous philosophy. Spinoza succeeds in thinking the one and only substance only by such an arrangement. It absorbs all the determinations of beingness and all the individuals corresponding thereto, to the point that it drowns the essentially finite horizon of Cartesian metaphysics in its infinitely saturated presence. To conceive it, it must multiply formally into attributes, all equally and differently infinite, each opening the possibility of an endless interpretation of modes, finite as well as infinite.[57] The substance can thus pass from the horizon of thought to that of extension, without omitting the unknown attributes, other potential horizons. Only this always reversible passage permits calibrating and easing, so to speak, the initial saturation, which would otherwise remain pure and unspeakable bedazzlement. With this, moreover, Spinoza does nothing more than revive, to be sure by overturning, the tactics elaborated by the doctrine of the convertibility of transcendentals. The irreducible plurality of *ens, unum, verum, bonum* (and sometimes *pulchrum*) allowed not only the ordinary phenomenon of a finite being to be translated into a unity (Aristotle, Leibniz), but especially the saturated phenomenon par excellence —the Principle—to be declined in perfectly autonomous registers, where it gives itself to be seen, each time, only according to a perspective that is total as well as partial, conceivable and always incomprehensible: being in the act of Being, one before unity, truth of oneself and of the world, invisible splendor, etc. (Plotinus, Proclus, Dionysius, etc.). The convertibility of these registers indicates that saturation persists, but is distributed into several rival, though compatible horizons. Finitude still describes the saturated phenomenon because it grants it the right to several horizons. Generalizing, I will say that it is fitting to admit phenomena of $n + 1$ horizons, as it was necessary to admit spaces of $n + 1$ dimensions—whose properties saturate the imagination. Here bedazzlement paves the way for an infinite hermeneutic. (iii) We cannot rule out a third case, one that is rare but inevitable (§23–24): that saturation redoubles the first two cases by lumping them together. If the hermeneutic of an infinite plurality of horizons is by chance not enough to decline an essentially and absolutely saturated phenomenon, it could be that each perspective, already saturated in a single horizon (bedazzlement), is blurred once again by spilling over the others—in short, that the hermeneutic adds the bedazzlements in each horizon, instead of combining them. Then, not only no single horizon, but no combination of horizons, could successfully tolerate the absoluteness of the phenomenon, precisely because it gives itself as absolute, that is to say, free from all analogy with common-law phenomena and from all predetermination by a network of relations, with neither precedent nor antecedent in the already seen or foreseeable. In short, there would appear a phenomenon saturated to the point that the world (in all senses of the word) could not accept it. Having come among his own, his own do not recognize it; having come into phenomenality, the absolutely saturated phenomenon could find no space there for its display. But this denial of opening, therefore this disfiguring, still remains a manifestation (§30).

Couldn't one fear that the very hypothesis of a phenomenon saturating a horizon is a danger—one that should not be underestimated since it is born from the most real experience: that of a totality without door or window, excluding every possible, every other, every Other? But this danger, while no doubt undeniable, results less from the saturated phenomenon itself than from the misapprehension of it. When this type of phenomenon arises, it is most often treated like a common-law phenomenon, indeed a poor phenomenon, one that is therefore forced to be included in a phenomenological situation that by definition it refuses, and it is finally misapprehended. If, by contrast, its specificity is recognized, the bedazzlement it provokes would become phenomenologically acceptable, indeed desirable, and the passage from one horizon to another would become a rational task for the hermeneutic. The saturated phenomenon safeguards its absoluteness and at the same time dissolves its danger when it is recognized as such, without confusing it with other phenomena.[58]

In this way, by giving itself absolutely, the saturated phenomenon also gives itself as absolute—free from any analogy with already seen, objectified, comprehended experience. It is freed because it does not depend on any horizon. In every case, it does not depend on this condition of possibility par excellence—a horizon, whatever it might be. I therefore call it an unconditioned phenomenon.

§22 SKETCH OF THE SATURATED PHENOMENON: I

According to Modality: Irregardable

Neither *visable* according to quantity nor bearable according to quality, but absolute according to relation, that is to say, unconditioned by the horizon (§21), the saturated phenomenon is spoken of as irregardable[59] according to modality.

We know that the categories of modality are distinguished from all the others in that they determine neither objects in themselves (quantity, quality) nor their mutual relations (relation), but only—Kant insists—"their relation to thought in general." These categories, in contrast to those that Aristotle deduces from, and leads back to, *ousia*, are the operators of the fundamental epistemological relation to the I; in short, they "express only the relation to the faculty of knowledge," "nothing but the action of the faculty of knowledge."[60] In fact, between the object of experience and the power of knowing, it is no longer only a matter of a simple relation, superadded, extrinsic and probably optional, but of the fact that these objects "agree" with the power of knowledge—and absolutely must if they are to be known. This agreement determines their possibility (therefore also their actuality and their necessity) to be and to be known as phenomena solely by the measure of their suitability to the I, for whom and by whom the experience takes place. "The postulate of the *possibility* of things requires [*fordert*] that the concept of the things should agree [*zusammenstimme*] with the formal conditions of an experience in general."[61] The phenomenon is possible strictly to the extent that it agrees with the formal conditions of experience, therefore with the power of knowing that fixes them, therefore finally with the transcendental I itself. The possibility of the phenomenon depends finally on its reconduction to the I. Not only is the phenomenon with an intuitive deficit (poor or common) not assured of its possibility by itself, but it is alienated in an external instance—that of the I—in order that it might perform its own appearing. Far from showing *itself*, it is staged only in a scene set by and for an other besides it, actor without action, submitted to a spectator and transcendental director. The Kantian sense of the categories of modality in the end produces the phenomenon's alienation from itself; far from giving *itself,* it lets itself be shown, made visible and staged. In short, it becomes constituted as an object, one that gets its status from a previously objectifying intentionality, like a still and always "well-grounded" phenomenon—therefore, on condition. Such a poor or common phenomenon lacks not only intuition with regard to its concept; it lacks phenomenal autonomy, since it renounces (according to the categories of modality) giving *itself* to whoever happens to see it, and instead lets itself be constituted (constructed, schematized, synthesized, etc.) by whoever precedes and foresees it. The "postulates of empirical thought in general" postulate that the phenomenon never appears except in response to requirements outside and anterior to it, requirements that it can, in the best of cases, satisfy only by submitting to. Alienated phenomenon, exercising a conditioned phenomenality, the poor or common phenomenon perfectly deserves its title—poor in intuition, poor especially in phenomenality.

This same extremity leads to reversing the Kantian situation so as to ask in return: what would happen if a phenomenon did *not* "agree with" or "correspond to" the power of knowing of the I? The likely Kantian response to this question is hardly in doubt: such a phenomenon quite simply would not appear; there would not be a phenomenon at all, but a confused perceptive aberration without object. I can admit that this answer remains meaningful for a phenomenon that is poor in intuition or a common-law phenomenon (which aim no higher than an equality between intuition and concept)—though even in these cases, it is perhaps necessary to imagine exceptions, as in quantum physics.[62] But is it still valid for a saturated phenomenon? In fact, the situation is very different here. In saturation, the I undergoes the disagreement between an at least potential phenomenon and the subjective condition for its experience; and, as a result, it does not constitute an object. But this failure to objectify in no way implies that absolutely nothing appears here. To the contrary, intuitive saturation, precisely insofar as it renders it *invisable,* intolerable, and absolute (unconditioned), is imposed in the type of phenomenon that is exceptional by excess, not by defect. The saturated phenomenon refuses to let itself be regarded as an object precisely because it appears with a multiple and indescribable excess that annuls all effort at constitution. The saturated phenomenon must be determined as a nonobjective or, more exactly, nonobjectifiable phenomenon; this denegation means in no way to take shelter in the irrational or arbitrary, since it is a question of a phenomenality that escapes not so much objectivity (one of the characteristics of the object, on the same level as subjectivity) as objectness—the property and status of the object, as it is opposed and abandoned to the gaze of a subject. The saturated phenomenon contradicts the subjective conditions of experience precisely in that it does not admit constitution as an object. In other words, though exemplarily visible, it nevertheless cannot be looked at, regarded. The saturated phenomenon gives *itself* insofar as it remains, according to modality, irregardable.

How does it give itself to be seen without letting itself be looked at? This difficulty is rooted in the presupposition that "to see" and "to gaze" [*"voir" et "regarder"*] are exactly equivalent and that the one cannot go without the other. But this is not the case, provided that we read "to gaze," *regarder*, literally: *re-garder* transcribes exactly *in-tueri* and should be understood in terms of *tueri*, "to guard or to keep"—but in the sense of "to keep an eye on, to watch out of the corner of one's eye, to keep in sight." "To gaze" [*regarder*] therefore implies something more or wholly other than simply "to see." In order to see, it is not as necessary to perceive by the sense of sight (or any other sense) as it is to receive what shows *itself* on its own because it gives *itself* in visibility at its own initiative (anamorphosis, §13), according to its own rhythm (unpredictable landing, §14), and with its essential contingency (incident, §16), in such a way as to appear without reproducing or repeating itself (event, §17). On the other hand, gazing, *regarder*, is about being able to keep the visible thus seen under the control of the seer, exerting this control by guarding the visible in visibility, as much as possible without letting it have the initiative in appearing (or disappearing) by forbidding it any variation in intensity that would disturb its inscription in the concept, and especially by conserving it in permanent presence through postulating its identical reproducibility. To gaze at the phenomenon is therefore equivalent not to seeing it, but indeed to transforming it into an object visible according to an always poor or common phenomenality—visible within the limits of a concept, therefore at the initiative of the gaze, enduring as long as possible in permanence, in short, visible in conformity with objectness. And it is not by chance that Descartes entrusts *intuitus* with the role of maintaining in evidence what the ego reduces to the status of *objectum*[63]—the gaze keeps objects in an objected state for the I. Therefore, the gaze sees, but more originally it possesses and conserves— it guards. Consequently it concerns only objects, that is, for the purpose of this study, phenomena whose visibility remains submitted to objectness. And since the excess of intuition over the foresight of the concept and the conditions of the I contravenes objectness, the phenomenon saturated with an excess of intuition can only be withdrawn from the gaze. Determining the saturated phenomenon as irregardable amounts to imagining the possibility that it imposes itself on sight with such an excess of intuition that it can no longer be reduced to the conditions of experience (objecthood), therefore to the I that sets them.

Counter-Experience

In what figure does it appear? For by definition it does appear, since it must appear in the measure of the excess of giving intuition in it. The irregardable saturated phenomenon must appear par excellence, but it also contradicts the conditions for the poor or common phenomenality of objects. If it appears counter to the conditions for the possibility of experience, how could the supposed excellence of its phenomenality not end up as a pure and simple impossibility of experience—not even an experience of the impossible? The response to this difficulty resides in its very statement: if, for the saturated phenomenon, there is no experience of an object, it remains for us to imagine that there might be a counter-experience of a nonobject. Counter-experience is not equivalent to a nonexperience, but to the experience of a phenomenon that is neither regardable, nor guarded according to objectness, one that therefore resists the conditions of objectification. Counter-experience offers the experience of what irreducibly contradicts the conditions for the experience of objects. Such experience to the second degree recovers the peculiarly Husserlian novelty of founded acts: like them, in order to appear, it depends on the very thing that it passes beyond but nevertheless renders intelligible. We could therefore say that, of the saturated phenomenon, there is founded experience. That is, confronted with the saturated phenomenon, the I cannot not see it, but it cannot any longer gaze at it as its mere object. It has the eye to see but not keep it. What, then, does this eye without gaze see? It sees the superabundance of intuitive givenness; or rather, it does not see it clearly and precisely as such since its excess renders it irregardable and difficult to master. The intuition of the phenomenon is nevertheless seen, but as blurred by the too narrow aperture, the too short lens, the too cramped frame, that receives it—or rather that cannot receive it as such. The eye no longer apperceives the apparition of the saturated phenomenon so much as it apper-

ceives the perturbation that it in person produces within the ordinary conditions of experience—in the way that an excess of light is not seen directly
on the photographic paper but is inferred indirectly from the overexposure,
or else—like the speed of something in motion, unrepresentable in a frozen image—nevertheless appears there in and through the smudge that its
very unrepresentability makes on the paper. In these cases, the eye does not
see an exterior spectacle so much as it sees the reified traces of its own powerlessness to constitute whatever it might be into an object. It sees nothing
distinctly (in particular not an object), but clearly experiences its own powerlessness to master the measurelessness of the intuitive given—therefore,
before all, the perturbations of the visible, the noise of a poorly received
message, the obfuscation of finitude. It receives a pure givenness, precisely
because it no longer discerns any objectifiable given therein.[64] It falls to
music, or rather listening to music, to provide privileged occurrences of
this sense of the phenomenon. The opening of a symphony—the *Jupiter*,
for example—reaches me in such a way that even before reconstituting the
melodic line or assessing the orchestral fabric (therefore constituting two
objects from two givens), I first receive in my ear the movement (nonobjectifiable because giving) of the sonorous mass, which comes upon me
and submerges me, then my very belatedness to the deployment of this
coming. A memory of previous performances no doubt allows me to identify the melody more quickly and to assess the orchestral ensemble, but it
does not allow me to abolish the arising, therefore the event. The music offers the very movement of its coming forward, its effect on me who receives it without producing it, in short, its arising without real content.
Consequently, it comes upon me in such a way that it affects me directly
as pure givenness mediated by almost no objectifiable given, and therefore
imposes on me an actuality immediately its own. The musical offering offers first the very movement of its coming forward—it offers the effect of
its very offering, without or beyond the sounds that it produces. Let me
name this phenomenological extremity where the coming forward exceeds
what comes forward a *paradox*.

The Paradox and the Witness

The paradox not only suspends the phenomenon's subjection to the I;
it inverts it. For, far from being able to constitute this phenomenon, the I
experiences itself as constituted by it. To the constituting subject, there succeeds the witness—the constituted witness. Constituted witness, the sub-

ject is still the worker of truth, but he cannot claim to be its producer. With the name *witness*, we must understand a subjectivity stripped of the characteristics that gave it transcendental rank. (i) Constituted and no longer constituting, the witness no longer enacts synthesis or constitution. Or rather, synthesis becomes passive and is imposed on it. As with constitution, the giving of meaning (*Sinngebung*) is inverted. The I can no longer provide its meaning to lived experiences and intuition; rather, the latter give themselves and therefore give it their meaning (a meaning that is for that matter partial and no longer all-encompassing). (ii) That is, in the case of a saturated phenomenon, intuition by definition passes beyond what meaning a hermeneutic of the concept can provide, a fortiori a hermeneutic practiced by the finite I, which will always have less givable meaning (concept, intentionality, signification, noesis, etc.) than the intuitive given calls for. (iii) The inversion of the gaze, and therefore of the guard it mounts over the object, places the I, become witness, under the guard of the paradox (saturated phenomenon) that controls it and stands vigilant over it. For the witness cannot avail himself of a viewpoint that dominates the intuition which submerges him. In space, the saturated phenomenon swallows him with its intuitive deluge; in time, it precedes him with an always already there interpretation. The I loses its anteriority as egoic pole (polar I) and cannot yet identify itself, except by admitting the precedence of such an unconstitutable phenomenon. This reversal leaves him stupefied and taken aback, essentially surprised by the more original event, which takes him away from himself. (iv) The witness is therefore opposed to the I in that he no longer has the initiative in manifestation (by facticity), does not see the given phenomenon in its totality (by excess of intuition), cannot read or interpret the intuitive excess (by shortage of concept), and finally lets himself be judged (said, determined) by what he himself cannot say or think adequately. In this way, the phenomenon is no longer reduced to the I who would gaze at it. Irregardable, he confesses himself irreducible. The event that comes up can no longer be constituted into an object; in contrast, it leaves the durable trace of its enclosure only in the I/me, witness constituted despite itself by what it receives. In short, the witness succeeds the I by renouncing the first person, or rather the nominative of this first role. In this witness, we should hear less the eloquent or heroic testator to an event that he reports, conveys, and defends—assuming again therefore a (re-)production of the phenomenon—and more the simple, luminous witness: he lights up as on a control panel at the very instant when and each time the information he should render phenomenal (in this case, the visible) arrives to him from a transistor by electric impulse without initiative or delay. Here the witness himself is not invested in the phenomenon, nor does he invest it with . . . ; rather, he finds himself so invested, submerged, that he can only register it immediately.

To introduce the concept of the saturated phenomenon into phenomenology, I just described it as *invisable* (unforeseeable) in terms of quantity, unbearable in terms of quality, unconditioned (absolute of all horizon) in terms of relation, and finally irreducible to the I (irregardable) in terms of modality. These four characteristics imply the term-for-term reversal of all the rubrics under which Kant classifies the principles of the understanding and therefore the phenomena that they determine. However, in relation to Husserl, these new characteristics are organized in a more complex way: the first two—*invisable* and unbearable—offer no difficulty de jure for the "principle of all principles"; for what intuition gives can quantitatively and qualitatively surpass the scope of the gaze. It is enough, therefore, that it give without common measure. This is not the case for the last two characteristics: the "principle of all principles" mentions the horizon and the constituting I as the two unquestioned presuppositions of anything that would like to be constituted in general as a phenomenon; and yet the saturated phenomenon, inasmuch as it is unconditioned by a horizon and irreducible to an I, claims a possibility free of these two conditions; it therefore contradicts the "principle of all principles." Husserl, who nevertheless surpassed the Kantian metaphysic of the phenomenon, must in turn be overcome if we are to reach the possibility of the saturated phenomenon. Even and especially with the "principle of all principles," he maintains a twofold reserve vis-à-vis possibility (the horizon, the I). Nevertheless, Husserl's reserve toward possibility can bespeak a reserve of phenomenology itself—which still keeps a reserve *of* possibility so that it may itself be overcome in favor of a possibility without reserve. Because it gives itself without condition or restraint, the saturated phenomenon would offer the paradigm of the phenomenon finally without reserve. In this way, following the guiding thread of the saturated phenomenon, phenomenology finds its final possibility: not only the possibility that surpasses actuality, but the possibility that surpasses the very conditions of possibility, the possibility of unconditioned possibility—in other words, the possibility of the impossible, the saturated phenomenon. Though paradoxical, or precisely for that very reason, the saturated phenomenon should in no way be understood as an exceptional, indeed vaguely irrational (to say it plainly, "theological"), case of phenomenality. Rather, it accom-

plishes the coherent and rational development of the most operative definition of the phenomenon: it alone appears truly as itself, of itself, and on the
basis of itself,[65] since it alone appears without the limits of a horizon or reduction to an I and constitutes itself, to the point of giving *itself* as a *self.* I
will therefore name this apparition that is purely of itself starting from itself,
this apparition that does not submit its possibility to any prior determination, an auto-manifestation. With this, it is purely and simply a matter of
the phenomenon taken in its full sense, in short, of the phenomenon's normative figure, in relation to which the others are defined and declined by defect or simplification.

Three Examples

This is also confirmed by the very history of philosophy, which has
long known such saturated phenomena, even if it rarely does them justice.
One could even go so far as to hold that no decisive thinker has omitted the
description of one (or several) saturated phenomena, even at the price of
contradicting his own metaphysical presuppositions. Among many fairly
obvious examples, let me select only Descartes, Kant, and Husserl. (a) Descartes, who everywhere else reduces the phenomenon to the idea that the
ego has of it, then this idea to an object, nevertheless thinks the idea of the
infinite as a saturated phenomenon. It indeed bears all the marks of one.
According to quantity, the idea of the infinite is not obtained by summation or successive synthesis, but "tota simul"; thus the gaze (*intueri*) becomes the surprise of admiration (*admirari*).[66] In terms of quality, it admits
no zero, or finite degree, but solely a *maximum*: "maxime clara et dis-
tincta," "maxime vera."[67] In terms of relation, it maintains no analogy with
any other idea whatsoever: "nihil univoce"; in effect, it exceeds every horizon, since it remains incomprehensible, capable only of being touched by
thought: "attingam quomodolibet cogitatione."[68] In terms of modality, far
from letting itself be led back to a constituting I, it comprehends the I
without letting itself be comprehended by it ("non tam capere quam ab ipsa
capi"),[69] in such a way that even the ego itself could perhaps be interpreted
as one who is called. But in any case, wouldn't it be enough to translate
"idea of infinity" term for term by "saturated phenomenon" to establish my
conclusion? (b) Kant provides an example of the saturated phenomenon
that is all the more significant as it does not concern, as does Descartes's, rational theology, but rather the finite exercise of the faculties; for him, it is a
question of the sublime. I based my argument above on the "aesthetic idea"

in order to contest the principle of the shortage of intuition and to introduce the possibility of a saturation (§20), but already with the doctrine of the sublime, it is an issue of a saturated phenomenon, whose characteristics it bears. That is, in terms of quantity, the sublime has no form or order, since it is great "beyond all comparison," absolutely and noncomparatively (*absolute, schlechthin, bloss*).[70] In terms of quality, it contradicts taste as a "negative pleasure" and provokes a "feeling of immensity," of "monstrosity."[71] In terms of relation, it very clearly escapes every analogy and every horizon since it is literally "limitlessness [*Unbegrenztheit*]" that it represents.[72] In terms of modality, finally, far from agreeing with our power of knowing, "it may appear in such a way as to contradict the finality of our faculty of judgment." The relation of our faculty of judgment to the phenomenon is therefore reversed to the point that it is the phenomenon that from now on "gazes" at the I in "respect."[73] The Kantian example of the sublime would thus permit us to broaden the field of application for the saturated phenomenon.

But without a doubt we owe it to (c) Husserl to have illustrated it in a perfectly universal occurrence: the internal consciousness of time corresponds to, and in a privileged way, the distinctive characteristics of the saturated phenomenon. In terms of quantity first, time proves *invisable* and therefore unforeseeable; that is, the flux admits no homogeneity in its parts, since each consists only in the "continual running-off"[74] of each moment, slipping from the future to the present and from the present into the past, modifying itself without pause. In terms of quality, then, time proves unbearable, since it does not admit degrees. First, because one cannot assign a zero point to the flux; that is, between the original impression and the first retention, nothing ever comes up but "an ideal limit, something abstract," and accordingly, "the ideal now is not something entirely different from the present non-now."[75] Next, because the flux constitutive of temporality has nothing in common with it, has itself "no duration [*kein Dauer*]" and therefore remains "nontemporal [*unzeitlich*]." At best, it would follow a "quasi-temporal order."[76] Degrees of quality (intensity) therefore cannot be set in a time that it precedes, surpasses, and exceeds. In terms of relation, time remains absolute. Nothing shows this better than the doubling of intentionality into, on the one hand, transversal intentionality—which, across the flux, is stubbornly oriented to the object-in-its-how to the detriment of time itself, a mere means or screen for an objectifying aim and of itself indifferent to time—and, on the other, longitudinal intentionality, which pushes from retention to retention so as to constitute without pause the unity of the temporal flux, that is to say, time itself without relation to or aim at even the slightest object. Henceforth, longitudinal intentionality works only in the "the self-apparition of the flux,"[77] before any object, before all real or even intentional immanence; it therefore deploys temporality without applying it to objects or the connection of objects among themselves. Contrary to Kant, time does not first have to ensure the necessary connections among the objects of experience and therefore the analogies. It shows itself in itself and by itself without relation to or among objects, in short, absolutely. In terms of modality, finally, time cannot be gazed at. For, as "original impression," time imposes itself starting from itself as "the absolute unmodified [*das absolut Unmodifizierte*]" which not only "is not produced," but "is the original production."[78] The original impression originally determines consciousness, which henceforth loses its status as origin and discovers itself originally determined, impressed, constituted—transcendentally taken witness.[79]

The saturated phenomenon is therefore by no means an extreme or rare hypothesis. It concerns a figure of phenomenality that is so essential that even barely phenomenological thinkers (Descartes, Kant), like those who are more phenomenological (Husserl), have recourse to it as soon as the thing itself calls for it—that is, when it appears according to excess and not shortage of intuition. In fact, only the saturated phenomenon can mark, by rendering visible to excess, the paradoxically unmeasured dimensions of possible givenness—which nothing stops or conditions.

§23 TOPICS OF THE PHENOMENON

Poor Phenomena, Common Phenomena

It now seems possible to lay out, if only in outline, a topics for the different types of phenomena. In every case, I will maintain the phenomenon's generic definition as what shows itself from itself (Heidegger) and does so only insofar as it gives itself in itself from itself alone; what shows itself does so only to the extent that it gives itself. To give itself means that the aspect that shows itself (shape, schema, species, concept, signification, intention, etc.) should also always give itself in person, though in a measure that varies (intuition, hyletic layer, noema, etc.). Givenness accomplishes manifestation by giving it fulfillment, a fulfillment that is intuitive in the majority of cases, but not necessarily all.[80] The different types of phenomena can be defined as different variations of auto-manifestation (showing itself in and from itself) according to the degree of givenness (giving itself in and from itself).

I will thus distinguish, in terms of their degree of givenness, three original figures of phenomenality. (a) First, the phenomena poor in intuition. They claim only a formal intuition in mathematics or a categorical intuition in logic, in other words, a "vision of essences" and idealities. For this type of phenomenon, what shows itself in and from itself does not need much more than its concept alone, or at least just its intelligibility (the demonstration itself), to give itself—of course, in the empty abstraction of the universal without content or individuation, according to an iterability that is perfect because unscathed by matter (even significative), but nevertheless in fact. Can we imagine, besides these phenomena poor in intuition, others that are absolutely deprived of intuition? The absence of intuition could be understood in two opposed senses. Either as a real shortage, which directly contradicts phenomenality: what in no way gives itself in no way shows itself either. Or, by contrast, as pure givenness coming to relieve intuition (manifestation)—which will demand other distinctions. But with poor phenomena, the essential point is found elsewhere—in the privilege that metaphysics has always accorded them over and above all other thinkable phenomena: the privilege of certainty. That is, admitting an intuition that is only formal or categorical, poor phenomena no longer admit anything "that experience might render uncertain,"[81] and therefore their very abstraction guarantees their certainty, therefore objectification. But this epistemological privilege inverts itself and becomes a radical phenomenological deficit—manifestation here does not give (itself), or only a little, since it conveys neither real nor individual intuition, nor the temporalization of an event, in short, no accomplished phenomenality. In opposition to metaphysics' constant decision, we should conclude that the privilege of poor phenomena (abstract epistemological certainty), far from qualifying them, forbids establishing them as secure paradigm for phenomenality in general. (b) The common-law phenomena should be defined by how much they vary in terms of givenness, not by reference to the poor phenomena. In their case, signification (aimed at by intention) is manifest only to the extent that it receives intuitive fulfillment. In principle, this fulfillment can be adequate (intuition equaling intention). At first and most of the time, however, it remains inadequate, and the intention, like its concept, remains partially unconfirmed by intuition, thus not perfectly given. Nevertheless, this deficiency is not enough by itself to disqualify the objectivity of common-law phenomena. By contrast, it alone establishes it. First, because, just as a bank guarantees the loans it makes with reserves that represent only a partial percentage of their total, so too does a weak intuitive confirmation of the concept reasonably suffice to give the corresponding phenomenon—provided it is confirmed by being repeated regularly. Next and especially, because the deficit of intuition secures the concept's mastery over the entire process of manifestation, thereby maintaining an abstraction thanks to a weak intuition, or else attaining a degree of certainty comparable (at least tangentially) to that of the poor phenomena. In this way, the common phenomenon can be accomplished according to objectivity. Obviously classed as common phenomena are the objects of physics and the natural sciences. In these cases, it is a question of establishing the objective certainty of conceptual maximums (signification, theories, etc.) on the basis of intuitive minimums (sense data, experimental protocols, statistical accounts, etc.). It should be possible to if not eliminate, at least reduce, "material" understood as the disturbance made by *hulē*. The physical law is true only by accounting for what disturbs it, that is to say only by correcting itself so as to integrate the factors that weaken it—only by calculating what makes an exception to its calculation. For example, Galileo's law of falling bodies is experimentally verified only if one eliminates in thought the friction, the resistance of the milieu, the noninfinity of the space crossed, etc. The objectification of the phenomenon itself demands restricting the intuitive given to what confirms (or rather does not diminish) the concept. The intention thus keeps mastery over the manifestation, and givenness is cut to the size of objectification. But this figure of phenomenality—the common-law variety, with possible but not realized adequation—finds confirmation in the case of technological objects. Here the intention and the concept take on the role of plan, schema, or drawing ("mechanical" or done with CAD), in short, exactly what industry names the "concept" of an object. It is defined by the fact that in principle it renders fully intelligible, that is to say, at least imaginable, the structure of the object, but also by the fact that it already integrates its feasibility (its industrialization) and the calculation of the profitability of its fabrication and commercialization—not only its technical definition (its essence), but also the conditions for its entering production and eventually the economy (existence). The concept (in the sense of the "concept" of a product) renders this product visible before production actually gives it, and sometimes even without any production following the manifestation of its "concept" (simulation, "concept car," etc.). To show in and through a concept (signification, intention, etc.) precedes, determines, and sometimes annuls intuitive givenness (actuality, production, intuition, etc.).

The inadequation between intention and intuition, which Husserl describes in terms of fulfillment by means of the continuous temporal flux of consciousness, is here declined in terms of delay and foresight. Of delay, first. It belongs essentially to the technological object (what I will from now on call the product) that its manifestation in "concept" radically precedes its givenness (its production in and for intuition); its "concept" therefore always gets the upper hand chronologically over whatever intuitive fulfillment might be, that is to say, over this product itself. The technological object would therefore not literally deserve its title "product" since production only completes its "concept" in the sense that, in metaphysics, existence contributes only a mere "complement to the possibility," therefore to essence. For the product never gives itself first, but by contrast always after and following its "concept," which is previously shown and demonstrated. And if it is thus necessary to consider the product on the basis of its "concept," it would therefore be necessary to define it more as induced (on the basis of an anterior "concept") than pro-duced, in advance or before. The incurable chronological gap between the manifest "concept" and its induced (given) production follows, in the field of the technological object, the factual inadequacy between intention and intuition. Above all, it confirms the derived, indeed alienated, phenomenal status of the technological object, which always comes after itself and continually recaptures in an always unequal actuality its own supposedly impeccable intelligibility. Foresight comes next. The theoretical and chronological preeminence of the "concept" of the product, in general of the concept over intuition, allows us to know at the outset and in advance the characteristics of what comes at the end of the chain of production. The product confirms—at best—the "concept," and the intuition, the intention, without any surprise, unpredictable landing, or incident ever arising. What we call, with some naivete in our satisfaction, the product's "total quality" here means this: the "concept" never undergoes even the least variation or incident during the course of its intuitive actualization; manifestation never suffers a counter-blow at the hand of givenness. Thus foreseen, production and intuition (therefore givenness) remain beneath the watchful gaze of the concept. From its vantage point, it sees them coming from afar, without surprise and without expecting anything new from them. The predictability of the technological object, therefore the perfect foreseeability of the product induced on the basis of its "concept," not only confirms that this concerns an alienated phenomenality, but permits (or demands) the product's repetition. That is, since intuition always comes after the fact and plays the role of actual confirmation of the plan's original rationality, and since it should make no difference ("flawless"), it also should not tolerate any innovation, modification, or, in short, any event. Thus the identical repetition of the product becomes possible since it makes no difference. Production already contains the reproduction, which in fact adds nothing to it, since intuition adds nothing real to the "concept." And, quite obviously, the quantity of the (re)production—the number of exemplary products of the product—doesn't add anything to the reproduction, either. It merely declines it. It follows that, like the poor phenomenon, the common-law phenomenon cannot, strictly speaking, be individualized. Wouldn't this happen at a minimum through the "material," the disturbance of *hulē*? But every productive business eliminates this disturbance as far as possible ("flawless," "total quality," etc.). Therefore, the product, common-law phenomenon par excellence, cannot be individualized—it must therefore be reproduced; that is to say, it must continually confirm the primacy of the concept over intuition, therefore the deficit of givenness.

Saturated Phenomena, or Paradoxes

Now it is possible to broach (c) the saturated phenomena, in which intuition always submerges the expectation of the intention, in which givenness not only entirely invests manifestation but, surpassing it, modifies its common characteristics. On account of this investment and modification, I also call saturated phenomena "paradoxes." The fundamental characteristic of the paradox lies in the fact that intuition sets forth a surplus that the concept cannot organize, therefore that the intention cannot foresee. As a result, intuition is not bound to and by the intention, but is freed from it, establishing itself now as a free intuition (*intuitio vaga*). Far from coming after the concept and therefore following the thread of the intention (aim, foresight, repetition), intuition subverts, therefore precedes, every intention, which it exceeds and decenters. The visibility of the appearance thus arises against the flow of the intention—whence the paradox, the counter-appearance, the visibility running counter to the aim. Paradox means what happens counter to (*para-*) received opinion, as well as to appearance, according to the two obvious meanings of *doxa*. But it also means what happens counter to expectation—"praeter expectationem offertur"[82]—what arrives against all that representation or intention, in short the concept, would expect. The paradox therefore belongs, indisputably, to the domain of the truth, with this minor qualification: that its givenness contravenes, in its intuition, what previous experience should reasonably permit us to foresee. That is, here the I of intentionality can neither constitute nor synthesize the intuition into an object defined by a horizon. The synthesis—if there must be one—is accomplished without and contrary to the I, as a passive synthesis, coming from the nonobject itself, which imposes its arising and its moment on and before all active intentionality of the I; for the passivity of the "passive synthesis" indicates not only that the I does not accomplish it actively and therefore suffers it passively, but above all that activity falls to the phenomenon and to it alone. Thus it does indeed show *itself* because it gives *itself* first—in anticipation of every aim, free of every concept, according to a befalling that delivers its self. Givenness, now to the measure of the excess of intuition over intention, is no longer defined in terms of what the concept or the horizon assign to it, but can be deployed indefinitely. The concept no longer foresees, for intuition fore-comes—comes before and therefore, at least once, without it. As a result, the relation between manifestation and givenness is inverted. For (a) poor and (b) common-law phenomena, intention and the concept foresee intuition, make up for its shortage, and set limits for givenness; on the other hand, for the (c) saturated phenomena, or paradoxes, intuition surpasses the intention, is deployed without concept and lets givenness come before all limitation and every horizon. In this case, phenomenality is calibrated first in terms of givenness, such that the phenomenon no longer gives itself in the measure to which it shows itself, but shows itself in the measure (or, eventually, lack of measure) to which it gives itself.

But if the paradox clearly emphasizes to the benefit of givenness the principle that a phenomenon shows itself only insofar as it gives itself, we must not conclude from this that it is an exception to the common rule, represented by the first two types. It falls to metaphysics alone to consider the paradox an exceptional (indeed eccentric) case of phenomenality, whose common law it organizes according to the paradigm of the poor phenomenon. With notable exceptions (Descartes, Spinoza, Kant, Husserl), metaphysics always thinks the common-law phenomenon (shortage of intuition) on the basis of the intuitively poor phenomenon (certain, but of little or nothing). My entire project, by contrast, aims to think the common-law phenomenon, and through it the poor phenomenon, on the basis of the paradigm of the saturated phenomenon, of which the former two offer only weakened variants, and from which they derive by progressive extenuation. For the saturated phenomenon does not give itself abnormally, making an exception to the definition of phenomenality; to the contrary, its ownmost property is to render thinkable the measure of manifestation in terms of givenness and to recover it in its common-law variety, indeed in the poor phenomenon. What metaphysics rules out as an exception (the saturated phenomenon), phenomenology here takes for its norm—every phenomenon shows itself in the measure (or the lack of measure) to which it gives itself. To be sure, not all phenomena get classified as saturated phenomena, but all saturated phenomena accomplish the one and only paradigm of phenomenality. Better, they alone enable it to be illustrated. This is why one can without much difficulty make each of the determinations of the phenomenon insofar as given (Book 3) correspond with one of the characteristics of the saturated phenomenon (Book 4), precisely because the latter lets the paradigm of the phenomenon as such swing to its full range. (i) Unforeseeability (in terms of quantity), therefore also the nonrepeatability of the saturated phenomenon (§21), consecrates the factuality of the fait accompli, such that it determines every given phenomenon (§15). (ii) The unbearable and intolerable (in terms of quality) character of the saturated phenomenon, therefore also the bedazzlement it provokes (§21), fully develops the unpredictable landing, determination of the given phenomenon in general (§14). (iii) The absoluteness of the saturated phenomenon, outside all relation and all analogy (even that of causality) (§21), demarcates to excess the incident, determination of the phenomenon as given (§16). (iv) Finally, the impossibility of constituting or gazing at (§22) accomplishes in saturation the anamorphosis that already characterizes the given phenomenon (§13). In other words, the two subversions that free the saturated degrees of phenomenality (submerging every horizon, the I reverting into a witness) do nothing other than push the universal determinations of the given beyond their limits—which the poor, common-law, or intermediary (the being given) variants still hide. The saturated phenomenon in the end establishes the truth of all phenomenality because it marks, more than any other phenomenon, the givenness from which it comes. The paradox, understood in the strictest sense, no longer runs counter to appearance; it runs with apparition.

It now becomes possible to trace, within the topics of the phenomenon insofar as given and in order to complete it, a topics of the saturated phenomenon itself. The guiding thread will no longer be the degree of intuition (since in all cases, there is on principle saturation), but the determination in relation to which saturation is each time accomplished (quantity, quality, relation, or modality). I will therefore distinguish, without intending any hierarchy, four types of saturated phenomenon. In each case, it will be question of paradoxes, never constitutable as objects within a horizon and by an I. We should not be surprised, then, that we have already seen these privileged phenomena in the previous analyses. With the determinations of the given phenomenon in general, and still more with the sketch of the saturated phenomenon, they were no doubt already at issue.

The Event

The saturated phenomenon is attested first in the figure of the historical phenomenon, or the event carried to its apex. It saturates the category of quantity. When the arising event is not limited to an instant, a place, or an empirical individual, but overflows these singularities and becomes epoch-making in time (delimits a homogeneous duration and imposes it as "a block"), covers a physical space such that no gaze encompasses it with one sweep (not a mappable "theater of operations," therefore, but a battlefield to canvass), and encompasses a population such that none of those who belong to it can take upon themselves an absolute or even privileged point of view, then it becomes a historical event. This means precisely that nobody can claim for himself a "here and now" that would permit him to describe it exhaustively and constitute it as an object. Put trivially, nobody ever *saw* the battle of Waterloo[83] (nor Austerlitz, to be fair). To be sure, it is plain that Fabrice saw only the fire of his own confused erring and barely the fire of the hail of bullets, barely the emperor passing, his horse in flight, or the barmaid in a flutter; but the emperor himself saw hardly more: he saw neither the advance of the enemy reinforcements nor the delay of his own, neither the ditch where his cavalry got bogged down nor the dying among the already dead. In fact, nobody will see more, not Wellington, any of the officers, or any of the men on the field—each will furnish confused and partial reports from an angle of vision taken in by panic or rage. The battle passes and passes away on its own, without anybody making it or deciding it. It passes, and each watches it pass, fade into the distance, and then disappear, disappear like it had come—that is to say, of itself. In history making itself (*Geschichte*), the battle makes itself of itself, starting from a point of view that it alone can unify, without any unique horizon. For those, by contrast, whom it enlists and encompasses, not one of their (individual) horizons will be enough to unify it, speak it, and especially, foresee it. Neither Fabrice, nor Flambeau, nor Chateaubriand, with an ear to the ground, saw it. Consequently, in recorded and transmitted history (*Historie*), the battle will demand additional horizons (this time conceptual) of an indefinite number: military horizons (the strategy adopted since the return from exile, the tactics concerning this place), diplomatic, political, economic, ideological (reference to the Revolution), etc. The plurality of horizons practically forbids constituting the historical event into *one* object and demands substituting an endless hermeneutic in time; the narration is doubled by a narration of the narrations. More: in this hermeneutic labor, the proliferation of horizons implies also the proliferation of the sciences used, as well as of the literary genres. The romantic fiction of Chateaubriand, Hugo, and Stendahl shows as much, better no doubt, than the factual reports of the memoirists or the quantitative historical analyses. The saturation of quantity in a paradox such as the historical event implies, therefore, in order to ensure the indefinite diversification of its horizons (testimonies, points of view, sciences, literary genres, etc.), not only a teleology without end, but above all an interobjectivity—knowledge of the historical event becomes itself historical, like the sum of the agreements and disagreements among subjects partially constituting a nonobject always to be re-constituted, like the history of an intersubjectivity mediated by a nonobject, the paradox itself. The hermeneutic of the (saturated because historical) event is enough to produce a historical community and, through its very inachievability, to render communication possible.[84]

The Idol

The saturated phenomenon appears secondly under the aspect of the unbearable and bedazzlement, insofar as they subvert the category of quality carried to the maximum. I will name this paradox "the idol." The idol is determined as the first indisputable visible because its splendor stops intentionality for the first time; and this first visible fills it, stops it, and even blocks it, to the point of returning it toward itself, after the fashion of an invisible obstacle—or mirror. The privileged occurrence of the idol is obviously the painting (or what, without the frame of the frame, takes its place), not to speak too generically of the work of art. Saturation marks the painting essentially. In it, intuition always surpasses the concept or the concepts proposed to welcome it. It is never enough to have seen it just once to have really seen it, in contrast to the technical object and the product. Totally opposite this, each gaze at the painting fails to bring me to perceive what I see, keeping me from taking it into view as such—so that it always again conceals the essential from visibility. No doubt, I can comprehend, conceptually or by means of information, as a theoretician or historian, a continually increasing part of its given; but the more this part grows, the less accessible givenness itself becomes, as the phenomenon's purely unpredictable landing in its totality and at its own initiative. The givenness of the visible gives rise to other questions. On the basis of what "self" is it given? According to what anamorphosis is it imposed? With what authority does it summon me to come see it? To these questions, all of which are provoked by the surplus of intuition, no concept will ever answer. The painting is definitively given "without concept"—Kant understood this perfectly—or idea (Hegel missed this). This unpredictable landing, whose intuition saturates every possible concept, is attested by the painting in its summoning not only to come and see it, but especially to come and see it again. To see the painting again does not mean adding one intuition to another (to complete one bit of knowledge with another) or reconsidering it (to revise information), but again confronting a new concept or a new intention with an indefinite intuition that the familiar habit of seeing one and the same painting tames. To see again is equivalent to trying to contain and resist the same saturating intuitive given by means of the grill of a new concept (or several of them), a different horizon (or several). The intuitive given of the idol imposes on us the demand to change our gaze again and again, continually, be this only so as to confront its unbearable bedazzlement. In the case of the idol, one point must be noted, which distinguishes it essentially from the previous saturated phenomenon: instead of presupposing an interobjectivity and an at least teleological communication, like the historical event does, the idol provokes an ineluctable solipsism. That is, since the painting summons *me* to see it, since above all I must see it again at the pace of *my* own changing horizon and concept, it shows itself only by arriving to *me*, therefore by individualizing me radically (*Jemeinigkeit* by the idol, no longer by Being). The sequence of gazes that I continually pose on the idol establish so many invisible mirrors of myself; it therefore describes or conceptualizes it less than it designates a temporality where it is first an issue of my ipseity. The idol marks me—traces the mark of the site where I stand—because in it intuition is always lacking the concept.[85]

The Flesh

The saturated phenomenon comes up a third time in the absolute character of the flesh, such that it is torn from the category of relation and carries the fait accompli to its excellence. The flesh is defined as the identity of what touches with the medium where this touching takes place (Aristotle), therefore of the felt with what feels (Husserl), but also of the seen and the seeing or the heard and the hearing—in short, of the affected with the affecting (Henry).[86] For before intentionality opens a gap between the intended and the fulfillment or between the I and its objective and even in order that consciousness might render this ecstasy possible, it must be admitted that it first has to receive impressions, original or derived, whatever they might be—intuitive impressions, but impressions that are significant as well. Now it can do so only inasmuch as, of its essence, it is susceptible to radical affection in itself (self-affection); but it can be affected in itself only inasmuch as its affection presupposes no external or preexisting affect, therefore inasmuch as it accomplishes itself unconditionally. In order to affect itself in itself, it must first be affected by nothing other than itself (auto-affection). Such an affection is at issue each time the paradox not only exceeds every constitutable object, but saturates the horizon to the point that there is no longer any relation that refers it to another object. The affection refers to no object, according to no ecstasy, but only to itself; for it itself is sufficient to accomplish itself as affected. It thus attributes to itself the privilege that *ousia* holds for Aristotle: not to arise from relative terms, *oudemia ousia tōn pros ti legetai.*[87] The flesh auto-affects itself in agony, suffering, and grief, as well as in desire, feeling, or orgasm. There is no sense in asking if these affects come to it from the body, the mind, or the Other, since originally it always auto-affects itself first in and by itself. Therefore, joy, pain, the evidence of love, or the living remembrance (Proust), but also the call of consciousness as anxiety in the face of nothing (Heidegger), fear and trembling (Kierkegaard), in short, the *numen* in general (provided that one assigns it no transcendence), all arise from the flesh and its own immanence. Two points allow us to distinguish the saturated phenomenon of the flesh. First, in contrast to the idol, but perhaps like the historical event, it cannot be regarded or even seen. The immediacy of auto-affection blocks the space where the ecstasy of an intentionality would become possible. Next, in contrast to the historical event, but no doubt more radically than the idol, the flesh provokes and demands solipsism; for it remains by definition mine, unsubstitutable—nobody can enjoy or suffer for me (even if he can do so in my place). Mineness (*Jemeinigkeit*) does not concern first or only my possibility as the possibility of impossibility (dying), but my flesh itself. More, it belongs only to my flesh to individualize me by letting the immanent succession of my affections, or rather of the affections that make me irreducibly identical to myself alone, be inscribed in it. In contrast with the interobjectivity to which the historical event gives rise and more radically than the indefinite revision that the idol demands of me, the flesh therefore shows itself only in giving itself—and, in this first "self," it gives me to myself.

The Icon

The saturated phenomenon is accomplished fourth in the aspect of the irregardable and irreducible, insofar as they are free from all reference to the I, therefore to the categories of modality. I will call this fourth type of saturated phenomenon the icon because it no longer offers any spectacle to the gaze and tolerates no gaze from any spectator, but rather exerts its own gaze over that which meets it. The gazer takes the place of the gazed upon; the manifested phenomenon is reversed into a manifestation not only in and of itself, but strictly by and on the basis of itself (auto-manifestation)— the paradox reverses the polarity of manifestation by taking the initiative, far from undergoing it, by giving it, far from being given by it. The saturation of the phenomenon stems first from the silent and probably poor reversal of its flux, more than from its likely excess. And in this way, anamorphosis reaches its ultimate point. It must be observed that intuition here takes an absolutely new turn. The gaze that comes upon me (lands unpredictably, event) provides no spectacle, therefore no immediately visible or assignable intuition; it resides precisely in the black holes of the two pupils, in the sole and minuscule space where, on the surface of the body of the Other, there is nothing to see (not even the color of the iris that surrounds them) in the gaze facing me. The gaze that the Other casts and makes weigh on me therefore does not give itself to my gaze, nor even to be seen—this invisible gaze gives itself only to be endured. The Other is charged to me: strictly speaking, he weighs on my gaze like a weight, a burden. It is the same with the face. To be sure, the Other assigns me by his face, but only if its essential invisibility is understood. This face, nobody has ever seen it, except by bringing about its death—since to see it would suppose at once reducing it to the rank of a constituted spectacle, therefore eliminating it as such—or dying oneself—by transferring oneself to its point of view, thereby nullifying each as individualized monad. The face of the Other is not seen any more than its gaze; it deploys its invisibility over a portion of the flesh where it radiates from the pole of two voids. This face, like this gaze, gives me nothing to see—but gives itself by weighing on me. By gaze and by face, the Other acts, accomplishes the act of his unpredictable landing as saturated phenomenon.[88] Such an inversion of phenomenality's polarity evidently implies that the I not only renounce its transcendental function of constitution, but that it pass to the figure of what we have already thematized as the witness (§22): me, insofar as I receive *myself* from the very givenness of the irregardable phenomenon, me insofar as I learn of myself from what the gaze of the Other says to me in silence. And in fact, the concept of witness finds its full phenomenological legitimacy only when related to the saturated phenomenon of the Other, who alone can constitute me as his own because he precedes me in the order of manifestation.

Finally, the icon offers a surprising (or rather, expected) characteristic: it gathers together the particular characteristics of the three preceding types of saturated phenomena. Like the historical event, it demands a summation of horizons and narrations, since the Other cannot be constituted objectively and since it happens without assignable end; the icon therefore opens a teleology. Like the idol, it begs to be seen and reseen, though in the mode of unconditioned endurance; like it, the icon therefore exercises (but in a more radical mode) an individuation over the gaze that confronts it. Like the flesh finally, it accomplishes this individuation by affecting the I so originally that it loses its function as transcendental pole; and the originality of this affection brings it close, even tangentially, to auto-affection. This gathering of the first three types in the fourth and last at least confirms the coherence of the region where phenomena saturate. It would also confirm its phenomenological legitimacy, if the strict correspondence between the determinations of the phenomenon as given (Book 3) and its degrees (Book 4) as far as saturation had not already established it. The definition of the phenomenon as given frees it from the limits of objectness and beingness. It also lets us think that it shows itself in and from itself only insofar as it gives itself in and from itself, indeed by quitting the "self." But it enlarges the field of phenomenality by admitting, beyond phenomena of the common-law type and those poor in intuition, the domain and privilege of saturated phenomena.

§24 TO GIVE ITSELF, TO REVEAL ITSELF

The Last Possibility—the Phenomenon of Revelation

Arranging the topics of the saturated phenomenon, I noted that the last type—the Other showing himself as icon—gathered within it the modes of saturation of the three other types (the historical event, the idol, and the flesh). One cannot help but conclude that, be it only within the privileged region of saturation, not all phenomena, saturated though they are, offer the same degree of givenness. The question of determining the degree to which saturation can be deployed thus presents itself. Does it attain a maximum, or does it, by hypothesis, always transgress it—but also, is there any sense in envisaging a phenomenon that gives (itself) according to a maximum of phenomenality? This question arises inevitably from the mere fact that it alone permits all dimensions of phenomenality to be glimpsed, explores the region of saturated givenness, thoroughly inventories it, and cannot be dodged. This constraint, however, is most often not enough to block its pure and simple denegation. Why is it challenged? Obviously not for a theoretical (phenomenological or not) reason, at least not at first, but out of a more banal, ideological fear: that the question of God might again arise. As we know, theology contradicts logic. We would therefore preserve rationality by banishing the question of a maximum point of phenomenality. The argument is so lacking in rigor and precision that, for now, I will not examine it as such. With the question of a phenomenon taking saturation to its maximum, it is not straightaway or always a question of debating the status of the theological in phenomenology, but at the outset and in the first place of a possible figure of phenomenality as such.

A possible figure of phenomenality—my entire project has been directed to liberating possibility in phenomenality, to unbinding the phenomenon from the supposed equivalencies that limit its deployment (the object, the being, common-law adequation, poverty of intuition). What remains is to determine just how far such a possibility goes and if we can assign a maximum to it. To be deployed without contradiction, this possibility posits two requirements: (i) the potential maximum must remain a phenomenon; that is to say, it must be inscribed within the already acquired definition of phenomenality (determinations in general, saturation in particular), as a variation of this one and only definition; (ii) the maximum must also remain a possibility, in the twofold sense of transgressing itself permanently without being fixed in a definite figure and also designing itself independently of all actual and worldly accomplishment of this maximum. The maximum of saturated phenomenality must remain an ultimate possibility of the phenomenon—the last, but still under the heading of possibility. This twofold and at first glance contradictory requirement is carried out with what I will now call the phenomenon of *revelation*. In effect, (i) it is a question of the last possible variation of the phenomenality of the phenomenon inasmuch as given. The phenomenon of revelation not only falls into the category of saturation (paradox in general), but it concentrates the four types of saturated phenomena and is given at once as historic event, idol, flesh, and icon (face). This concerns a fifth type of saturation, not that it adds a new one (arbitrarily invented in order to do right by the supposed right of the "divine") to the first four (the sole describable ones), but because, by confounding them in it, it saturates phenomenality to the second degree, by saturation of saturation. From the common-law phenomenon there followed, through a variation of intuitive possibility, the saturated phenomenon or paradox; likewise, from the latter, there follows, as an ultimate variation on saturation, the *paradoxōtaton*, the paradox to the second degree and par excellence, which encompasses all types of paradox.[89] Nevertheless, (ii) the phenomenon of revelation remains a mere possibility. I am going to describe it without presupposing its actuality, and yet all the while propose a precise figure for it. I will say only: if an actual revelation must, can, or could have been given in phenomenal apparition, it could have, can, or will be able to do so only by giving itself according to the type of the paradox par excellence—such as I will describe it. Phenomenology cannot decide if a revelation can or should ever give itself, but it (and it alone) can determine that, in case it does, such a phenomenon of revelation should assume the figure of the paradox of paradoxes. If revelation there must be (and phenomenology has no authority to decide this), then it will assume, assumes, or assumed the figure of paradox of paradoxes, according to an essential law of phenomenality. In this sense, since revelation remains a variation of saturation, itself a variation of the phenomenality of the phenomenon inasmuch as given, it still remains inscribed within the transcendental conditions of possibility. Would I have come all this way only to recover precisely what I wanted to destroy—conditions preceding possibility and delimiting it a priori? Better, wouldn't I have recovered precisely, in regard to revelation, the very type of phenomenon that neither can nor should submit to them? In fact, it's nothing like this—here (as in §1), the condition of possibility does not consist in rendering the phenomenon possible by delimiting it a priori from the impossibilities, but in freeing its possibility by destroying all prerequisite conditions for phenomenality, therefore by suspending all so-called impossibilities, indeed by admitting the possibility of certain ones among them. The phenomenon of revelation would be defined, it too, as the possibility of impossibility—on condition of no longer understanding impossibility confiscating possibility (being toward death), but possibility assimilating impossibility (incident, fait accompli). Simply put, this freeing of possibility as revelation and through revelation is always deployed solely by means of a second variation (paradox of paradoxes) on a first variation (saturated phenomenon) of the initial determination of the phenomenon as what shows itself only insofar as it gives itself. The phenomenon of revelation is therefore officially inscribed within the one and only figure of the phenomenon that, ever since the beginning and without interruption, I have been seeking—the given. In this sense, formally, the paradox of paradoxes offers no extraordinary phenomenological trait. Though exceeding the common-law phenomenon, it does not make an exception to the original determination of what shows itself: it gives itself—and without common measure.

The phenomenon of revelation (§24) is therefore defined as a phenomenon that concentrates in itself the four senses of the saturated phenomenon (§23), where each alone sufficed to pass beyond the common-law phenomenon (§§21–22). I am obliged *here*—in phenomenology, where possibility remains the norm, and not actuality—only to describe it in its pure possibility and in the reduced immanence of givenness. I do not *here* have to judge its actual manifestation or ontic status, which remain the business proper to revealed theology.[90] If I therefore privilege the manifestation of Jesus Christ, as it is described in the New Testament (and in conformity with the paradigms of the theophanies of the Old), as an example of a phenomenon of revelation, I am nevertheless proceeding as a phenomenologist—describing a given phenomenological possibility—and as a philosopher—confronting the visible Christ with his possible conceptual role (as Spinoza, Kant, Hegel, or Schelling dared to do), with an eye toward establishing it as paradigm. The manifestation of Christ counts as paradigm of the phenomenon of revelation according to the paradox's four modes of saturation. According to quantity, the phenomenon of Christ gives itself intuitively as an event that is perfectly unforeseeable because radically heterogeneous to what it nevertheless completes (the prophecies). It arises "as the lightning comes from the East and shows itself [*phainetai*] as far as the West" (Matthew 24:27), saturating the visible at one fell swoop. This character of event that happens is not added extrinsically to the figure Christ assumes, but by contrast determines its first aspect, since he comes intrinsically as "he who must come [*ho erkhomenos*]" (John 1:15 or 27). He arrives under the banner of an advent and advances only his own advance, which counts as one of his names. The coming, according to which he comes forward, defines him so essentially that it embraces him and precedes him—he himself depends on it without determining it; and he arises from this eventfulness because it attests that he does not come forward from himself ("I have not come of my own," John 8:43), but at the bidding of the Father ("You have sent me," John 17:18, 23). Christ therefore submits to his own unforeseeable eventfulness, in the same sense that he submits to the Father. As a result, the end of the world is as unforeseen by him, by him the Son, as his own coming as the Christ surprises those who inhabit this same world. The unforeseeability comes to an end only for the Father: "As for the day and the hour, no one knows them, neither the angels in heaven, nor [even] the Son, except the Father" (Mark 13:33), "except the Father alone" (Matthew 24:36). And this is why, for the men of the world, the impossibility of knowing the hour, therefore of foreseeing (the end of time and the coming of Christ, which in fact are one), demands renouncing the anticipatory calculation that would allow them to appropriate this event par excellence; they must instead await it insofar as it remains unforeseeable, that is to say, as if each moment was and was not the right one. This expectation without foresight, characteristic of the unpredictable landing, defines the phenomenological attitude appropriate to the event—vigilance: "Open your eyes, be vigilant, for you do not know when the [right] moment [*kairos*] will come" (Mark 13:33), "Be vigilant, for you do not know the day when your Master will come" (Matthew 24:42). Vigilance and expectation invert foresight; thus the event itself escapes all preparatory anticipation in the past, is concentrated in its pure fait accompli, arises without genealogy and can even be established after the fact as a new beginning: "He who must come after me is before me" (John 1:15). The past now comes after (and not before) the event, which happens solely in terms of its arising: "Before Abraham was born, I am" (John 8:58). The figure of Christ therefore offers the characteristic of a paradox that is perfectly unforeseeable because intuition saturates every prior concept quantitatively. It is a case par excellence of the event.

In terms of quality, the figure of Christ obviously attests its paradoxical character because the intuition that saturates it reaches and most often overcomes what the phenomenological gaze can bear. Does he not say to his own: "I still have many things to say to you, but you do not yet have the power to bear them [*ou dunasthe bastazein*]" (John 16:12)? But what is to be borne? The visible and its excess, like the whiteness that absorbs the entire prism of colors and is excepted from the world of objects: "He was transformed before them, and his clothes became resplendent, excessively white [*leuka lian*], the likes of which no fuller on earth could bleach" (Mark 9:3). And also the voice from beyond the world, which comes from the heavens and does not belong to space, and which therefore terrifies: "A cloud came and overshadowed them; as they entered it, they were afraid. And a voice came out of the cloud, saying, 'This is my beloved Son, listen to him'" (Luke 9:34–35; see Matthew 7:5–7). In fact, the unbearable stems from nothing less than the pure and simple recognition of Christ as such. For example, when he declines his identity and pronounces his name before those who come to arrest him, he becomes visible to them as Christ and therefore unbearable in all senses; they therefore collapse: "When he said to them: 'It is me (I am),'[91] they recoiled and fell to the ground" (John 18:6–7). The unbearable therefore suspends perception in general, beyond the difference between hearing and sight, because it results from the thorough saturation of the figure of Christ. And this paradox culminates in the resurrection itself; for, since it by definition passes beyond what this world can receive, contain, or embrace, it can let itself be perceived only by terrifying, to the point that this terror sometimes suffices to designate it by denegation: "[The women in the tomb] said nothing to anybody; for they were terrified" (Mark 16:6). This terror implies neither refusal nor flight. It is allied with its opposite, joy ("They left the tomb with terror and joy," Matthew 28:8), in marking two registers of the same intuitive saturation— beyond terror and joy, as well as beyond touch ("Put out your finger . . . put out your hand," John 20:27) and the avoidance of touch ("Do not touch me," John 20:17), beyond union ("And behold I will be with you for all days until the consummation of time," Matthew 28:20) and separation ("And it happened that while blessing them, he parted from them," Luke 24:51). Christ thus accomplishes the paradox of the idol as well: saturation of the gaze by excess of intuition renders its phenomenon unbearable; vision—fulfilled—no longer sees by dint of seeing.

In terms of relation, Christ appears as an absolute phenomenon, one that annuls all relation because it saturates every possible horizon into which relation would introduce it. It saturates every possible horizon not only because its "moment" escapes the time of the world (saturation in terms of the unforeseeable event) and its figure the space of the "earth" (saturation in terms of the unbearable), but because "his kingdom is not of this world" (John 18:36). The world of common-law phenomenality is not for him and eventually would turn against him and condemn him to not appear in it or to appear in it only disfigured (which was indeed the case). From this principal characteristic, we can draw two arguments establishing that this is a question of saturation pertaining to the flesh. (i) The death of Christ offers the apex of his visibility—"Truly this was the son of God!" (Matthew 27:54), "They shall look upon him whom they have pierced" (John 19:7, citing Zechariah 12:10)—and of his visibility as royal (John 19:19–22). This paradox would remain unintelligible if we did not see in it the flesh that is all the more manifest as such as it auto-affects itself more radically in its agony. Only the flesh suffers, dies, and therefore can live. (ii) If the paradox of the flesh consists in the fact that it affects itself by itself, it also manifests itself without having to be inscribed in any relation, therefore in an absolute mode, outside or beyond any horizon. It follows that the saturated phenomenon of Christ assumes the paradox of the flesh by always subverting the supposedly unique horizon of phenomenality, thereby demanding a never definite plurality of horizons. This is indicated perfectly by a similar formulation in the two final chapters of John: "Jesus did still more signs and others in the sight of his disciples, but these are not written in this book" (20:30–31); "There are also many other things Jesus did; but if it were necessary to write every one of them, I do not know if the world itself could receive all the books to be written" (21:25). The world cannot welcome the writings that would describe what Christ did; it is clear that the acts of Christ, even reduced to writings, exceed the horizon of this world, are not of this world, demand other horizons and other worlds. This principle of the plurality of worlds, or rather horizons, governs all dimensions of the phenomenality of Christ's flesh. His royal character, which is not of this world, is therefore spoken in three tongues, not just one (Luke 23:38; John 19:20). The writers who attempt to offer witness to the paradox they have seen are at least four and necessarily in partial disagreement on account of the finite aspect and horizon that each was able to take into view and put into operation. Scripture itself traditionally admits four concurrent meanings, something that recent exegesis confirms by according it an unlimited number of different literary genres, each of which in fact offers a new horizon in order to welcome a new aspect of the one and only paradox. In this context, the fact that Christ can receive a plurality of names, none of which says his essence, does nothing more than reproduce the property of God himself of admitting all names and refusing each of them (*poluōnumon kai anōnumon*)—the property of summoning an infinity of nominative horizons in order to denominate he who saturates not only each horizon, but the incommensurable sum of the horizons. Consequently, the absolute marked by the paradox of Christ's flesh can be deployed in the limited visibility of worldly horizons only by their indefinite temporal and spatial proliferation in so many fragmented and provisional approaches to the same bursting absolutely without compare, common measure, or analogy. It could even be that history (in the case of time), civilizations (in the case of space), and spiritualities, literatures, cultures (in the case of horizons) are set forth only to decline, unfurl, and discover the paradox of Christ, which his absoluteness renders inaccessible as such to all sight, contact, and speech.

In terms of modality, finally, Christ appears as an irregardable phenomenon precisely because as icon he regards me in such a way that He constitutes me as his witness rather than some transcendental I constituting Him to its own liking. The inversion of the gaze lacks no textual references. In effect, the I loses primacy as soon as the "the servant is not greater than his master" (John 15:19). Next, Christ constitutes his disciples as witnesses by electing them; he can do this legitimately only because he sees them first—before they see themselves ("He saw two brothers," Matthew 4:18)—and foresees them "from afar" (Luke 14:20). He therefore names them with a borrowed proper name (John 1:42) and can dispatch them as witnesses (Matthew 28:18). A text illustrates perfectly how the inversion of the gaze produces saturation (Mark 10:17–22). Consider a rich young man. He "runs and kneels before" Christ, that is to say, exposes himself to his gaze and implicitly recognizes his primacy. He asks him, in the name of his "goodness," to teach him access to eternal life—that is to say, to perfection, therefore to a, indeed the, saturated phenomenon par excellence. Christ answers him by denying goodness for himself and referring it to his Father, then by enumerating the known commandments of the Law, at least all those that demand respect for the Other inasmuch as Other (do not commit adultery, do not kill, do not steal, do not give false testimony, honor your mother and father). Thus the saturated phenomenon comes from the counter-gaze of the Other (Christ) such that it constitutes me its witness. The young man acknowledges this phenomenon as saturated; he lets himself be measured with neither reserve nor dissimulation by the requirements of the gaze of the Other, and he conforms to this icon: "Master, all this have I observed from my youth." Now it is precisely at this point, where the saturated phenomenon is acknowledged and admitted, that two essential characteristics are accentuated. (i) First, the irregardable paradox provokes and identifies its witness by the gaze that it casts over him: "Jesus gazed upon [*emblepsas, intuitus*] him and loved him"—to gaze upon is of course not equivalent to just casting one's gaze (otherwise the text would have said nothing at all), but to instituting what one gazes upon. In effect, the gaze is not cast indifferently on just anyone, but differently on this one or that one, each time another Other. The gaze recognizes, establishes, and individualizes what it thus takes under its wing; and for all that, this electing gaze does not objectify or reify since it ends up loving, therefore letting what it just posited be set forth by its own withdrawal. The irreducible saturated phenomenon therefore transforms the I into a witness, into its witness. (ii) Accordingly, the paradox, far from being spread thin, will be redoubled. To the first saturation (accomplishing the commandments of the Law concerning the Other), the irregardable gaze adds a saturation of saturation—sell your goods "whatever they might be" and "give [the proceeds] to the poor." The last type of saturation implies its redoubling: one must not only respect the gaze of the poor (not objectify them, but recognize their originarity) and, doing that, come to stand before the irregardable gaze of Christ; one must also annul all possession and all originarity in order to "give [oneself] to the poor," therefore to the first among them. Thus, when the young man decides to stay rich, he confesses to remaining stuck between two states of the paradox: intuitive saturation and saturation beyond itself, saturation to the second degree.

We therefore recover, in the figure of Christ, not only the four types of paradox, but the redoubling of saturation that defines the last among them.

Either... Or...

The saturated phenomenon therefore culminates in the type of paradox I call revelation, one that concentrates in itself—as the figure of Christ establishes its possibility—an event, an idol, a flesh, and an icon, all at the same time. Saturation passes beyond itself, exceeds the very concept of maximum, and finally gives its phenomenon without remainder or reserve. We thus possess for the first time a model of phenomenality appropriate to phenomena that are neither poor nor common. In effect, when these phenomena appear fully, that is to say, when they are given without reserve, they do so neither according to the Cartesian evidence that applies solely to objects, nor according to the manifested being (*geoffenbart sein*) of the concept (to

which Hegel, without reason, reduced revelation, *Offenbarung*), nor according to the opening with withdrawal of the *Ereignis* (to which Heidegger pretends to confide the advent of a possible "god"). If the Revelation of God as
showing himself starting from himself alone can in fact ever take place, phenomenology must redefine its own limits and learn to pass beyond them following clear-cut and rigorous procedures. That is to say, it must design one
of its possible figures as a paradox of paradoxes, saturated with intuition to
the second degree, in a word, a phenomenon of revelation. Otherwise, it will
repeat the absurd denegation on which metaphysics and the "question of Being" stubbornly insist: better to erase or disfigure the possibility of Revelation than redefine the transcendental conditions of manifestation in order to
admit the mere possibility of a phenomenon of revelation. The debate is
summed up in a simple alternative: is it necessary to confine the possibility
of the appearing of God to the uninterrogated and supposedly untouchable
limits of one or the other figure of philosophy and phenomenology, or
should we broaden phenomenological possibility to the measure of the possibility of manifestation demanded by the question of God? One should
not, once again, pose as an objection to the phenomenon of revelation the
argument that the transcendence of God is bracketed by Husserl. Though
apparently incontestable, it does not stand up, for the following reasons. (a)
Husserl submits what he names "God" to the reduction only insofar as he
defines it by transcendence (and insofar as he compares this particular transcendence with that, in fact quite different, of the object in the natural attitude); and yet in Revelation and *theo*-logy, God is likewise, indeed especially,
characterized by radical immanence to consciousness, and in this sense
would be confirmed by a reduction. (b) Husserl aims to reduce the transcendent "God" only by identifying him with a "'ground,' *Grund*"; and yet
this metaphysical denomination par excellence would not concern the *theo*-
logical names of God, to which the phenomenon of revelation means to do
justice.[92] (c) Here it is a matter of admitting only the *possibility* of the phenomenon of revelation (and not, once again, the *fact* of a Revelation), and
yet this possibility does not put the reduction into question, since it is designed entirely within and on the basis of the radical immanence of the phenomenon. Not only does the phenomenon of revelation show itself only insofar as it is given, but it owes the excellence of its visibility only to the
givenness beyond the common (law) that its saturation of saturation ensures
to it. In other words, as paradox of paradoxes, the phenomenon of revelation
does nothing more than accomplish the immanence of the given phenome-

non by carrying it first to saturation and then to saturation redoubled. It thus does no less than produce the ultimate variation of the one and only figure of the given phenomenon, all of whose determinations it maintains (anamorphosis, unpredictable landing, fait accompli, incident, event), carries to saturation (historical event, idol, flesh, icon), and gathers into one single apparition. (d) If danger there must be here, it would reside more in the formal and, in a sense, still transcendental phenomenalization of the question of God than in some sort of theologization of phenomenality. It could be that the fact of Revelation provokes and evokes figures and strategies of manifestation and revelation that are much more powerful and more subtle than what phenomenology, even pushed as far as the phenomenon of revelation (paradox of paradoxes), could ever let us divine. Whatever the case might be, there is nothing astonishing in the fact that one inquires after God's right to inscribe himself within phenomenality. What is astonishing is that one should be stubborn—and without conceptual reason—about denying him this right, or rather that one is no longer even surprised by this pigheaded refusal.

But another objection arises, one that is much more serious because less polemic and better focused on what is at stake. It distinguishes a contradiction between, on one hand, the description of the phenomenon of revelation according to intuitive saturation and, on the other, the ongoing tradition of apophaticism in which God is known only as unknown, in the "night" of the senses and concepts, therefore in a radical intuitive shortage.[93] The response to this objection will also permit me to explain the saturation of saturation in more detail. (a) First, a saturated phenomenon cannot by definition be seen according to a definite intuition that would be simply lacking or sufficient. The saturating intuition cannot not bedazzle and give to see, at first, only its bedazzlement rather than some certain spectacle (§22). Hence, intuitive saturation can be perfectly translated by the (at least provisional) impossibility of seeing some *thing*, and so appears as a lack of intuition. To stick with just one of the paradigms of the saturated phenomenon (without going so far as its redoubling), let us consider the face. It uncontestably saturates phenomenality, since it reverses intentionality and submerges my gaze with its own; and yet this counter-gaze comes to meet me only while remaining invisible, at least as object or being—strictly speaking, there is nothing to see. And this, for that matter, is why the majority of the time I do not see the face of the Other as the face of the Other: the invisible of his gaze escapes me. As soon as this invisible has disappeared, I can once again begin to see his face as a simple object and a being available in visibility (a face that is beautiful or ugly, desirable, contemptible, etc.). The same paradox can be found in the historical event, the painting (the idol), and the flesh. There is, properly speaking, nothing to see when they give themselves as such. In effect, intuitive saturation is never equivalent to giving a great (or too great) quantity of intuition for the purpose of simply fulfilling a concept that lets us better perceive an object, for this first degree of excess can still define a common-law phenomenon in which objectivity would be simply blurred but not overcome. By contrast, if saturation gives too much intuition, it therefore gives even less objectivity. From the perspective of objectivity, one can and should say— without any contradiction—that the saturated phenomenon gives nothing to see. (b) Next, it will be observed that the deception of the senses and of the understanding obviously indicates that there is nothing (no thing) to perceive, but not that intuition is lacking. Simply the paradox and, especially, the phenomenon of revelation are never used to construct an object, but always to provoke the unforeseeable, the excess, the absolute, or the assignation to witness—in short, to affect the flesh and saturate it with intuition. The moments and the movements of this nonobjectifying saturation become, to different degrees, the affair of mystical theology, as well as novels or the analytic cure—in all these cases, intuitive saturation in no way concerns objectness, or rather, in no way concerns the object, and therefore is equivalent to its lack. But the lack of an object is not equivalent to a shortage of givenness, for saturated givenness gives much more (and better) than objects. (c) Finally, it will be observed that if shortage (thus understood as a shortage of objects) was absent and lack was lacking, manifestation not only would not increase—it would decrease. What is at issue here is the possibility of the phenomenon of revelation, in which an excess of intuition is redoubled in a paradox of paradoxes. It is therefore a question of letting a phenomenon come to manifestation, which is given in such a way that nothing more manifest can be given—*id quo nihil manifestius donari potest*. So I ask: Does the moment of denegation that the redoubled excess of intuition imposes diminish *this* phenomenon, confirm it, or even add to it? If the *phenomenon* of revelation could be seen without lack, indeterminacy, or bedazzlement, would it be manifest more perfectly as phenomenon of *revelation* or, on the contrary, would it be disqualified? Doesn't it belong essentially to the paradox and its apparition to contradict the course of apparition in general, to give itself as a *para*-dox and not only as a para-*dox*? Here finally it is necessary that we no longer define the saturated phenomenon simply by the inversion of the determinations of the common-law phenomenon. With the phenomenon of revelation, we come to the point where it is necessary to free ourselves not only from these (metaphysical or phenomenological) determinations, but even from their destruction. The paradox of paradoxes does not have to choose between cataphasis and apophasis any more than between saturation and shortage of intuition; it uses them all in order to push to its end the phenomenality of what shows itself only insofar as it gives itself.

The Given Without Intuition—a Question

Now I can confront a difficulty that, since the opening of our study, I have continually run up against and dodged at the same time. It can be put in this way: if the privilege of intuition stems from its character of givenness (§20), how are we to explain that givenness is often accomplished without intuition?[94] The response is deduced from the principle just laid out—when givenness no longer gives an object or a being, but rather a pure given, it is no longer carried out by intuition; or rather, the alternative between a shortage and a saturation of intuition becomes undecidable. Among these pure givens, at once empty of and saturated with intuition, we can distinguish three types. (a) The cases where givenness brings it about that phenomena show themselves that are by definition nonobjectifiable, therefore without intuition fulfilling an intentional aim at an object. For example, "giving time" gives nothing (no thing, no object), therefore mobilizes no intuition; and yet, in giving the nonobject par excellence, time, givenness grants to all the things that benefit from it the possibility of giving and re-giving themselves. To give time amounts to giving nonactuality itself, which is not nothing since it ensures possibility to all that is. Likewise, "to give life" in fact gives nothing, since the flesh intrinsically avails itself of its power to live and "life" remains what is absent par excellence from all biological science; and yet this "nothing" does not say nothing. He to whom it was given, and for as long as he receives it, keeps the possibility of living in and for himself; life never has objective status, and so it must give itself without intuitive fulfillment (or a concept to be fulfilled); but in this way it appears all the more as a pure given possibility, since it itself gives possibility to objective and being phenomena. Givenness without intuition by default. (b) Next, there are cases where givenness brings it about that phenomena of nonbeings, of what by definition should not be, show themselves, phenomena which can appear only insofar as they give themselves outside Being. For example, "the gift of death" amounts to giving not only no being, but to the state of no longer Being, since even death itself cannot be any more than it can let Be what it reaches. It is not merely a matter of giving the impossibility of being, but giving impossibility itself as directly nonbeing. Similarly "to give one's life" (which sometimes strangely enough equals "giving death," "giving oneself death") for the Other (whether it be individual, collective, abstract, finite, or infinite) implies giving to him (therefore giving oneself to him as) a non-being. Givenness consists precisely and explicitly in this disappearance of all beingness, and it would in turn be annulled if "death" or "my life" recovered an ontic positivity. Givenness without intuition by definition. (c) Finally, cases present themselves in which givenness lets phenomena that exceed, and therefore include, all beingness and objectness show themselves. For example, "to give one's word" indicates a gift always still to come, all the more still to come as it has already been accomplished for a long time. The soldier or the lover, equally engaged in risking their life in a hard struggle, should stick to their word even more as they have already not only given, but maintained it. The more they realize it, the less they are dismissed from keeping it. The more it was, the less it is ensured of still being. In effect, it bears on no object, nor any being, but on the very temporality of what shows itself thanks to the given word. The same is true when one "gives peace," "gives meaning (*Sinngebung*)," or "gives a face to...." Givenness without intuition by excess. All these givennesses succeed in giving paradoxes (saturated phenomena) without intuition or without one being able to decide between excess and shortage. I will name the phenomena of revelation (saturation of saturation), where the excess of the gift assumes the character of shortage, with the name the *abandoned* [*l'abandonné*].[95]

Thus I have not only set out a topics of the phenomenon in general. I have above all broadened it to the point of doing justice to a heretofore repressed or denied type: the paradox, or the saturated phenomenon, including even its most complex figure, the phenomenon of revelation. The principal result of this broadening is not that we can now accord a phenomenological possibility to the possible fact of Revelation (though this is indeed a remarkable advance in relation to metaphysics). Rather, its essential effect is to extend the previously won definition of the phenomenon—what shows itself in the measure to which it is given (Book 1, §6)—to its fullest extent, so that we end up at this last definition: what gives itself in the measure to which it reveals itself. To be sure, this radicalization does not count for every given phenomenon (Book 3), nor even for every saturated phenomenon (paradox, Book 4, §§20–22), but only for phenomena saturated to the second degree (paradox of paradoxes, §24). And yet, this exceptional phenomenon is inscribed within the general definition of the phenomenon as given, under the heading of a simple though remarkable variation of the originary phenomenological givenness. It accomplishes it, but because it comes from it.

Book V

THE GIFTED

§25 THE APORIAS OF THE "SUBJECT"

From the Subject to the Receiver

The phenomenon therefore manifests itself insofar as it gives itself
(Book 3) and inasmuch as it gives itself (Book 4). To manifest itself as well
as to give itself, it is first necessary that the "self" with which the phenomenon is deployed attest itself as such. It does this only by appropriating the
gravitational center of phenomenality, therefore by assuming the origin of
its own event. Only in this way can it tear itself away from the alienated
status of the object—a status wherein it remands all mastery for its own
visibility to the rule of a constituting I, who from the outside defines and
produces it. The phenomenon gives itself and shows itself only by confirming itself as a "self"; and this "self" is attested only counter to every ex-
clusively transcendental claim of the I. For the "self" of the phenomenon
in person to recover initiative in its own phenomenality, we are obliged to
redefine the I according to the guiding thread of its anamorphosis (§13), as
well as its mere witness (§22). This change would lead to confusion, indeed
would lead us to stray into the most trivial psychologism, if it were not governed strictly by the very phenomenality that the "self" renders to the phenomenon. If the phenomenon gives itself in order to show itself, it must
designate the point (blind, blinded, or patent and illuminated point) where
and to which it gives itself. In giving itself, what shows itself also, necessarily, designates that to whom or to which it abandons itself and without

which it could no longer appear. And we must not be hasty here in decid-ing whether the given phenomenon shows itself to an "unto whom" (al-ready too psychological) or an "unto which" (still too neutral), for both must be understood on the basis of the emergence of a function of pure re-ceiver of givenness.[1] The "self" of the phenomenon—as soon as it is es-tablished against objectness—transforms the I into a witness, according to a compulsory anamorphosis, because it first inverts the nominative (the subject, such as grammar posits it) into a more original dative, which des-ignates (grammatically again) the "unto whom/which" of its receiver. To be sure, such a receiver is the successor of what metaphysics means by "sub-ject" only because it stands clearly opposed to it. And yet, this opposition does not stem only from the fact that the receiver comes after the phenom-enon, whereas the "subject" foresees or provokes it, but especially from the fact that, as such, the receiver can no longer claim to possess or produce phenomena. It no longer stands in a relation of possession to the phenom-enon, but in a purely receiving relation—they are no doubt contiguous, but irreducibly separated—in short, in a relation of unlimited usufruct, but without any guarantee. This dispossession is all the more radical as the more the phenomenon is given continually and without return the more it proves that it shows itself of itself, therefore attests the phenomenological priority of its "self" over every possible receiver. The receiver therefore comes after the "subject" in the double sense of succeeding its metaphysical figure and, especially, of proceeding from the phenomenon, without coming be-fore it or producing it.

To the thus original figure of the receiver, it seems nevertheless possi-ble to address two objections—one metaphysical, the other phenomeno-logical. (a) The metaphysical objection would be stated in this way: at the very least, though it may be in the one-dimensional and alienated mode of objectness, the "subject" ensures a phenomenality for the phenomenon by "accompanying" every objective representation with the more originary representation of the "I think." For, according to Kant, "it must be possible for the 'I think' to accompany all my representations, for otherwise some-thing would be represented in me which could not be thought at all, and that is equivalent to saying that the representation would be impossible, or at least would be nothing to me."[2] Phenomenality here dwindles to repre-sentation, which implies an I, but even impoverished thus, it is accom-plished. The phenomenon actually appears, though lowered to the level of objectness and alienated in the "subject." Couldn't we ask in turn if the receiver still secures the phenomenality of the phenomenon when it no longer synthesizes, like the I, the manifold of intuition by an act of the spontaneity of the understanding? But, is it self-evident that the necessary link between every representation and that of the "I think"—what Kant calls accompaniment—is equivalent to the synthesis of the represented manifold (of the phenomenon) by the unity of the concept, therefore by the understanding and finally by the spontaneity of the I? For it is one thing to say that no phenomenon escapes its representation (understood in the broadest sense of a presentation to . . .), and consequently that every phenomenon presentable to . . . also implies "the representation 'I am,' which expresses the consciousness that can accompany all thought,"[3] since even phenomena that emerge from the paradox always admit an essential (though blurred) relation to representation (§23). But this is something completely different from interpreting the accompaniment of each thought (presenting to . . .) by the thought of the I as a synthesis of the phenomenon according to an "act of spontaneity,"[4] therefore as its production by the imagination (indeed, concept of the understanding). Why set aside another possibility— that the representation which accompanies all representation is not said in an "I think" (therefore in the spontaneity of the understanding), but in an "I feel" (in terms of the affection of sensibility)? Even sticking to the double a priori formality retained by Kant, why couldn't the accompanying representation of phenomenality *also* consist in the receptivity of sensibility vis-à-vis intuition? Shouldn't it even consist *first* in this sensible representation, since precisely for Kant himself, intuition alone benefits from the privilege of givenness? And since Kant himself defines it as "that representation which can be *given prior to* all thought,"[5] why does he subordinate it to the originarily synthetic unity of apperception rather than according it the unconditioned anteriority of an attribution calling forth a receiver [*un attribution qui provoque un attributaire*]? By contrast, if on one hand sensibility gives inasmuch as it is receptive passivity, if on the other the thought (can one still say "representation" here?) accompanying all other presentations to . . . can consist more originarily in an "I feel" or "I am affected" than in an "I think," then shouldn't we admit, within the very framework of the Kantian hypotheses, that the so-called transcendental, spontaneous, and productive "subject" should yield to what I am calling the receiver—the "unto whom/which" the phenomenon gives itself such as it shows itself on the basis of itself and as the "self"? If, therefore, a pure a priori anteriority intervenes in both cases, for an "I am affected" as well as an "I think," it is not enough for establishing a hierarchy in favor of the second. It must be admitted, therefore, that for Kant the difference in fact stems from another criterion, one more deeply veiled. In fact, it is because synthesis and spontaneity are implicitly accorded an originary character that understanding precedes sensibility and the "subject" obscures the receiver. Now, since the originarily synthetic unity of apperception presupposes the givenness of the intuitive manifold, shouldn't we invert the hierarchy and define the a priori by the passivity of sensibility, recipient of givenness (§1), therefore by the receiver—and no longer by the apperceiving "subject"? In absolutely no way is it self-evident that the synthetic unity of apperception—or the "subject" of the synthesis—deserves the title "origin." The I could exert the originary function equally well, if not more legitimately, as an "I am affected" than as an "I think." Thus, the metaphysical objection provides the argument that refutes it.

There remains (b) the phenomenological objection. The phenomenon shows itself insofar as and inasmuch as it gives itself, but the gift, which gives itself equally (though in the particular, improper, mode of exchange), can be read without givee (§9) as well as without giver (§10) or gift given (§11). That being the case, why privilege here, under the heading of receiver, solely the determination of the gift by the givee "to whom/which" it gives itself? If we maintained, as would be perfectly legitimate, the determination of the gift given by a giver without givee, wouldn't its phenomenality end up requalifying its author and its agent, thereby restoring something like a "subject" knowing (itself) how to give? The coherence of this argument should not hide its limit. I have established that the description of the phenomenon of the gift does not govern that of givenness but depends on it, because the phenomenality of pure givenness destroys and is free of the reversibility of the exchange model that restrains and warps the economy of the gift (and it alone). More precisely, if the gift can, by abstraction from commerce (§8), be described from the perspective of the giver (without givee) as well as from the perspective of the givee (without giver), as soon as it is finally completely grasped in terms of the given phenomenon and as one of its (optional) derivatives, it must, in rigorous phenomenology, be described resolutely and essentially from a precise situation—that of the givee (possibly without giver or gift given) receiving the phenomenon (§12). Why? Precisely because it belongs to the ultimate definition of the phenomenon to show itself only insofar as and inasmuch as it gives itself; and if it gives itself starting from its "self," as irreducible phenomenological basis, it therefore shows itself intrinsically as to be received. Accordingly, if one claims to produce it, or merely to assign or deliver it by pretending to exercise the function of giver, it immediately slips away from its own visibility and is obscured as given. The parity of giver and givee counts only for the gift (and again, seen abstractly in terms of commerce), not for the given phenomenon. Insofar as and inasmuch as it gives itself, the given phenomenon, by contrast, shows itself only to a givee—in this case, a receiver—never to a giver (in this case, a "subject" who is supposedly the producer of the object). The phenomenological objection thus leads to removing the ambiguity that burdened the merely provisional similarity between the phenomenologies of the gift and the given.

The receiver is thus imposed in the place of and counter to the "subject" as a strict consequence of the givenness of the phenomenon. But this breakthrough would have only relative importance if it did not permit (i) taking a step back outside the subjectivity of the "subject" supposed by metaphysics so as to see and mark its aporias clearly; (ii) assuming these very aporias in order to break through them and thus sketch the irreducible traits of the receiver "to whom/which" alone what gives itself shows itself.

Formal Objections to the Transcendental I

The "subject" does not owe its contemporary disqualification to some stubbornly negative or ideologically biased polemic, as several recent reactionary hermeneutics would lead us to believe. It owes it to its continually confirmed powerlessness to do justice to the most patent characteristics of its own phenomenon. To take stock of these insufficiencies, I will first distinguish four formal aporias of the "subject" reduced to the "I think"—two insofar as it is considered a transcendental "subject," two others when considered an empirical "me." These then boil down to one sole phenomenological aporia. (a) As transcendental I, the "I think" accomplishes *no individuation*. Because it exerts a pure abstract function, "the representation 'I' does not contain in itself the least manifoldness and it is absolute (although merely logical) unity." It unifies the manifold precisely because it remains an empty unity, orphan of all particularity. It therefore intervenes as "one and the same in all consciousness" so as to prevent it from happening that "I should have as many-coloured and diverse a self [*ein so vielfarbiges verschiedenes Selbst*] as I have representations of which I am conscious to myself."[6] The "subject" secures its transcendentality at the price of its deprivation of all quality; it therefore establishes its universality to the detriment of its identity. It reproduces the oneness of the agent intellect that Averroes's interpretation of Aristotle had already opposed to the (empirical) multiplicity of passive but individualized understandings. The fact that in this very tradition, one obstinate about eradicating even the merest claim to an individual "self," individuation should in the end be quite logically abandoned to matter and therefore condemned without appeal to unintelligibility simply confirms that the "I think," understood transcendentally, can never say or be called "I." Or if it says it, it cannot accomplish it as its own because it cannot achieve any "self." Everything happens as if the "I think," which claims as its function and foundation alienating the "self" of the phenomenon by objectifying it, lost in this destruction first and above all its own "self." Hence an obvious dilemma: if the "I think" as transcendental does not permit—better, forbids—the individuation of the "I," must we renounce thinking subjectivity as far as its irreducible individuation, or renounce thinking the individuality of the "I" in terms of the transcendental figure of the "I think?" Of course, between these two ways, I will choose the second—thinking the "I" according to a determination more originary than the "I think" and asking the receiver to lead me as far as the ultimate individuality of a "self." (b) As a transcendental I, the "I think" also cannot free itself from *solipsism*. It is not just a matter of the classic difficulty demonstrating the existence of the outside world (Descartes, Malebranche, Berkeley, Kant, etc.), a difficulty limited to a region of being and by right always surmountable (Husserl, Heidegger). It is above all a matter of the transcendental implications of the primacy of an "I think" that would accompany every other representation. Such a situation would suppose that all representation equals, at bottom, self-representation, that all *cogitatio* harbors a *cogitatio sui*, therefore that all "I think" implicitly develops an "I think myself"—an implication I will note henceforth with "I think (myself)." Such circularity does not only produce the formal tautology of the "I think" as "I am";[7] it above all imitates the identity of essence and existence deployed by the so-called "ontological argument" and by the *causa sui*: all thought (of whatever essence) includes in it the existence (the ontico-epistemological) of the I as "I think" whose essence is enough to cause its own existence. Whence this consequence: no thought comes up that does not first give to be thought, before itself, the "I think (myself)." And even if we admitted the groundedness of this solipsism (Berkeley), we could not tolerate the inadequacy that it brings to the simple description of the "subject." In itself, that is, the primacy of the "I think (myself)" not only does not let us take into account the finitude of the "subject"; it radically forbids it. For if Kant maintains this finitude, it is because he pairs the spontaneity of the "I think" with the receptivity of sensibility, while Husserl by contrast lets his transcendental I drift toward indefiniteness and universal oneness because he always maintains the primacy of activity over and above passivity and the intentional aim over and above intuitive fulfillment. Inversely, Heidegger reestablishes finitude so precisely only because he first uproots Dasein from the prestige of the theoretical attitude and the "I think (myself)" by means of Being-in-the-world, involvement [*Bewandtnis*], and facticity. For that matter, Descartes—before anyone else—would not have maintained the finitude of the ego if he had not taken care to frame the *cogitatio sui* by, on one side, doubt and the creation of eternal truths and, on the other, its formally infinite will. It therefore seems clear that the privilege accorded the "I think" in the description of subjectivity ends up contradicting or ignoring its essential trait—finitude. Here again, a dilemma arises: is it necessary to renounce thinking the finitude of the subject in order to maintain the privilege of the "I think," or should we have done with the "I think" in order to do justice to the finitude of the "subject," or rather the receiver who comes after it? I am inclined toward the second solution.

Formal Objections to the Empirical Me

These two aporias (nonindividuation, solipsism) flow directly from assigning to the "I think" the function of transcendental I. Would they be avoided by sparing it this function and interpreting it as an empirical me? Perhaps, but at the price of a radical consequence: such a supposedly empirical me would in fact already bear certain characteristics of what I am introducing with the term *receiver*, rather than those of the I, even an I reconsidered in terms of empiricity. Whence two final aporias. (c) The essential empiricity of the me stems from the fact that the first act of the "I think," in short of the spontaneity of the understanding, consists in a synthesis of the manifold, therefore from the fact that it comes after (or as) this manifold has come forward in intuition. The first act—"I think"—can only "accompany," second in line, the unpredictable landing of intuition. It therefore depends on it. What Kant suggested—if intuition precedes the understanding according to givenness, then the empirical me comes before the originary synthetic unity of the "I think" (apperception)—it falls to Husserl to formalize in an exemplary way: the originary does not belong to the transcendental I of intentionality or constitution, but to the ever new temporal impression, which arises *in advance of* what it thus renders immediately bygone, though retained in the first presence. Only the *original impression* of living time is first, no longer the apperception of the synthetic unity. Therefore the originary is displaced from the "I think" of self-representation, according to the understanding, to the "I am affected" in intuition by the ever renewed, but absolutely without precedent, instant, which bursts, so to speak, upon the screen of my consciousness—awakening it, disappearing in it, and thus opening it to the following impression, charged in turn with originarity. Such a transfer of the origin to the temporal impression does not only relativize the transcendental pretension of the I (formally, though partially maintained by Husserl); it above all exposes it to the radical givenness that time exercises over consciousness, which at once changes status. In effect, the empirical me is not just added, as if optionally, to the transcendental "I think," for the originary impression, which alone gives access to temporality, could not happen within an already originally synthetic unity or a transcendental constitution of objects (both presupposing this temporality that they receive and manage, but neither produce nor provoke). In contrast, the originary impression happens only because it gives itself from top to bottom and without anything objectifiable. It thus enters into phenomenality only inasmuch as its givenness is received as the unique originary event. It therefore requires that the I, unless the I totally ignores it, renounce the status of accompanying and originarily synthesizing representation in order to assume the function of receptivity, in short, that it quit the "I think" in favor of the "I am affected." With the empirical me, therefore, it's not a question of a simple stand-in or rival of the transcendental I; already, under this ambiguous and obscure title, it's a matter of a complete return imposed on subjectivity as a whole by the irreducible phenomenality of the originary impression of time. This particular absolute phenomenon requires not only that the transcendental I yield definitively to the empirical me, but above all that the empirical me secure its primacy in terms of its receptivity to givenness, therefore that it completely submit itself to it. More: this receptivity, instituted as the sole a priori suitable to the (temporal) givenness that is here at issue defines exactly, instead of and in the place of the I and even the me, the instance that is entirely exhausted in the function of receiving: the "to whom/which," the receiver. The aporia of empiricity thus leads to reversing the two sides of metaphysical subjectivity in favor of the new figure, whose dative succeeds the (nominative) "subject." (d) The final aporia would stem from the very *splitting* of the "subject" into a pure transcendental I and an empirical "me." This splitting means, at the most basic level, that what gives itself in fact (the me) has no standing as origin (not transcendental) and that reciprocally what exercises the transcendental function can never and should never give itself. In short, it directly denies givenness the title of last principle—of a principle that is first insofar as it is a posteriori (§1). As a result, this splitting acknowledges, in the mode of a denegation, that the "subject" defined by the "I think" (i) slips from the status of given, since by fixing the conditions of experience it immediately removes itself from the ranks of the objects of experience, at the risk of contradicting "the highest principle of all synthetic judgments," which it claimed to secure;[8] and (ii) renders givenness itself secondary, and therefore impugns it as such. But the very fact that it is fixed and frozen thus without given or givenness could stand in a quite close relationship to the aporias previously stigmatized, for the impossibilities of individuation, openness to alterity, and exerting originary receptivity all arise from a deficit of givenness. That is, individuation amounts to oneself giving oneself according to the facticity of a given phenomenon (§15); openness to alterity is equivalent to exposure to the unpredictable landing (§14) and the incident (§16) of the given phenomenon, while anamorphosis (§13) assigns the receiver its receptive function vis-à-vis the event (§17) of one and the same unique given phenomenon. To be individualized means to be put at stake in the heart of the given (empiricity) as receiver of originary givenness (transcendentality), therefore to break solipsism by virtue of a "self" itself given and understood in terms of givenness. Inversely, the aporias of the "subject" all flow from the denegation of its particular status as given, namely its function as receiver; this denegation itself becomes inevitable through ignorance of givenness as universal phenomenological characteristic of what shows itself as such. The formal aporias that disqualify the "subject" thus cover exactly its phenomenological shortfall in givenness and being given.

"... *like the other phenomena* ... "

It now becomes possible to confront the properly phenomenological aporia of the "subject," an aporia stemming from a unique deficiency: its mode of apparition remains essentially determined by that of objectness. In effect, by being reduced to an "I think," the "subject" is focused on the object, whose presenter and representer it alone becomes by virtue of the essence of representation—to the point that, when it wants to represent itself directly to itself, it has no other possibility but to assume one more time (and one time too many) the poorest phenomenality—that of the object. "I

think" is so organized by the object that it itself can no longer appear or
show itself except as another object, or at least within the horizon of objectness. Kant marked this aporia unambiguously: "How, therefore, can I say:
'I, as intelligence and *thinking* subject, know myself as an object that is
thought, in so far as I am given to myself (as something other or) beyond
that (I) which is (given to myself) in intuition, and yet know myself, like
other phenomena [*gleich anderen Phänomen*], only as I appear to myself,
not as I am to the understanding'—these are questions that raise no greater
or less difficulty than how I can be an object to myself at all, and, more particularly, an object of intuition and inner perceptions."[9] It must be concluded from this extraordinary passage that I am therefore an object to myself, or rather that the I is an object as soon as it must appear to me. That is,
since appearing admits only one modality, that of objectness, I appear "like
the other phenomena," therefore like "in general an object for me." This
causes "neither more nor less difficulty" in my own case than for that of any
phenomenon whatsoever—"*nulla difficultas*," Descartes already said.[10] The
role of accompaniment to every representation, assigned to the representation of "I think" (or "I am"), in fact ends up at an ontology and a phenomenology of imitation. The I is and appears only in the same mode as objects,
which it should merely accompany but in fact ends up assimilating. Such an
"I think" cannot therefore claim to secure the characteristics proper to a
genuine subjectivity. And Kant was perfectly right: from *his* "I think" we
can derive neither personality nor simplicity (nor individuality either); but
far from that obliging us to disqualify these characteristics as paralogisms, it
could be by contrast that their very inaccessibility definitively marks the
radical impotence of all phenomenality of the object to make some sort of
"subject" appear.

   No one saw and denounced better than Heidegger this insufficiency,
which is found equally in Husserl and in Kant, namely that the mode of
Being, and therefore phenomenality, appropriate to what says "I" should be
essentially lacking because always borrowed from that of the object.[11] To
overcome this deficiency, Heidegger substitutes Dasein for the "I think"
such that, in the figure of care [*Sorge*], it identifies itself properly: "Dasein
becomes 'essentially' Dasein in that authentic existence which constitutes
itself as anticipatory resoluteness [*vorlaufende Entschlossenheit*]."[12] It is fitting therefore to examine whether or not this ultimate determination of the
meaning of its Being permits Dasein to overcome the "subject," or if we
should still expect another. There would be no sense in contesting the fact

that *Sein und Zeit* puts into question not only the Kantian transcendental I (such as it reappeared in 1913), but also the phenomenological I in the ground definitively assigned to it by the *Logical Investigations*, by accomplishing a radical revolution. The "subject" no longer confesses its objective to be the objectification of the object, because the ultimate instrument of this objectification—intentionality—no longer has as its task to constitute objects, but rather to open a world. The intentionality that constitutes objects no doubt remains, but it is reduced to the level of a case derived from the fundamental determination, namely Being-in-the-world affecting he who is no longer in the world as a spectator, especially not a constituting one. He is in the world as one taking part in it, eventually taken apart by what meets him. The world is no longer summed up in the sum of constituted objects, since it itself consists in nothing, not even everything, but opens (by becoming wholly) a world. This world nevertheless opens only in that, previously, it is incumbent on Dasein to make the opening in general by means of its own ecstasy. This ecstasy resides in the fact that, far from being grounded in its essence or grounding its essence in a substratum (according to the two postulations, Kantian and Aristotelian, of subjectivity), Dasein is the being for whom nothing less than its Being is at issue each time—indeed better: it is the being for whom, when *its* Being is at issue, it is also an issue of *the* Being of all the other beings. Such an appropriation of Being to the I—"The Being of any such entity is *in each case mine* [*je meines*]"[13]—should not be interpreted as a subjection of Being to the figure of the ego, still less to a transcendental egoism (contrary to the unjustified criticism of Levinas). Rather, it results from the impossibility for other beings to attain their Being and especially from the impossibility of Dasein reaching Being otherwise than by putting itself at stake in the first person—in risking itself as one is exposed to death. Being opens to Dasein as death affects it with possibility: in person, in the first person, in the mode of nonsubstitutability. The "mineness" of Being no longer indicates that the I would subsist in an essentially unshakable subjectivity, but rather that Being remains inaccessible to Dasein (and therefore absolutely hidden) so long as the latter does not risk itself in exposure without reserve or certainty, as the possibility of impossibility. Being-toward-death therefore accords Dasein what the "I think (myself)" always lacked: unsubstitutable individuation, irremissible ipseity. Here for the first time the chief ambiguity of the Cartesian ego—its transcendental and empirical duality—is dissipated.

The Constancy of the Self

This accomplishment, however remarkable it might be, is not enough to break through all the metaphysical aporias of the "subject." Dasein is still exposed to solipsism and the objectness of a substratum. (a) On what condition does its "mineness" individualize Dasein? The answer is found in a formulation: "Resoluteness [*Entschlossenheit*] is a distinctive mode of Dasein's disclosedness [*Erschlossenheit*]."[14] Anticipatory resoluteness lays bare the Being of Dasein as care [*Sorge*] and allows us to reach the meaning of its Being on the basis of the future. The question therefore is to determine how the ecstasy of care is accomplished. In short: On what is resoluteness resolved? What does it give to Dasein? On what does the decision that Dasein receives from it bear? Resoluteness can be spotted concretely in several phenomena that it organizes: anxiety, consciousness of indebtedness, and being-toward-death (as anticipation). All have one characteristic in common: the nothingness of alterity.

(i) Anxiety arrives at the ordeal of the nothing/nothingness of every being, ready-to-hand as well as present-at-hand: "In that in the face of which one has anxiety, the 'nothing and nowhere' becomes manifest."[15] That this nothing/nothingness should be understood as the world does not mitigate the fact that anxiety opens to the nothing/nothingness, with nothing more than this nothingness itself. (ii) The consciousness that experiences its indebtedness perceives a call therein, whatever it might be. This call evokes and requires no response, no reparation, nor any ontically assignable price: "*What* does the conscience call to him to whom it appeals? Taken strictly, nothing. The call asserts nothing, gives no information about world-events, has nothing to tell."[16] The consciousness of debt therefore does not open Dasein to any being of the world whatsoever, except to itself inasmuch as it transcends beings. (iii) Being-toward-death seems at first glance to be an exception: never does Heidegger suggest that it too would open onto nothing/nothingness (which nevertheless the entire study seems to intend), but only onto the possibility of impossibility. Nonetheless, anticipating toward being-toward-death finally opens Dasein to absolute possibility—absolute since it even includes the impossible where it fully accomplishes its transcendence toward every being and is therefore undergone as such. As a result, since in "Being-towards-death, Dasein comports itself *towards itself* as a distinctive potentiality-for-being,"[17] it must be concluded that it relates itself to nothing other than itself, therefore to nothing of beings, to the nothing/nothingness. In this way, the three phenomena that determine the Being of Dasein as care exhibit anticipatory resoluteness as an ecstasy open strictly onto nothing. Dasein is disclosed, at the very moment of risking and individualizing itself as the being in which its very being is at issue, as an empty identity to itself. What is formulated at the outset of the analytic as "mineness [*Jemeinigkeit*]" is said, at its end, as "selfhood": "Dasein's Selfhood [*Selbstheit*] has been defined formally as a *way of existing*."[18] Dasein therefore exists insofar as itself, and its resolution resolves nothing because there is nothing it has to resolve, since for Dasein it was only a matter of risking itself in its own Being. Selfhood has to do with it alone. Whence a new solipsism, no longer ontic (being-in-the-world preserves it), but ontological (the transcendence of Dasein secures it). This requirement is doubtless based on the neutrality of Dasein (without ethics, face, or sex), but it is also a remnant of the metaphysical transcendental "subject." (b) This remnant explains why selfhood can also be understood as a self-constancy-in-person or an auto-constancy (*Selbst-standigkeit*):

Selfhood is to be discerned existentially only in one's authentic potentiality-for-Being-one's-Self [*Selbstseinkönnen*]—that is to say, in the authenticity of Dasein's Being as *care*. In terms of care the *constancy of the Self* [*Ständigkeit des Selbst*] as the supposed persistence of the *subjectum* gets clarified. But the phenomenon of this authentic potentiality-for-Being also opens our eyes for the *constancy of the Self* [*Ständigkeit des Selbst*] in the sense of its having achieved some sort of position. *The constancy of the self* [*Ständigkeit des Selbst*], in the double sense of steadiness and steadfastness, is the *authentic* [*eigentliche*] counter-possibility to the non-Self-constancy [*Unselbst-ständigkeit*] which is characteristic of irresolute falling. Existentially, "*Self-constancy*" signifies nothing other than anticipatory resoluteness.[19]

In this way, selfhood is deployed in the self-constancy of the self, which is prolonged in auto-constancy, thus confirming that care leads Dasein back to a sort of self-identity. Thus arises the wonder of 1927: the ecstasy of care, which radicalizes the destruction of the transcendental "subject" (Descartes, Kant, and Husserl) and all the while mimics the subject by reestablishing an autarchy of Dasein to the point that its individuated selfhood is stabilized in auto-positing itself. Without a doubt, Heidegger abolishes the permanence of *ousia* and the *res cogitans* in Dasein; and yet the autarchy of the Self, which he maintains, goes so far as to just touch the strange title "constantly present-at-hand ground":

If the ontological constitution of the Self is not to be traced back either to an "I"-substance or to a "subject," but if, on the contrary, the everyday fugitive way in which we keep on saying "I" must be understood in terms of our *authentic* potentiality-for-Being, then the proposition that the Self is the constantly present-at-hand ground of care [*ständig vorhandene Grund der Sorge*] is one that still does not follow.[20]

Not only does just a fragile denegation, by the way advanced without reason, keep Dasein from drifting toward the level of a subsisting ground, but it is difficult to see what true phenomenological criteria separate this metaphysical "constantly present-at-hand [*ständig vorhanden*]" from a ground and from the "constancy of Self [*Ständigkeit des Selbst*]" proper to Dasein, which will follow. In fact, the reflective characteristics of Dasein—to resolve *itself*, to put *itself* at stake, to precede *itself*, to agonize over *itself*, and each time for nothing other than itself (for the nothing and the Self)—are such good imitations of the transcendental subject's reflexivity that they should also suggest the character of subsisting ground for Dasein. The aporia of solipsism implies that of subsistence. As a result, wouldn't individuation itself also become problematic? Being does indeed put me at stake by playing itself out in me; but can one ever assign it a singularity and not imagine it as unique for all beings? Doesn't it sometimes assume a collective identity? Can we ever base an individuation on it? Dasein's "mineness" defines it so intrinsically that Dasein can neither multiply it nor individuate it. The aporias of the "subject" forever haunt Dasein. It could be that Dasein does not designate what succeeds the "subject" so much as its last heir, such that it offers less an overcoming than the path toward possibly overcoming it.

These aporias will remain as long as we claim to begin with the ego, the "subject," or Dasein presupposed as a principle or, to speak like Aristotle, as a that "from which one would start first" in general.[21] They will eventually dissipate only if, by a radical reversal, we substitute an "unto whom/which," a receiver to which/whom the phenomenon that shows itself by giving itself always ends up arriving. For in receiving what gives itself (the phenomenon), the receiver receives its effects, therefore receives itself from it—it is individualized by facticity (§15), breaks solipsism by the alterity of the unpredictable landing (§14) and the incident (§16), overcomes the spontaneity of the "I think" in the receptivity of the "I am affected" by the effect of the event (§17), and receiving itself as a being given (§18), frees itself from the subsistence of a substratum, in short, from the subjectivity of the "subject." The receiver remains—if you will—a "subject," but one emancipated from all subjectivity because first free of all subjectness and through with all substrata.

But if the receiver does not arise from its own basis or rest on its own substratum, whence does he come to himself? What (or who) therefore precedes him?

§26 TO RECEIVE ONE'S SELF FROM WHAT GIVES ITSELF

From Givenness to Manifestation

From where does the receiver arise, or—which amounts to the same thing—from where does what, giving itself, institutes it as a receiver come to him? Formally, the answer leaves no doubt: what gives itself shows itself, and the given phenomenon brings it about that the receiver arises by happening to him. My task therefore is only to describe this scene, where what comes after the "subject" is in the end *born*—that is to say, finally admits its inability, or especially its unobligedness, to constitute itself by the *cogitatio sui* or *causa sui*, but receives itself from the given phenomenon and from it alone. Describing it is difficult enough, however, that I will do so twice. The birth of the receiver will be described first on the basis of the given phenomenon as such (according to Book 3), then on the basis of the phenomenon given insofar as saturated (according to Book 4, §23). In this way, I can attain its ultimate denomination, that of the *gifted*.[22]

Consider the event of what shows itself inasmuch as it gives itself, or rather any one of the phenomena that give themselves—for example, since Descartes has already explained it to us, a piece of wax. What does it give when it enters into the field of possible experience by means of an *inspectio mentis*? According to the Cartesian doctrine of the code, the "thing" itself gives nothing other than elementary concepts, the "simple natures," whose combinations in principle suffice to define it. The piece of wax gives, strictly speaking, only (i) the chemical formula for the composition of this type of *wax* in general, (ii) the quantity of molecules so defined corresponding to the physical body that constitutes this *piece* of wax, and (iii) the spatio-temporal coordinates of *this* piece of wax. These characteristics are all described in terms of extension, shape, and *Mathesis Universalis*. The likely difference between the concepts that Descartes used and those that the contemporary sciences prefer (supposing such a thing can be fixed) is less important than what they share: the intuitively poor givenness realized by the formula, and the quantity and coordinates of the piece of wax, which enable it to be defined but in no way seen. The concept of the wax does not yet show it; its intelligibility does not always phenomenalize it. Metaphysics, by the way, used to admit this gap; it even claimed it. Descartes (after Galileo and before Locke) formalizes it by investigating a radical solution of continuity between the truth of the "thing" (namely, its concept, such that the simple natures organized by order and measure suffice to constitute it) and the "idea" or "feeling" that we conceive of it (namely, what of it appears to us subjectively). This chasm ought not to be trivialized by reducing it to a mere opposition between the "first qualities" (simple natures, supposedly intrinsic to the thing) and the "secondary qualities" (extrinsic to the thing and therefore supposedly proper to the "subject"), since the concept constructed by the simple natures arranged by measure breaks definitively with all quality and no longer has recourse to anything but quantities or quantifiable givens.[23] No doubt, the chasm between the "thing" and the "feeling" finally opposes the object to what perceives it, but it does so only by first recognizing the phenomenological difference that alone justifies it—the difference between what gives itself by means of a poor intuition (the concept that models and measures the "thing"), therefore without showing itself (without entering into visibility, or more generally, into any of the sensible dimensions of phenomenality), and what gives itself only by showing itself in full intuition (the "feeling" of the wax). For, the wax—before and without its being modeled or quantified by the simple natures—gives itself first and especially by showing itself to "feeling." It gives itself to sight (with a color that veers from yellow to red), but it also gives itself to touch (passing from cold to hot), to hearing (passing from a rapping to a silent flow), indeed to taste and smell (taste and odor of honey); in short, it manifests itself in terms of sensible immediacy, that is to say, in terms of my five senses. *Mine?* What me insinuates itself here? Obviously not the constituting ego that exercises this pure and spontaneous *cogitatio* synthesizing an object, which Descartes will discover *over and against* the receiver of the sensible manifold, but precisely this receiver itself—who constitutes no object unified by a concept, but to whom are attributable as many fragmentary "feelings" as are demanded by the rhapsody of the manifold that shows itself. The me that here comes to light indirectly is therefore not distinguished, contrary to what Descartes (and all metaphysics with him) leads us to suppose, by a defect in the modality of knowledge—the uncertainty, passivity, and "subjectivity" of sensible experience. It is characterized rather by an uncontestable, unstoppable, absolute phenomenological *privilege*. While what gives itself by concepts, order, and measure is merely constituted under the gaze of the ego and therefore no longer appears to it (one will say that a noumenon, empty representation, gives itself), while what is grasped in the mode of the object gives itself too poorly to show itself in its full phenomenality (one will say that a model, a type, or a "concept" gives itself), by contrast, what metaphysics savagely disqualifies as a nonobjectified phenomenon is the sole thing to give itself in plenitude—that is, to give itself to the point of showing itself from itself, of phenomenalizing its givenness to the point of rendering manifest its unsubstitutable selfhood. As a result, the me who feels by "feeling" loses its constituting spontaneity (I, ego) only in order to regain receptivity vis-à-vis the manifestation of what shows itself ("me," "to whom/which"). The receiver, who alone is put in the situation of feeling and impassioned affection, suffers the very flesh of the phenomenon in a state of manifestation. Counter to metaphysics, it must be said that "feeling" does not result from the "thing" as its effect, does not double it as its appearance, but that it shows it as its one and only possible apparition—it manifests it like a public demonstration makes manifest, by attesting and imposing. The receiver therefore does not only receive what gives itself—it allows the given to show itself insofar as it gives itself. The piece of wax shows itself only to the "feelings" of the receiver and is hidden from the gaze, which reconstitutes it according to order and measure. Phenomenality is not grasped; it is received.

To receive, for the receiver, therefore means nothing less than to accomplish givenness by transforming it into manifestation, by according what gives itself that it show itself on its own basis. It goes without saying that this receptivity cannot be defined within the framework of a trivial opposition between passivity and activity, since it is privileged to mediate them. This mediation lets us specify two essential characteristics of the receiver. (a) The receiver, in and through the receptivity of "feeling," transforms givenness into manifestation, or more exactly, he lets what gives itself through intuition show itself. In receiving what gives itself, he in turn gives it to show itself—he gives it form, its first form. Beyond activity and passivity, reception gives form to what gives itself without yet showing itself. The receiver is therefore put forward as a filter or prism, which brings about that the first visibility arises, precisely because it does not claim to produce it (as would, if it could be admitted, a schema without synthesis) but submits to it without interfering or causing a disturbance. This filter thus defines a function: manifesting what presents (gives) itself, but which must still be introduced into the presence of the world (show itself). It's not surprising that this function should characterize the consciousness-pole (or whatever one would like to call it) in that it manages the phenomenological opening where the given must show itself. But this characteristic function also lets us finally remove the ambiguity that has until now haunted the "to whom/which." To be sure, any "to whom/which" will be enough to welcome what gives itself, but only a "to whom" (and never a "to which") can assume the full role of receiver—presenting what gives itself in such a way that it shows itself in the world. For this presentation implies reception in "feeling," and it aims precisely at showing for thought, manifesting for a consciousness, forming for vision what, otherwise, would give itself to the blind. Therefore the receiver who presents and renders visible should see. He is in play like vision, exerts an aim, exposes a face, which one will have to look in the face as a personal other. He must therefore also say the "I" that says it all.[24] (b) The receiver does not precede what it forms by means of its prism—it results from it. The filter is deployed first as a screen. Before the not yet phenomenalized given gives itself, no filter awaits it. Only the impact of what gives itself brings about the arising, with one and the same shock, of the flash with which its first visibility bursts and the very screen on which it crashes. Thought arises from pre-phenomenal indistinctness, like a transparent screen is colored by the impact of a ray of light heretofore uncolored in the translucent ether that suddenly explodes on it. It is itself received in the exact instant when it receives what gives itself in order to, thanks to its own reception, finally show itself. The thought of the consciousness-pole is born with the manifestation that it renders visible without knowing or wanting it, and perhaps without even being able to do so. Consequently, it is "nothing more than the feeling of an existence [Dasein] without the slightest concept,"[25] indissociable from the "feeling" wherein the given shows itself that it accedes incidentally to itself, and this concerns neither knowledge of an object nor a subjective impression, since the originarily receptive thought here plays on this side of the distinction between the phenomenon and the in-itself: "[This proposition] the 'I think' expresses an indeterminate empirical intuition. . . . An indeterminate perception here signifies only something real that is given, given indeed to thought in general, and so, not as appearance, nor as thing in itself (*noumenon*) but as something which actually exists and which in the proposition 'I think' is denoted as such."[26] This actual existence is not represented but undergone by feeling prior to squaring the circle of the constituted phenomenality (noumena, phenomena, objects, etc.) instituted by the phenomenality that givenness claims. The receiver answers for what shows itself because he answers to what is given—first by receiving itself from it.

If the receiver is determined as a thought that transforms the given into the manifest and is received from what it receives—in short, if it is born from the very arising of the phenomenon inasmuch as given, that is to say, from a given exerting the mere impact of its event—what will happen when a phenomenon given as saturated arises? The impact will be radicalized into a *call*, and the receiver into *the gifted*.

The Call

Reference to the call has sometimes been troubling. Here, however, it is nothing less than obvious and almost inevitable; and besides, some arguments testify to it. (a) As has been shown elsewhere, Heidegger was finally obliged to thematize the ontically ontological character of Dasein, once the ontological difference had been rendered problematic, by direct reference to Being. To describe this reference, he supposed that Being itself could exert a claim (*Anspruch des Seins*) over the one who, as "man" and more than Dasein, then assumed the title "claimed [*Angesprochene*]." Now, as has also been shown, the phenomenality of the call could not be described directly in terms of the "question of Being," which is not necessarily implied by it, indeed is ignorant of it; and for that matter, how could the call belong to the "question of Being" or the ontological difference, seeing as it comes up precisely for the sake of relaying or at least buttressing them? The call and the claim therefore have their own singular and irreducible phenomenological figure, one that demands being described for itself, that is to say, without having to accept a series of authorities (Being, "the Father," the Other, etc.), from which different doctrines would have leased it.[27] That being the case, the call as such, without any other identification of origin (see §29), suffices to provoke the *interloqué*,[28] hence the gifted. Let us consider this point established. (b) What we understand by call comes out of the reversal of intentionality, which is perhaps an essential characteristic of intentionality itself. Hence, Levinas has, in an exemplary fashion, opposed to intentionality—which arises from the I in order to aim at and posit an object—"an inversion of intentionality," "the contrary of intentionality," in short, "counterconsciousness, reversing consciousness,"[29] thematized under the heading counter-intentionality. In his work, it is first a question of "responsibility for the Other, going against in-tentionality."[30] In effect, the face of the Other benefits from a formidable property: if I can aim at it intentionally and inscribe it like other objects within a common horizon whose center I remain (in this way, the portraits painted by Cézanne or Picasso close men's faces by leading them back to mineral or animal nature), I should also and especially undergo the counter-aim that he addresses to me silently, but more clearly than in a cry. For, as face, he faces me, imposes on me to face up to him as he for whom I must respond. But if I must respond for him, I must also respond to him. I have therefore received (and suffered) a call [*un appel*]. The face makes an ap-peal [*un appel*]; it therefore calls me forth as gifted. But having reached this point, we can no longer dodge a question: isn't the call Levinas recognizes in the Other just as much exhausted therein as the call Heidegger assigns to Being is confined to it? For that matter, didn't Husserl himself already describe counter-intentionalities, therefore sketches of the call apropos of neither ethical nor ontological phenomena?[31] Wouldn't it therefore be ap-propriate to disconnect once and for all the figure of the call (therefore of the receiver and the gifted) from its successive uses? (c) The call in fact characterizes every saturated phenomenon as such. That is, we have seen that the saturated phenomenon is characterized as such by the excess of in-tuition in it, which subverts and therefore precedes every intention that it exceeds and decenters. The visibility of the appearing now arises against the flow of the intention—following a para-dox, a counter-appearance, a visibility counter to the aim.[32] And in fact, each type of saturated phenom-enon (or paradox) inverts intentionality, therefore makes a call possible, indeed inevitable. (i) The event, unforeseeable according and counter to quantity, comes to pass by passing over the I, which yields to an infinite hermeneutic and lets itself be encompassed by it. (ii) The idol, unbearable according and counter to quality, stops and returns intentionality by filling it with its first visible, in such a way that I find *myself* summoned to see it (as with the painting), more than aiming at a visible. (iii) The flesh, abso-lute according and counter to relation, is enacted as an auto-affection; it therefore saturates all intentional ecstasy and aim at an object by the I. (iv) As for the icon, irregardable according and counter to modality, and which inverts the gaze gazing at a gaze gazed upon by the Other, we have already seen that it accomplishes counter-intentionality par excellence. It is there-fore the saturated phenomenon as such that inverts intentionality and sub-mits the receiver to the presence of the call.

The Gifted

Thus is born the gifted, whom the call makes the successor to the "subject," as what receives itself entirely from what it receives. The call institutes the gifted phenomenologically in terms of the four characteristics of its own manifestation. (a) *Summons*: The interloqué suffers a call so powerful and compelling that he must surrender [*s'y rendre*] to it, in the double sense of the French *s'y rendre*: being displaced and submitting to it. Thus he must renounce the autarchy of self-positing and self-actualizing. It is insofar as altered by originary hearing that he acknowledges himself possibly identified. The pure and simple shock (*Anstoss*) of the summons identifies the I only by transforming it without delay into a *me* "*to whom.*" The passage from the nominative to the objective cases (accusative, dative) thus inverts the hierarchy of the metaphysical categories. Individualized essence (*ousia prōtē*) no longer precedes relation (*pros ti*) and no longer excludes it from its ontic perfection. In contrast, relation here precedes individuality. And again: individuality loses its autarchic essence on account of a relation that is not only more originary than it, but above all half unknown, seeing as it can fix one of the two poles—*me*—without at first and most of the time delivering the other, the origin of the call (for the call can be exercised without coming into evidence). Individual essence thus undergoes a twofold relativization: resulting from a relation and from a relation of unknown origin. Whence a primordial paradox: in and through the summons, the gifted is identified, but this identification escapes him straightaway since he receives it without necessarily knowing it. He therefore receives himself from what he thinks neither clearly nor distinctly; he is, despite the failure in him of the "I think (myself)." Subjectivity or subjectness is submitted to an originally altered, called identity. (b) *Surprise*: The interloqué, resulting from a summons, is taken and overwhelmed (taken over or surprised) by a seizure. But this seizure determines him all the more radically as it remains (or can remain) of indeterminate origin. The call surprises by seizing the gifted without always teaching him what it might be. It reduces him to merely watching for, freezes him in place, puts him in immobile availability for what might not finally come or indeed ever begin. The gifted gives all his attention to an essentially lacking object; he is open to an empty gap. Such a gap, imposed on the *self/me* without giving him knowledge of it, therefore contradicts all ecstasy of knowledge, by which the transcendental I constituted, in front of itself and in an on principle transparent evidence, the object. Surprise, this obscure and suffered seizure, contradicts intentionality, this known and knowing ecstasy deployed by the I at its own initiative. Far from surveying with its gaze the pure land of the objectivity to be known, the I transformed into a *self/me* is overwhelmed by the unknowable claim. The inversion of the overwhelming (*sur*-prise) is but one with the disqualification of objectifying comprehension (sur-*prise*). Both are confused in the same loss of knowledge, in the double sense of losing all original self-knowledge and being powerless to grasp the original pole of the claim as an object. Descartes can here serve as a guide, thanks to his definition of wonder: "When our *first* encounter with some object *surprises* us and we find it novel, or very different from what we formerly knew or from what we supposed it ought to be, *this causes us* to wonder and to be astonished at it. Since all this may happen *before we know whether or not* the object is beneficial to us, I regard wonder as the first of all the passions."[33] This rapprochement has its limits, however. The surprise of wonder is for Descartes still a first passion of the ego, therefore of the "subject." I am describing here a more originary affection, which precedes the metaphysical subjectivity/ness. Even if the latter could still proceed from it, surprise would leave it destitute of its privilege of metaphysical ground, since it puts into operation the originary a posteriori of the last principle (§1). (c) *Interlocution*: By no means is it a question of a dialogical situation in which two speakers converse with one another in an equal relation, but of the unequal situation in which I find myself *interloqué*, that is to say called, indeed assailed as the "unto whom" of an addressed word. It is no longer a case of understanding oneself in the nominative case (intending the object—Husserl), nor in the genitive (of Being—Heidegger), nor even in the accusative (accused by the Other—Levinas), but in terms of the dative: I receive *my self* from the call that gives me to myself before giving me anything whatsoever. It is almost necessary to suppose that this strange dative is no longer distinguished from the ablative, since the *myself/me* makes possible (as worker, means), as first gift allocated by the call, the opening for the givennesses of all other particular givens. Receiving himself from the call that summons him, the gifted is therefore open to an alterity, from which the Other can be lacking, but who thus appears all the more. As surprise opens even onto the unknown or failing object, interlocution opens onto the indeterminate or anonymous Other. Thus the gifted is delivered straightaway—with its birth —from solipsism.

Undeniable Facticity

There remains (d) *facticity*: The interloqué endures the call and its claim as an always already given fact. This given fact of the call (§15) leads into the undeniable facticity of the interloqué. For not one of us mortals has ever lived, if only for an instant, without having received a call and being discovered interloqué by it. Or, what this amounts to, strictly speaking: never has a mortal lived, be it only for an instant, without discovering himself preceded by a call already there. The paradigm for this irreparable facticity resides in the fact, always already completed, of the word itself: for every mortal, the first word was always already heard before he could utter it. To speak always and first amounts to passively hearing a word coming from the Other, a word first and always incomprehensible, which announces no meaning or signification, other than the very alterity of the initiative, by which the pure fact gives (itself) (to be thought) for the first time. Not only is the first word never said by the I, which can only undergo it by receiving it; not only does it not give us any objective or rational knowledge; but it opens only onto this very fact that some gift happens to *me* because it precedes *me* originarily in such a way that I must recognize that I proceed from it. Man deserves the title mortal (or, what is equivalent, animal) endowed with speech on condition that we understand "endowed with speech" in the strictest sense: having received the gift of speech, therefore, in phenomenological rigor, endowed by the gift of the heard word, heard insofar as given. Whence a decisive paradox: the call gives *me* to and as *myself*, in short, individualizes me, because it separates me from all property or possession of the proper by giving it to me and letting this proper anticipate its reception by me and as me. It is not necessary to say only that the call, in and through its facticity, imposes authenticity as the original (or rather originally nonoriginal) posture of the *myself/me*. Above all it must be admitted that the facticity of the call renders the called's access to itself as a *myself/me* (therefore its selfhood) equal to its originary difference with itself as an I, therefore its inauthenticity. The originary and irreducible posture of the *myself/me*—its selfhood—is thus accomplished in inauthenticity, originally nonoriginary. Authenticity hides the fact of the call—the fact that the call alone always already gives (me) (as) to myself. The call, and not the I, decides *myself/me* before myself—the I is only insofar as the call has always already claimed and therefore given to itself something like a *myself/me*. Authenticity dissimulates after the fact the inauthenticity that alone is originarily giving.

The result of this is the birth of the gifted, a subjectivity or subjectness entirely in conformity with givenness—one that is entirely received from what it receives, given by the given, given to the given.

A new paradox also results from this: the call can be neither negated nor denied since all who would pretend to impugn it must first admit that they come from it. That is, before knowing an object (surprise), before seeing the Other (interlocution), I always find myself already transformed into a *me* under the impact of the call (summons). Accordingly, my sole individuation or selfhood is found only in the facticity imposed on me by the word originally heard from the call, not pronounced by *myself.* To deny the call thus amounts to confirming it twice: first by recognizing that one must respond to it, therefore that it in fact precedes; next by refusing, with each response, the word that it said and that we could never pretend to recuse, if we hadn't already, in fact, heard it. The call, by definition undeniable, therefore accomplishes the privilege of givenness (§15) without remainder or loss. The gifted receives himself as the call that he receives is given—undeniably.

§27 TWO CALLS IN METAPHYSICS

Descartes—the Ego Cogitatum

That the call is given undeniably, that it cannot be denied, that no instance ever precedes it, aren't these theses that—by hypothesis—metaphysics should undermine? If it is defined, actually and as it should be, by the precedence of a formal a priori to experience, one that delimits its conditions from the outset, doesn't it disqualify the call's claim to exercise primacy? In fact, metaphysically, it goes like this: the a priori principle of analytic judgments boils down to the principle of identity, for which the equality $A=A$ culminates in the equality $I=I$, while the principle of synthetic judgments (that the conditions for the possibility of objects of experience are reducible to the conditions for the possibility of experience, therefore to the "subject" itself) is accomplished in the equality of the I and the "I think." However, it could be that, even in the privileged moments when it installs the finite subjectivity that is in principle an a priori of experience, metaphysics itself does not succeed in reaching its goal and thus confirms, despite its declared intention, the unconditional anteriority of the undeniable call. Or rather, it could be that metaphysics, even when it is accomplished as such by grounding (itself) (as) an "I think," still attests, by masking it, the more originary instance of the call; for, alone undeniable and unconditioned, the call arises even there where it should disappear. At least that is what I will try to demonstrate regarding the two things that metaphysics could suppose to be most demonstrative of the priority of the "I think" (or the *I=I*): the ego established by Descartes and the I established by Kant. In these two cases, where the a priori characteristic of metaphysics is exercised in an exemplary fashion, the ego and the I are nevertheless discovered to be instituted a posteriori by two anterior instances (respectively, what deceives me and respect), which suffice to overdetermine them as gifteds defined by the call (either as persuaded, or as considered with respect).

Descartes established the ego in 1644 as existing in terms of the tautological identity "Repugnat enim, ut putemus id quod cogitat, eo ipso tempore quo cogitat, non existere [It is a contradiction to suppose that what thinks does not, at the very time when it is thinking, exist]"—in accordance with the principle of contradiction (of analytic judgments); in 1637, he established the ego as existing with the status of a "substance whose whole essence or nature is simply to think"—in accordance with the transcendental authority (of synthetic judgments).[34] But these formulations, which conform strictly to the metaphysical (therefore Kantian) sense of the "subject," do not correspond to the demonstration of the ego's existence that is ushered in by the *Meditationes* in 1641.[35] In this unique but indisputably normative text, Descartes does not use the classic formulation "Ego cogito, ergo sum" (at least not for the main interpretation). He instead prefers another formulation, one that omits the thought of self by the self (of the type "Cogito me cogitare")[36] in favor of the redoubled affirmation of existence: "Denique statuendum sit hoc pronuntiatum, *ego sum, ego existo*, quoties a me profertur, vel mente concipitur, necessario ese verum [I must finally conclude that this proposition, *I am, I exist*, is necessarily true whenever it is put forward by me or conceived in my mind]."[37] Where has the thought that thinks itself in such a way as to gain its own existence disappeared to? This question can receive a quick and apparently (indeed, to a certain extent, really) exact response: the *cogitatio* does not intervene in this utterance precisely because it thinks it, accomplishes it, in short performs it (in the figure of the "a me profertur, vel mente concipitur") according to the act ("pronuntiatum") and temporality ("quoties") characteristic of the performative.[38] Actor of existence, the *cogitatio* would not be enacted as a premise, nor even as a previous utterance; thought—even thought of self—does not think *itself* as thought thought, but as thought thinking. It does not show itself since it does itself. Even when this thesis is admitted, however, shouldn't we object that the performative of my existence in the act of my thought perfectly achieves—and even better than a thought of the self by the self—the originary equality *I=I*? As a result, by emancipating it from the constraints of representation, the performative interpretation of the *cogito* would strengthen the metaphysical tautology all the more.

Now, it is precisely this interpretation that is invalidated by the reasoning of *Meditatio II*, such that we nevertheless arrive at the performance of the *ego*. To see this, we have only to follow the thread of the demonstration in its four moments. (a) A first passage[39] tries to contest the conclusion of the previous arguments, claiming one can know nothing with certainty. It asks if, in addition to the uncertainties already counted, there might not be "something else [*aliquid diversum*]." Since this cannot be one of the bodies cast into doubt, it could be an other, even an Other, "a God or whatever I may call him [*aliquis Deus, vel quocumque nomine illum vocem*]." In this way, even before the ego appears, there arises another instance, an other a priori, indeed an Other that is all the more irreducible as he does not need existence or even essence ("some deceiver, I know not what, *deceptor nescio quis*")[40] to precede the ego and its self-performance itself. From this hypothesis—that of an originary alterity—an inevitable consequence follows: this other would certainly secure my existence, but at the same time, it would render it necessarily derivative. We thus understand why, logically enough but strangely, Descartes tries at first to escape such an existence, one that is certain but secondary, by evoking the counter-hypothesis that these thoughts put in my mind ("*mihi ipsas cogitationes immittit*") by the still-anonymous other could have I myself as their unique "*author*, capable of producing them myself." For this primary debate about primacy bears not on my existence but on the priority that the ego disputes in thought with I know not whom, before all existence (since neither myself nor this Other yet exist): Am I in and through myself thinking me, or does an other think me before I do by sending me my first thoughts from the outside? Whence a counter-hypothesis, one that is strange because it seems to mobilize a sort of unconsciousness: I could produce my first thoughts even without being conscious of them. But this counter-argument immediately implies that I can think without depending on what I had until now considered the sole thinkable reality—the bodies (or material simple natures). Could I therefore imagine, within hyperbolic doubt, another object of thought, this time nonmaterial, but pure thought? (b) The second passage[41] is based precisely on the ignorance in which the ego finds itself regarding the reality of whatever might be outside itself (including "*nullas mentes,* no minds" that *Meditatio I* did not include in the hyperbolic doubt limited to the material simple natures); for if this ignorance, justified or not, forbids me from imagining bodies that transcend me, and therefore convinces me of inexistence, it should have for its other consequence, at the very least, that "I am myself persuaded, *mihi persuasi.*" If *I* am *myself* persuaded of it, then this persuasion, even without true content, is secured on its own; it therefore ensures me of myself in the figure of an ego become *mihi,* as an act that produces itself simply because it pairs the uncertain (because without certain object) subject with a certain (because he receives a certain persuasion, even without certain object) receiver. Strange situation, where I persuade myself of nothing true, therefore where there is no objective performative—but where I nevertheless accomplish an act (void of object) inasmuch as *I* persuade *myself.* This performative remains inverted, as it were, since it bears on an ignorance or uncertainty of content—I am inasmuch as I don't know whether what I give myself to think is true or false. And since this quasi performative rests on the indeterminacy of its content, it forbids me from positing myself in the posture of a certain and originary "subject." Me too, I am by deficiency inasmuch as I persuade myself of what I do not know, for example of my possible nonexistence ("nonne igitur etiam me non esse"). I am inasmuch as I persuade myself that I am myself persuaded of something or other, even of my uncertain nonexistence.

Consequently (c) the third passage[42] makes this deficiency explicit by deploying the failure of the "I am myself persuaded" to the point of the ego's clear dependence on some anonymous instance that assures it its existence: "There is therefore no doubt but that I am [*also*], if he is deceiving me, *haud dubie igitur ego etiam sum, si me fallit.*" I am, not first because I think myself (according to the identity formula *ego cogito, ergo sum*), but because an other (or an Other, I don't yet know) intervenes first (since I am only "also, *etiam*") in order to deceive me, that is to say, to persuade me that I am myself deceived, since he is deceiving me. In short, I am because he thinks me by deceiving me. I am, to be sure, but I am only after and according to the thought that is addressed to me, that possibly assails me by deceiving me with its hostile address. I am inasmuch as originarily thought by an other thought, one that always already thinks me, even if I cannot yet identify its essence or demonstrate its existence. I am already a *res cogitans,* but as a thought that an other thinks, a thought thinking thought by another thought thinking—*res cogitans cogitata.* The certain ego, as first truth, is therefore not a first authority—not so much because it would depend on the supposed "veracity" of the existing God (here it is a question of neither one nor the other), but because it results from its originary interlocution by what deceives it, persuades it, and therefore thinks it. The first thought of the ego in effect bears neither on an object (certain or false) nor on myself, but on the thought in and through which an other (indeed an Other) thinks it (persuades it or deceives it). The ego is therefore instituted as originarily a posteriori. (d) To be sure, it can even, in the fourth passage,[43] lay claim to assuming directly the role of what thinks it ("every time that I utter it or that I conceive it in my mind, *quoties a me profertur, vel mente concipitur*"), but it will not in this way abolish the divide between self and originary thought. In contrast, it renders the divide still more manifest by marking the essential absence of actual thought thinking from the statement of merely thought thought, *ego sum, ego existo,* now void of origin.[44] The ego thinks itself, but after the fact. At the origin, it finds itself persuaded and deceived by another *cogitatio,* which weighs on it by persuading it or deceiving it—"ego eram, si quid mihi persuasi," "ego etiam sum, si me fallit." That eventually it should perform this itself (self-persuasion), without a real Other (a *deceptor nescio quis*), changes nothing. The first *cogitatio* happens to the ego as what thinks it, not as what it thinks. It is named *res cogitans* only first as *cogitata.* Or, to use Descartes's own words, the ego should first acknowledge itself persuaded before exercising its own persuasion over others: "Ego persuasus sum, alios *etiam* possim persuadere."[45] The ego thought, insofar as thinking, reaches its first existence on the basis of a call that persuades it, *ego persuasus.*

Confirmations

However original this formulation might be, it finds at least three noticeable confirmations. (a) *Meditatio II,* which first used it to prove the existence of the ego, takes it up again to establish its essence. The determination of the ego's essence remains problematic since it derives from the *ego persuasus.* To successfully identify it as *res cogitans,*[46] it is wise to proceed step by step. (i) Defining it as a "rational animal" is not appropriate because it supposes we know the meanings of the two terms composing this definition, which doubt forbids. (ii) The Aristotelian definitions in terms of the properties of the *psukhē*—to feed, to move, indeed to feel (itself), vegetable, mobile, and sensitive soul—are not appropriate since they can be reduced; the ego can be without them. (iii) The *cogitatio* remains, alone indispensable since without it I would totally cease to be. Whence the second occurrence of the proper formulation in 1641: "Haec sola a me divelli nequit. Ego sum, ego existo; certum est [This alone is inseparable from me. I am, I exist. This is certain]." In this sense, I am inasmuch as I am thinking: "Sum igitur praecise tantum res cogitans [I am then in the strict sense only a thinking thing]." It should not be objected that here the *res cogitans* is instituted in thought as if in a tautologically possessed property, equivalent to the "I think" of an I=I. In effect, the thinking ego is certain only on a restrictive temporal condition. I am only "as long as, *quamdiu,*" I am thinking.[47] There is nothing trivial about this temporal condition; it indicates that even the ego, the first certain knowledge and ground of all others, is not confused with temporality, therefore does not exercise it in the role of transcendental principle as the condition of possibility for the other phenomena; rather, the ego submits to it—it is inscribed in it, depends on it. It too is temporalized, not as mere "empirical self," but already insofar as the very principle of experience. Thus it admits the essential facticity that the call imposes on what it provokes. Thought, the essential property (attribute) of the ego *in actu*, arises as a fact and an event that produces *itself* of itself—that produces me more than (or at least as much as) I produce it. My *cogitationes* come upon me; I fall over and into them: "priusquam in has cogitationes incidissem [before I fell into these (doubting) thoughts]," "dubiis, in quae . . . incidi [all the doubts into which I have fallen]," "quamvis non necesse sit ut incidam unquam in ullam de Deo cogitationem [though it may not be necessary that I ever fall into any thought of God]."[48] The ego, inasmuch as *persuasus,* does not produce all its thoughts—those of doubt, itself, and God come upon it, determine it, and so to speak, think it by permitting it to think itself as *res cogitans cogitata.*

Two other confirmations appear in *Meditatio III.* (b) First, the sequence that repeats the existence of the ego within the framework of the thematization of the "general rule" of truth: "When I turn toward the things themselves which I think I conceive very clearly, I am so persuaded by them that of my own I declare: let whoever can do so deceive me, he will never bring it about that I am nothing, so long as I continue to think I am something [*Fallat me quisquis potest, numquam tamen efficiet ut nihil sim, quamdiu aliquid esse cogitabo*]."[49] What is remarkable here is the juxtaposition of the two formulations Descartes uses. As in the scholarly writings (*The Discourse* and *Principles*), we rediscover the thought of self—"I think myself to be something [*aliquid esse cogitabo*]"—where nothing precedes or relativizes thinking thought. But as in *Meditatio II*, this exoteric and simplified formulation is preceded by the originary interlocution: "let whoever can do so deceive me [*fallat me quisquis potest*]." The ego thus appears first in the objective case (*me*, me), submitted to what deceives it and therefore thinks it first; the ego is thought by its deceiver insofar as it gives itself to it as thinking it originarily. Of all these thoughts, the first that happens to me, "*mihi occurrit*—presents itself to me," is not the thought of my thought, but the "*praeconcepta de summa Dei potentia opinio*—preconceived belief in the supreme power of God."[50] The repetition of my existence is accomplished in and through resistance, therefore in response to the first thought—that of an Other whose omnipotence would perhaps deceive me and therefore think me first. (c) The conclusion of *Meditatio III* reproduces this arrangement, but it substitutes for the preconceived opinion of an anonymous and hypothetical deceiver the true idea of an omnipotent, infinite, and incomprehensible God who obviously is not deceiving. The thinking and thought thought of myself always remains a response to the originarily thinking thought of the infinite over me, no longer in the mode of conflict, but in that of image and likeness. The exercise of the "I think" finally takes place within the infinite horizon of thought such as it is opened and secured by God alone. *Horizon* here means that the ego accomplishing its own (finite) existence amounts to it recognizing the anteriority of the infinite existence and thought that makes it possible. In other words: "I perceive that likeness, which includes the idea of God, by the same faculty with which I perceive myself"; the Latin emphasizes this paradox even more: "Illamque similitudinem, in qua idea Dei continetur, a me percipi per eandem facultatem, per quam ego ipse a me percipior." This should be understood as follows: the "faculty" with which I perceive myself—that is to say, the classic way of formulating the notion that my existence results from the thought of myself by myself, for which the Latin has no fear of an almost incorrect redundancy of egoness (*ego ipse a me*) and the French even dares to introduce a "réflexion sur soi"—is also equivalent to, at once and "at the same time—*simul etiam*," the knowledge of the idea of God. The convertibility of each to the other operation in one sole faculty rests on a presupposition that is evident for Descartes: the positive infinity of God is immediately conceived in contrast to the created's consciousness of its finitude, in this case the ego who doubts: "I also understand at the same time [*simul etiam*] that he on whom I depend has within him all those greater things (to which I aspire)."

In discovering itself to be "an imperfect, incomplete thing dependant on an Other—*rem incompletam et ab alio dependentem*," the ego not only repeats the perception *a contrario* of its existence in thinking doubt (if he deceives me, I am); it grounds this perception in its own dependence on and aspiration toward the infinite that thinks it (if I am finite, he is therefore infinite, there is therefore an infinite). This is to say that the ego recognizes its existence only at the heart of an interlocutionary plot, in response to the originary call come this time not from a "nescio quis" deceiver, but a "revera Deus" "subject to no defects whatsoever."[51] The single "faculty" lays bare not only the hierarchy of two beings, nor even just the transcendental function of the infinite horizon in the perception of the finite; it fully brings to light the originary model of the call and response—the call is attested in the first thinker thinking (the infinite interlocutor); the response is carried out with the finite, first existent thinking, to be sure, but especially, first of all *thought*, because at the outset interloqué.

Kant—the Decentering

Kant's determination of the transcendental I was and still is, even in its aporias (§26), the counter-model of the gifted. But perhaps this does not exhaust all that Kant contributed to elaborating what comes after the "subject." For when pure (theoretical) reason becomes (pure) practical reason, when the noumenon becomes the rule and the sensible constitution of the object disappears, the I itself veers off. Its theoretic schizophrenia (split between "empirical self" and transcendental I) gives way in favor of another opposition, one susceptible of resolution. To reach the status of a free actor, that is to say, of an actor acting according to pure reason in the role of noumenal intelligence, the I must be rid of every act determined by sensibility; that is to say, it must be free of its condition as one phenomenon among all other phenomena, therefore of its determination by empirical inclinations. But according to Kant, these "inclinations taken together . . . constitute the egoism, *Selbstsucht.*" Kant assimilates this "self-regard" to "solipsism [*Solipsismus*]" in general, and to "benevolence toward one's self [*philautia*]" or "self-love [*Eigenliebe*]" in particular. What are we to understand by such a solipsism? No doubt a moral attitude that consists in loving only oneself or at least first of all one's self, with all the "injustice" Pascal denounced in it; but this moral ramification would not be possible without a more radical determination of the "subject" such as to permit an (in principle perfect) return of the self to the self. This presupposes the possibility of the equality I = I, precisely what we had previously thematized as the aporia of solipsism.[52] In this way, Kant tries to contest, using the term solipsism, the metaphysical figure of the I and not only its moral (or immoral) avatar, egotism. The line of argument that he deploys will therefore reach its particular goal (defining the freedom of the moral agent) only by contesting from the ground up the theoretical definition of the I in general. He contests it, or better, "demolishes" it: "Pure practical reason simply demolishes [*tut Abbruch*] self-love [love of self by the self, *Eigenliebe*]."[53] What is meant by such a crumbling or clearing away, such a demolition (*Abbruch*)? No doubt, what will later be called a destruction—or the deconstruction of a conceptual figure so as to let another, more originary and more fecund, appear: destroying subjectivity as self-love for oneself, therefore the equality of self to self and finally the identity I = I accomplished in the "I think (myself)," and undertaking this destruction with a view toward laying bare a "subject" that is morally free because acting solely in accordance with pure (practical) reason; however, this freedom implies that he be directly determined by it (noumenally) and not by sensible and pathological (phenomenological) inclinations. Here arises the greatest difficulty: how can the I not return (pathologically) to itself, not love itself according to the model of its thought of itself? And inversely, how can it ex-center itself in the direction of the moral law and its noumenal universality? In short, how can the I not amount to I = I? Kant claims to secure this decentering by recourse to the feeling inspired by the moral law, a feeling that offers the subjective side, but without anything pathological—namely, the feeling of respect. That is, "respect for the law is not the incentive to morality; it is morality itself regarded subjectively as an incentive, inasmuch as pure practical reason, by rejecting all the rival claims of self-love, that gives authority and absolute sovereignty to the law."[54] Hence, respect appears as the essential argument permitting the self-equality of the I to be subverted in view of reaching a "subject" always already preceded by what renders it free (here, the moral law).

Respect

I will therefore follow the guiding thread of respect in order to reconstitute a Kantian anticipation of the gifted. (a) Respect has the status of a feeling, but a feeling that is strangely "known a priori," "not of empirical origin . . . and known a priori."[55] This is not a contradiction in terms; for if all other feelings come a posteriori, they owe it to their double empirical dependence—toward the "self" (therefore the I) who is affected by them and toward the flux of phenomena that cause them. And this dependence reinforces the transcendental dignity of the a priori conditions of experience (forms of intuition, categories of understanding). By contrast, respect does not intervene in the course of experience, as the effect of a phenomenon acting on a "subject" by means of its sensibility, but as the effect on the I's sensibility of the moral law itself, that is to say, the effect of a nonsensible cause, of a pure noumenon. Respect does not cause the law; rather, the law, in actually positing itself for the I, causes a feeling without phenomenal origin, without sensible requisite.[56] Respect is thus known a priori because it never comes from any phenomenon a posteriori, but solely from a noumenon, the categorical imperative, known par excellence a priori. This noumenon, in contrast to all the others and all the while remaining a priori, must first be able to have an effect on the I, then (and especially) make itself known. Kant satisfies these two requirements by postulating that we have a priori consciousness of the categorical imperative—in the double sense that we comprehend it (objectively) and respect it (subjectively). This postulation "may be called a fact of reason." But can a fact ever be enough to establish that we comprehended a noumenon and that it affects us? For that matter, can a fact intervene a priori? And even, has the fact of this facticity been well established? To these questions, Kant offers no response except the fact itself of facticity, which proves itself: "The fact just indicated is undeniable [*unleugbar*]."[57] Undeniable, like the call,[58] the categorical imperative is given as a fact of reason. That one cannot deny it is seen in the practical field: the very one who transgresses it grasps it perfectly and could not do so without this transgression. But the practical impossibility of its denial flows more essentially from its theoretical status: it shows itself perfectly a priori because it remains unscathed by the subjective conditions of experience and is given solely by its fact without having to become the object of any sensible intuition. Without any other condition besides itself, the fact of reason is not inscribed in the I's experience of the world, but precedes and exceeds it. Its a priori is therefore not confused with that put into operation by the I, which follows it and comes after it. In short, the I knows a priori the fact of reason, but nevertheless it discovers this fact always already done; the I never constitutes it. The I therefore receives it a posteriori. The fact of reason thus includes one of the radical determinations of the call and last principle—an a priori always already given, always a posteriori.

There follows (b) another character of respect. It consists precisely in stripping the I of its position as transcendental a priori and relativizing the self-identity that secures it its definition as an "I think (myself)." This happens by affecting it counter to itself. Respect affects, but this "strange feeling" affects only negatively; for the "negative effect on feeling (through the check on the inclinations) is itself feeling."[59] Without origin in the world or pathological content, it could not affect positively; it therefore negatively affects the consciousness by "humbling" it before the law that it receives as an incommensurable a priori: "The moral law inevitably humbles [*demütigt*] every man when he compares the sensuous propensity of his nature with the law." To humble (*demütigen*) is equivalent to undoing the spirit (*Gemüt*), deconstructing the "subject" equal to itself, rendering it impossible for it to say "I think (myself)" and to believe itself found, grounded. No doubt, in order to limit the radicality of this violence, one can immediately add that this representation "humiliates us in our self-consciousness, it awakens respect for itself so far as it is positive and the ground of determination. The moral law, therefore, is even subjectively a cause of respect."[60] It could thus be imagined that humiliation and respect go together like two sides of the same coin, emitted into the sensible by the one and only authority of the fact of the moral law; but their balance remains unstable, first because the moral law most often inspires the humiliation of not being able to enact it, then because respect itself adds next to nothing to the humiliation—I respect the moral law all the more as I know that I am not able, or don't want, or cannot want to accomplish it. Duty itself is always announced as a "duty contrary to my self," which diverts me from my essence itself.[61] For, to face up to respect, that is to say, to face up to a feeling without *pathos*, a direct effect of the facticity of practical reason, requires interrupting the self's self-inspection (*inspectio mentis*), to look at oneself from on high (*despicere*), by taking the noumenal point of view of myself, therefore to undo the I's transcendental reign over the objects of experience in order to experience only pure reason as practical. Thus, what remains of the "subject" in the situation of respect, before—in fact after—the fait accompli of the a priori a posteriori, clearly corresponds to what I was thematizing as the surprise (before the radical a posteriori) of the interloqué (exiled from his solipsism) by a summons. Kant does not hesitate to subsume the entire mechanism opened by respect under the heading of a voice: "In the boundless esteem for the pure moral law, removed from all advantage, as practical reason presents it to us for obedience, whose voice [*Stimme*] makes even the boldest sinner tremble . . . , there is something so singular"—tremble at its voice, since in effect "the duty here is only to cultivate one's conscience, to sharpen one's attentiveness to the voice [*Stimme*] of the inner judge."[62] Silent and insensible, the "voice" of pure practical reason achieves the fait accompli of the call, for which the humility of respect describes the interlocution more precisely. Kant thus anticipates the fundamental traits of the gifted.

The "I think (myself)" is therefore not enough to describe the phenomenality of what can no longer be recognized as a "subject," but which is itself received from what gives itself. Even in situations as radically metaphysical as those of Kant or Descartes, when the call is operative (by the "nescio quis" or by the "fact of reason") for the purpose of appointing its *persona*, the I must disappear and clear the field for the gifted. No doubt I cannot reach this result without a bit of violence in my reading, but the violence consists only in taking seriously signals betraying the fact that, in two classic theories of the "subject," the I cannot be reduced to the "I think (myself)" or its own equality with itself, I=I. Before self-consciousness, it is an issue of the a posteriori fait accompli of the call given a priori, therefore also of the possible response to its surprise. Interloqué, the "subject" knows from the start that he will find himself only in what gives itself insofar as it gives itself to him. From this point forward, I must pass beyond the sketches that actual phenomenology and metaphysics have, despite themselves, traced in symptomatic form and describe directly the gifted as such, as he who is himself received from what gives itself.

§28 THE CALL AND THE RESPONSAL

The Call Shows Itself in the Response

Formally, I mean by the gifted a figure of what comes after the "subject," distinguished by three specifics. (i) The gifted is exposed not only to what shows itself insofar as it gives itself (the phenomenon in general), but more essentially to a paradox (the saturated phenomenon), from which he receives a call and an undeniable call. (ii) The gifted, thus letting the given arise unreservedly, receives it so radically (receiver) that in addition, he frees givenness as such. He is thus marked as the sole given in which the fold of givenness is unfolded. (iii) Fully offering himself to givenness, to the point that he delivers it as such, the gifted finally attains his ultimate determination—to receive himself by receiving the given unfolded by him according to givenness. Consequently, the gifted is defined entirely in terms of givenness because he is completely achieved as soon as he surrenders unconditionally to what gives itself—and first of all to the saturated phenomenon that calls him. The gifted is privileged to surrender to the evidence—in the double sense of bearing the burst of the given and of not denying the undeniable.

And yet, this formal definition is not enough, for it still leaves undetermined the point where the given is articulated (according to the fold of givenness) with the gifted, who receives it and receives himself in it. I have of course already identified this point of articulation: it is the call, already characterized as the undeniable par excellence. I have also sketched its essential traits: summons, surprise, interlocution, and facticity. What remains is to describe the call solely in terms of its origin—the paradox—and always in the encounter with its receiver—the gifted—who thus seems constrained to suffer its impact and record its fait accompli; if, in addition, the call assumes the fundamental phenomenological figure of counter-intentionality, it seems it must inevitably lead to two aporias. (i) How can it ever offer a precise significative aim, that is to say, an aim susceptible to an identifiable intuitive fulfillment, seeing as it can be carried out without presupposing any "consciousness" (indeed by excluding it) and by transgressing all objective character (§§21–23)? In short, won't the call thus defined remain definitively empty? (ii) As a result, how could an empty call be received, that is to say, make itself heard? And if it allows no real hearing, how will one ever be able to respond to it? In a word, if the call says nothing, the response will be lacking on principle. This double objection does not impose its evidence—the call does not have the phenomenological qualification that would permit describing the articulation of the gifted with the given—unless one admits the hidden presupposition, namely that the call precedes the response and is distinguished from it. Now, this presupposition must be contested.

Let me at first follow the clues laid down by a painting. Take the canvas in which Caravaggio tries to bring about the appearance of "the calling of Saint Matthew."[63] The difficulty confronted by the painter resides in the fact that he must show in silence a call that is invisible. He can only show, without making anything heard, by means of the only phenomenality available, that of the silence of the forms, colors, shadow and light. But he must use the phenomenality of the visible to make appear what belongs first to a phenomenality of the audible, a call that is officially invisible—and doubly invisible for that matter: first of all, like every call that does not appear first to the eye but to the ear; next, like a vocation or calling in the strict sense—a call that decides the choice of a spirit, a soul, a life, in short, of what is by definition nonvisible. The calling of Saint Matthew therefore signifies an invisible call (since to be heard, not seen) destined to an invisible (nonsensible) hearing. To paint *The Calling of St. Matthew* requires a double invisible to be rendered visible, without recourse to the sound that would render it manifest. Caravaggio thus confronts the only thing that is at stake in a painting worthy of the name: to render the invisible manifest. How does he succeed in doing this? Let us consider what is being staged in this painting: a ray of light traverses the space on a diagonal, designating the line where two beams of opposed gazes cross. In the upper right, in the shadows, a man with his back turned (Saint Peter, perhaps) follows the gaze and gesture of another, facing forward (Christ), whose almost hidden eyes and outstretched arm point toward the left, where a group seated around a table are busy counting coins—Matthew is levying the tax on a couple of people, surveyed by two witnesses. So far, Caravaggio has not yet shown the call, but rather, in the best case, the gesture of one man in the direction of another—strictly speaking, an attitude void of meaning, one that neither the spectator nor the opposite group have any reason to read, consider, or even see; in the best of cases, it could be a mere signal, a deictic that is imprecise and abstract (as they all are without an accompanying word), a signal that would concern Matthew no more than any of his other companions at the table (and why not the innkeeper, who could be imagined outside the frame). And yet, we only have to look for a minute at the phenomenon that Caravaggio has put into visibility to sense that Christ's gesture is not addressed generally to the indistinct group surrounding Matthew—where three out of five notice and even look at this outstretched arm—but rather to Matthew and Matthew alone, who sees in it *his* calling. By what do we see it—by what do we see that this gesture in fact exercises a call, that this call constitutes a calling and is therefore addressed to one alone, whom it identifies and who is recognizable by it? We see it—this call —appear in Matthew's gaze infinitely more than we do in Christ's gesture. For Matthew, who lifts his eyes from the table and turns away from the coins, does not perceive Christ so much as the gaze of Christ, which is intended for him. Not Christ as another spectacle to be seen, but Christ's gaze as a weight that weighs on his own gaze and holds it captive. Then—and here is the decisive moment—caught in the crossing of the gazes, Matthew, with his left hand, makes the merest suggestion of a gesture pointing to himself in silent response to the call, which is neither said nor heard, and asks or else announces: "Me?" What makes us see the calling, that is to say the doubly invisible call, does not come from a visible signal (in fact, always indistinct), but from the response itself. While around the table three (two cannot tear their attention from the coins) saw the signal, only Matthew read a call therein because he alone took it for himself—in the sense that a guest, a soldier, or a player says, each in his own way, "The next one's mine!" He alone asked himself, "This is mine? This is for me?"—thus he is at once given over as the "unto whom" of what gives itself and, with this very fact, notifies him of the call. If Matthew alone suffers the silent call of his calling, even though everyone indifferently could see its indistinct signal, this is because he alone answered it straightaway. Matthew received the call of his calling by taking it upon himself—and this taking it upon himself already constituted the first response. One could perhaps understand in this way the (at first glance redundant) function of the character (Saint Peter) who shadows Christ from behind: he would in fact respond to Matthew's response by confirming his silent question "Me?" with a second hand sign: "Yes, you!"—unless he is asking Christ to confirm that Matthew's first question ("Me?") indeed accomplishes the expected response ("Him?" "Yes, him!"). In this way, without breaking the silence of the painting, Caravaggio succeeds in making visible the in itself invisible call by choosing to construct not the indistinct phenomenon of a signal (the outstretched arm), but that of a mute and singular response (Matthew designating himself with his hand). This call is painted in this response: the painter's gaze saw (and now shows us) that the call gives itself phenomenologically only by first showing itself in a response. The response that gives itself after the call nevertheless is the first to show it.

The same result can be established according to the guiding thread of what I will call, for convenience's sake, intersubjectivity. (a) Let us consider the most ordinary situation: seduction. Take a conversation between two, professional, friendly, or simply boring; one speaks of everything, therefore of nothing and certainly not the two conversants; no call cuts across the dialogue about . . . transforming it into a dialogue of the one facing the other and for him. They each chat: it's not about him, or her. And yet, it could happen that, imperceptibly, the until now loose web of this conversation about some third or a neutral object is drawn tighter, without anyone saying anything about it; for this to occur, one has only to try by allusions, too well chosen examples, or false generalities, etc., to direct the conversation's center of gravity to the other himself. At one fell swoop, from partner to the discussion, this Other imperceptibly becomes also what's at stake in it. The call of the seduction thus begins. Nevertheless, this call remains as such null and does not happen as long as its target does not grasp or, more often, does not want to grasp what new game you are playing with him, what new role you would like to make him play. As long as this call remains (at least apparently) implicit, it will remain absolutely in vain, for it will never take place, so long as it has not been explicitly heard, recognized, admitted—so long as nothing will have happened. But what more is needed for "something to happen" or to have happened? First and almost uniquely, that the target of the proposition acknowledge having heard a call, that he admit that this call was indeed addressed to him, in short, that he assume unambiguously the role of he who knows himself subjected to a seduction—and therefore that he even silently utter this "Me?" which brings it about that "now, it is for me" and that it is necessary to decide if you want it or not.[64] But as long as the target is unaware, can stay unaware, or wants to believe himself unaware of the attempt whose object he has become, every seductive enterprise will be null and void and won't happen. For seduction, like the calling, stems from a call, therefore plays itself out by constituting it first in and through the response, which alone can attest it by rendering it, for the first time, audible and visible. To seduce consists first in getting the Other to admit not that I seduced him, but that I tried to seduce him and that he let me try it—this is the response ratifying the fact that a call was given. That this call then be received or not is less important, provided it was heard. (b) Since the vocation always happens as a seduction (though it might be regretted that the reciprocal is not so frequent), we can therefore analyze the vocation in the same terms as seduction. For example, the prophetic vocation of the young Samuel obeys the logic of seduction. Three times, "The Lord called Samuel, and Samuel responded, 'Here I am [*Me voici*].'" Each time, Samuel remains in the situation of a dialogue about some third term—he imagines an order that his master Eli would give him; he does not see and does not know that the "lord" who speaks to him does not speak to him about something or as an equal. Eli himself is therefore obliged to advise Samuel that the "lord" is here the "Lord" and that the only answer is this: "I hear." And Samuel responds to the fourth call of the Lord: "Speak, Lord, because your servant is listening to you." But then, not only must he hear and repeat to Eli the announcement of the punishment that the "Lord" will inflict on the latter, not only must he himself become a prophet ("the Lord was with him, and none of his words fell by the wayside")[65] instituted and constituted entirely by the word heard (gifted over), but above all he renders the call "because" he listens to it. These words "because your servant is listening to you," words that make the call (and every prophetic message to come) possible, in fact state the (first) response. Samuel's response (called, seduced, who "takes it upon himself") brings it about that the call sounds for the first time—without this response, the Lord would not have been able to call. Thus, in the loving intersubjective situation, as well as in that of election, the word that takes the initiative (the word that elects, that seduces) begins to be understood only when and if the response accords it having been heard—the a priori call awaits the a posteriori of the response in order to begin to have been said and to phenomenalize itself. The response states what the call had continually recalled to it.

The Delay of the Responsal

I have established the essential determination of the call—it is heard only in the response and to its measure. I here concur with the opinion of Emmanuel Levinas—"the call is heard in the response"—and especially the principle posited by J.-L. Chrétien: "All radical thought of the call implies that the call be heard only in the response."[66] This determination makes several other traits of the gifted more intelligible. (a) The gifted (the "unto whom") was previously[67] characterized as the screen that transcribes the colorless light of what gives itself in the visible phenomenon of what shows itself. This transcription had been accounted for in terms of a phenomenological prism, but that prism was still too abstract. I can now analyze it more exactly: the call remains as such always unheard and invisible because no receptor awaits it or welcomes it; it arises so originally that no hearing can in advance outline a horizon of manifestation for it, since, as paradox (saturated phenomenon), it makes an exception to every possible horizon. But it is nevertheless transcribed in visibility by way of the response. By admitting itself to be the target of the call, therefore by responding with the simple interrogative "Me?" the gifted opens a field for manifestation by lending itself to its reception and the retention of its impact. The gifted holds the place of a horizon of visibility for the paradox that gives itself. It makes the call visible by accepting it in its own visibility; it manifests the a priori in the prism of its a posteriori. What gives itself (the call) becomes a phenomenon—shows itself—in and through what responds to it and thus puts it on stage (the gifted). (b) The facticity of the call was defined by the fact that the first word, enjoyed by the "animal endowed with logos," is never uttered but always received by him.[68] The remaining problem was to understand more precisely how a word can be heard before being said. This difficulty finds its solution here: the originary word is said, probably (but not necessarily) by an Other who precedes me. I therefore cannot hear it because it speaks an unheard language and sounds in a space whose horizon I cannot fix in advance. In short, the word originarily said holds the status of call—inaugural, it remains inaudible. In contrast, the response, which is heard in the space of my hearing and its horizon, perfectly accomplishes the second word, originarily heard and not uttered, since by definition it says only what it received, as if being said without it and to it. But, for me, the gifted, it is the first to speak, since it alone can make itself heard—give itself to my hearing inasmuch as it comes from it. It speaks of the here in order to try saying the elsewhere in the mode of response. The gifted does not have language or *logos* as its property, but it finds itself endowed with them—as gifts that are shown only if it regives them to their unknown origin. Thus, only the response performs the call, and the gifted renders visible and audible what gives itself to it only by corresponding to it in the act of responding, "Here I am!" (c) If the call resounds only in the response, it follows that the response becomes phenomenologically first—the first manifestation of the call. The response comes after (echoes, returns, corresponds), but for the I become a gifted, it makes the first sound of the call heard, delivers it from the original silence, and hands it over to patent phenomenality. Such a response, which opens visibility and lets the call speak, which renders it a phenomenon instead of giving as good as it gets and degrading it, I will call the *responsal*. It follows that the responsal begins as soon as it has rendered the call phenomenal. The call begins to appear as soon as it finds an ear in which to settle, as soon as the first "Here I am!" (seduction, vocation). To lend an ear and open an eye already succeed in giving attention to the call—a responsal that gives what gives itself to show itself. The responsal and listening show the unheard and unseen call that already gave itself. Consequently, one could not decide to respond or even to refuse it; the response begins with the responsal and the responsal with the hearing. Hearing has always already begun. It is necessary to have already heard something to deny that a call was heard. It is necessary to have already tried to hear (awaited) in order to be disappointed with silence. The responsal has always already tried to speak because the call has always already—silently—summoned the gifted. The meanings invested by the responsal can be chosen, decided, arrive by accident, but the responsal is nothing like an optional act, an arbitrary choice, or a chance—in it we are, we live, and we receive ourselves.

If the call is always given straightaway, but does not show itself—does not become a phenomenon—except in the responsal, an essential paradox follows: the responsal completes the call, but it is belated—late for what gives itself, it delays its monstration. In a word, the responsal delays the call. This delay attests a double property of the call. First: its irreparable excess over and above all possible responsal.[69] In effect, each responsal confirms a possible call, one of the possible faces of the call, without any prejudice as to what the call still holds in reserve. The exhaustion of phenomenality never concerns the givenness of the call—invisible by definition—but only the respondent's fatigue—limited in his power of manifestation. The responsal wearies of showing what the call never grows weary of giving. Next: its fait accompli. No mortal can claim to have already responded to, heard and attended, the call, if only because he speaks with a word originarily received and thinks thoughts first impressed. Even and especially the denegations do nothing but confirm the impact of the beginning—for what would be refused if nothing (be this only a pretext, three times nothing) had been offered to the refusal? This double property is attested in the unique phenomenon of birth. The gifted is late ever since his birth precisely because he is born; he is late from birth precisely because he must first be born. There is none among the living who did not first have to be born, that is to say, arise belatedly from his parents in the attentive circle of waiting for words that summoned him before he could understand them or guess their meaning. This observation is not at all trivial since it inscribes before and more essentially than mortality the gifted in his gap from the call. My birth, which fixes my most singular identity even more than my existence, nevertheless happens without and before me—without my having to know about it or say a word, without my knowing or foreseeing anything. All my slow coming to consciousness, stubborn about rising to the $I=I$ of "I think (myself)," has no other ambition than to absorb my delay in responding to my birth (call) and to contain the initial excess with the fragile poverty of solipsism. Metaphysical subjectivity could even be defined as the denegation tripped up by the always already accomplished fact, fait accompli, of my birth: "As regards my parents, to whom it *seems* I owe my birth, . . . that does not mean that it is they who make and produce me insofar as I am a thinking thing, *nec . . . me, quatenus sum res cogitans, effecerunt.*"[70] But is it self-evident that I am ultimately a *res cogitans*, and not first and rather the gifted? What is more, metaphysical subjectivity does not dismiss birth so much as its irreducibility to every principle, every known origin, every horizon of foresight.

In effect, not only am I born as if from a call, but this call even precedes my birth, which constitutes only its first responsal. Before my birth, words were said around me and I heard them without understanding; even before my conception, words were exchanged by others, words ranging from joy to violence and from which I no doubt come. I therefore was said and spoken before being; I am born from a call that I neither made, wanted, nor even understood. Birth consists only in this excess of the call and in the delay of my *responsal*.[71]

Inauthenticity

It follows that the gifted forever bears the marks of his delay to the call. I will suggest three of these marks, from among many others: inauthenticity, the proper name, and responsibility. (a) The gifted turns up by extricating himself from the "I think" and its pretension to positing on principle *I*=*I*. This self-equality, supposing it accessible and accomplishable, would allow the I to appropriate itself, to become its own property (*Eigentum*), and therefore to authenticate itself without remainder (*Eigentlichkeit*). For authenticity supposes self-appropriation, without remainder or distance. This is why metaphysics pretends to reach it by abstracting from objects and phenomenology by reducing beings. But the gifted knows that this appropriation cannot, on principle, be accomplished. Distance and remainder do not come along and separate the I from itself as if after the fact, when it goes out of itself in intentionality toward objects or beings. Distance arises in the I itself, with it and even before it, since it is hollowed out as soon as the call gives itself, even before the responsal shows it. The delay of the responsal to the call structures the gifted from the outset by this inequality that gives it to itself inasmuch as not proper to itself, inasmuch as inauthentic. The gifted does not contest, complicate, or destroy a supposedly more simple and more originary I. By contrast, the delay of the responsal to the call (the a posteriori) defines the origin (a priori). The complex of the gifted (call/response) precedes the simplicity of the I because the latter only simplifies—by mistake or denegation—the originary phenomenological given, namely that the origin itself belongs under givenness, and therefore unfolds according to an irreducible inauthenticity and nonpropriety. What absolutely must be contested is the originary character of authenticity as self-appropriation: not because establishing this would carry with it an ethical injustice toward the Other or an illusion of self-transparency without unconscious, etc., but because it simply cannot be established or justified phenomenologically. It would even be necessary to redirect suspicion back against every pretense to authenticity. For in the ambition of accomplishing self-appropriation in and through the equality *I=I*, what it's really all about is at best an illusion and at worst, if it's stubborn, a lie. Meanwhile, acknowledging a fundamental inauthenticity, originary inappropriateness, lets us reach the truth of the gifted. I is an other—this is almost like saying: I appear only by dissimulating the gifted, instituted by the irreparable delay in it of the responsal to the call.

The Improper Name

This is confirmed by (b) the strange function of the proper name. In principle, nothing lays a greater claim to authenticity and self-appropriation than the proper name, which has no other role than to guarantee them for me. I am me, as my proper name is enough to indicate. Each of us bears one or two, sometimes three names (a given or Christian name, a family name, and possibly a surname, second given name, second surname, or toponym). Their combination suffices to designate Everyman without confusion as to his final individuality (*haecceitas*). This designation of final individuality by a supposedly proper name remains nevertheless illusory de facto and de jure. De facto, because this combination of names never avoids perfect homonyms. In order to avoid ambiguities, it has to be complemented by information that escapes nomination and the symbolic because it comes from the realm of numbers: the calendar of the civil state, geographic coordinates, banking, communication codes, in short, a collection of information transcribed into numbers that undertake an indefinite empirical description and abandon the pretension of pure nomination. Socially, my identity is not read in my name, but in my cards and papers. This factual failing of the proper name is deepened by its de jure failing, since no proper name can happen to me properly. Because, first of all, quite obviously, my family name always names a host of others besides me: Mr. Jones is always put in the plural straightaway—the Joneses; for directly or not, I inherit a family name that is mine only insofar as it does not belong to me and is not proper to me. It identifies me precisely insofar as it attaches me to a family, a line of descent, a site, indeed a nation—in short, it masks my individuality (*haecceitas*) in order to render it socially presentable, receivable, recognizable under another name, already known because common. My family name accords me an identity only by denying it as my own; it dispossesses me of my identity to myself as soon as it attributes it to me; or rather the family name that calls me is on principle not identical to me. It calls me by another name besides mine. In short, with this family name, I am called by a name that I am not, have not chosen, and perhaps do not want (a name "difficult to bear"). Therefore that by which one calls me precedes me and happens to me; it has the function of a call that will occupy my whole life with the office of responsal. What goes for the family name goes even more for the given name since, in contrast to the family name, which is imposed on the entire lineage without discussion or choice, the given name is explicitly chosen by others (the parents) and so is imposed on me without me, as if more me than me. What is more, in the case where the given name has the status of a baptismal name (a Christian name), the disqualification of the identity appropriate to the self becomes intentional. One explicitly assigns the given name as a borrowed name (mine by definition), borrowed from a saint, whose perfection gives me the model to which my life should respond. My life, as soon as, indeed before, it begins or falls to me, is identified not with me, who am not yet anybody, but with another besides myself. Better: I identify myself in an other besides me. In this way, the baptismal given name, the "proper" name par excellence, results from a call (one calls me with the name of such a saint) because, more essentially, this name constitutes a call in itself—I would not be called simply by this name, but indeed to this name. This "proper" name was given to me before I chose it, knew it, or even heard it; it precedes me and defines me in the role of my call, as the stranger par excellence. But this name was given to me in such a way that I was given as me and to myself—in short, in such a way that I discover myself as the gifted, therefore as identified par excellence with myself. Thus, in the "proper" first name, still more than in the family name, the stranger (the call) coincides with the identity (responsal). Never can I say that I call myself by this (proper) name. In order to say myself (present myself), I will always have to say names that others have always already given me, names of which I am just the receiver (representing the absent proprietors). When I name myself, I represent myself more than I present myself. I am therefore constituted as the responsal responding for and to a call—the name with which others have first called me.[72] In this way, I call myself with my name only insofar as others have always already appropriated for me a name that, without their summons, could never name me properly. What is proper to me is the result of an improper appropriation; it therefore identifies me only by an originary inauthenticity. Before the supposedly proper name, the de facto and de jure improper name, is appropriated to me by others (summons), it is necessary for this call to precede it. The name with which one calls me, more than an appellation, fixes a call for me. From this it follows that the anterior call constitutes the real first name of the name (composed of the given name and the family name, indeed a third), which becomes its responsal. In this sense, the given name precedes the name as the call of my name precedes and establishes me as its respondent. Don't we say that I respond to my name? It is therefore necessary that it call me—as the call of all my responsals.

Responsibility

Responsibility can now be redefined. (c) Nobody will deny that responsibility, understood as the property of a juridical "subject" having to respond for his acts and an ethical "subject" having to respond to what the face of the Other demands (seeing him as such), can be deduced from the most general figure of the responsal that a gifted makes to a call. For that matter, since the call always arises from a paradox (saturated phenomenon) and since the face of the Other belongs officially to the paradoxes (under the heading, icon), it is self-evident that the face gives itself as a call and shows itself (phenomenalizes itself) only to the degree that the gifted responds to it. For, what of the Other shows itself, puts on a good or a bad face, depends precisely on the response that I address to his living call: depending on whether I see him or not, kill him or love him, he changes his face. I am responsible for him since he changes from one phenomenon to the other according to the response I consent to make. But does this responsibility toward the call of the Other exhaust all responsibility? The other types of saturated phenomena (the event, the idol, and the flesh, and a fortiori the paradox of revelation that combines them all) also deploy a call; they too therefore provoke responsals. To be sure, faced with the gaze of the Other, the gifted grasps that he cannot not respond *for him*. But he responds as well, though in a different mode, *for* the event as its witness, charged with its reconstitution and its hermeneutic. He responds equally *to* the affection that his flesh undergoes first in and through itself. He responds finally for the scope of his own gaze *before* the idol, which fills it. In short, the gifted stands as collateral responding for all the saturated phenomena, which happen to him as so many calls. Responsibility cannot be restricted to just one of the paradoxes—the icon, however privileged it might be—nor confined to just one horizon, be this the ethical. Responsibility belongs officially to all phenomenality that is deployed according to givenness: what is given (the call) succeeds in showing itself as a phenomenon only on the screen and according to the prism that the gifted (the responsal) alone offers it. All the determinations by which the phenomenon gives *itself* and shows *itself* starting from *itself* to the point of exerting a call (impact, counter-intentionality, unpredictable landing, anamorphosis, fait accompli, incident, event, etc.) are concentrated and transcribed for the gifted in the responsibility that he suffers from them. The pertinent question is not deciding if the gifted is first responsible toward the Other (Levinas) or rather in debt to itself (Heidegger), but understanding that these two modes of responsibility flow from its originary function of having to respond in the face of the phenomenon as such, that is to say, such as it gives itself.[73]

To Differ/Defer

The delay of the responsal behind the call characterizes the gifted so radically that it lets us redefine difference. In effect, the dominant role that phenomenology has always assigned to difference has rendered even more aporetic the question of knowing from where and how difference differs. Heidegger, intending difference as ontological, attempted to think this difference in terms of givenness; but in the end he renounced this victory in favor of the *Ereignis*, whose advance does not render the withdrawal visible, and so hides difference (§3). Levinas collapsed difference into the relation to the Other, but by keeping a temporal horizon for it, which presupposes, more than it shows, that the Saying differs from the said according to a lapse of time.[74] There is therefore nothing illegitimate in Derrida's line of questioning when he asked how difference differs. His answer is well known: difference differs [*differe*], in the logical sense of undoing self-identity and self-equality, only in that, more radically, it delays (defers [*differe*]) self-presence, as a differance. "*Differer* in this sense is to temporize, to take recourse, consciously or unconsciously, in the temporal and temporizing mediations of a detour that suspends the accomplishment or fulfillment of 'desire' or 'will.'" Full presence, either of signification or of intuition, is always put off until later, in fact endlessly referred. Presence never comes in person, but is always represented by the trickery of linguistic substitutes, formalisms, and the imaginary. Difference, by deferring presence, thus compromises from the outset the metaphysical project of a substance present without reserve, as well as the phenomenological goal of a presence that shows itself without remainder. As radical as it pretends to be and as it remains, this reconduction of difference to differance still suffers from a basic indeterminacy.

That is, since here it is always a question of "difference as temporization-temporalization,"[75] how can we not ask if temporalization flows from temporization (time from differance, the "logical" position) or temporization from temporalization (differance from time, the "Husserlian" position)?[76] Put otherwise: Can the delay, which imposes on presence that it be continually represented and therefore renders it possible (or rather impossible), be conceived simply on the basis of its inverted present and temporality? Difference differs by its withdrawal (Heidegger), its lapse (Levinas), or its delay (Derrida)—but do these come from temporality or should they be thought in and through themselves? If they stem from temporality, for which they merely invert the primacy of the present, wouldn't they again be inscribed in the most metaphysical conception of presence? If, by contrast, they determine temporality and the modes of temporalization, they need to be described as such, according to their own procedures of differance; they should not be reconducted to a still uninvestigated, indeed squarely metaphysical temporality. It is not self-evident that the delay, which opens all difference, can and should be understood first temporally—in other words, that the delay is equivalent to a pure and simple temporization. It is precisely here that the play of call and responsal marks a difference without compare—because it provokes differance on the basis of itself alone, before time. The call precedes the responsal, which continually confesses and fulfills its delay by multiplying its responses, whose series opens nothing less than a historicity proper to the gifted. The history of the gifted is due to the sum of its responses, which draw it near to and distant from the call. But for all that, the call and responsal are not defined temporally, as is proven by the fact that they assume equally and in turn each of the ecstasies of time. We can consider the call the immemorial past, but also the future toward which the responses are directed, and just as well the present, which summons the gifted in each instant. Reciprocally we can take the responsal for the sole present of the call (which shows itself only therein), and again for its indefinite past (the fabric of accumulated responses tracing its historicity), and therefore for the unique manifest future of the call—which sounds only to the degree that the responses continually recall it. Temporalization therefore does indeed flow from temporization, though in multiple rival figures, but temporization itself is not temporized; it resonates with call and responsal. Its delay belongs to the very simultaneity of the responsal and the call—precisely because the call resonates only with and in "the moment" of the responsal, it is delayed behind it and delays it. The belatedness has nothing of a temporizing or temporalized delay; it stems from the gifted's strictly phenomenological conversion of what gives itself (the call) into what shows itself (the responsal). This conversion imposes a delay—a slowness, but a ripening slowness that puts the given on the path of showing itself by filtering through the prism of the gifted. The belatedness of what shows itself to what gives itself stems from the phenomenological work that the responsal exercises over the gifted. Only givenness, unfolded in all its instances, differs/defers. Differing and deferring, it shows itself. The visible is late in hatching, but it hatches only in this very delay. Temporality itself delays only in order to attest it.

§29 THE NAMELESS VOICE

Anonymity

The call and responsal are articulated as what gives itself and what shows itself, by the mechanism of a prism—the gifted—who converts the one into the other because he himself receives himself from what gives itself.

This thesis is open to an objection that no doubt presses upon it with great urgency since it has been made often. The summoning of the gifted by the call, even if it is accomplished only in the responsal, supposes some instance that performs it, a first or last pole that claims and whose initiative tears, by silence or sound, what comes after the "subject": the gifted. It is of course necessary that the gifted give itself over to. . . . And therefore, we inevitably have to ask: who or what summons, invokes, and surprises the gifted? This question develops into a double suspicion. First, concerning the identity of what could exercise the claim: God (in and through revelation), the Other (in and through obligation), Being (in and through the event), life (in and through auto-affection), etc. Doesn't the simple and abstract description of the call in general hide—quite poorly, for what it's worth—one of these authorities, here probably the first, the nostalgic aim of the entire project, censured so as to better free it? On this hypothesis, wouldn't the call and responsal, such as they lead givenness to its term, aim at restoring a quasi-metaphysical arrangement? A transcendent, indeed self-grounding, principle would sustain a subjectivity that is derived, but nevertheless privileged, since in charge of phenomenality in general. The next suspicion bears on the status of the gifted: in all these cases, doesn't the gifted, instituted by and after a principle, obligatorily regress to the ordinary rank of a regional, anthropological, indeed psychological and plainly subjective given—without rightful necessity, purely factual, empirically de-scribable, but conceptually indeterminate? To these two suspicions, I will oppose first the notion that the call remains and must remain phenomeno-logically anonymous in such a way that, secondly, the gifted responds to it in accordance with a reduction to the pure immanence of givenness.[77]

Let us consider the first point: it belongs essentially and on principle to the call to be given without, however, giving its name. Several arguments establish this. (a) The call comes from the saturated phenomenon (para-dox). The paradox is conjugated in several strictly distinct types (event, idol, flesh, and icon), and yet each of them can accomplish the same and unique type of call. Therefore the description of the call as such (§§26 and 28) does not depend on specifying this or that paradox. Consequently, one cannot, starting from a call, go back directly to this or that type of paradox, still less to identifying its name. This indifference of the call to the type of saturated phenomenon that provokes it finds another confirmation in the possibility of a paradox of paradoxes, revelation, which would concentrate all types of paradox. Here, the call—if it turns up—would bear no name because it would assume them all. The anonymity would be reinforced by the very excess of the paradox, which would require an infinite denomina-tion. In this way, no call would offer *less* of a name than that of a phenom-enon of revelation. What is more, the highest name of God, such as he re-veals it to Moses, attests precisely the impertinence of every essential name or description by summing it up in an empty tautology—I am who I am—which opens the field to the endless litany of all the names. The voice that reveals reveals precisely because it remains voiceless, more exactly nameless, but *in* the Name. The Name gives itself only in saying itself without any name, therefore in all. Far from fearing that such a call should lead surrep-titiously to naming a transcendent *numen* and—what's worse—to "theol-ogy," it must be concluded that every phenomenon of revelation (as possi-bility) and especially a Revelation (as actuality) would imply the radical anonymity of what calls. Anonymity therefore, in terms of the paradox that calls. (b) The second argument for the anonymity of the call is drawn from the definition of the gift in general according to givenness. The gift appears as such when it is recovered in the reduction, and one of the figures of the reduced gift is realized by the bracketing of the giver (§10)—and therefore of his name. In this way, the reduced gift, that is to say, the phenomeno-logically legitimate gift, is deployed according to an immanent and intrin-sic givenness that owes nothing to the giver, not even its identity. It must be said again that a gift bears the contingency of the pure given (among others, the determinations of unpredictable landing, fait accompli, and the incident) all the more as it arises without a known, identified, or named giver. Anonymity again, according to the reduced gift.

Whence a third argument to justify the first two, one drawn from the same articulation of call and responsal. (c) Phenomenologically, the call must remain anonymous because its function is never to name itself, only to call the respondent and thus arouse him. That is, before the call, there is no listener yet to be found—no witness and no gifted who can already hear the name of the call. Therefore the first and sole function of the call is nothing more than to summon such a witness, and in no way to say itself by speaking its name—an enterprise that is not only vain, but impossible in phenomenological rigor. And if it is ever necessary to give a name to the call, this will not be the job of the call itself (nor of the giver), but of the responsal (or the givee). The responsal recognizes what the call gives to it, and thus identifies it. As a result, it can go through the named gift and thereby succeed in naming the call for the first time. The call calls the responsal, never itself; it therefore receives its possible name only from the responsal, which gives a name to it after the fact. The "Here I am!" of the responsal is the only thing that can give the status of "There you are!" to the call, therefore attribute a name to it. This rule is verified, for example, in the political call (the event): he who issues it is still, at the moment when he issues it, abstract, indeed almost perfectly unknown—"It used to seem to me that I was alone and destitute of all;"[78] but those who take this call upon themselves (therefore the gifteds) name it strictly to the extent that they are named by it: "republicans" (because "the Republic calls us"), "gaullists" (those called by "Gaul"), indeed "bonapartists," "leninists," etc. As a result, they give, in and through their response, a full name to the caller of the call. And inversely for those who have heard nothing, or who, having heard, wanted to hear nothing, the absence of the responsal maintains the anonymity of the call. Likewise for the lover's call (the icon): when it appears and enters into public visibility, whatever charm it might have (even mediocre), it exerts (or attempts to exert) a call; but though all see it (or can see it), not all consider it equally gazable. Some gazes slide over it, do not see it, in short, do not put a name to this face. The anonymity of the call always results from the deficiency of the responsal, but let one of the listeners take upon himself the call of this face (if their gazes truly cross), and "it was like an epiphany"—the responsal will confer its unique name (possibly a surname) on the call because the gifted will have let himself be entirely governed by what he will receive: "She was seated in the middle of a bench all alone, or at any rate, he could see no one dazzled as he was by her eyes."[79] The same goes for hearing the painting or seeing the melody (the idol), for affection by anxiety, joy, or suffering (the flesh)—all name their call only to the measure of the gifted, therefore in the responsal. The same procedure can also be described according to clues provided by the entry into phenomenality: what gives itself (call) at first does not yet show itself, and therefore remains anonymous. It shows itself only if the gifted converts it into a phenomenon (responsal) where from now on it has a visibility and probably receives a name. Anonymity therefore, according to the responsal.

The anonymity of the caller (what or who?) therefore does not weaken the concept of the call, but strengthens it. Since *I* acknowledge *myself* summoned and interloqué before all consciousness of my subjectivity—which is precisely its result—all knowledge of the caller's identity will be added to the claim after the fact and will never precede it like a presupposition. At the origin is accomplished the claim, not the consciousness of this claim by the interloqué, still less the knowledge that allows some caller to be identified in the call. What is more, surprise, therefore the loss of consciousness, forbids the interloqué from grasping and knowing his summons as a determined and denominated object. To find *myself* summoned would lack all rigor if surprise did not deprive *me*, at least for awhile and sometimes definitively, of knowing, in the instant of the summons, by what and by whom the call is exercised. Reciprocally, if I knew in advance that it is Being or the Other or God or life that was summoning me, then I would escape the full status of the gifted since I would be free of all surprise. Knowing in advance (or at least immediately) with what and with whom I am dealing when dealing with the word heard, I would know (what) or I would respond (who) according to the surplus of constitution or the equality of dialogue, but without the interlocuted passivity of surprise. In short, I would again become an *I* who delivers itself from the status of a *me*. Anonymity therefore belongs strictly to the conditions for the possibility of the call because it defines its unconditioned poverty. In conformity with the principle of insufficient reason, the call does not have to make itself known in order to be acknowledged, nor identified in order to be exercised. This poverty alone succeeds in wounding the "subject" and exiling him from all authenticity as a gifted. By right, a call that would say its name would no longer call, but would put the caller at center stage, reconduct him to the visibility of an occupant of the world, smother the voice with the evidence of a spectacle.[80] The only things, by contrast, that truly make a call resound are voices that show absolutely nothing, not even the image incited by a sonorous vibration—in short, "the noiseless trumpets that we all hear."[81]

The Child and the Father

Strangely enough, the nameless call is attested in the situation that, at first glance, would most clearly seem to be an exception—paternity. It seems obvious that, since the father uses his own name to name the one he engenders, supposing this is how he calls the child, this call always bears a name, his own. However, this description is inadequate to the things themselves, since it approaches them neither from the perspective of the father nor from that of the one engendered, but rather from a phenomenologically unjustifiable point of view—that of a third who inexplicably avails himself of information proper to each of the two poles, which, as such, remain irreducible. If, by contrast, we stick to a real description in terms of one or the other of the two poles, the situation is transformed. The father calls his child, gives him a name, his own; his call therefore has a name and consists in giving a name—these are what ordinary appearances show. What still remains to be understood is this: Why does he thus give him a name? One obvious reply might be because the child does not yet have one and remains anonymous. But in this case, how and with what right does the father call a nameless child by his own name, thereby literally offering no sign that he is from this father? The obvious reply to this is because the father knows, through intimate experience, that this child is born from his own deeds, from his own wife, in his house, in front of him, etc. These excellent reasons nevertheless suffer from a well-known weakness: by definition, in fact on account of the temporal delay of birth's initial belatedness to conception, biological paternity remains without immediate and direct proof, always doubtful (and technologically it will become more and more so in the near future). Every child is born naturally from its mother, but strictly speaking, it always remains of unknown father; there is no child who is not a foundling—that is to say, received. As a result, it has been admitted since time immemorial that the sole proof of paternity resides in the juridical recognition of the child by the father; paternity is accomplished symbolically, not first of all or always biologically. The father becomes one, in all cases and not only in adoption, only by his decision to recognize, ask for, and claim as his own the foundling and natural child. At this point, the question becomes: For what reasons does the father recognize a child who does not bear his name and is therefore sill nameless? Why, as is the rule in certain species of animals, indeed as is a frequent practice in certain sections of the so-called developed societies, not deny paternity and leave the child without paternal name? One will say, obviously and justly, that powerful ethical authorities (responsibility, fidelity, altruism, construction of his destiny, etc.) are operative here, but we could still ask how these authorities become compelling motives for a personal and voluntary decision, since sometimes they are not enough. In the final analysis, there is only one correct response: the father decides to be father because the child (and the context surrounding his birth) exerts over him a call to recognition in paternity. The child silently calls the father to call him with his name—with the name of the father, with the name that he does not have, which is not and never will be his own. The child thus exercises an anonymous call on the father. When the father recognizes himself as father to the point of recognizing the child as his own, to the point of giving him his name, he does nothing other than, by calling him in this way, offer a response to a call. The name by which the child is called is only the father's response to a nameless call. The anonymity of the call (and of the child) neither contradicts nor interdicts paternity, but constitutes its terrain, stakes, and condition of possibility. The father will therefore be born into his own paternity to the extent that he responds to the child's anonymous call with a naming response. This nomination is laid out in a history: first, the father gives his own name (last name), then the first name (Christian name), both borrowed (§28); next he gives real identity, through word, speech, and language, then through the community, religion, "*Weltanschauung*," etc. Continually giving him a name through the indefinite succession of his responses, the father will never annul the anonymity of the initial call enacted by the child. He will, by contrast, only emphasize it, since he will swallow all these identities in the gulf of the original absence of the name. And therefore in the end, the child "will leave his father and mother"; that is to say, he will pass beyond the names given in response in order to confront his own anonymity. At this moment, the child becomes an adult—one who knows his own anonymity and that he should make a name for himself. Thus, from the father's point of view, the child is given as an anonymous call and remains so.

Reciprocally, we customarily say that the child calls his father all the more easily as he bears his name as his own. If he is called as his father is called and as he calls him, then the father is to him a call endowed with a name, one who calls him to and by a name—these are admittedly how things appear. They remain to be understood, for as the father has no biological certainty of his paternity, the child has no immediate and direct proof of his filiation; he must accept it, on the faith of the father, following the symbolic argument of his being recognized by him. This is in fact translated by adopting the father's name as collateral for his own adoption by the father. Therefore, the child bears—as a heavy burden and a tiresome yoke — a name that is not his. This name (and the other names that complete it) comes upon him as a fait accompli always already done for and without him, indeed counter to him. For the proper name, we saw (§28), has as its own proper characteristic to remain improper. It is alienating. How is this improper name exerted? First as a call—in calling me after my father, the name refers me to him as an obsessing paradigm. It matters little that I love or hate him, that I admire or condemn him, since in every case I can identify with myself only by referring myself to him. Before me, more within me than myself, this name calls me and thus calls me to him. My historicity is declared to the degree that I add varying responses to the name's singular unique call, ranging from acceptance to refusal, adherence to forgetting. But this name that calls thus still remains strangely anonymous. First, because it does not tell me who I am, since it belongs originarily to another, the father; in this sense, its anonymity results directly from the alienation that it imposes on me. Next, because it does not tell me who my father is; far from identifying him, it hides him and even establishes him as unknown father. All that I will ever know about my father I will learn from his stories, his confessions, his lies, strange tales; in short, I will learn it counter to his name, by deconstructing it or corroborating it each time by what it does not say. The name of the father hides his identity and endlessly substitutes for his empirical individuality. Not only does this name show nothing; it conceals. We will therefore call this call, by which I am called, an anonymous, or better, antonymous call. The father gives himself to the child only as a call that does not even say his name, even though it says nothing besides a name—and another name.

Historicity

This anonymity of the voice that calls could easily be seen in other situations belonging to what we call improperly intersubjectivity, but still more in those of the painting, the flesh, or the event. I will not insist on this here, leaving others to complete the analysis in each case. It is important to emphasize, however, that just as the delay of the responsal to the call permitted difference to differ (§27), so too does the anonymity of the call open a historicity for the responsal. That is, as the call does not secure the nomination of its identity any more than what gives itself succeeds on its own in showing itself, the responsal can never, even by proliferating indefinitely, do justice to the anonymity of the call. The responsal will always be suspected of having poorly or partially identified the call, of not having perfectly accomplished its injunction, of not having exhausted all its possibilities. The call excites the responsal but is never appeased by it. Each advance remains a beginning, and the responsal never finishes beginning (like desire). It alone begins to say what the call silences, but it never succeeds in saying it all the way. Thus its historicity opens. The call gives, or rather, of itself constitutes, what is given, but it does not yet show itself. It can therefore be considered a destiny—that is to say, a sending that is not seen, a voice that is veiled. The responsal that the gifted gives and in which he receives himself entirely tries to make it such that the destiny, which gives itself without showing itself, finally does show itself. But, as the self-given by definition does not manifest itself, it hides whether it dissimulates or shows itself and just how far its given holds back from appearing. As a result, the responsal never knows if and just how far it succeeds in bringing about that what gives itself also shows itself. The response can no more annul its originary belatedness to the call than what shows itself can claim to exhaust what gives itself. Therefore the responsal always remains to be completed. With this delay continually still to be completed, it opens to its historicity, which is therefore radically temporalized on the basis of the already given and not yet shown, therefore on the basis of the past. It could be that if difference differs in terms of call and response and not first temporally, it is temporalized no longer in terms of the present (as in metaphysics) nor in terms of the future (as in the existential analytic), but well and truly in terms of the past —according to the anonymity of the call that the responsal never ceases to rename. For the responsal, which comes after the call, returns toward it inasmuch as it confers a name on it and thereby shows what is given in it. Each responsal arises in the present for the purpose of returning toward the past call, in order to receive the always already accomplished given; but since this returning toward the originary given can only show what it receives from it, without ever proving that it exhausts all that lands unpredictably, the responsal on principle comes up short, in withdrawal. It continually slips back behind the call; relapse of the given, it thus lets a lapse of delay arise, a belated time—the time of the delay. And this time of delay is continually re-produced, in proportion as the responsal returns toward the call, repeatedly and stubbornly responding to it in an always different mode, and therefore in an always deferred adequation. The future (*Zukunft*) arrives in the pres-ent (*Ankunft*) on the basis of the each time insufficient information (*Aus-kunft*) that the responsal delivers in regard to the call. The repetition—the resumed search—of the call by the responsal, the re-putting —into play and on stage—of what gives itself without name by what shows itself, in short, the recall of the call, sets in motion a historicity and frees a temporal-ity. The history of the gifted consists only in the uninterrupted, but finally suspended, series of its responsals. And the gifted dies as soon as he no longer has a respondent and no longer succeeds in once again naming the nameless call.

Immanent Decision

We can now see the second properly phenomenological characteristic of the call (besides its anonymity): the gifted responds to it in accordance with a reduction to the pure immanence of givenness. The gifted receives the call without exiting immanence because givenness itself remains intrin-sic (§12) and the call is inscribed as an impact without depth (§26) or name. To be sure, the gifted assigns it a name to be reassumed and completed without end, but this nomination always belongs to it as its own risk, one that no transcendence can verify by some unthinkable *adequatio rei et intel-lectus*, since the thing is deployed precisely only in the hearing of the gifted. What gives itself gives itself on the plane of immanence (this is why it bears anonymity), and what shows itself appears on the plane of immanence (un-der the heading "response"). This radical immanence means that before launching the demonstration (the staging of the phenomenon) of the given, the gifted sees nothing; it means that no light precedes the birth of what gives itself into the visible; and it means that what shows itself emerges into the light without any foresight. How could a pre-phenomenality emerge on this side of immanence (of "consciousness") before the screen and the prism by which the gifted converts the anonymous given into what shows itself? Where could the given show itself prior to the instance of manifestation— the immanence that receives it? Before the phenomenon, there is nothing to see or foresee. Therefore the responsal sees nothing before naming the call. Properly speaking, it does not know what it says before saying it, as it sees nothing before giving itself over to it. This situation is better grasped by opposing it to the metaphysical principle that the will wants what the understanding sees in its own light and to the extent that this light illuminates, "quia ex magna luce in intellectu magna consecuta est propensio in voluntate [because a great light in the understanding was followed by a great inclination in the will]." But to claim that what is firmly willed should first be conceived in evidence, in short, to claim to know what one wants, one first has to admit that one sees without wanting and before wanting. Now, we know that we see without wanting only the poorest phenomena, indeed those that are barely constituted. As soon as a phenomenon is enriched with intuition, therefore as soon as its degree of givenness grows, it is necessary that we constitute it and bear it for it to be seen, therefore wanted—truly wanted, not denied or evaded. In order to see, one must first want to see. There is no worse blind man than the one who does not want to see. It is therefore necessary that we say instead that a great light in the "understanding" always follows from a great inclination in the "will." This, in any case, is what must be said in the obviously privileged case of God, where in conformity with the creation of the eternal truths, nothing shows itself that "we can suppose to have been the object of understanding before its nature was constituted as such by the determination of the will." But, in fact, this is also the case for the finite mind, since error, at least, results from the fact that "voluntas latius patet quam intellectus [the scope of the will is wider than that of the understanding]" and that therefore I can extend it "etiam ad illa quae non intelligo [to matters which I do not understand]."[82] In this way the will determines what the understanding can attain.

What metaphysics stigmatizes as error defines in phenomenological terms the basic function of the responsal: it converts what gives itself into what shows itself. For, in order to phenomenalize the given, one first has to admit it (to "want" to receive it) and receive oneself from it as given over to it so as thus to see (eventually, to grasp by "understanding") what it shows. The decision to respond, therefore to receive, precedes the possibility of seeing, therefore of conceiving. The more the given is saturated with intuition and rises toward the paradox, the more difficult, as well as fruitful, this decision becomes, because the response turns out less and less adequate, more and more insufficient, and therefore endlessly repeated. The excess of the given over and above the response provokes not only the bedazzlement (§22) of the gifted by imposing on it a visible that is ever more powerful than expected, nor only the suffering of bearing an impact too powerful to convert into the unfurling visible. The given humbles the gifted, like respect but more universally than respect, since each saturated phenomenon humbles. This humiliation can be specified in an alternative: What should we privilege—a nonsaturated phenomenon (poor in intuition or common) susceptible to a response that is adequate or quasi-adequate because in fact it has only to be constituted into an object, or a saturated phenomenon that shows what it gives only inadequately, in an endless series of always partial and provisional responses, marking the irrevocable shortcoming of the gifted? In other words, should we consent to receiving and seeing only the poor or common given of an object in order to gain the enjoyment of a power adequate to constituting, or should we expose ourselves to the humiliation of never constituting and endlessly repeating the responses in order to gain the enjoyment of a givenness of paradoxes and win the full standing of a gifted? Humiliating the power to constitute can also be read as satisfying the full and total receptivity open to the paradox, therefore the phenomenalization of what gives itself in excess. The excess of givenness obviously implies the endless belatedness of the response. Nevertheless, it is possible to understand this belatedness not as a defeat but as a consecration of the gifted by what happens to him. Between these two interpretations of a single phenomenological situation, interpretations that define the two irreconcilable tendencies cutting across the entire history of philosophy (either constitute the object poor in intuition or receive the excess of givenness without objectifying it), no reason could decide. For since it is still and always a question of receiving the given or not, the response alone should decide, without relying on the visibility of what does not show itself before the response. The responsal does not know what it wants because it must first want it in order to see it, therefore to know it. Here opens a space of indecision that cannot be imagined without fright: the decision in favor of staging the given as a phenomenon, therefore also that in favor of the reason of things, can be made only without vision or reason since it makes them possible. The responsal decides with nothing other than itself alone. With the birth of the visible (the conversion of what is given into what shows itself), there is at play, in a pre-phenomenological and pre-rational obscurity, the choice or the refusal of "the great reason"—of unconditioned givenness. This decision recovers and radicalizes what Descartes meant by indifference, but redoubled. Descartes opposed the negative indifference of the finite mind, where the shortcomings of the understanding leave the will undecided, to the positive indifference of God, where the initiative of creation precedes every level of rational thing. Here the gifted, finite by defi-

nition and originarily a posteriori, finds itself in charge of receiving or denying the given, that is, the a priori of givenness. It is inasmuch as it remains
negatively indifferent (by a deficiency of sight) that it receives the burden
of positive indifference (to bring it about that what gives itself shows itself,
or not). The gifted, inasmuch as finite, has nothing less than the charge of
opening or closing the entire flux of phenomenality.

This investiture of the responsal, set up as gatekeeper for the ascent
into visibility of all that gives itself, can and should be troubling. However,
it does nothing more than radicalize the fundamental character of Dasein—to be the being in which its Being, and therefore the Being in general of all beings, is at stake. Here the gifted is characterized as the being
given that puts in play, in the given, itself, which is received, and thereby
the givenness of all beings and their ascent into visibility. Nothing of what
gives itself can show itself except to the gifted and through it—not by constitution, anticipatory resoluteness, or exposure to the Other, but by the
will to see, originally derived from givenness itself. This responsibility toward all the given and prior to all visibility (or reason) clarifies by analogy
a better-known existential situation of the gifted. When the gifted is, hypothetically, condemned to decide a saturated phenomenon, for example
the paradox of the icon, in short, when he must decide to expose himself
without protection to the gaze that crosses his own and the face that sees
him clearly, in a word, when he must resolve himself to love (or to not deny
loving), he finds himself in such an indifference. The more passion increases, the more indifference does, too. There is nothing surprising in that:
passion develops an imperial hermeneutic, where reasons are born that are
as incontestable as the phenomena shown therein; but at the same time,
other hermeneutics also become possible, with, if not the same force, at
least the same right. It is enough to question the loving given for what
shows itself to disappear, for its reasons to fade and other visibles to emerge,
even ones that are blurry and indistinct with their counter-reasons. In this
conflict of white on white, of the gifted with itself, who will decide, since it
is a question of deciding the reasons to decide, of the abandon given over
to the gift, and of receiving the vision? Here givenness enters into conflict
with the gifted, the given with its reception, the call with the responsal. No
advice or counsel, no friend or enemy, can do anything for the gifted in the
situation of giving itself over or not. It depends only on his indifference that
the given give itself to him and become visible in glory, therefore that it be
received. This given itself can do nothing about it, since its call sounds only

with the responsal. The responsal remains in suspense, and this very suspense offers the last truth of givenness—that the first is also the last. Givenness traces, perhaps in sand, but ineffaceably, the most rigorous hermeneutic circle. We do not have to enter into it because we are always already taken up in it, but we should not try to leave it because its very denegation leads back into it.

Givenness therefore exercises the play of the call and the responsal solely on the level of its radical immanence. It protects this immanence by the lateness of the responsal (§28) as well as by the anonymity of the voice that calls (§29). The greatest divides that the gifted can cross, his historicity and his indifference, are only deployed there. As givenness produces the phenomenon absolutely reduced to what shows itself inasmuch as it gives itself, it reduces the "subject" to what receives itself without remainder from what it receives—the given. Privilege of givenness.

§30 ABANDON

The Remainder

I was able to determine the gifted starting from the fait accompli always already done of the call, such as it is addressed to him, only by basing my determination on its most proper characteristic—that of receiving itself entirely from what it receives (§26). The gifted can therefore be understood by definition only insofar and as long as it receives and thus receives itself. Better, it must receive in order to receive itself. Everything that contradicts the reception of the given not only would render it unintelligible, but would make it disappear. Without reception of the given, nothing more—no gifted —comes after the "subject." We have already encountered such an impossibility, however, since the topics of the phenomenon already admitted explicitly two exceptions to the reception of the given: one by shortage of intuition (poor phenomenon), the other by its excess (paradox). At that time, I admitted that the given without intuition can take the figure of the abandoned.[83] Don't these two propositions contradict each other? What is more, doesn't the second also contradict the last principle, that nothing makes an exception to the universal privilege of givenness, established since the beginning (§5)? And for that matter, can I reasonably avoid this double contradiction when I claim to have reconducted all that is possible to phenomenality and all phenomenality to givenness? Can I affirm that all, without remainder, gives itself and that all given is received in order that it might, across the singular gifted, show itself (§6)?

The answer to these fearsome difficulties, if there is one, can be found only by examining at greater length the touchy issue in what I have said. For the two theses, incontestable in my eyes—nothing makes an exception to givenness, all that shows itself gives itself—do not necessarily end up imposing a universal manifestation, with neither limit nor remainder. They should sometimes be co-posited with another thesis, it too incontestable— the given also gives itself in the figure of the abandoned when it is deprived of intuition, either by shortage or by excess. And this third thesis could possibly let us disconnect the strict implication of phenomenality and givenness: if all that shows itself must first give itself, it sometimes happens that what gives itself does not succeed in showing itself. Does this mean that I am once again putting into question the principle that all that gives itself finishes by showing itself (§6)? Not at all, for these limits do not affect the phenomenological principle of the given's monstration, but attest that it is always put into operation in the essential finitude of the gifted. The operator of phenomenalization for what gives itself should stage a given that accomplishes itself on the basis of its irreducible self, therefore one that sometimes, indeed often, is not governed by the receptive capacity of the gifted and thus frees itself of these limits. The given respects neither the conditions for the possibility of objects of experience (because it is not always submitted to objective status [§23]), nor the conditions for the possibility of experience (because it never recognizes any a priori to experience [§1]). Since its finitude essentially determines the gifted, it cannot by definition adequately receive the given such as it gives itself—namely, without limit or reserve. The finitude of the phenomenalization operated by the gifted, therefore, does not necessarily succeed in rendering visible all that comes upon it. The phenomenological principle that what gives itself shows itself remains intact, but it is accomplished for us only within the limits that the finite gifted puts into operation. That these limits can recede, indeed recede continually and endlessly (which I would gladly admit as a new definition of what Kant named "genius"), does not invalidate this essential finitude, but on the contrary confirms it. It is extremely important that phenomenology, especially when it has the audacity to free visibility to the measure of givenness, maintain respect for the finitude of its operator—not only so as to avoid the intoxication of constituting ever wider regions, an intoxication to which Husserl was not the only one to succumb; but above all because what comes after the "subject," the gifted, is characterized properly by the submission of its undeniable activity and live spontaneity to the passivity of an absolutely originary receptivity. The given comes, on its own, upon the gifted, whose structural secondariness attests an absolute finitude. Precisely because the principle "What gives itself shows itself" remains intact, it becomes possible to observe the finitude of phenomenality in the realm of givenness. For what gives itself shows itself only insofar as it is received by the gifted, whose proper function consists in giving in return that the given show itself; and such a conversion of the given into a shown phenomenon can therefore be realized only in the field, obviously finite, where the gifted receives and stages. If the gifted always phenomenalizes what gives itself to him and receives himself from it, nothing establishes that the gifted always can or wants to receive *all* that is given. We can never exclude some cases in which a given would not succeed in showing itself because the gifted could or simply would not receive it; we need only imagine those unpredictable landings in which the gifted fails before the excess of the given or remains idle in its shortage. This hypothesis must therefore be examined in order to see if it is phenomenologically legitimate and how it might remain coherent with the privilege of givenness. This is equivalent to closing my determination of the phenomenon as given with an inventory of marginal givens, those that do not phenomenalize themselves—on the model of the appendix to Kant's *Analytic of Principles*, where he examines the meanings of "nothing," that is to say, of what never phenomenalizes itself as an object. I will therefore examine two figures of a given that does not show itself owing to its reception by the gifted—first by lack of intuition, then by excess of intuition. I will try to confirm that these two shortcomings are always inscribed within the phenomenality of givenness, since they occupy its extreme limits.

By Deficiency

The given can lack intuition. It is therefore possible that, lacking intuition, the given is not received in such a way that it does not show itself. I do not dispute this evident possibility. But this lack itself does not escape the phenomenality of givenness, even though it remains marginal. That is, the deficiency of intuition does not obscure every possibility of staging the very phenomenon of lack. The lack of intuition can, as lack, still be given, and the given lack can, if not appear as a phenomenon that shows itself, at least show itself as a lack. Therefore the gifted can still give itself over to the absent. Let me enumerate the clearest examples of this situation. (a) I tried to establish it at the outset by studying the privilege of givenness (§5), in which the nothing and death are not describable without intuition in terms of (non)givenness, and therefore appear at the limit, without objectification. These analyses are still valid here, and I will not recount them. (b) What I called purely formal (logical) phenomena or poor phenomena (mathematical idealities) are given, therefore thought and calculated, without any other intuition besides the categorical (analogical) or "pure" (space, time) (§§20 and 23). Not only does this intuitive shortage, which excludes them from the world of life, not forbid them from being received, manipulated, and constructed; but the very fact that they offer "nothing to see" in the changing world installs them in an unchanging universe, so protected from perturbations that they no longer maintain anything that "experience renders uncertain," and thus attain the status of the unshakeable (Descartes). This givenness, so poor in intuition, thus becomes their exceptional epistemological privilege. They give themselves almost without showing themselves intuitively and, by that very fact, they receive a certainty that would have been denied to them by a more rich, therefore sensible and changeable, intuition. Without exactly reaching the status of abandoned (since they keep a minimal degree of intuition), formal or poor phenomena already indicate that givenness is accomplished in this shortage and is even objectified more easily as material disturbances are missing from it.

But the phenomenality of the abandoned is not restricted to just these extreme cases. (c) We have already encountered another of its occurrences, one perfectly well known by the metaphysical tradition under the nonetheless ambiguous rubric *cogito*. For Descartes (and no doubt also for Husserl), this is not a matter of intuition, not even intellectual intuition. In contrast, the staging of this incomparable phenomenon can be accomplished only by the progressive and systematic elimination of every objective intuition— first of all, sensible intuition of worldly phenomena; then intellectual intuition of formal, logical, mathematical, or mathematized phenomena (simple natures), indeed analogizing intuition of the alter ego. In the realm of doubt (if not of the reduction), nothing remains really given that can, through the prism of thought, reach phenomenal monstration. But it is precisely this total suspension of the world and its givens that lets a last given arise, one that is transcendental and unconditioned—the gifted itself. He alone finally "feels" himself directly, based on the fact that every sensible has disappeared because he knew how "to detach his thought from sensible things."[84] The ego appears more or less to itself (supposing that it truly does appear), not despite the deception of intuition but thanks to it. And therefore, the abandoned—in actual fact the ego itself—gives itself only by paying the price of this intuitive lack and to the extent of it, lack of the world as much as of the self, to the point that it is directly identified with the gifted. The privilege of givenness is not only confirmed in the case of the abandoned, but—at least in metaphysics—it claims to erect it as ultimate ground. This pretension, no doubt unacceptable in phenomenology, attests at the very least that the given can still be accomplished even in intuitive shortage and therefore that the abandoned maintains a thinkable and practicable phenomenological function by means of the gifted. (d) But it is not enough just to admit the figure of the abandoned as noncontradictory and useful; it is also appropriate to recognize it as indispensable to a description of all the phenomena that are essentially determined by absence in the ways we have already discussed (§11). When a phenomenon becomes an object of desire, it is defined at once by the lack of intuition in it and, inseparably, by its obsessional givenness. It is intuitively deficient, but this deficiency continually troubles him to whom it is addressed; the latter (and not just any other) desires this phenomenon (and not some other) because he apperceives it as lacking. The lacking remains simply absent for everybody, but for the one who desires it, its intuitive absence still gives it, indeed more intensely. What is lacking shines by its absence—the latter, without intuition, gives itself all the more. Desire thus confronts the pure abandoned—which gives itself only insofar as it *disappoints* the expectation of an intuition.

> This great desire for my forgotten good,
> As the Author of my immortal death,
> Gnaws my mind with such a fury
> That, consumed by so hot a pursuit,
> Hope makes it, not for my own good, revive.[85]

Desire is deployed between an already accomplished givenness and a still deficient intuition; it would disappear if the latter were lacking lack or if the former filled it. It therefore endures as its ownmost given what it can never receive or render visible. In a word, only the desiring gifted gives himself over to the abandoned as such; it alone safeguards the extreme mode of phenomenality—that of a given that remains given even and especially when it is lacking. A major consequence follows from this: never can a finite gifted (and we know of no other kind) pretend, before a phenomenon of the type of the abandoned, to experience its own abandon, since the abandoned, by definition, finds itself always already given to the gifted despite or by virtue of its intuitive lack. No mortal can ask, "Why have you abandoned me?" For us, all abandon like all abandoned, even in intuitive desertion, remains under the watchful eye of givenness.

By Excess

The given can equally (or rather, unequally) give itself with an excess of intuition. This excess can saturate the capacity of the concept, therefore the reception of the gifted. As a result, the given that the gifted cannot stage cannot show itself. We have already encountered this figure of givenness, but we had until now always maintained its positivity. To be sure, the saturated phenomenon, nonconstitutable in terms of objective phenomenality, escaped the grasp of the constitutive I; but in its place and instead of it, it summoned what I named the witness.[86] The witness not only gives himself over to the given; he gives himself over par excellence, even offering the first real accomplishment of the gifted. Consequently, the witness permits the saturated phenomenon to show itself as an official phenomenon, precisely as paradox, and the paradox itself achieves, by means of the gifted (the witness), the passage from what gives itself to what shows itself. In fact, the saturated phenomenon shows itself clearly and distinctly as paradox, just as the witness fills precisely the function of the gifted. What is strange about this arrangement resides in the fact that its phenomenality breaks decisively with that of the object and constitution, but this very rupture, in the form of the paradox, makes the saturated phenomenon. This description therefore treats the excess of intuition within the paradigm of the saturated phenomenon such that the given not only shows itself to the gifted, but shows itself par excellence. Here the gifted again assumes its role of phenomenalization, with a rigor so strict that even intuitive saturation succeeds in showing itself paradoxically through its finitude. Finitude does not pose an obstacle to intuitive excess; it does justice to it according to the paradox. This figure is obviously still privileged, and for that matter it renders intelligible the whole phenomenality of givenness, whose landscape it lets us sketch. Here is not the place to question it, but to complete it. That is, there remains one last possibility opened by (and to) the excess of intuition. Instead of the saturated phenomenon still being inscribed within phenomenality because the gifted still receives it, the gifted might no longer be able or might decide not to bear the given, to no longer convey it to the visible. In short, the gifted might no longer put intuitive excess into operation in a phenomenon, not even in a saturated phenomenon. Saturation would block phenomenality; the distance (*para-*) from the norm would obscure apparition (*doxa*), even that of a paradox. This possibility is distinguished from the previous one (intuitive shortage) not only because it occupies the other extreme in the spectrum of givenness, but first because it introduces, in addition to the powerlessness of the gifted (already constitutive of the witness), his will not to stage the intuitive excess given to him. As we will see, the intervention of this authority turns out to be indispensable for the description of this new phenomenological situation. It is all the more important to avoid two equally harmful confusions. (i) The willing required here should not be too quickly assimilated to what metaphysics means by "will," for one very clear reason: what the metaphysical will wants is that it be based on an evidence of the understanding (Descartes, Leibniz) or reason (Kant), indeed with the intention of resisting and reversing its primacy (Schopenhauer, Nietzsche), while the willing here tries only to dodge the excess of intuition, and therefore the evidence. The willing that the gifted opposes to the intuitive excess does not contest it any more than it follows it—it flees it. The gifted avoids the given, becomes the absent gifted delivered. Willing indeed makes a decision, but a decision to desert, not to resist, an act of defeat, at the opposite extreme from a defiant will, a will to power, or a will to will. (ii) If this willing can abandon the given to itself (§9) by refusing it the phenomenal assistance that would allow it to show itself, as one abandons a battle, a party, or a business, its abandon does not belong to the moral or practical disposition. At issue is an abandon of phenomenality that would be qualified as theoretical if the phenomenality of givenness did not overstep the boundary between theory and practice. This abandon marks only one of the intrinsic possibilities of this phenomenality—for if every phenomenon appears because it first gives itself, it belongs to phenomenality that this gift can be exposed to abandon, to what no gifted would succeed in receiving in order to render it visible. What remains then is to examine how this failing deploys one of the extreme figures of givenness confronted with intuitive excess. I will do this by confronting this failing with the four figures of the saturated phenomenon, or paradox, already articulated (§23).

Fainting and Idle Talk

The saturated phenomenon appears first (a) in terms of quality, as the idol, so intense that the gaze can no longer bear it. When the gifted can no longer bear (or doesn't want to bear) this unbearable enough to let it appear in the paradox of the idol, it slips away from this too "deep contemplation."[87] Thus Zarathustra himself, confronted with the task of "enduring the idea of (eternal) recurrence," begins by crying, "Nausea, nausea, nausea —woe unto me!" and then faints. For the intensity of this thought attains such a degree of freedom (with regard to resentment), as well as horror (before the repetition of all things past without exception or selectivity), that it is necessary either to find a "means of enduring it" (the eternal return itself) or a "means of disposing of it" (fainting).[88] For that matter, Nietzsche himself, in his own life, no doubt bounced continually back and forth between these two dispositions; and when he decided ultimately to give himself over to the unbearable thought, he fainted definitively—not by evasion, but by collapsing beneath the weight of the idol. But fainting does not always remove the gifted from the intensity of nausea or horror; it can also remove him from happiness. For example, Rimbaud: if one dares to say "I embraced the summer dawn," then one must bear the fact that "precious stones gazed upon (me)," that "a flower . . . told me her name"; one must be able to see "a goddess" atop the pines, "pursue the dawn" "on the plains" and "in the city," "in the path" as on "the road"—in short one must "one by one, lift her veils" or surround her "with her massed veils" until the time comes when "I sensed a little her immeasurable body." At this very instant, this "a little" already gives much too much, and the gifted faints: "Dawn and the child plunged to the bottom of the wood."[89] Thus by fainting before happiness as well as horror, the gifted disappears as givee of the excessive given, givee charged with its crushing rise into visibility. He decides to abstain, to absent himself, to take refuge in an absence—that is to say, to prolong into a permanent state the absence that he experiences in the instant. If Lot's wife "becomes a pillar of salt" (Genesis 19:26), it is not only because she looked back at God's destruction of Sodom and Gomorrah, but no doubt also because this petrifaction alone permitted bearing its saturated phenomenon. The unbearable givens do not always happen in the figure of the thought of eternal return, but often as sorrows and joys too heavy to bear. We slip away and we faint as much as we can (or cannot) so as to no longer be there, as their gifted, when they burst forth. (b) The saturated phenomenon appears next in terms of quantity, as the event that happens without the gaze ever being able to foresee it, because the indefinite sum of its parts is continually increasing and never equals its final sum. Submerged by the excess of this flux, the gifted can renounce rendering visibility to the given, even the visibility of a paradox. Here the denegation takes on the style of false witness. Not the witness that is deliberately falsifying (which constitutes only its trivial side), but the witness that reports the event, in such a way as to take from it its dignity as saturated phenomenon. To tell stories, "to give his testimony," to play the reporter speaking from the field, in short, to blur the paradox by dissipating it in so many little stories, true details, and insignificant anecdotes that in the end it will have to lose its excess of meaning and destinal signification. This informed idle talk means to "treat" the event as if it were not one, as if it had objectifiable causes, a familiar unfolding, a definite temporality—as if the sum of gapers, spectators, and journalists had, in the end, the power to go "see it," to know all about it, to review it all. But when one has the pretense of having "seen it all," one has hidden everything since the event gives to see infinitely more than any gaze can receive and bear. In this way, the disciples at Emmaus sincerely claim to instruct Christ in his own Passion: "You are indeed the sole inhabitant of Jerusalem not to know the things that have happened here these days" (Luke 24:18). To be sure, the gifted is not deceived, but he seeks precisely this disqualification of the event in an almost finite sum of "true little facts" so as to evade the excess of intuition that renders it unforeseeable, not reducible to what could show itself—the event was, finally, "only that." Provided one brings to light a minuscule anecdote, a trivial detail, a limited statistic, one masters the event, whose unforeseeability vanishes.[90] Such curiosity (in response to fainting) denies the event its paradoxical character in order to dismiss the gifted from having to lose itself in its excess of intuition.

Denegation and Contempt

The saturated phenomenon appears next (c) absolute in terms of relation, like the flesh. It could seem contradictory to imagine that a gifted denies what gives itself to it as flesh, since this paradox is by definition carried out in perfect immediacy. In admitting that such an immediacy ends in an auto-affection—affection of oneself by the self alone—it is self-evident that no separation would remain any longer in the phenomenon of flesh—a separation with which the gifted could play in order to remove itself from its excess. I am, without the least remove, what affects me—my flesh, or rather: the flesh, which can be deployed only as mine; for another flesh (or the flesh of an Other) ceases immediately to count as flesh and again becomes, in the best case, an animated body. However, a gifted can challenge even the absolute immediacy of a given saturated in terms of the flesh. That is, such a phenomenon, appearing by definition only in my flesh (or in that of the Other as his ownmost), strengthens its phenomenality only by the confession or narration that communicates it. The more the phenomenon in terms of the flesh is saturated with intuition, the more it requires, to be visible to others, the word; sorrow, of course, but even enjoyment is not an exception. They must be said to this Other, who gives them to me in order that they don't smother me. This is what happens in the case of compassion in the midst of sorrow, grief before the deceased, solidarity in struggle, etc. In principle at least, for it can be that the gifted no longer says what its flesh attests, as a saturated phenomenon, and must (then wants to) deny it—with a denegation that blocks the phenomenalization of a given that is only visible through the word that says and confesses it. The model for such a situation is tragically self-evident: the survivor of the extermination camps. They were affected in their (biological, therefore phenomenological) flesh by a suffering so intense, so durable, and so all-encompassing (physical, psychological, spiritual) that one can justly call it absolute—with neither comparison, competition, nor possible relation with another or with an Other—in short, a suffering become a world unto itself. What is more, according to this saturated phenomenon of suffering, they were submerged in the intimate and daily experience of death and evil, to the point that they left the shared world for an other world and its indescribable logic. As soon as they returned—those who did return—to our world, where, even after the war or under real socialist regimes, we live, breathe, eat, take pleasure, in short, speak, they immediately saw that the phenomenon that had saturated them in their flesh—evil and suffering—could not be said, understood, or therefore appear in our world, that our world could not do justice to theirs—that it was not necessary to try and superimpose these two worlds separated by an abyss. Almost despite himself, the survivor, even the one closest to us— even my father—therefore denies: he says nothing because we could not imagine it or form the least idea of it—in short, because we could not phenomenalize what is nevertheless given to the survivor. And we thus see that the denegation comes as much from us, the spectators, as from him, the survivor: the gifted who denies the given is the one who shies away from the task of phenomenalizing it, therefore us first of all. For the survivor was and remains given over to what gives itself to him (how could he shy away from it?). If he does not stage the given that affects him carnally, this is because he lacks the stage; but who would open this stage to him, if not the spectators? But the spectators are lacking because we implement the denegation, better than and before the survivor—we do not want to see, hear, or have to know anything about it.[91] We hope the given (that saturates the gifted) will stay buried in the unseen and spare us its manifestation. In this way, the denegation of the carnal absolute recedes from the public space where the phenomenon can show itself to the still unseen saturated givenness. The unsayable often designates only a saturated phenomenon about which nobody wants to hear anything spoken—consequently one that nobody dares to say—the invisible, a saturated phenomenon whose sight nobody wants to bear: consequently one that nobody dares to show. What obviously counts for suffering and evil also counts for the other paradoxes according to the flesh: enjoyment, joy, and jubilation also risk denegation—and justly so, for they can hardly be separated.

The saturated phenomenon appears finally (d) absolute according to modality, like the icon that is irregardable and faces me. The paradox here stems from the fact that the relation of knowledge (modality) is inverted. Far from being able to keep the phenomenon under my sight as my object, I receive its gaze, which faces me. I find myself given over to the given of this gaze in such a way that I let it show itself in the face that he assumes so as to envisage me. In this scheme of things, the way in which what gives itself could be unable or unwilling to show itself is obvious. If I find myself given over to the gaze of the Other, I should, to see him show himself, gaze at this gaze (then this face). Such a counter-gaze and facing require of my gaze that it bear the gaze of the Other—that I take him in view. At this point, all possibilities open, therefore also the one suggesting that I cannot or don't want to take him into view. Not to take a gaze into view is to have contempt for it. Contempt for the gaze of the Other here does not have first an ethical meaning, but the strictly phenomenological sense of challenging, refusing, and avoiding the face-to-face that exposes me to a paradox of the type of the icon. I do not take into view the gaze of the Other. I never enter into the crossing of gazes and mutual regard. I avoid it, bypass it, and avert it. I let it be mistaken about me (it takes me for another) so as to better be mistaken about it (I take it for another). Neither he nor I accord a gaze to the other or recognize the other, and therefore see a face. We go side-by-side in the strictest sense, without seeing each other. This contempt dismisses the Other from appearing as the icon that he could deliver if his saturated given had found a counter-gaze in which to show itself. But this contempt has nothing exceptional about it, nor necessarily anything violent or frustrating. It actually defines the daily life of commerce between economic, institutional, and even familial actors. We have no need of the face nor regard for the Other, as an icon, in order to work, traffic, exchange with him. By contrast, the obligation to let such a saturated phenomenon show itself in every moment would practically forbid social life, seeing as it calls for the anonymity, interchangeability, and speed of exchange. Contempt therefore does not suspend sociability, but rather makes it possible by dismissing us from the obligation of seeing the other man for what he gives himself—a saturated phenomenon of the type of the icon. But, in this way, givenness remains in suspense: given to the gifted who condemns it, it cannot show itself. The gaze, left without regard for it since without counter-gaze, awaits its phenomenality—it is given as abandoned. The case is the same for the other paradoxes: the idol gives itself without showing itself before those who faint, the event gives itself without manifesting itself for the curious spectator, and the flesh gives itself without appearing in denegation.

Givenness often gives the given without measure, but the gifted always keeps within its limits. By excess or by default, givenness must in many cases renounce appearing—be restricted to abandon. Phenomenality always admits limits, precisely because givenness, which transgresses them, gives itself over only to my finitude.

Nevertheless, even abandoned, a gift remains perfectly given. I am therefore obsessed by what I cannot or don't want to let show itself. A night of the unseen, given but without kind, envelops the immense day of what already shows itself. And thus the gifted remains in the end the sole master and servant of the given.

OPENING ONTO A QUESTION

Several conclusions can be drawn from the investigation I have just completed.

Phenomenology does not break decisively with metaphysics until the moment when and exactly in the degree to which—a degree that most often remains in flux—it names and thinks the phenomenon (a) neither as an object, that is to say, not within the horizon of objectness such as, starting with Descartes, it defines the epistemological project of constituting the world and excludes from phenomenality, and therefore from the truth, all that, whether by lack (the pure sensible) or by excess (the divine and the insensible), does not fall under the order and measure of the *Mathesis Universalis*; (b) nor as a being, that is to say, within the horizon of Being, whether we understand this in the sense of the metaphysical *ontologia* or claim to "destroy" it in the name of the Dasein analytic or protect it under the cover of *Ereignis*—for a number of phenomena simply are not, or just don't appear inasmuch as they are. To let phenomena appear demands not imposing a horizon on them, whatever the horizon might be, since it would exclude some of them. The apparition of phenomena becomes unconditional only from the moment when they are admitted as what they give themselves—givens, purely.

The phenomenality of the given suggests that the phenomenon does not appear only when an other besides it (the I) constitutes it (Kant, Husserl), but first when it shows *itself* in itself and from itself (Heidegger). What remains is to take the most perilous step: thinking this *self/itself*—

which alone permits the phenomenon to show *itself.* For this project, I turn to the phenomenology of givenness because it opens at least a way of access to the *self/itself.* The phenomenon shows itself inasmuch as it unfolds in it the fold of givenness; it always keeps, at the end of this unfolding, the mark of the passage, trajectory, or movement that it accomplished in order to come forward. The given testifies, by the trembling with which it still and always vibrates, not only to its irreversible and intrinsic difference, but also to its incessantly lost and repeated happening. It therefore attests that if it appears (shows itself), it owes this only to itself, only to its *self* (which gives itself).

No doubt, the object can be received as a phenomenon—but as a handicapped or challenged phenomenon. Its intuition is limited to its concept, and therefore hides its givenness. Its coming forward submits to constitution, and therefore represses the *self* according to which its givenness would be outlined. Its apparently identical reproduction dissimulates its coming forward since its extrinsic finality as equipment destroys its anamorphosis and fait accompli. No doubt, too, all beings appear only as given —even though their submission to the concept of being imposes on them the yoke of representation, which hides their determinations as event and incident. But not every given shows itself reciprocally as a being. The majority of the time, it manifests itself precisely beyond or without the ontic categories. From now on, it is necessary that we learn to see what shows itself simply and strictly inasmuch as it shows itself, in the absolute freedom of its apparition. There is nothing easy about this apprenticeship, for what shows itself first gives itself and to see what gives itself, we must first renounce constituting and "grasping" it (in the Cartesian sense), in favor of simply receiving it. But to receive, in philosophy as elsewhere—what could be more arduous?

Along this way, however, opens the possibility of reintegrating into an official phenomenology saturated phenomena or paradoxes. In contrast to the classic doctrines of phenomenality, which were constructed according to the paradigm of phenomena poor in intuition (logical utterances, mathematical objects, the doubting ego, the I of the reduction, indeed Dasein in anxiety), the phenomenology of givenness follows the paradigm of the unconditional given, quite possibly saturated with intuition and therefore unobjectifiable. It can therefore do justice to the unconstitutable, which constitutes for us what is essential in our world (the idol, event, flesh, and face), indeed in what passes beyond it. Far from underestimating the most recent advances in phenomenology—hermeneutics, differ*a*nce, auto-affection, and the gaze of the Other—I am only trying to confirm them by assigning each a precise site within givenness. These advances have actually accomplished such triumphant breakthroughs that they have gone almost too far, almost to the point of cutting themselves off, so to speak, from their foundations. Pressed by the thing itself, they have not always taken care, first, to reach a decisive decision about their rupture with the horizons of the object or Being and, next and especially, to justify this rupture by elaborating the definition of phenomenality that permitted them in each case to accede to phenomena as radically new as theirs. For it is not enough to win new territories; it is still necessary to justify one's right to occupy them. I dare to propose that the definition of the phenomenon as what shows *itself* only inasmuch as it gives *itself* is the sole one to secure this justification.

A new question follows. The phenomenology of givenness has finished radically—in my eyes, for the first time—with the "subject" and all its recent avatars. It succeeds in this, however, precisely because it tries neither to destroy nor to suppress it. For such attempts have all failed; indeed they have reinforced the return of the repressed, because no knowing, however positivistic it might pretend to be, can do away with such a supposedly knowing and seeing *x*. To tear down this *x* would be a performative contradiction since whoever says or understands the apparently triumphant attack (and it is triumphant only for such a witness) annuls it by the very movement by which he consecrates it. Destroying the "subject" by denying it all actuality amounts to assigning it all the more an ideal definition; but the ideas of reason remain "inevitable" and continually stake a claim to existence in objectivity. The "subject" therefore always rises again from each of its pretended destructions. To have done with the "subject," it is therefore necessary not to destroy it, but to reverse it—to overturn it. It is posited as a center: this will not be contested, but I will contest its mode of occupying and exercising the center to which it lays claim—with the title of a (thinking, constituting, resolute) "I." I will contest the claim that it occupies this center as an origin, an ego or first person, in transcendental "mineness." I will oppose to it the claim that it does not hold this center but is instead held there as a recipient where what gives itself shows itself, and that it discloses itself given to and as a pole of givenness, where all the givens come forward incessantly. At the center stands no "subject," but a gifted, he whose function consists in receiving what is immeasurably given to him, and whose privilege is confined to the fact that he is himself received from what he receives.

The institution of the gifted by the given immediately implies reconsidering in new terms the question of access to the Other. The conditions in which the "subject" was instituted raise many obstacles to such access. For, if the "subject" is defined as constituting objects, then it can only objectify the Other (Descartes, perhaps Sartre) or appresent him in ordinary interobjectivity and therefore miss him as such (Husserl). If, by contrast, he accomplishes this purely by his own self-resolution, he only comes across the Other according to his own for-the-Other, without joining him (Heidegger). It's entirely different with the gifted: defined as he who receives and receives himself from the given, he can receive, according to the ordinary procedures of givenness (no predetermined horizon, no a priori principle, no constitution), among other givens, the paradox classified as icon, the face. For in the realm of givenness, the phenomenon of the Other, for the first time, no longer counts as anything like an extraterritorial exception to phenomenality, but belongs to it officially, though with the title paradox (saturated phenomenon). To receive the Other—that is equivalent first and before all to receiving a given and receiving oneself from it; no obstacle stands between the Other and the gifted. There is more: the gifted himself belongs within the phenomenality of givenness and therefore, in this sense, gives itself, too, in a privileged way. (i) It gives itself first inasmuch as, like every phenomenon, it arises from the given. (ii) It gives itself next par excellence, since it alone can and should respond in turn to the givens that appear as such only by showing themselves to it. (iii) Above all, the gifted can glimpse the possibility of giving itself to an exceptional given—the given that would show itself in the mode of the gifted, it too accustomed to receiving itself from what gives itself to it. When the Other shows itself, it is a case of one gifted giving itself to another gifted: first as a common given (a phenomenon given), next as a gifted (to whom givens are given). The difficulty no longer consists therefore in deciding if the Other can appear (traditional solipsism, the supposedly definitive "noncommunicability of consciousnesses"), but in grasping how the Other shows himself by giving himself to the gifted that I remain. And it could be that much attention and effort is needed to describe and understand the exceptional phenomenological situation in which a gifted shows himself, therefore gives himself, to another gifted according to several levels of the one and only givenness. This would no longer concern intersubjectivity or interobjectivity, but intergivenness—less an exception to ordinary phenomenality than one of its most advanced developments and, perhaps, its completion.

This situation, still unspoiled by exploration, not only allows and requires reconsidering the thematic of ethics—of respect and the face, obligation and substitution—and confirming its phenomenal legitimacy. It would
also perhaps authorize broaching what ethics cannot attain: the individuation of the Other. For I neither want nor should only face up to him as the
universal and abstract pole of counter-intentionality where each and every
one can take on the face of the face. I instead reach him in his unsubstitutable particularity, where he shows himself like no other Other can. This
individuation has a name: love. But we have for a long time now been without the concept that would do it justice, and this name remains the most
prostituted of words. Nonetheless, phenomenology claims to make it its
privileged theme—"Love, as basic *motive* for phenomenological understanding" (Heidegger).[1] Could the phenomenology of givenness finally restore to
it the dignity of a concept?

REFERENCE MATTER

NOTES

PREFACE

1. Paris: P.U.F., 1989.

2. Paris: P.U.F., 2001. English translation forthcoming from Fordham University Press.

3. Besides the debate "Autour de *Réduction et donation* de J.-L. Marion," *Revue de Métaphysique et de Morale*, 1991/1 (Henry, Greisch, Laurelle), see Dominique Janicaud's polemic *Le tournant théologique de la phénoménologie française* (Combas: Editions de l'Eclat, 1991), chap. 3 [English translation in Dominique Janicaud, J.-F. Courtine et al., *Phenomenology and the "Theological Turn"*].

4. Paris: Fayard, 1982, then P.U.F., 1991. Translated as *God Without Being*.

5. With an intermediary step, "Le phénomène saturé," in *Phénoménologie et théologie*, ed. J.-F. Courtine (Paris: Critérion, 1992), with contributions from Paul Ricoeur, Jean-Louis Chrétien, and Michel Henry, and a step beyond in "Au nom: Ou comment ne pas se taire," in *De surcroît* [English translations in Dominique Janicaud, J.-F. Courtine et al., *Phenomenology and the "Theological Turn,"* and John D. Caputo and Michael Scanlon, eds., *God, the Gift, and Postmodernism*].

6. He has already worked wonders in translating *Sur le prisme métaphysique de Descartes* [*On Descartes' Metaphysical Prism*] and *Phénoménologie et théologie* [in Dominique Janicaud, J.-F. Courtine et al., *Phenomenology and the "Theological Turn"*].

7. See his work, which I highly recommend: Jeffrey L. Kosky, *Levinas and the Philosophy of Religion* (Bloomington: Indiana University Press, 2001).

PRELIMINARY ANSWERS

1. Novalis, *Das Allgemeine Brouillon*, §902, in *Schriften*, ed. P. Kluckhorn, R. Samuel (Stuttgart, 1960) vol. 3, p. 441.

2. Must we be reminded again that the term *étant* (unheard of in the dictionaries of Littré, Lalande, and Robert) appears in Scipion Dupleix, *La logique ou art de discourir et raisonner* (1603), I:7, ed. R. Ariew (1984), p. 45 *et passim*.

3. *Poem*, fragment 6, in *Die Fragmente der Vorsokratiker*, ed. Diels-Kranz (Zürich, 1966), 12th ed., t. 2, p. 232. This is translated, in French: "Nécessaire est ceci:

dire et penser de l'étant l'être" (trans. J. Beaufret [Paris, 1955], p. 81), or more clearly: "Il faut dire et penser l'étant être" (trans. M. Conche [Paris, 1966], p. 102).

4. Shakespeare: "I have done the deed," *Macbeth* 2.2, *The Yale Shakespeare*, ed. W. L. Cross, T. Brooke (New York, 1993), p. 1133.

5. M. Henry, "Quatre principes de la phénoménologie," *Revue de Métaphysique et de Morale*, 1991/1.

6. Jacques Derrida, *Donner le temps: 1. La fausse monnaie* (Paris, 1991) [translated as *Given Time*].

7. A question posed by Paul Ricoeur during a debate about *Réduction et donation* held June 10, 1994, at the Centre Sèvres in Paris.

8. J. Benoist, unpublished paper, during this same debate or, more recently, "Qu'est-ce qui est donné? La pensée et l'événement," *Archives de philosophie*, 1996/4; F. Laurelle, "L'Appel et le Phénomène," *Revue de Métaphysique et de Morale*, 1991/1; and D. Janicaud, *Le tournant théologique de la phénoménologie française*. In the last mentioned, the questions address most often, though without skill, precisely what I did *not* say.

9. J. Greisch, "L'herméneutique dans la 'Phénoménologie comme telle,'" *Revue de Métaphysique et de Morale*, 1991/1; and J. Grondin, "La phénoménologie sans herméneutique," *Internationale Zeitschrift für Philosophie*, 1992/1.

10. Pietro Bembo, "Rime XLIII," in *Prose e rime*, ed. C. Dioissoti (Turin, 1960), p. 542.

11. My thanks to those whose intelligence and patience followed, along with their criticisms, my lengthy effort: A. Bonfand, V. Carraud, C. Cayol, J.-L. Chrétien, D. Franck, and M. Henry, as well as all those who have borne me.

BOOK I

1. In this sense, the phenomenological method is always practiced as a deconstruction (*Abbau*) or a destruction. Between these two terms, which are in fact both derived equally from the reduction, the difference stems solely from the nature of the obstacles cleared away: objectivity, Being as presence, the "history of Being," etc.

2. I have spoken at least once, with regard to *Réduction et donation*, of a "sort of negative phenomenology," along the lines of the negative theology set forth in *Dieu sans l'être*" ("Réponses à quelques questions," *Revue de Métaphysique et de Morale*, 1991/1, p. 68). This formulation seems to me today to be inexact and inappropriate. Inexact, because in Christian theology (as in my work of 1982), there is, properly speaking, no "negative theology," merely a negative way, inseparable from the affirmative way and the way of eminence; the attention paid today to so-called "negative theology" often misses this essential point. Inappropriate, then, because the phenomena that I mentioned (boredom, the call, etc.) in fact have nothing negative about them; Heidegger and Levinas had already offered perfect descriptions of certain characteristics that I confined myself to completing; in this sense, it was an issue of the most positive of phenomenologies, and some prejudice is necessary not to recognize it as such. However, it seemed to me at that time that

these same phenomena were considered in a still merely negative description, since the call remained anonymous, the interloqué unspecified, boredom by definition in suspense, etc. In *this* sense, they call for a new attempt at bringing them to light, an attempt that *Réduction et donation*, a strictly methodological work, could not and should not have risked; whence my formulation, unnecessarily problematic, which I now retract.

3. Michel Henry, "Quatre principes de la phénoménologie."

4. Originally introduced by J. F. Herbart (1776–1841): "Soviel Schein, soviel Hindeutung aufs Seyn" (*Hauptpunkte der Metaphysik* [Göttingen, 1806] in *Sämtliche Werke*, ed. K. Kehrbach, O. Flügel [Langensaltza, 1887; Frankfurt am Main, 1964], vol. 2, p. 187), cited inexactly by Husserl, *Erste Philosophie* II, §33, Hua. VIII, p. 47. This formula is passed along to the *Cartesian Meditations*, §46, Hua. I, p. 133, then into Heidegger, *Prolegomena zur Geschichte des Zeitbegriffs*, GA 20, p. 119, and *Sein und Zeit*, §7, p. 36. Let me emphasize that Herbart does not introduce this motto by chance, but in a previous question (*Vorfragen II*) explicitly titled: "What is given (*was ist gegeben*)?" He answers by asserting that "originally Being should be posited in the given [*ursprünglich würde das Seyn in das Gegeben gesetzt werden*]." This represents an essential thesis, one which he deduces from the analysis of appearance as a nothing which, inasmuch as unconditioned, does not remain any less of a real appearing: "Let us deny all Being. There then remains at the barest minimum the undeniable simplicity of sensation. But what remains after the Being [thus] eliminated is the appearance. This appearance, as appearance, is [*Dieser Schein, als Schein, Ist*]! But it belongs to the concept of appearance that it not be what it seems. Its content, what it reflects, is denied in the concept appearance. Thus it is everywhere explained as a nothing, as long as one does not attribute to it a new Being (totally foreign to that which is reflected by it). But from the latter, appearance has also been deduced. As a result of which: so much appearance, so much suggestion of Being" (Herbart, "Soviel Schein"). Herbart's project deserves more attention.

5. Nietzsche, "To impose upon becoming the character of being—that is the supreme will to power," *Wille zur Macht*, §617 = *Fragment* §7 [54], *Nietzsche Werke*, ed. Colli and Montinari, vol. 8/1, p. 320 [English trans., p. 330]. On the comparison of Nietzsche and Husserl, see *Réduction et donation*, pp. 30–33 [English trans., pp. 17–19].

6. Husserl, *Ideen I*, §19, Hua. III, p. 43 [English trans., p. 35]. See *Philosophie als strenge Wissenschaft*: "We must question things [*Sachen*] themselves. Back to experience, to intuition, which alone can give meaning and rational justification to our words. Very much to the point! But what, then, are things [*Sachen*]? And what sort of experience is it to which we must return in psychology?" (Hua. XXV, p. 21 [English trans., pp. 96–97]). In both cases, however, Husserl criticizes those who would restrict this return to "things" to those things that empiricism conceives. Thus: "One must in no instance abandon one's radical lack of prejudice, prematurely identifying, so to speak, such 'things' ['*Sachen*'] with empirical 'facts' ['*Tatsachen*']" (Hua. XXV, p. 61 [English trans., p. 146]).

7. Husserl, *Ideen I*, §24, Hua. III, p. 52 [English trans., p. 44 (modified)]. In his note to the French translation, Paul Ricoeur observes that the rapprochement of "giving intuition" and "what gives itself" not only is "striking," but above all "contains in miniature all the difficulties of a philosophy of constitution that must remain at the same time and from another point of view an intuitionism." In fact, the two formulations converge easily enough in givenness alone. But another difficulty then arises: is givenness measured solely by intuition (and constitution)?

8. On this liberation and its limits, see also *infra* Book 4, §20.

9. According to Didier Franck's demonstration in *Chair et corps: Sur la phéno-ménologie de Husserl* (Paris, 1981), chap. 1, p. 24.

10. Michel Henry, "Quatre principes de la phénoménologie," p. 11.

11. In point of fact, the *Ideas* define the "principle of all principles" in §24 while they spell out the reduction only beginning with §30.

12. Without going so far as to speak of "murder" (M. Henry, "Quatre principes de la phénoménologie," p. 12), one can certainly speak of a *betrayal* of phenomenality by intuition. By serving it and displaying its dignity, intuition lowers phenomenality to the status of mere fulfillment of the intentional aim at an object.

13. *Philosophie als strenge Wissenschaft*, Hua. XXV, p. 31 [English trans., p. 108].

14. I introduced this formulation in the conclusion of *Réduction et donation*. It goes without saying that I would not dare elevate it to the rank of principle of phenomenology if Michel Henry had not validated it in his commentary ("Les quatres principes de la phénoménologie," pp. 3 and 26). In fact, one could also refer to Michel Henry himself if one wanted to acknowledge the principial role of givenness: "Because [ipseity] belongs, inasmuch as its self-givenness, to all givenness whatsoever . . . , any being can have in this givenness, and through it alone, as phenomenon, a 'self'" (*Phénoménologie matérielle* [Paris, 1990], p. 74).

15. *Die Idee der Phänomenologie*, Hua. II, 7, 11–14 [English trans., p. 5 (modified)].

16. Ibid., Hua. II, 9, 14–20 [English trans., p. 7 (modified)].

17. Ibid., Hua. II, 44, 19–22 [English trans., p. 34 (modified)].

18. Ibid., Hua. II, 50, 30–32 [English trans., p. 40 (modified)]. Other formulations from this text could also be cited. For example: "If we restrict ourselves to the pure phenomenology of cognition, then we will be concerned with the *essence of cognition* as revealed in direct intuitive showing, i.e., with a showing that is carried out by way of intuition [*schauende . . . Aufweisung*] in the sphere of phenomenological reduction and self-givenness [*Reduktion und selbstgegebenheit*]" (Hua. II, 55, 1–5 [English trans., p. 43 (modified)]). Or else: "The absolute phenomenon, the *cogitatio* that has undergone reduction [*reduzierte cogitatio*], counts as an absolute self-givenness [*absolute Selbstgegebenheit*] not because it is a particularity but because it displays itself in pure 'seeing' after phenomenological reduction [*nach der phänomenologischen Reduktion*], precisely as absolute self-givenness [*absolute Selbstgegebenheit*]" (Hua. II, 56, 25–29 [English trans., p. 44 (modified)]). On this point, one can also consider the "reductive givenness" that Eugen Fink has excellently de-

fined as "possible accessibility through . . . the phenomenological reduction" (*VI. Cartesianische Meditationen. Teil 1. Die Idee einer tranzendentalen Methodenlehre* [Dordrecht, 1988], pp. 63–64 [English trans., p. 57]).

19. See *Réduction et donation*, p. 303 [English trans., p. 203].

20. That is to say, without *ecstasy*, in the sense that Michel Henry writes: "Therefore sight in its ecstatic structure (the eye and its mirror) does not constitute phenomenality's first actuality and upswelling. On the contrary, seeing can see what is seen only if it is first possible as seeing, that is, is apperceived in itself. So this apperception is inherent to ek-stasis and precedes instead of being constituted by it" (*Généalogie de la psychanalyse: Le commencement perdu* [Paris, 1985], p. 33 [English trans., p. 24]).

21. Michel Henry: "The reduction opens and gives. And what does it give? Givenness" ("Quatre principes de la phénoménologie," p. 13).

22. *Die Idee der Phänomenologie*, Hua. II, p. 61, 9 [English trans., p. 49 (modified)].

23. Heidegger, "Was heisst 'gegeben,' '*Gegebenheit*'—dieses Zauberwort der Phänomenologie und der 'Stein des Anstosses' bei den anderen," *Grundprobleme der Phänomenologie*, WS 1919–20, GA 58, p. 5. Here, it seems to me, Heidegger suggests that the "magic" of a supposedly mystical enchantment would offer no more an attitude appropriate to what givenness would demand than would the "scandal" of ordinary rationalism. He adds, lest one underestimate the difficulty of givenness, something which still remains to be broached: "Die Dialektik ist blind gegen die Gegebenheit" (ibid., p. 225). In fact, the blind are not lacking, as we have seen. In thus recognizing the privilege of givenness, Heidegger obviously transmits Husserl (note 22), but one will also find echoes of him in all the descendants he makes possible. Thus Merleau-Ponty: "The central phenomenon . . . consists in the fact that I am given to myself. *I am given*, that is, I find myself already situated and involved in a physical and social world—*I am given to myself*, which means that this situation is never hidden from me" (*Phénoménologie de la perception* [Paris, 1945], p. 413 [English trans., p. 360 (modified)]). Or Jean-Paul Sartre: "The truth cannot remain the property of the unique absolute-subject. It is in order to be given. . . . The truth is a *gift*" (*Vérité et existence*, 1948, posthumous edition [Paris, 1989], p. 28 [English trans., p. 27]). And especially Emmanuel Levinas, who maintains (contrary to Husserlian usage) the term *givenness* (in French, *donation*), even when it is no longer a question of immanence: "Transcendence is not a vision of the Other, but a primordial givenness" (*Totalité et infini* [The Hague, 1961], p. 149 [English trans., p. 174 (modified)]). Givenness thus determines equally, if not indifferently, the phenomenality of the self, the Other, and the truth. This is not, evidently, a matter of chance nor of a homonym.

24. *Die Krisis der europäischen Wissenschaften und die tranzendentale Phänomenologie*, §68, Hua. VI, p. 237 [English trans., p. 234 (modified)].

25. *Die Idee der Phänomenologie*, Hua. II, 14, 11–14 [English trans., p. 11 (modified)].

26. *Die Krisis der europäischen Wissenschaften und die tranzendentale Phänomenologie*, §48, Hua. VI, p. 169 [English trans., p. 166, note (modified)]. See also §§46 and 68 (as well as my commentary in *Réduction et donation*, p. 51ff [English trans., p. 31ff]).

27. *Die Idee der Phänomenologie*, Hua. II, 11, 21–24 [English trans., p. 9 (modified)].

28. *Die Idee der Phänomenologie*, Hua. II, 13, 1–5 [English trans., p. 10 (modified)].

29. Descartes, *IIIae Responsiones*, AT VII, p. 194, 12; Husserl, *Die Idee der Phänomenologie*, Hua. II, p. 70, 23–24 [English trans., p. 55 (modified)].

30. *Die Idee der Phänomenologie*, Hua. II, p. 11, 4–8 [English trans. p. 8 (modified)]. See also *Ideen I*, §44: "We therefore hold fast to the following: the essence of everything that gives itself by appearances [*zum Wesen der Gegebenheit*] implies that no appearance gives [*gibt*] the thing as an 'absolute,' but only in a one-sided way; by contrast, the essence of immanent givenness [*zum wesen der immanenten Gegebenheit*] implies giving an absolute [*ein Absolutes zu geben*]" (Hua. III, p. 102 [English trans., pp. 96–97 (modified)]).

31. *Die Idee der Phänomenologie*, Hua. II, p. 74, 25–31 [English trans., p. 59 (modified)]. I am here correcting the translation, truncated and therefore incorrect ("la donation est partout [givenness is everywhere]"), that I had given for this passage in *Réduction et donation*, p. 29 [English trans., p. 16]. This error did not provide surreptitious support for my thesis (the universality of givenness), but undercut it. For givenness is all the more universal as it is enacted in a "noetic phenomenon," by definition universal because singular. Givenness thus recovers "in some way all things," even more so as it is always enacted by the noetic, which, according to Aristotle, knows only by being assimilated "in some way to all things."

32. *Die Idee der Phänomenologie*, Hua. II, p. 5, 22–26 [English trans., p. 3].

33. Ibid., Hua. II, p. 10, 22–23 [English trans., p. 8].

34. Ibid., Hua. II, p. 55, 22–26 [English trans., p. 43 (modified)].

35. Ibid., Hua. II, p. 55, 16–21 [English trans., p. 43 (modified)].

36. *Ideen I*, §57, Hua. III, p. 138 [English trans., p. 133 (modified)], and *Cartesianische Meditationen*, §41, Hua. I, p. 117, 3–5 [English trans., p. 84 (modified)]. See also *Pariser Vorträge*: "*Transcendence is an immanent mode of Being, that is, one that constitutes itself within the ego*" (Hua. I, p. 32 [English trans., p. 32]). But in contrast to the text of 1907, these three texts no longer think transcendence in immanence explicitly on the basis of givenness.

37. *Die Idee der Phänomenologie*, Hua. II, p. 9, 8–9 and 13; 9, 16 and 19–20 [English trans., p. 7].

38. Ibid., Hua. II, p. 73, 9–10; p. 31, 15–17 [English trans., p. 58 (modified); then p. 24 (modified)].

39. Ibid., Hua. II, p. 12, 23–25 [English trans., p. 10 (modified)].

40. Unless one considers the essay on *The Idea of Phenomenology* in its entirety as research dedicated to defining givenness. Following this hypothesis, should we

conclude that the thought of givenness precedes the transcendental turn of 1913 (and especially of 1929) and could, in part, be opposed to it?

41. Pascal, *De l'esprit géométrique*, p. 351 [English trans., p. 195].

42. *Die Idee der Phänomenologie*, Hua. II, 74, 8–25 [English trans., p. 59 (modified)].

43. In fact, after 1907, Husserl discovers other "modes of authentic givenness," in particular the flesh, the passive syntheses, intersubjectivity, and teleology. Subsequent phenomenology has not stopped adding to this list (Being/beings, Dasein and its fundamental moods, the face, self-affection, hermeneutics, and difference, etc.). I claim that each falls within givenness, whether they admit it or not.

44. *Die Idee der Phänomenologie*, Hua. II, 73, 19–26 [English trans., p. 58 (modified)].

45. Ibid., Hua. II, 32, 3–4 [English trans., p. 25 (modified)].

46. *Ideen I*, Hua. III, p. 155, 18–19, and p. 156, 18–26 [English trans., pp. 153–54 (modified)].

47. *Die Idee der Phänomenologie*, Hua. II, 70, 23–24 [English trans., p. 55 (modified)].

48. Ibid., Hua. II, 12, 23–25 [English trans., p. 10 (modified)].

49. Ibid., Hua. II, 31, 11–17 [English trans., p. 24 (modified)]. See: "How can consciousness posit as a being something [*etwas als seiend*] which is not really and directly given in it [*in ihr gegeben*]," Hua. II, 35, 29–30 [English trans., p. 28 (modified)].

50. Ibid., Hua. II, 31, 25–30 [English trans., p. 24 (modified)].

51. Ibid., Hua. II, 73, 31–34 [English trans., p. 58 (modified)].

52. Ibid., Hua. II, 76, 1 [English trans., p. 60 (modified)]. *Ideen I*, §55, Hua. III, 134–35. The fact that *givenness* [*donation*] here translates *gebung* as well as *Gegebenheit* does not indicate any ambiguity, but foreshadows what will soon be thematized as the fold of the given (§6).

53. Only by taking the standpoint of givenness can one understand how Husserl does not contradict himself any more than he hesitates in postulating successively that "all ontologies . . . fall under the blow of the reduction" and that nevertheless "phenomenology claims no less to harbor within itself all ontologies" (*Ideen III*, successively §§13 and 14, Hua. V, 76 and 77 [English trans., pp. 65 and 66 (modified)]). See the texts and discussion in *Réduction et donation*, chap. 5, §§1, 2, 6, p. 235ff [English trans., p. 157ff], the conclusions of which I no longer subscribe to today in their totality. The one-sided insistence on submitting "ontology" to the reduction hides the fact that this same ontology arises from givenness.

54. *Ideen I*, §49, Hua. III, p. 116, 35–36, p. 117, 2, and p. 116, 39 [English trans., p. 111 (modified)].

55. *Ideen I*, §10, Hua. III, p. 27, 29–32, and p. 26, 12–13 [English trans., pp. 21 and 20 (modified)].

56. Which Husserl suggests: "We observe, however, that '*object*' is an accolade for various formations that nonetheless belong together—for example, 'thing,'

'property,' 'relationship,' 'predicatively formed affair-complex,' 'aggregate,' 'ordered set.' Obviously they are not interchangeable but rather in every case refer to one kind of objectness that, so to speak, takes precedence as the *originary objectness* [*Urgegenständlichkeit*]" (*Ideen I*, §10, Hua. III, p. 27, 7–13 [English trans., p. 20 (modified)]). Why then collect them together under this accolade if they cannot be assimilated to the "originary objectness," not even analogically? No doubt, this sole concept assembles them insofar as they are not assemblable. But how can it do so unless in it noetic indifference gets the upper hand over intentional differentiation? In this case, doesn't the primacy of the noetic simply repeat in phenomenology that of the *conceptus entis* in metaphysics? This at least is how we can understand the following pronouncement: "In reflection, the *cogitatio*, the appearing itself, becomes an object" (*Die Idee der Phänomenologie*, Hua. II, p. 14, 17 [English trans., p. 11]). For that matter, every attempt to oppose *in fine* objectness in terms of Husserl's "formal logic" to the metaphysical theory of the object not only will be driven mad by the "accolade" which here joins the configurations of the object under the rubric of objectness, but will blatantly contradict the results of several recent works on the deployment of objectness from the medievals to Kant and beyond (K. Twardowski, A Meinong, etc.).

57. *Die Idee der Phänomenologie*, Hua. II, p. 74, 8–11 [English trans., p. 59 (modified)]. I underline precisely the terms that Husserl does not emphasize in this passage, no doubt because for him the equivalence was self-evident.

58. Ibid., Hua. III, p. 55, 18–20 [English trans., p. 43].

59. Ibid., Hua. II, p. 73, 31–34 [English trans., p. 58 (modified)].

60. The customary translation of "es gibt" by "il y a" or "there is," no doubt admissible in everday usage, is no longer justified when one wants conceptual precision. It actually hides the semantics of givennness which structure the "es gibt." I really do not understand the inverse argument of F. Fédier: "Every place in the translation where the *Es gibt* is developed along the lines of *to give*, the translation goes a bit too far" (note in *Questions IV* [Paris, 1976], p. 49). Why? Can such a harsh denunciation get by without the least bit of justification? We will see that in refusing to translate what is nevertheless literally written, it often does not go far enough. As for the authority of Rimbaud ("Il y a . . . ," "Enfance, III," *Illuminations*, in *Oeuvres complètes*, ed. A. Rolland de Renéville [Paris: Pléiade, 1963], p. 177), whom Heidegger invoked on his own behalf ("Summary of a Seminar on the Lecture 'Time and Being,' in *Zur Sache des Denkens* [Tübingen, 1969], p. 42 [English trans., p. 40]), it seems to have been used arbitrarily. It does not seem that this poem is particularly illuminating or that it puts givenness as such into operation; at the very least, this would have to be established. Other references from Rimbaud would perhaps be more to the point. For instance, if one thinks givenness in the register of Being: "It is repose illuminated, neither fever nor languor, on the bed or on the meadow" ("Veilles," *Oeuvres complètes*, p. 192 [English trans., p. 143]); or if one thinks it as advent: "May it come, may it come, / The time of which we'd be enamored" ("Alchimie du verbe," *Une saison en enfer*, in *Oeuvres complètes*, p. 234ff [En-

glish trans., p. 83]) For that matter, Heidegger himself, more reserved than his commentators, does not deny what is evident: "The perfectly exact translation of Rimbaud's *il y a* would be the German *Es ist*" (*Zur Sache des Denkens*, p. 43 [English trans., p. 40 (modified)]). He therefore implicitly concedes that "il y a" does not perfectly translate "es gibt." I will therefore stick with "cela donne [it gives]," exact though unusual; it at least permits us to have recourse to several idiomatic formulae of indisputable phenomenological import, which we will encounter soon enough.

61. *Sein und Zeit*, §2: "Sein liegt im Dass—und Sosein, in Realität, Vorhandenheit, Bestand, Geltung, Dasein, im 'es gibt'" (p. 7, 1–3 [English trans., p. 26 (modified)]).

62. *Sein und Zeit*, §43: "Allerdings nur solange Dasein *ist*, das heisst die ontische Möglichkeit von Seinsverständnis, 'gibt es' Sein" (p. 212, 4–5 [English trans., p. 255 (modified)]).

63. *Sein und Zeit*, §44: "Sein—nicht Seiendes—'gibt es' nur, sofern Wahrheit ist. Und sie *ist* nur, sofern und solange Dasein ist" (p. 230, 5–6 [English trans., p. 272 (modified)]). This should be compared with §63: "Wenn es aber Sein nur 'gibt,' sofern Wahrheit ist [If, however, 'it gives' Being only insofar as truth 'is']" (p. 316, 21–22 [English trans., p. 364 (modified)]).

64. *Sein und Zeit*, §62: "Eine vollständige 'Gegebenheit' des ganzen Daseins" (p. 309, 28–29 [English trans., p. 357 (modified)]).

65. *Sein und Zeit*, §2, p. 6, 24–25 [English trans., p. 26 (modified)]. It is already a matter of the ontological difference (see *Réduction et donation*, p. 47 [English trans., p. 28]).

66. *Zur Sache des Denkens*, p. 47 [English trans., p. 44].

67. *Zeit und Sein* in *Zur Sache des Denkens* (Tübingen, 1969), pp. 4–5 and 6 [English trans., pp. 4–5 and 6 (modified)]. It is useless to emphasize here the bottleneck into which one is led by stubbornly refusing to translate "es gibt" by "cela donne" or "it gives"—unless one adds an unjustifiable gloss, the French and the English become unintelligible while the German remains insipid/limpid.

68. *Zeit und Sein*, p. 8 [English trans., p. 8].

69. *Nietzsche II* (Pfullingen, 1961), p. 355. Concerning the inscription of the history of metaphysics as nihilism in the "es gibt," see my sketch "Du pareil au même, ou: comment Heidegger permet de refaire de l'histoire de la philosophie,'" in M. Haar, ed., *Martin Heidegger* (Paris, L'Herne, 1983).

70. *Zeit und Sein*, p. 8 [English trans., pp. 8 and 9 (modified)]. See "the giving showed itself as sending" (p. 10) and "the sending in the destiny of Being has been characterized as a giving [*Geben*] in which the sending source keeps itself back and, thus, withdraws from unconcealment" (p. 23) [English trans., p. 10 and p. 22].

71. "Dieses Phänomen 'Sein,'" *Prolegomena zur Geschichte des Zeitbegriffs*, §32, GA 20, p. 423 [English trans., p. 307]. I have not invented this (rare and all the more significant) phrase.

72. *Zeit und Sein*, p. 23 (*ansichhalten* does not suspend, but retains) [English trans., p. 22].

73. *Zeit und Sein*, p. 17 [English trans., p. 16]. See also: "Thus the 'it' continues to be undetermined, enigmatic" (p. 18 [English trans., p. 17 (modified)]). See *Protocole*, p. 43 [English trans., p. 40].

74. *Zeit und Sein*, pp. 18 and 19 [English trans., pp. 17 and 19].

75. *Zeit und Sein*, p. 5 [English trans., p. 5]. Heidegger's insistence should be taken seriously, and it is the best confirmation of my translation. Whether the "es" or rather "Es" should be translated by "il" rather than "cela" matters little. Though the latter shows more respect for the neuter form, the difference does not change what is essential: it concerns the instance provoking the givenness of beings on the basis of Being. The official translation hides, here as elsewhere, everything that is at stake.

76. *Ideen I*, §58; *Metaphysische Anfangsgründe der Logik im Ausgang von Leibniz*, GA 26, pp. 177 and 211.

77. *Zeit und Sein*, p. 20 [English trans., p. 19 (modified)]; "Summary of a Seminar on the Lecture 'Time and Being,'" pp. 29 and 42 [English trans., pp. 27 and 38].

78. *Zeit und Sein*, p. 22 [English trans., p. 22 (modified)]. No doubt other texts from Heidegger could complete, confirm, or correct this analysis of the "it gives." I will not take them into account here for two reasons: (a) My project is not in the history of philosophy, but in philosophy. I walk with Heidegger as long as he guides us, fix the limits of his farthest advance, and forge ahead. I do not have to describe exhaustively the terrain crossed. (b) It is appropriate to privilege *Zeit und Sein* when considering the "it gives" because Heidegger explicitly claimed that he reconsiders the "it gives" in *Sein und Zeit* (see *supra*, n. 2).

79. I am not obliged, here at least, to specify the best formulation. See *infra* §4, §5, and §18.

80. Dominique Janicaud posed a fair condition for the approval of our project: "If the paradoxes of *Reduction and Givenness* were restricted to questioning the notion of givenness and interrogating its phenomenological sense . . . , we would have no objection" (*Le tournant théologique de la phénoménologie française*, p. 51 [English trans., pp. 65–66]). But, as is evident here (and already in 1989), I have set out to do nothing but construct the question of givenness in its strictly phenomenological sense. There should therefore no longer be anything to object to.

81. This requirement will be developed subsequently in the analysis of anamorphosis (§13).

82. I have, in this analysis, privileged the painting rather than other figures of the work (music, the poem, film, or dance) because it assumes the characteristics of an object more obviously than they do—seeing as it subsists and is actually manipulated (it is put in the hands of a "conservationist"). It therefore transgresses them all the more clearly.

83. Kant, *Kritik der Urteilskraft*, §17, conclusion; §15 (twice), Ak. AV, respectively, pp. 236, 226, and 228 [English trans., pp. 120 (modified), 111 (modified), and 112].

84. And if the frame in itself appears decorative, indeed beautiful, then it di-

rects the gaze to itself and becomes a work in its own right, on which the analysis can be repeated.

85. Heidegger: "So wäre das Wesen des Kunsts dieses: das sich-ins-Werk-Setzen der Wahrheit des Seindes," "Der Ursprung des Kunstwerkes," in *Holzwege*, GA 5, p. 25 [English trans., p. 36].

86. Heidegger: "Schönheit ist eine Weise, wie Wahrheit als Unverborgenheit west," "Der Ursprung des Kunstwerkes," p. 43. Likewise: "Art lets truth originate. Art originates as the founding preserving in the work of beings" (ibid., p. 64 [English trans., p. 77 (modified)]).

87. Husserl, *Ideen II*, §56, Hua. IV, p. 236 [English trans., p. 248]. This character of "objects invested with spirit" can be applied to the painting: "A spiritual being that essentially includes the sensuous but that, once again, does not include it as a part, the way one physical thing is part of another" (p. 239 [English trans., p. 251]). The beauty of a being does not belong to it in a "thinglike," real mode—and, may I add, not even in the ontic mode. On the considerable importance of this teaching, see Didier Franck, "L'objet de la phénoménologie," *Critique* 502 (March 1989).

88. On this eventness, see below §§14, 17, and, on the event of the painting, 23. The ontic exception of the painting was pointed out by Alain Bonfand, *L'expérience esthetique à l'épreuve de la phénoménologie: La tristesse du roi* (Paris, 1995).

89. Baudelaire, "Salon de 1845," *Oeuvres complètes*, ed. Y.-G. Le Dantec and C. Pichois (Paris: Pléiade, 1966), p. 863.

90. On this ascent of the unseen into the visible, see my analysis in *La croisée du visible* (Paris, 1991), chap. 2, p. 51ff.

91. Paul Cézanne, *Conversations avec Cézanne*, ed. P. M. Dorian (Paris, 1978), pp. 37, 125, 107, and 106.

92. Wassily Kandinsky, *Du spirituel dans l'art et de la peinture en particulier* (Paris, 1998), pp. 198, 107, 126, and 198 [see English translation in *Concerning the Spiritual in Art*]. I am obviously referring to the studies of Michel Henry in *Voir l'invisble* (Paris, 1988) whose interpretation, in its essential parts, I here make my own. I should note that Heidegger saw this phenomenological situation perfectly: "The event of its being created . . . reverberates through the work" (*Holzwege*, GA 5, p. 53 [English trans., p. 65]); however, he immediately misconstrued it by collapsing it into the ontic status of the work.

93. Maurice Merleau-Ponty: "It [the painting] gives visible existence to what profane vision believes to be invisible" (*L'oeil et l'esprit* [Paris, 1964], p. 27 [English trans., p. 259]). It could not be said any better: the painting makes the invisible effect as such visible. But painting does so only because it itself remains partially invisible, so as to be able to introduce as much visibility: "It is visibility itself, which includes a nonvisibility" (*Le visible et l'invisible* [Paris, 1964], p. 300 [English trans., p. 250]). To this invisible, indispensable operator of the visible, Merleau-Ponty assigns four principal meanings: (1) "what is not actually visible, but could be"—the as yet potential visible, still to come, that we call the unseen—then (3) what can-

not be seen, though it exists (for example, objects of the other senses, the tactile, etc.), and (4) the *lekta*, or mere thinkables—this concerns what does not have to be seen or made visible—but especially (2) "what, relative to the visible, could nevertheless not be seen as a thing" (ibid., pp. 310–11 [English trans., p. 257])—that is to say, literally what I mean by the arising, the effect, the "what it gives," which cannot appear like the things they are not, but which nevertheless makes possible the real visible to which they are essentially related.

94. Kant, at the very moment when he attributes to intuition the privilege that properly speaking characterizes intuition alone, nonetheless feels obliged to add—thereby ruining his own thesis: "Intuition takes place only in so far as the object is given to us" (*Kritik der reinen Vernunft I*, A 19/B 33 [English trans., p. 65]). In fact, seeing as the object is given to us only insofar as the intuition (object of the act) is too (in the act of intuition), both the one and the other therefore depend on the singular givenness, though in different ways. Husserl repeats this in his own way: "In the case of *complete unclarity*, the polar opposite of complete clarity, nothing at all has become given [*Gegebenheit*]. The consciousness is blind; it *is no longer in the least intuitive*, is no longer 'giving'" (*Ideen I*, §67, Hua. III, p. 156 [English trans., p. 154 (modified)]). What remains is to specify whether consciousness is no longer giving because it is no longer intuitive, as Husserl seems to assert, or the inverse, as I suggest.

95. *Denegative, but not negative givenness*—by definition, givenness excludes negation (see *infra*, n. 101).

96. *Sein und Zeit*, §40, p. 187, 25 [English trans., p. 232].

97. Bergson approaches this conclusion when he criticizes the idea of nothing with the argument that "I am always perceiving something, either from without or from within" (*Evolution créatrice*, chap. 4, in *Oeuvres*, ed. H. Gouhier and A. Robinet [Paris, 1959], p. 731 [English trans., p. 278]). But two presuppositions keep him from going from perception back to givenness: he does not admit that givenness can still give even without giving "something," and he always assigns its "perceiving" to it by means of a prior "I" or "consciousness" (p. 730 [p. 278]). Givenness, however, is not limited to the real given and does not proceed from an anterior pole of consciousness (which, in contrast, proceeds from it).

98. *Die Idee der Phänomenologie*, Hua. II, p. 74 [English trans., p. 59].

99. See *infra*, Book 5, §28. It is not certain that Jacques Derrida, in his classic study *La voix et le phénomène*, maintained the distinction between intuition and givenness. The inevitable consequence of this indecision in his interpretation of Husserl was the establishment, shortly thereafter, of difference outside all phenomenality, in the belief that he had overcome givenness (phenomenality) because the poorly secured pretensions of intuition had been deconstructed. But phenomenology does not come to an end when it is set free from the primacy of intuition—it begins. On this decisive point, see my discussion in *Réduction et donation*, I, §§4–5.

100. *Ideen I*, §67, Hua. III, p. 157 [English trans., p. 154].

101. For example, the case of Eugen Fink, whose use of the term "nongivenness" could be disconcerting: is he trying to limit the unconditioned universality of givenness, or is he risking a phenomenological contradiction in terms? Neither the former nor the latter. It is simply a question of designating the nonintuitive: "Der 'Gegenstand'—oder beser: die Gegenstände—der konstruktiven Phänomenologie sind nicht 'gegeben'; das darauf gerichtete Theoretisieren ist nicht ein 'anschauliches Gegebenen,' ist nicht 'intuitiv' (The 'object'—or better, *the objects*—of constitutive phenomenology are not '*given.*' The theorizing directed to them is not an 'intuitive having given' [*anschauliches Gegebenhaben*], is not intuitive [*intuitiv*])," *VI Cartesianische Meditationen, Teil 1: Die Idee einer transzendentalen Methodenlehre*, ed. H. Ebeling, J. Holl, and G. Van Kreckoven (Dordrecht, 1988), p. 62. Fink here makes an unfortunate terminological choice, but he fundamentally changes nothing in the Husserlian conceptuality. It should never be forgotten that Husserl applies the term "givenness" even to significations, however deprived of intuition they might be by definition. Should we correct his text by speaking of nongiven significations? Obviously not, so great and blatant a misreading would this be.

102. See *infra* Book 2, §§9 and 11.

103. *Sein und Zeit*, §53, p. 262 [English trans., p. 307].

104. Epicurus, *Lettre à Ménécée*, §125. See also *Letters and Maxims*, II.

105. Epicurus, *Sentences vaticanes*, §31.

106. La Fontaine, "La mort et le bûcheron," *Fables*, Book I, 15/16, in *Oeuvres complètes*, ed. J. Marmier (Paris, 1965), p. 79 [English trans., p. 27]; Ronsard, "Hymne de la mort," in *Oeuvres complètes*, ed. J. Céard, D. Ménager, and H. Simonin, vol. 2 (Paris: Pléiade, 1994), p. 609.

107. I am making no judgments here as to the legitimacy of a givenness (and a gift) not received by any givee. It is not necessary here to appeal to this figure of givenness, one that I will, however, study later (see Book 2, §9), since, whatever the case may be, death as possibility does not suppress the givee, but renders him possible in every sense of the term.

108. Descartes, AT IX-1, 19 ("Haud dubie igitur ego etiam sum, si me fallit, et fallat quantum potest, numquam tamen efficiet, ut nihil sim quamdiu me aliquid esse cogitabo," *Meditationes de prima Philosophia*, AT VII, 25, 8–10 [English trans., p. 17]).

109. On the reasons for bringing together and distinguishing these formulae—of which only the second is literally Cartesian—see my book *On Descartes' Metaphysical Prism*, chap. 2, §§8–9.

110. *Ideen I*, §35, Hua. III, p. 79 [English trans., p. 69 (modified)].

111. [The ambiguity of which Marion speaks is less evident, indeed hardly evident at all in the English translation he has proposed. As Marion explains below, the French *donation* is a noun that designates both the verbal action of giving (a nominalization formed from *donner*) and the substantive result of this action. The same ambiguity inheres in the English *donation*, though in English *donation* loses on the level of the signifier its connection with *giving*. In the English *givenness*,

both the verbal and the substantive senses of *donation* are hidden behind a nominalization drawn from the past participle (*given*) used adjectivally to designate quality.—Trans.]

112. In other words, don't I "exploit the ambiguity of the notion of givenness [*donation*]" (Janicaud, *Le tournant théologique*, p. 51 [English trans., p. 65]) or "play on a certain equivocality in the term 'givenness' [*donation*]" ("Question de la rédaction," *Revue de métaphysique et de morale*, 1991/1, p. 65, to which I have already made an effort to respond on pp. 65 and 68)? But the ambivalence of *givenness* (*donation*) (and its semantic network) remains a fact. To admit this fact implies no exploitation nor even the slightest game; it amounts to not neglecting a glaring question.

113. The declaration "I'm a self-made man!" approaches in the register of everyday talk what is conceptually called *causa sui*; but it offers a negative definition for the given: the phenomenon that not only is not self-made, but which makes itself visible only by also making visible the arising from which it comes.

114. The same analysis could be made, almost without modification, in terms of concepts comparable to the *givens* [*données*] of a problem. (a) The deal [*donne*] that passes out cards at the beginning of a hand (playing cards, but also financial, political, etc.), without saying anything about the anecdotal identity of the dealer, emphasizes even more the accidental necessity that is irrevocably imposed on the parties to the game, begins a new temporal sequence, and brings it about that a new, unheard-of interrelation of forces arises. (b) The genetic givens of an individual obviously remain forever without identifiable giver, without a giver that could be designated as original cause. It is indeed a matter of the given given to this individual, but especially giving it to himself, because it befalls him without choice or appeal, as a fact that upbringing and culture can never annul, a fact that they must, by contrast, presuppose in order to open a possible space for freedom. (c) Same analysis in terms of the artistic (or other) *gift*: he who receives it receives it without any cause that can be identified with a giver (genealogy being only one cause among others, sometimes not even). This given, precisely because it is one, always bears the stigma of its extraordinary inexplicability, and yet it irrevocably defines its beneficiary, to the point of radically individualizing him ("there's no one like him"). Givenness is marked by the impossibility of distinguishing in the gift between its actuality and its origin (see *infra*, Book 3, §17).

115. Spinoza, *Ethica III*, §1, dem. [English trans., p. 104]. Causal relation is, on principle, thought in terms of givenness: "Ex data causa determinate necessario sequitur effectus [From a given determinate cause there necessarily follows an effect]" (*Ethica I*, axiom 3). R. Misrahi makes the relevant remark: "*Dari* means to be given, to exist. Spinoza intentionally employs the expression in order to insist on the actuality and the existential reality of the envisaged cause. 'To be given' therefore does not here mean *to be given to someone* (as Gueroult thinks) nor simply there is (as Caillois thinks)" (Spinoza, *Ethique: Introduction, traduction, notes et commentaires*, [Paris, 1990], p. 332). Rather than actuality and existence, one should say facticity

(see *infra*, Book 3, §15), but the immanent givenness of the given is noticed in the double exclusion specified here.

116. Spinoza, *Ethica I*, §33, dem. and scholia 2 [English trans., p. 54 (modified)]. The transition from axiom 3 is mediated by §16 (cited in §33, dem.), where the deduction of *infinita infinitis modis* on the basis of the necessity of divine nature relies on the principle "Ex data cujusque rei definitione plures proprietates intellectus concludit, quae revera ex eadem (hoc est, ipsa essentiae) necessario sequuntur [From the given definition of any one thing, the intellect infers a number of properties which necessarily follow in fact from the definition (that is, from the very essence of the thing)]."

117. [The German *Gegebenheit* would be transcribed into English literally as *givenness*. My decision to render Marion's *donation* as *givenness* reflects, in addition to Marion's own preference, the fact that the French term is meant to render the German *Gegebenheit*. I am thus perhaps translating the German and not the French. Marion could very well have coined a neologism in French, just as *Gegebenheit* is itself not standard German. That is, he could have written *donéité*, comparable to his following the standard practice of using *étantité* [beingness] and *objectité* [objectness] where the French suffix -*ité* would be added to render the past participle an abstract noun, exactly as in the formation of the German *Gegebenheit* from the participle *Gegeben* and the suffix -*heit*, and the English *givenness* from the participle *given* and the suffix -*ness*.—Trans.]

118. Concerning the *es gibt* used by Heidegger, its transposition into the French *il y a* and the English *there is* cannot be justified despite usage. The analysis of *Sein und Zeit* aims only to play on the fold between the gift given (or *Gabe*) and a giving (*Geben*), in which Heidegger wants to avoid confusing givenness with some form of gift giving. Now, since all thought of Being without regard for beings, therefore all thought of Being in terms of the *Ereignis*, supposes that the *Geben* is still implied in the *Gabe* that explicates it, but which it in turn governs, the intervention of an *il y a* or *there is* totally conceals the explication of this fold of the given, which in contrast is maintained literally in the *cela donne* or *it gives* (see *supra*, §3). What leads the translation astray stems less from some pretended insufficiency of French or English to render the German than from the recoil before the radicality of the concept of givenness.

119. Note from A. Lowith in his otherwise quite remarkable translation of *Die Idee der Phänomenologie* (*L'Idée de la phénoménologie*, p. 54). Same commentary, with the same ultimate contradiction, on his translation of *Selbstgegebenheit*: "A term that designates what is given in person as well as the characteristic of being given in person; as with *Gegebenheit*, I therefore translate with either *given-in-person* or *presence-in-person*, or else by juxtaposing the two" (p. 55). This indecision unfortunately renders certain pages almost unintelligible (for example, Hua. II, 73–76; French translation, p. 98ff).

120. Though privileging the translation *given* (*Idées directrices pour une phénoménologie* [Paris, 1950], p. 538), Paul Ricoeur clearly marks the fold of the given:

"The rapprochement of the two expressions—*giving* intuition and what gives *itself*
—is striking. It contains in a nutshell all the difficulties of a philosophy of constitution that has to remain at the same time and from another point of view an intuitionism" (ibid., p. 78, n. 1 in §24); and "Here the *being-given* [*être-donné*] for 'naïve'
intuitionism and the givenness of meaning for transcendental consciousness converge" (ibid., p. 162, n. 2; see p. 183). A. Lowith followed this path, as did D. Souche-
Dagues (*Expérience et jugement* [Paris, 1970], pp. 21, 312, 438, etc., but *donation/
givenness*, pp. 303, 304, etc.); E. Escoubas (*Idées II* [Paris, 1982], p. 412); J. English
(*Problèmes fondamentaux de la phénoménologie* [Paris, 1991], p. 331), who also suggests
donnéités (p. 201); and M. B. de Launay et al. (*Méditations cartésiennes* [Paris, 1994],
p. 139). Opting inversely for *donation* are S. Bachelard (*Logique formelle et logique
transcendentale* [Paris, 1957], pp. 249 and 380), A. L. Kelkel (*Philosophie première*
[Paris, 1972], p. 301), and D. Tiffeneau (*Idées III* [Paris, 1933], p. 280).

121. Note of A. Lowith, *L'Idée de la phénoménologie*, p. 54.

122. Husserl, *Die Idee der Phänomenologie*, Hua. II, pp. 14 and 11 [English
trans., pp. 11 and 9].

123. *Sein und Zeit*, §7, "Das Sichzeigende," p. 35 [English trans., p. 59]; "Das
was sich zeigt, so wie es sich von ihm selbst her zeigt, von ihm selbst her sehen
lassen," p. 34 [English trans., p. 58].

BOOK II

1. Janicaud, *Le tournant théologique*, pp. 50 and 51 [English trans., pp. 63 and
65] (no precise reference mentioned). How can one reproach a philosophical and,
in general, scientific procedure or statement with abstraction? Must we be reminded
that abstraction not only characterizes all fundamental philosophical statements—
science of beings in their being, act of Being, *ego cogito*, monad, transcendental I,
spirit, eternal return, reduction, etc.—but that even the most "attenuated," far
from annihilating, actually permit certainty and access to the things themselves.
To reproach a philosophical thesis with abstraction is often equivalent to re-
proaching it with its truth.

2. *Le tournant théologique*, p. 40 [English trans., p. 52]. Elsewhere Janicaud
(p. 40) hesitates to formally acknowledge the utterances of revealed theology in *Reduction and Givenness*. I see two reasons for that: (i) This book (in contrast to others that are explicitly theological) remains by design strictly philosophical, without
a word of theology, to the point that one of its final pages expressly brackets the
question of God (p. 302 [English trans., p. 202]), which I *oppose* to Levinas's use of
Deuteronomy 6:4 (contrary to Janicaud, p. 49 [English trans., p. 63]); (ii) next, theology, a serious and scholastic enterprise, does not recognize itself in a "thought of
the Highest Being" (p. 88 [English trans., p. 102]), of "contents" (p. 86, author's
quotation marks [English trans., p. 100]), in general, of any vague realm. Why not
maintain the initial prudence? Why instead choose to find a "too obvious . . . theological veering" at the very moment of citing a passage from *Réduction et donation*,
which expressly says the opposite (p. 53 [English trans., p. 68], likewise p. 51)?

3. *Le tournant théologique*, p. 81; see pp. 44 and 89 [English trans., pp. 94, 56, and 103].

4. *Ideen I*, §58, Hua. III, p. 138ff [English trans., pp. 133–34]. Again it must be noted that here the bracketed "God" is defined only as the ground (*Grund*) of the facticity of the world, therefore according to its metaphysical sense as a transcendent being outside the world. This narrow sense would therefore leave intact any definition of God not based on a transcendence of this (metaphysical) type. Now, it is precisely the case for revealed theology that it approaches God by immanence as well as by transcendence: for instance, according to Saint Augustine, God is discovered as "interior intimo meo" (*Confessions*, 3.6.11). Would this immanence more radical than the region of consciousness also fall beneath the blow of the reduction? At the very least, this would have to be demonstrated (see *infra*, Book 4, §24, and note).

5. This statement appears in the conclusion of Janicaud's most theoretical work: "This genealogy of rationality is not metaphysical in the sense of special metaphysics, in the sense that it is not supported by any fundamental principle of the justification of the real. What remains for it of general metaphysics is only the desire for intelligibility" (*La puissance du rationnel* [Paris, 1985], p. 340 [English trans., p. 237]). This rash definition of the special metaphysics that burdens phenomenological givenness believes it can oppose general metaphysics to special metaphysics, as if one could separate the two aspects of the onto-theo-logical constitution of metaphysics, or even just the two fundamental disciplines in the system of metaphysics. It also assumes, in a hardly critical way, the supposed metaphysical innocence of the mere "desire for intelligibility."

6. *Le tournant théologique*, p. 51 [English trans., p. 65]. Of course, *Réduction et donation* never applies these terms to givenness, so obvious is it that they define *causa sui* to the exclusion of all else. See my clarification of this point in *Sur la théologie blanche de Descartes* (Paris, 1981), §18, and more recently in "The *Causa Sui*—Responsiones *I* and *V* ," in *Questions cartésiennes II* (Paris, 1996), chapter 5.

7. Jacques Derrida, *Donner le temps: 1. La fausse monnaie* (Paris, 1991), p. 24 [English trans., p. 13]. The rapprochement of Mauss and Derrida was outlined by D. Giovannangeli, "Die absolute Möglichkeit der Freiheit: Marcel Mauss' *Gabe* in der Rezeption bei Sartre und Derrida," *Fragmente* 30/40 (December 1992).

8. Marcel Mauss, *Essai sur le don*, first appearance in *L'Année sociologique*, 1923–24, reprinted in *Sociologie et anthropologie* (Paris, 1950, 1995), pp. 153, 197, and 161 [English trans., pp. 7, 35, and 13]. See Marcel Mauss: "This system presupposes (1) the obligation to give; (2) the obligation to receive; (3) the obligation to repay," in *L'obligation à rendre les présents, Oeuvres*, ed. V. Karady, vol. 3 (Paris, 1969), p. 45.

9. Leibniz, *Texts et opuscules inédits*, ed. G. Grua (Paris, 1948), p. 605. See: "Justitia est charitas sapientis seu charitas quae prudentiae congruit," p. 516 (see pp. 579, 583, 604, and 622).

10. J. Derrida, *Donner le temps*, p. 24 [English trans., p. 12].

11. M. Mauss, *Essai sur le don*, pp. 143 and 145 (my emphasis) [English trans.,

title page and p. 1]. The so-called gifts are always obligatory, despite the appearance of gratuitousness: "The aim of all this is to display generosity, freedom, and autonomous action, as well as greatness. Yet, all in all, it is mechanisms of obligation, and even of obligation through things, that are called into play" (p. 177 [English trans., p. 23]).

12. J. Derrida, who adds: "The simple *recognition* of the gift *as* gift, *as such*, [annuls] the gift as gift even before *recognition* becomes *gratitude*" (*Donner le temps*, p. 26 [English trans., pp. 13–14]). And also: "There is no more gift as soon as the other receives" (p. 27 [English trans., p. 14]). The last point can be disputed: it could in fact be the case that the gift survives the refusal to receive it (a way of ignoring it), as Derrida even seems to suggest in the logic of his third and fourth arguments. Whatever the case might be, this requirement is enough to disqualify as gift what Mauss names as such when he says, "Every contract begins with an exchange of presents that one is obliged to repay in one form or another and, in certain more or less defined cases, with a certain surplus" ("L'obligation de rendre les présents," p. 44).

13. Derrida, *Donner le temps*, p. 38 [English trans., p. 23]. See "the intentional significance" of the gift (pp. 157–58). One can, however, dispute the claim that the consciousness of giving *always* leads to the giver's narcissism. This path is verified only if the consciousness of giving is first of all the consciousness that it is I who gives, consciousness of the giving self, more than consciousness of the giving. But does this transfer of the gravitational center from givenness to the self ever reach an authentic consciousness of the gift? Derrida's argument thus presupposes what it is a matter of demonstrating: that the consciousness of the gift annuls *as such* the gift.

14. Mauss, *Essai sur le don*, p. 269ff.

15. Descartes in fact speaks of an "inner satisfaction" (*Passions de l'âme*, §43, AT XI, p. 377): "Happiness [*la béatitude*] consists, it seems to me, in a perfect contentment of mind and inner satisfaction" (*To Princess Elizabeth*, 4 August 1645, AT IV, p. 264 [English trans., p. 257]). He makes it the result of the will, or rather, of self-consciousness as good will: "The good use of free will is what produces the greatest and most solid contentment in life . . . the peace of mind and inner satisfaction felt by those who know they always do their best" (*To Queen Christina*, 20 November 1647, AT V, pp. 84–85 [English trans., pp. 325–26]). On this twofold reflexivity, see my analysis in *Questions cartésiennes*, chap. 5, §5.

16. Derrida, *Donner le temps*, p. 39 [English trans., p. 24].

17. Ibid., p. 26 [English trans., p. 14].

18. Ibid., p. 26 [English trans., p. 13].

19. Ibid., p. 26 [English trans., p. 13]. Or, "It cannot be gift as gift except by not being present as gift," and "If it presents itself, it no longer presents itself" (ibid., pp. 27 and 28 [English trans., pp. 14 and 15]).

20. Ibid., p. 42 [English trans., p. 27].

21. Formally, one could distinguish two meanings of this formulation. (a) If *or* is taken in a conjunctive sense, you get "nongift" = "nontruth," therefore, by sub-

tracting the negatives, "gift=truth"; (b) if *or* is taken in a disjunctive sense, you have "nontruth" or else "nongift," therefore "either gift or truth." Thus the formulation can be understood either as the equivalence of gift and truth or as their mutual exclusion. If one must choose, Derrida would probably lean toward the second interpretation; and I would do the same, though the first remains thinkable. But what is strange is found elsewhere—the fact that the gift maintains in both cases a privileged relation with the truth.

22. Derrida, *Donner le temps*, p. 76 [English trans., p. 54].

23. Moreover, here it would be a matter of the ground of a "present in general." It can be suspected that it itself would remain caught in this presence. Here again the two objections made to the gift, even in terms of givenness (founding causality, permanent presence), are collapsed (as *supra*, §7).

24. Derrida, *Donner le temps*, p. 24 [English trans., p. 12].

25. The conclusion of the *Essai sur le don* (pp. 271, 278, etc.) clearly shows that Mauss did indeed mean to draw out a contemporary model of economy from his ethno-sociological investigation. Moreover, emphasizes Lévi-Strauss, exchange (therefore economy) comes into play as an interpretation, not as an empirical observation: "But this exchange is not observed by him [Mauss] in the facts. Empirical observation does not provide exchange, but only 'three obligations: to give, to receive, to repay' [see *Essai sur le don*, p. 161]. The entire theory thus lays claim to the existence of a structure for which experience offers only the fragments, the scattered members, or rather the elements. If exchange is necessary and if it is not given, it must be constructed" ("Introduction à l'oeuvre de Marcel Mauss," in *Sociologie et anthropologie*, p. xxxviiff.). I want to emphasize this very specific formula: exchange is not given (it is an interpretive choice, nothing more), and reverse it: the given is not exchanged (is not interpreted in terms of exchange, economy). The recent work of M. Godelier, *L'énigme du don* (Pairs, 1996), also confirms this economic perspective.

26. "A gift . . . is literally a giving that can have no return, i.e., it is not given with the intention of being repaid": Saint Thomas Aquinas, *Summa theologiae* Ia, q. 38, a. 2, c [English trans., vol. 17, p. 95].

27. It should not be surprising that I stick with *one single* giver, *one* object given, *one* givee, without ever glimpsing the possibility that one or the other should multiply. It is not my ambition to broach the so-called question of intersubjectivity—which would certainly demand that the third be included—only that of givenness. I therefore stick with the most basic figure of the former; it is enough, we shall see, to raise great difficulties.

28. I will use *the Other* [*autrui*] hypothetically when it is a question of intersubjectivity, and not *the other* [*autre*], which is reserved for ontic alterity in general.

29. This ignorance can go far: without lingering over the diversions, wastes, and losses possible, it can happen that humanitarian aid is diverted from the victims to the executioners, that food sent ruins local agriculture, that it increases the exodus to urban centers, etc. It can also be the case that I don't even comprehend

what's at issue—assimilating aid for man to the defense of animal or plant life ("nature"). There are also the delirious excesses of the gift, with their dangers.

30. This operation, before being valid in phenomenology, is carried out in the name of pure charity: "For if it is in the expectation of a reward that you give, where is your grace [*poia hymin kharis estin*]?" (Luke 6:33). In contrast to friends "who repay each other equally [*apobalōsin ta isa*]" (Luke 6:34), enemies repay nothing; they therefore guarantee the nonreciprocal gratuity of love. In fact, the theology of the New Testament contradicted the Aristotelian description of friendship, defined by the reciprocity of services (given and especially) repaid in accordance with equality, and which thus excluded the gods (*Nicomachean Ethics* 8.9).

31. Saint Augustine evoked this paradox: "What is the perfection of love? To love even our enemies and to love them so much that they become our brothers— et inimicos diligere, et ad hoc diligere ut sint fratres. . . . Love thine enemies in the hope that they become your brothers; love thine enemies while hoping that they be called to enter in communion with you." Or: "Extende dilectionem in proximos, nec voces illam extensionem, prope enim te diligis, qui eos diligis qui tibi adhaerunt. Extende ad ignotos, qui tibi nihil mali fecerunt. Transcende et ipsos; perveni, ut diligas inimicos.—Extend [your love] to those strangers who have done you no wrong. Go farther: to the point of loving your enemies" (*In primam Epistulam Ioannis* 1.9 and 7.10.

32. On this point, there are some good suggestions in P.-M. Hasse, *Le mémorial de l'éternel* (Paris, 1983).

33. *Matthew* 25:37, 44.

34. *Matthew* 25:40.

35. *La jeune fille Violaine* (2nd version), in *Théâtre I*, ed. J. Madaule (Paris: Pléiade, 1964), p. 390.

36. For that matter, the unknown and powerful benefactor is helpful more often on account of dubious motives (Vautrin's vis-à-vis Captain Nemo and Lupin) than noble ends (Valjean). Even providence can sometimes play the role of anonymous giver—I think here of Robinson Crusoe, who spontaneously puts into operation a quasi-phenomenological reduction. Alone on his island, observing nevertheless that a benevolent power saves him at each moment, he recognizes it as unknown: "All that reawakened a reflection which often came into my mind when I began to understand Heaven's gentle view of the dangers we face in this life: How many times are we wonderfully delivered without knowing anything about it! How many times, when we are left hanging—as it is said—in doubt or hesitation about which we way we must take, a secret wind pushes us toward another route besides the one to which we are inclined, the one we call our own, our inclination, and perhaps even our obligations!" (Daniel Defoe, *Vie et aventures de Robinson Crusoë et autres oeuvres*, ed. F. Ledoux [Paris: Pléiade, 1959], p. 172).

37. See *supra* Book 2, §4.

38. This indeed is why it is so important to the giver (athlete, lover, artist) that the pleasure given be confessed, acknowledged, spoken by its beneficiary; for the

giver and the giver alone knows nothing about it. He has to hear confirmation that "he was good," that "it was good," that he climbed, ran, jumped, rode, touched, caressed well. He has to be assured that he "gave it his all" because he alone is unaware and should be unaware. He gives *himself* without knowing it.

39. *Matthew* 6:3. Almsgiving demands un-consciousness, ignorance, nonreflection. In contrast to commerce, which records (in its ledgers or cash register), almsgiving does not calculate, spends "impulsively," does not keep count—by which it joins up with sumptuous luxury, over which it nevertheless maintains the paradoxical superiority of sometimes fully accomplishing itself by giving nearly nothing and nevertheless almost everything (necessary).

40. It will not be objected that the majority of debts can be reimbursed and that the giver (in fact, the creditor) remains, however anonymous, operative, nor that we must distinguish debts that are reimbursable, because they bear on (finite, repeatable) objects, from debts that are irreversible, because they bear on nonobjects (the gift of life, of death, of time, etc.). In effect, even reimbursable debts require time in order to be free of them; that is to say, they are converted from objective to nonobjective. They are thus made worse (or deeper) by passing from the repeatable (object) to the irreversible (time). All debt, like all credit, amounts finally to time given and lost—but never repaid. In short, all debt is temporalized, whatever its object might be; therefore one is never free of it.

41. I will come back to the status of the consciousness of debt analyzed by Heidegger—"*das Dasein ist als solches schuldig*" (*Sein und Zeit,* §58)—but arbitrarily to the benefit of the horizon of Being. This one-sided analysis could be corrected by the counterinterpretation offered by Claude Bruaire, *L'être et l'esprit* (Paris, 1983). It deserves not to be forgotten.

42. One sees what opposes the metaphysical interpretation of givenness to the bracketing of all transcendence in the gift. In the first case, what precedes, like a first principle or first cause, is the presence of the giver, while in the second, what precedes is his absence; however, this absence does not abolish the giver, since he still intervenes in givenness as reduced. In this way, he is just as much involved in laying bare the essence of the gift because he permits describing it without presupposition, as received in the aspect of debt.

43. See *infra,* §9.

44. The reduction does not disturb this requirement. It could even be the case that it does justice to it. That nonknowledge (absence of intuition, absence of presence) defines the horizon where only access to the Other is in play was established by Husserl with the utmost precision by opposing his appresentation to intuitive presence (*Zur Phänomenologie der Intersubjektivität,* §§4 and 39 and appendix 27, Hua. XIII, pp. 114ff, 189ff, and 263ff; *Ideen II,* §44–45, Hua. IV, p. 162ff; and *Cartesianische Meditationen* V, §50, Hua. I, p. 157ff.

45. Molière:

> Harpagon: I'm finished with you!
> Cléante: Right. Be finished then.

H: I disown you as my son!

C: Very well!

H: I hereby disinherit you!

C: As you wish.

H: And I give you my curse!

C: I'll have nothing to do with your gifts."

L'avare IV:5, *Oeuvres complètes*, ed. P. A. Touchard (Paris, 1962), p. 455 [English trans., p. 201 (modified)]. There is here a double refusal of objectness: that of Harpagon, who gives only his curse (privation, the denegation par excellence, ontically empty) and that of Cléante, who refuses even the gift of nothing, even the anti-object. This execration of the blessing remains a gift, but manifested as perfectly unreal.

46. To assume the obscene conceptual formula put forward by Kant: "*Marriage* (*matrimonium*), that is, the union of two persons of different sexes for life-long possession of each other's sexual attributes." This concerns a "contract" (*Metaphysik der Sitten* I, §24 [English trans., p. 62]), therefore, no longer a gift, but commerce (literally, carnal commerce), because, hand in hand with this first failing of the gift (exchange), a second supports it: the objectification of the gift, here of the person, in a real object: "[Each] person is acquired by the other, *as if it were a thing*" (§25, Ak. A., VI, 277 and 278 [English trans., p. 62] [my emphasis]).

47. On the basis of these three examples, it would be easy to show that other gifts are even more obviously given in excess of all objectness: to give life, to give one's own life, to give death, to give peace, to give time, to give one's time, to give meaning, etc. I will have to consider them later (*infra*, Book 4, §24, p. 340ff).

48. I thus recover an admirable formula from St. Thomas Aquinas: "Donum non dicitur ex eo quod actu datur, sed inquantum habet aptitudinem ut possit dari . . . in nomine doni importatur aptitudo ad hoc quod donetur—[It is not called a gift based on the fact that it is actually given, but insofar as it has an aptitude for being given (or giving itself). . . . With the name *gift*, it is a question of this aptitude for being given]" (*Summa Theologiae* Ia, q. 38, a. 1). In an intriguing parallel, this aptitude is also privileged by Mauss: "Originally the *res* need not have been the crude, merely tangible thing, the simple, passive object of transaction that it has become. It would seem that the best etymology is one that compares the word to the Sanskrit *rah, ratih*, gift, present, something pleasurable. The *res* must above all have been something that gives pleasure to another person" (*Essai sur le don*, p. 233 [English trans., p. 50]). "Something that gives pleasure to another person" is like having-to-be-given, what I name givability, and is opposed to "the simple, passive object of transaction," exactly what I name the object of economic exchange. The gift bears par excellence on the ready-to-hand (*Zuhandene*), not on the subsistent (*Vorhandene*), but to the point that these ready-to-hand can even sometimes (in fact often) dispense with all real beingness.

49. Paul Claudel, *La jeune fille Violaine*, p. 590.

50. Chrétien de Troyes, *Le conte du Graal ou le roman de Perceval*, ed. C. Mela

(Paris, 1990), lines 3140–50 [English trans., pp. 416–17]. This refusal to ask is insisted upon in ll. 3182–83, 3230, and 3242.

51. Ibid., ll. 6325–27 [English trans., pp. 458–59].

52. Corneille has offered an exemplary staging of the refusal of a recognized and confessed gift. For example, the character of Alidor stoops to loving only on condition of being able to keep the power of not loving:

> The rules that I follow are quite different:
> I want freedom in the midst of chains.
> I cannot avail myself of an object that I possess,
> I cannot feed myself on a love that yields to me.
> I hate it, if it forces me; and when I love I want
> To give when it pleases me and withdraw my faith.

La place royale, I:4, lines 203–12. It is literally a matter of impugning the acceptability of a gift offered in fact: "One wants to smother a fire with one's burning eyes / And not love it when one is loved" (V:3, lines 1304–5). So as to refuse the gift insofar as it is given, Alidor imagines transmitting the supposedly beloved woman to a third party and clearly emphasizes that: "This is not to obligate him, but to satisfy me, / Not to give it [happiness] to him, but to take it from me" (IV:1, lines 897–98).

53. Racine, *Bérénice*, IV:5, l. 1070 [English trans., p. 426 (modified)].

54. It must be remarked that when a theologian of Anselm's caliber dares to think the Incarnation in terms of satisfaction—the dignified exchange between the fault for sin and its retribution in the Redemption (*Cur Deus homo*, I:12)—he finds himself bearing the brunt of objections that are all the stronger as they remain strictly theological. The model of the gift as transcendent exchange cannot stand, especially not in revealed theology.

55. It assumes it but modifies it essentially, as we will see soon enough in Book 5. But at this point in the analysis, this modification remains too radical for me to even be able to sketch its principal characteristics. It belongs to givenness that the one who receives the given can be described only on the basis of and therefore after this very given (Books 3 and 4).

56. Spinoza, *Ethica I*, §18: "Deus est omnium rerum causa immanens, non vero transiens."

BOOK III

1. Gilles Deleuze establishes this point clearly: "Empiricism is by no means a reaction against concepts, nor a simple appeal to lived experience. On the contrary, it undertakes the most insane creation of concepts ever seen or heard. Empiricism is a mysticism and a mathematicism of concepts" (*Différence et répétition* [Paris, 1968], p. 3 [English trans., p. xx]). Phenomenological empiricism, however, stands at an equal distance from this excess and this lack, in order to remain strictly within the realm of intuition and, here, of givenness.

2. This restriction, may it be remembered (see Book 2, §§7 and 12), is justified by the demand to maintain, in each reduction of the given phenomenon, a (quasi) consciousness that undergoes the lived experience of this gift: either a giver for the lived experience of givability, or a givee for the lived experience of acceptability. It would be absurd to pretend to reduce the gift to conscious lived experiences without, in each case, assigning them to a consciousness. It is for consciousness, in the figure of a giver, that the lived experience of givability becomes visible; it is for consciousness in the aspect of givee that the lived experience of acceptability becomes visible. The two difficult questions of their respective modes of intentionality and the identity of this "consciousness" can be broached only on this basis (Book 5, §§26 and 28).

3. Aristotle, *Metaphysics* I, 1003 a 21ff, and E, 1, 1026 a 23–32.

4. Saint Thomas Aquinas: "Hoc enim dari nobis quod aliunder habemus" (*Summa Theologiae* Ia, q. 38, a. 1, ad 1 m).

5. See §12. The famous example of anamorphosis, provided by Holbein the Younger, *The Two Ambassadors* (National Gallery), is remarkable in that the *same* painting can be seen (a) without anamorphosis, in frontal perspective—as an affirmation of objectness and beingness, and in the same frame, (b) with anamorphosis (the skull and crossbones, therefore a *vanitas*, therefore a givenness) if the viewer consents to move a little to the right, slightly downward, as anticipated by the way it is hung. Two phenomenalities in a single phenomenon.

6. Passing from aesthetics to phenomenological analysis, it becomes possible to broaden this concept, to include for example listening to music. The scholarly works and the virtuoso experimentation of I. Retznikoff have proven that the vaults of Romanesque churches (and even certain prehistoric caves) could resonate like stringed instruments, provided they were made to vibrate, by chanting, at a precise point. In each case, it was necessary, by a more and more precise approximation, to detect this point. The singer or the musician (and also the listener) had to move himself physically in such a way that the sound emitted would occur by itself in its fullness, would rise toward its total sonorous form. There is indeed sonorous anamorphosis. See I. Retznikoff, "Sur la dimension sonore des grottes à peintures du paléolithique," *Comptes rendus de l'Académie des Sciences de Paris*, vol. 304, 2nd series, no. 3 (1987); and "On the Sound Dimension of Prehistoric Painted Caves and Rocks," in *Essays in the Semiotic Theory and Analysis of Music*, ed. E. Tarasti (Berlin/New York, 1995). See also *Le chant de Vézelay* and *Le chant de Fontenay* (disques Studio SM 12 21.16 and 12 16.40).

7. Husserl, *Ideen I*, §2, Hua. III, p. 12 [English trans., p. 7 (modified)].

8. ["Comes upon me" here translates the French "m'advient."—Trans.]

9. Descartes: "Intellectum a nullo umquam experimento decipi posse, si praecise tantum intueatur rem sibi objectam, prout illam habet vel in se ipso, vel in phantasmate" (*Regula XII*, AT X, 423, 1–4 [English trans., p. 47]). This is in fact a recovery of Aristotle, *On the Soul*, III, 3, 427 b 11ff and *Metaphysics* G, 5, 1010 b 2.

10. Utility (*Zuhandenheit*) is therefore spotted not only in the extreme situation

of a breakdown or deficiency, but also and first in the (supposedly normal) one of functioning properly. Heidegger's analysis (*Sein und Zeit*, §16) should therefore be completed and resumed: equipment, when it belongs thoroughly to the mode of Being of technological objects, can never be forgotten, even when it works; for this working properly is itself carried out only by radically implicating the one to whom it happens (indeed all his potential aides and audiences) so that he watches over security, the controls, the instrument panel, etc. The utility maintained in each instant of its functioning (not only in breakdowns) remains a happening repeated in each instant.

11. To make the phenomenon appear, it is necessary that first "je m'y fasse"—literally that "I make myself over," more idiomatically that "I accustom myself to it." This admirable turn of phrase suggests two essential points. (a) First, that I model myself on equipment, without becoming it or it becoming nothing, but by working on myself to adapt myself to it. (b) Next, that I do not accustom myself to the equipment itself (since nothing real in it demands apprenticeship; in contrast everything dispenses with it), but to what I do not yet understand about it, that is to say, its usage, its utility, which is precisely irreal. To accustom *myself* [*me* faire] to the phenomenon (to its utilization) is therefore equivalent to making it (or letting it) come upon *me*.

12. Aristotle, *On Interpretation*, 9, 19 a 27–32 [English trans., p. 30]. For example, "It is necessary for there to be or not to be a sea battle tomorrow." See G. E. M. Anscombe, "Aristotle and the Sea Battle," *Mind* 65 (1965); and Pierre Aubenque, *Le problème de l'être chez Aristote* (Paris, 1962), p. 322ff.

13. ["Unpredictable landing" here translates the French "arrivage," a term from everyday, colloquial usage. This French term appears in everyday life when one dines at a restaurant featuring fresh fish. A literal translation would be something like "catch of the day" or "according to the market," which lose too much of the meaning Marion here intends. The unpredictability and uncertainty of what will arrive to market each day is, as any traveler knows, mirrored in the guesswork that surrounds the landing of a jet at any major airport. I have therefore chosen to shift the register from dining out to air travel and render *arrivage* as *unpredictable landing*—intending no slight, or homage, to the airline industry.—Trans.]

14. One thinks here of the monads, which arrive like so many "continual fulgurations of the Divinity" (*Monadology*, §47 [English trans., p. 186]). And of Descartes, defining surprise as a "sudden and unexpected arrival" (*Passions de l'âme*, §72 [English trans., p. 353]). [And, of course, of the arrival of a jet at any major airport.—Trans.]

15. Spinoza: "At res aliqua nulla alia de causa contingens dicitur, nisi respectu defectus nostrae cognitionis," *Ethica I*, §33, sc. 1 [English trans., p. 54 (modified)].

16. Spinoza: "De natura Rationis non est, res ut contingentes, sed ut necessarias contemplari." Leibniz will note still more precisely the relativity of the distinction between contingency and necessity. On the one hand, "Discrimen inter *veritates necessarias et contingentes vere idem* est, quod inter numeros commensura-

biles et incommensurabiles; ut enim in numeris commensurabilibus resolutio fieri potest in communem mensuram, ita in veritatibus necessariis demonstratio sive reductio ad veritates identicas locum habet." On the other hand, to erase it, it is enough to call on an infinite calculation, therefore on God: "At quemadmodum in surdis rationibus resolutio procedit in infinitum, et acceditur quidem utcumque ad communem mensuram, ac series quaedam obtinetur, sed interminata, ita eodem pariter processu veritates contingentes infinita analysi indigent, quam solus Deus transire potest. Unde ab ipso solo *ap riori* ac certo cognoscuntur" (*Die philosophischen Schriften*, ed. Gerhardt, vol. 7, p. 200).

17. Descartes: "Quid enim ad nos, si forte quis fingat illud ipsam, de cujus veritate tam firmiter sumus persuasi, Deo vel Angelo falsum apparere, atque ideo absolute loquendo, falsum esse? Quid curamus istam falsitatem absolutam, cum illam nullo modo credamus, nec vel minimum suspicemur? [What is it to us that someone may make out that the perception whose truth we are so firmly convinced of may appear false to God or an angel, so that it is, absolutely speaking, false? Why should this alleged 'absolute falsity' bother us, since we neither believe in it nor have even the smallest suspicion of it?]" (*IIae Responsiones*, AT VII, 145, 1–6 [English trans., p. 103]).

18. Saint Thomas Aquinas: "Utrum possibile sit aliquid fieri, quod semper fuerit," *De aeternitate mundi contra murmurentes*, in *Opuscula omnia*, ed. P. Mandonnet (Paris, 1927), vol. 1, p. 22 [English trans., p. 19].

19. "In hoc ergo tota consistit quaestio, utrum esse creatum a Deo secundum totam substantiam, et non habere durationis principium, repugnent ad invicem, vel non" (ibid., p. 23 [English trans., p. 20 (modified)]).

20. "Patet per inductionem, in omnibus mutationibus subitis, sicut est illuminatio et hujus modi" (ibid., p. 23 [English trans., p. 21]). Likewise, "Non repugnat intellectui, si ponatur causa producens effectum suum, subito non praecedere duratione causatum suum [No intellectual absurdity is implied if we suppose that a cause which produces its effect instantaneously does not precede its effect in duration]" (ibid., p. 24 [English trans., p. 21]).

21. "Esse autem non habet creatura nisi ab alio; sibi autem relicta in se considerata nihil est: unde prius naturaliter inest sibi nihil, quam esse . . . natura ejus est talis, quod esset nihil, si sibi relinqueretur" (ibid., p. 25 [English trans., p. 23]). The theme of *nihil*'s anteriority in the creature comes from, among others, Augustine: "Deus qui de nihilo mundum istum creasti [O God, who from nothing hast created this world]" (*Soliloquia* 1.1.2 [English trans., p. 344]); "Etsi de terrae pulvere Deus fixit hominem, eadem terra omnisque terrena materies omnino de nihilo est, animamque de nihilo factam dedit corpori, cum factus est homo [Although God fashioned man from the dust of the earth, the earth itself and all earthly matter are derived from nothing at all; and when man was made, God gave to his body a soul which was created out of nothing]" (*De Civitate Dei*, XIV, 11 [English trans., p. 568]). It is not merely a matter of a creation "*ex* nihilo" (starting from nothing and leaving it), but "*de* nihilo" (starting from nothing holding the place of matter

and definitively). See S. Kuki: "The profound meaning of disjunctive contingency is to be a possible nothing" (*Le problème de la contingence*, French trans. and introduction by H. Omodaka [Tokyo: Editions de l'Université de Tokyo, 1966], p. 191).

22. To be sure, in St. Thomas, this is formulated in terms of creation, causality, and ontic dependence. That is not enough, however, to disqualify it for my purposes. I retain phenomenologically only a necessary contingency, which remains precisely intrinsic to the phenomenon of the world. It is the remarkable success of this Thomist doctrine that it accomplishes a sort of reduction of contingency to the immanence of the lived experience of the world (lived experience as created in itself) instead of interpreting it as an extrinsic and transcendent relation (to consciousness or the creator). That eternity does not contradict the created character itself attests the immanence of the contingency, henceforth intrinsic to the phenomenon.

23. One certainly could, at the risk of surprising, hold that the same goes for the finite modes in relation to substance, according to Spinoza. For if "In rerum natura nullum datur contingens; sed omnia ex necessitate divinae naturae determinata sunt ad certo modo existendum et operandum [Nothing in nature is given as contingent, but all things are from the necessity of the divine nature determined to exist and to act in a definite way" (*Ethica I*, §29 [English trans., p. 51 (modified)]), it has to be admitted that (i) without this divine necessity, they would remain in themselves contingent; (ii) this necessity happens to them only through an efficient cause, therefore one actually distinct from them, the substance (§16 cor.); (iii) this necessity becomes immanent to them, despite its divine provenance, inasmuch as it remains in them *causa immanens* (§18). As the necessity of the mode is borrowed from that of the substance, it remains as such contingent, but with a contingency rendered intrinsically necessary by the immanent character of the necessary cause that produces it. If Spinoza thus thinks the necessity of the modes, shouldn't it therefore be admitted that he thinks it first in terms of an otherwise radical contingency?

24. Husserl, *Erste Philosophie* II, §33, Hua. VIII (The Hague, 1959), p. 50.

25. Ibid.: "Despite and during the experience itself" (pp. 49, 27). See pp. 50, 7, and 9 (ibid., p. 69); and §34 (p. 55, 11).

26. Ibid., §34: "The proposition that the world is a pure nothing, a pure transcendental illusion is *compatible* [*verträglich*] with our perceptive certainty of the existence of the world, which is empirically indubitable" (p. 54).

27. Ibid., §33, p. 48.

28. Ibid., §33, p. 49. On this possibility, see also §34, p. 53.

29. *Ideen I*, §46, Hua. III, p. 108 [English trans., p. 102 (modified)]. This text lets me answer a question that the texts from *Erste Philosophie* seem to leave undecided: does the contingency of the world precede the reduction or result from it? The *Ideas* here connect it unambiguously to the reduction, which in fact renders it definitively visible and unsurpassable (for the transcendent will always remain contingent, even once constituted). But *Erste Philosophie* in fact thinks the contingency

of the world on the basis of the reduction. (a) First, because §§33–34 of chapter 1 are separated from chapter 3 (dedicated to the reduction) only by a chapter 2 that develops the argument from madness (therefore intersubjectivity), which, in fact, takes up and criticizes the way borrowed from Descartes, and therefore directly prepares for the reduction. (b) Next, because chapter 3 explicitly takes up the contingency of the world from §§33–34 in order to oppose it, as clearly as had the *Ideas*, to the absolute necessity of the I: "In contrast to the possibility of the not being [*Nichtseinsmöglichkeit*] of the experienced world, or as Descartes preferred to express it, the possibility of doubting it, the *ego cogito* is set apart as absolutely indubitable to me" (§38). The contingency of the fact of the world prepares for the reduction, but takes on meaning only on the basis of it.

30. *Erste Philosophie* II, §33, p. 50; "Der Sinn dieser Zufälligkeit, die da Tatsächlichkeit heisst," *Ideas* I, §2, Hua. III, p. 12 [English trans., p. 7].

31. *Erste Philosophie* II, §33, p. 50.

32. I thus foreshadow §17, *infra*.

33. [Throughout this section, Marion plays on the French signifier *fait*. As a noun, *fait* would be translated as *fact*, but *fait* is also the past participle of the verb *faire*, "to do" or "to make."—Trans.]

34. Schelling, *Philosophie de la mythologie* VIII, ed. S. W. Cotta, vol. 12, p. 152 (modified). See K. Hemmerle, *Gott und das Denken nach Schellings Spätphilosophie* (Freiburg, 1968). The modifications that I have made to this text in repeating it stem from the fact that Schelling means only one fact (Revelation), just as Husserl took into view only the *Weltfaktum*, while I am trying to extend facticity to phenomenality in general.

35. Kant, *Kritik der praktischen Vernunft*, §7, Ak. A. V, 31 [English trans., p. 31].

36. Ibid., Ak. A. V, 47 [English trans., p. 48 (modified)].

37. Ibid., Ak. A. V, 42 [English trans., p. 43 (modified)].

38. *Sein und Zeit*, §39, p. 181, 4; §57, p. 276, 8–9; §41, p. 192, 21–24 [English trans., pp. 225; 321; 236].

39. *Sein und Zeit*, §29, p. 135, 20–24 [English trans., p. 174].

40. *Sein und Zeit*, respectively, §57, p. 276, 12–13 and §12, p. 56, 1–5 [English trans., pp. 321 and 82]. On the first formulations of the ontological difference in 1927, see *Réduction et donation*, chapter 4, §2.

41. *Sein und Zeit*, §12, p. 56, 8–11 [English trans., p. 82]. See: "This is a definite way of Being, and it has a complicated structure, which cannot even be grasped *as a problem* until Dasein's basic existential states have been worked out" (ibid., p. 56, 5–8 [English trans., p. 82]. It is remarkable that Heidegger, at the moment of thematically introducing facticity, recognizes a "*problem*" with it (the italics are his). What problem? This one no doubt: the factuality of worldly beings defines merely these beings, while facticity designates not only Dasein but the situation of all possible beings in relation to it and thus radically their mode of coming forward: they are encountered only to the extent that Dasein meets them. Thus, without a reinterpretation of the customary concept of fact/facticity in terms of the structures of

Being fundamental to Dasein, one risks falling into anthropology and losing one-self in the "*problem*." The equivalence between facticity and being-in-the-world is sealed by the canonic definition of care [*Sorge*]: "Ahead-of-itself-Being-already-in (the world) as Being-alongside entities that we encounter (within-the-world)." The first part (ahead-of-itself) defines existence in particular; the third clarifies falling (*Verfallen*); but the second—Being-already-in the world)—designates facticity (§50, pp. 249, 12–250, 2 [English trans., p. 293].

42. To translate *sich begegnen* by "bring about the encounter" appears to me to be a misreading, for the one who brings it about is solely and uniquely Dasein, not beings within the world that are only encountered, and only when Dasein first brings about the encounter with them.

43. *Sein und Zeit*, §50, p. 250, 1 [English trans., p. 293]. See the passage cited above, n. 38.

44. Please excuse me for preferring this declaration to the venerable: "Hic saltus, hic Rhodus." One could, in the same familiar register, compare it with the almost identical formulation of he who wants or claims to want to pay everybody's bill: "It's my turn!" But the differences are so obvious—the last example concerns a decision that is (i) free, (ii) temporary, in which I am still (iii) substitutable for the others, and which will be (iv) "repaid"—that the comparison doesn't count. It would even weaken the connection that I want to establish between facticity and the fait accompli (see *infra*, §28).

45. See the similar analysis made above, §13.

46. Descartes, *A Mesland*, 2 May 1644, AT IV, 118, 25–119, 1; *VIae Responsiones*, AT VII, 482, 14–18 (my emphasis) [English trans., p. 235; p. 291 (modified; my emphasis)].

47. Husserl attempted a comparable reduction with regard to logical state-ments, which he reconducted to the fait accompli of givenness, in *Erfahrung und Urteil* §4, §7, §8. He concludes: "Every objectivity of the understanding is pre-constituted in the judgment insofar as a judgment produces it as pre-given [*erzeugt als Vorgegebenheit*]" (§63, *Erfahrung und Urteil* [Hamburg, 1954], 2nd ed., p. 300 [English trans., p. 251 (modified)]).

48. Stéphane Mallarmé, *Oeuvres complètes*, ed. H. Mondor and G. Jean-Aubry (Paris: Pléiade, 1945), pp. 457, 459, 464, and 472 [English trans., p. 124, 126, 132, and 140].

49. Aristotle, *Metaphysics*, D 30 1025a 14–15; 5 (see E, 2, 1026 b 31–32); E, 2, 1027 a 13 [English trans., p. 1619, p. 1619, and p. 1621 (modified)]. As a general rule, I understand (and translate) *sumbebēkos* as *incident*. I use *accident* only when I stick to the narrow and metaphysical concept within the limits that Aristotle often sought to restrict it. The translation by *incident* corresponds to that of the German *Zufälligkeit, zufällig*, "what falls and arrives upon."

50. Aristotle, *Topics*, I, 5, 102 b 5 [English trans., p. 170]. Pierre Aubenque il-lustrates, without disputing, Aristotle's metaphysics position: "A being who can al-ways become other than it is, a being whose form is always affected by a matter

that blocks it from being perfectly intelligible, a being finally who is revealed to us only through the irreducible plurality of the categorical discourse" (*Le problème de l'être chez Aristote*, 4th ed. [Paris, 1962], p. 456). This faithful gloss suffices to pose my question: Does always becoming other and appearing in an irreducible plurality forbid or accomplish phenomenality? If "matter" multiplies the figures of apparition, in what sense does it block phenomenality? Henceforth, what reproach can be made, except to complicate not the conditions for appearing but—this is something quite different—those for intelligibility? But is it self-evident that phenomenality should have the limits of intelligibility as its norm? Couldn't we inversely put into question the span of intelligibility according to the range of phenomenality? Here, at least, Aristotle remains more Greek than phenomenologist.

51. Aristotle, *Metaphysics* D, 30.1025a5–25.

52. Aristotle, *Metaphysics* D, 30.1025a28–29. See Remi Brague, *Aristote et la question du monde* (Paris, 1988), p. 358ff.

53. Pierre Aubenque: "Contingency and what it implies, that is to say, a suspension of the principle of contradiction" (p. 492).

54. See *infra*, §16, n. 1.

55. Aristotle, *Metaphysics* D, 30.1025a25–30. The translation of *sumbebēkos* by *accident* (indeed *attribute*) obscures its phenomenality more than necessary to the benefit of the metaphysical lexicon. The phrase *what works with* (indeed *travelling companion*), though tempting, is, however, preconceptual and too familiar. *Coincident* has recently been proposed (M. P. Duminil and A. Jaulin, *Aristote, Métaphysique: Livre Delta* [Toulouse, 1991], p. 113). The reproduction of the Greek is literally impeccable, but the concept thus taken up into French or English clearly contradicts what the Greek meant, unless the meaning of *coincidence* is inverted for the sake of recovering the conflict of two incidences, one with reason, the other without. I have just sketched this solution (see §16).

56. Aristotle, *Metaphysics* D, 30,1025a30–34 [English trans., p. 1619 (modified)].

57. In particular following the *Posterior Analytics* 1.8 and *Metaphysics, Z*, 5. Alain Badiou's assertion concerning "the absolute nonBeing of the event" (*L'être et l'événement* [Paris, 1988], p. 337) can hardly be of help here, so lacking in precision and scope is the concept of Being he invokes.

58. Maimonides, *The Guide of the Perplexed* I, §57 [p. 132 (modified)]; Avicenna, *Philosophia prima*, 1.8, in *Opera in lucem redacta*, ed. 1508, reed. (Frankfurt am Main, 1961), f. 74 v. (see V, 2, t. 2, p. 238, and IX, 1, t. 2, p. 440ff and *La métaphysique du Shifa'*, 1, 5 and 1, 7; French trans. G. Anawati [Paris, 1978], t. 1, p. 108ff, 119ff). See also J. Jolivet, "Aux origines de l'ontologie d'Ibn Sina," in J. Jolivet and R. Rasehd, *Etudes sur Avicenna* (Paris, 1984).

59. Thomas Aquinas: "Creatio . . . si sumatur passive, sic est quoddam accidens in natura," or "Creatio aliquid est et est accidens" (*In Sententiarum libros* II, d. 1, q. 1, a. 2, as 4 m and a. 1, ad 1 m).

60. Thomas Aquinas: "Quicquid enim non est de intellectu essentiae vel quidditatis, hoc est adveniens extra. . . . Omnis autem essentia vel quidditas potest in-

telligi sine hoc quod aliquid intelligatur de esse suo . . . ; ergo patet quod esse est aliud ab essentia vel quidditate" (*De ente et essentia*, 4.5 [English trans., p. 55]—following the text of *Opera omnia*, vol. 43 [Rome, 1976]). Put otherwise, the most proper subsistence of essence is radically received from God, from the outside: "Esse suum receptum a Deo est id quo subsistit" (p. 158). See T. O'Shaughnessy, "St. Thomas' Changing Estimation of Avicenna's Teaching on Existence as an Accident," *The Modern Schoolman* 36 (1958–59); L. B. Geiger, *La participation dans la philosophie de saint Thomas d'Aquin* (Paris, 1942), c. XIV; and F. Brown, *Accidental Being: A Study in the Metaphysics of Thomas Aquinas* (Notre Dame, 1985).

61. Thomas Aquinas: "In Deo autem esse suum est quidditas sua; aliter enim accident quidditas et ita esset acquisitum ab alio et non haberet esse per essentiam suam" (*In Sententiarum libros* I, d. 8, q. 4, a. 2, c.).

62. This could be the reason why Aristotle, at the precise moment of defining the original sense of the first *ousia*, abandons the term and substitutes *tode ti*, designed to be ontically neutral, which almost mimics a nonessence, a pure incident (*Categories*, 2).

63. I retranslate the Latin text (*Principia Philosophiae* I, §52, AT VIII-1, p. 24), because Picot's translation glosses it excessively, though quite intelligently: "But when it is a question of knowing if some one of these substances really exists, that is to say, if it is at present in the world, it is not enough that it exist in this way for us to notice it; for that alone discloses to us nothing that would excite some particular knowledge in our thought. But in addition to that, there must be some attributes that we can notice" (*Principes de la philosophie* I, §52, AT IX-2, p. 47). On this Cartesian treatise concerning substance, and in particular on the medieval antecedents of this aporetic response (Suarez, Tolet, Duns Scotus, etc.), see my study "Substance et subsistance—*Principia Philosophiae*, §51–54," in *Questions cartésiennes* II, chap. 3.

64. Suarez clearly formulates the lack: "Substantia non immutat immediate intellectum nostrum ad aliquam intellectionem sui, sed tantum accidens sensibile" (*Disputationes Metaphysicae*, XXXVIII, s. 2, n. 8, O.o., ed. Berton, Paris, 1856, t. 26, p. 503). *Immutare*, which replaces *afficere*, also marks the arrival, the unpredictable landing that substance lacks.

65. *Principia Philosophiae* I, §§51 and 52, AT VIII-1, pp. 24 and 25 [English trans., p. 210].

66. *Vae Responsiones*, AT VII, p. 249, 10–15.

67. Descartes: "A conceptu rerum adaequato, qualem nemo habet, non solum de infinito, sed nec forte etiam de ulla alia re quantumvis parva" (*Vae Responsiones*, AT VII, p. 365, 3–5 [English trans., p. 252 (modified)].

68. See *supra*, Book 2, §11.

69. Aristotle, *Metaphysics* D, 30.1025a30.

70. Suarez: "Nullam autem est ens quod non sit vel effectus, vel causa" (*Disputationes Metaphysicae*, XII, prol., t. 25, p. 372); Pascal, *Pensées*, §199; Kant, *Prolegomena zu einer jeden künftigen Metaphysik*, §17, Ak. A. IV, p. 296 [English trans.,

p. 40]. Or else: "Everything that happens has its cause [Alles was geschieht, hat seine Ursache]" (*Kritik der reinen Vernunft*, A 9/B 13, Ak. A. III, p. 35 [English trans., p. 50]). To the contrary, Nietzsche states: "Es gibt weder Ursachen, noch Wirkungen. . . . In Summa: ein Geschehen ist weder bewirkt noch bewirkend," *Posthumen Fragmente*, 14 [98], ed. Colli-Montinari, vol. 8, 1, p. 67.

71. Descartes, *Responsiones, IIae*: "Nulla res existit de qua non possit quaeri quaenam sit causa cur existat. Hoc enim de ipso Deo quaeri potest" (AT VII, p. 164, 28–165, 1 [English trans., p. 116]); *Iae*: "Dictat autem profecto lumen naturae nullam rem existere, de qua non liceat petere cur existat, sive in ipsam causam efficientem inquirere, aut si non habet, cur illa non indigeat, postulare" (AT VII, p. 108, 18–22 [English trans., p. 78 (modified)]). In French: "La raison ne nous dicte point que ce que nous voyons ou imaginons ainsi soit véritable. Mais elle nous dicte bien que toutes nos idées ou notions doivent avoir quelque fondement de vérité [Reason does not dictate that what we thus see or imagine is true. But it does dictate that all our ideas or notions must have some foundation of truth]" (*Discours sur la méthode*, AT VI, p. 40, 6–10 [English trans., p. 131]). On these points, see, in addition to my study *Sur la théologie blanche de Descartes*, §18, *Questions cartésiennes* II, chap. 4.

72. Descartes, *Meditatio III*: "Jam vero lumine naturali manifestum est tantumdem ad minimum esse debere in causa efficiente et totali, quantum in ejusdem causae effectu. Nam, quaeso, undenam posset assumere realitatem suam effectus, nisi a causa? Et quomodo illam ei causa dare posset, nisi etiam heberet?" (AT VII, p. 40, 21–23 [English trans., p. 28]).

73. Descartes, *Discours de la méthode*, AT VI, p. 76, 21–22, and 29 [English trans., p. 150]. Nietzsche described perfectly—in its intention, which is enough to criticize it—the paradoxical ontic and phenomenal subordination of the cause to the effect in *Twilight of the Idols*, "The Four Great Errors" (particularly §§1–4).

74. Kant, *Kritik der reinen Vernunft*, A 194/B 239, Ak. A., III, p. 170 [English trans., p. 232].

75. One could almost accept Alain Badiou's formulation: "If an event exists, *its belonging to the situation of its site is not decidable from the perspective of the situation itself*" (*L'être et l'événement*, p. 202).

76. François Furet, *Le passé d'une illusion* (Paris, 1995), p. 49. See Paul Ricoeur: "An absolute event cannot be attested in historical discourse" (*Temps et récit*, vol. 1 [Paris, 1983], p. 140; and commenting on Raymond Aron: "The past, conceived as the *sum* of what has actually arrived, is outside the scope of the historian" (ibid., p. 141 (my emphasis). See H.I. Marrou [Davenson], *Bergson et l'histoire* (Paris, n.d.), p. 210.

77. Charles Péguy, *Clio, dialogue de l'histoire et de l'âme païenne*, in *Oeuvres en prose complètes*, ed. R. Burne, vol. 3 (Paris: Pléiade, 1992), pp. 1208 and 1209.

78. Donald Davidson, in particular in *Essays on Actions and Events* (Oxford, 1980), has observed that (i) "we are justified in believing that events exist" (French translation, p. 243), therefore in acknowledging the priority of the event as "fun-

damental category" (French translation, p. 242); (ii) "the redescription of an action by a reason" in virtue of which "events are often redescribed in terms of their causes" (French translation, p. 24) implies a reversal such that "it is not *events* that are necessary or sufficient as causes, but events *inasmuch as they are described* in one way or another" (French translation, p. 231)—in short, the event provokes its causes by interpretation after the fact; (iii) but his initial thesis—"the primary reason for an action is its cause" (French translation, pp. 16, 26, etc.)—in the highly laudable concern to "rationalise" action, admits too quickly the legitimacy of extending causality and ends by recovering the most classical metaphysical aporias.

79. Marcel Proust, "Du côté de chez Swann," in *A la recherche du temps perdu*, ed. P. Clarac and A. Ferré (Paris: Pléiade, 1954), p. 45 [English trans., p. 34 (modified)].

80. I do not understand how Davidson can on one hand define events, justly, as "particular, nonrepeatable entities" (*Essays on Actions and Events*, French translation, pp. 245, 248, etc.) and, on the other hand, posit that "events are identical if and only if they have exactly the same causes and the same effects" (p. 240). For (1) if they have causes, they are no longer events; (2) if they are identical in terms of their causes, they become repeatable and are once again no longer events; (3) in any case, the debate is pointless since causes and effects that are exactly identical are impossible, according to both time and space.

81. C. Wolff, *Ontologia* (Frankfort/Leipzig, 1730), §174. See, however, the recent clarification from J. Ecole: "La définition de l'existence comme complément de la possibilité et les rapports de l'essence et de l'existence selon Christian Wolff," *Les Etudes philosophiques*, 1996/1–2.

82. See *supra*, §13.

83. Paul Claudel, *Grandes odes* V, in *Poésie*, ed. J. Petit (Paris: Pléiade, 1967), p. 281 (my thanks to J. Colette for having pointed out this verse).

BOOK IV

1. See *supra*, Book 1, §§4–5.

2. Kant, *Kritik der reinen Vernunft*, A 218/B 265; A 220/B 267; A 219/B 266 [English trans., p. 239 (modified)].

3. *Principles of Nature and of Grace*, §7 [English trans., p. 199].

4. *New Essays on Human Understanding*, 4.2.84, in *Die philosophischen Schriften*, ed. C. Gerhardt, vol. 5, p. 355 [English trans., p. 375].

5. *Letter CXXIII to Des Bosses*, in *Die philosophischen Schriften*, vol. 2, p. 506.

6. *Letter VI to Des Bosses*, ibid., p. 306.

7. Schopenhauer, in *On the Fourfold Root of the Principle of Sufficient Reason*, §13, can cite only a secondary text, in which it is his polemic against Eberhard that leads Kant to repeat that: "*Everything must have a reason* [*Grund*], this is the (material) transcendental principle that no man has ever proven nor ever will prove on the basis of the principle of contradiction (and in general on the basis of simple concepts without relation to sensible intuition)" (Ak. A. VIII, p. 194).

8. *Kritik der reinen Vernunft*, A 158/B 197 [English trans., p. 194 (modified)]. See: "The a priori conditions of a possible experience in general are at the same time conditions of the possibility of objects of experience" (A 111 [English trans., p. 138]).

9. *Monadology*, §38 [English trans., p. 185].

10. *Kritik der reinen Vernunft*, §17, B 136 [English trans., p. 155].

11. *Ideen I*, §24, Hua. III, p. 52 [English trans., p. 44 (modified)].

12. See the reservations previously expressed in Book 1, §1.

13. *Ideen I*, §83, Hua. III, p. 201 [English trans., p. 197 (modified)]; ibid.; and §44, p. 100 [English trans., p. 94 (modified)].

14. *Ideen I*, §63, p. 150 [English trans., p. 148]. See *Erfahrung und Urteil*, §8: "[Every object] has, accordingly, its own empty horizon of familiar unfamiliarity, which is to be described as the universal horizon 'object'" (p. 35 [English trans., p. 38]).

15. *Ideen I*, §44, p. 101 [English trans., p. 94 (modified)]. No doubt, it is no small matter that Kant too used the concept of horizon in a similar sense (*Kritik der reinen Vernunft*, A 658/B 686ff and *Logic*, introduction, VI, Ak. A., t. IX, p. 40ff).

16. According to the interpretation advanced by H. Kuhn, "The phenomenological concept of 'Horizon,'" in M. Farber, ed., *Philosophical Essays in Memory of Edmund Husserl* (Cambridge, Mass., 1940).

17. One could remark that Heidegger, after having posited time as the "horizon" of all understanding of Being (*Sein und Zeit*, p. 1, and §5, pp. 17 and 34 [English trans., pp. 19 and 39]), ends his work with the aporia of this horizon (and no doubt every other): "Does *time* itself manifest itself as the *horizon* of Being" (§83, p. 437, 40–41 [English trans., p. 488 (my emphasis)]). Everything happens as if, at least in the case of time, Heidegger in the end renounced imposing a horizon on the phenomenality of Being.

18. *Ideen I*, §82, Hua. III, p. 200 [English trans., p. 196]. See also *Formal and Transcendental Logic*, §99, Hua. XVII, p. 257.

19. *Die Idee der Phänomenologie*, Hua. II, p. 14 [English trans., p. 11 (modified)]. See *Logische Untersuchungen*, III, §3: "Phenomena [*Erscheinungen*] in the sense of objects appearing [*erscheinenden*] as such, but also in respect of phenomena as the experiences in which the phenomenal things appear [*erscheinen*]"; and V, §2: "We cannot too sharply stress the equivocation that allows us to characterize as a phenomenon [*Erscheinung*] not only the lived-experience in which the appearing [*das Erscheinen*] of the object consists . . . but also the object appearing [*erscheinende*] as such" (t. 2, pp. 231 and 349 [English trans., vol. 2, pp. 439 and 538 (modified)]).

20. *Logische Untersuchungen*, VI, §37, vol. 3, p. 118 [English trans., p. 762 (modified)]. It is important to emphasize the persistence here in phenomenological territory of the most metaphysical definition of truth as *adaequatio rei et intellectus*.

21. Ibid., §37, vol. 3, p. 116 [English trans., p. 761]. See p. 118 [English trans., p. 762].

22. Ibid., §39, vol. 3, pp. 122 and 123 [English trans., pp. 765 and 766 (modified)].

23. Ibid., §39: "Ideale Fülle für eine Intention," p. 123; title of §37: "Ideal der letzen Erfüllung," p. 118; title of chapter 5: "Das Ideal der Adäquation," p. 115 [English trans., pp. 766, 761, and 760].

24. "It is obvious that reason, in achieving its purpose, that, namely, of representing the necessary complete determination of things, does not presuppose the existence of an essence [*nicht die Existenz eines solchen Wesens*], but only the idea [*nur die Idee*] of this essence, and this only for the purpose of deriving from an unconditioned totality of complete determination the conditioned totality, that is, the totality of the limited" (*Kritik der reinen Vernunft*, A577/B606 [English trans., pp. 491–92 (modified)]). This definition of the ideal by Kant—the unconditioned but nonexistent totality that permits reason to determine the conditioned but existing limitation—recovers, anachronistically, the Husserlian ideal of fulfillment: the unconditioned and complete, but not actualized, equality in relation to which and in comparison with which the intended, actualized, but intuitively deficient is measured. The difference stems from the fact that the ideal of reason coincides strictly with God for Kant, while Husserl will have to await the ultimate developments of his teleology to identify the ideal of fulfillment with God. See, besides the classic work of A. Ales Bello, *Husserl: Sul problema di Dio* (Rome, 1985), the texts collected and commented upon by J. Benoist, "Husserl: Au-delà de l'onto-théologie," *Les Etudes philosophiques* 4 (1991).

25. *Logische Untersuchungen* VI, §§40 and 63, vol. 3, pp. 131 and 192 [English trans., pp. 775 and 825]. Heidegger, too, speaks of "a surplus of intentions [*ein Ueberschuss an Intentionen*]," *Prolegomena zur Geschichte des Zeitbegriffs*, §6, GA 20, p. 77 [English trans., pp. 57–58]. This shortage of intuition is in part directly connected with the recourse to a horizon: "There is always more co-intended apperceptively than actually is given by intuition—precisely because every object is not a thing isolated in itself but is always already *an object in its horizon* of typical familiarity and pre-cognizance" (*Erfahrung und Urteil,* §25, p. 136 [English trans., p. 122]).

26. Plato, *Symposium*, 203 b.

27. See *Cartesianische Meditationen*, §§50–55. Let me emphasize that appresentation—"the surplus [*Ueberschuss*] in the perception of what is not authentically perceived"—does not only come up when it is a matter of knowing the Other, but for "absolutely every perception" of objects in the world (§55, Hua. I, p. 151 [English trans., p. 122 (modified)]). Descartes too admits that adequate knowledge remains impossible not only for the idea of the infinite (AT VII, 368, 1–3), but also for that of any object whatsoever, however limited it might be (AT VII, 365, 3–5).

28. *Kritik der reinen Vernunft*, A 58/B 82 [English trans., p. 97].

29. Ibid., A 51/B 76 [English trans., p. 93 (modified)].

30. Ibid., A 50/B 74 [English trans., p. 92]. See: "There are two conditions under which alone the knowledge of an object is possible, first, *intuition*, through which it is given, though only as phenomenon [*nur als Erscheinung, gegeben wird*];

secondly, *concept*, through which an object is thought corresponding to this intuition" (A 92/B 125 [English trans., p. 126 (modified)]).

31. Ibid., A 239/B 298, then A 253 and A 93 [English trans., pp. 259, 271, 129].

32. Ibid., A 247/B 304 [English trans., p. 264].

33. [*Visable*, from *viser*, designates what can be aimed at, meant, or intended. —Trans.]

34. In succession, Kant, *Kritik der reinen Vernunft*, A 327/B 383 ("notwendig") and A 339/B 397 ("unvermeidlich Schein") [English trans., pp. 318 and 327], then Mallarmé, *Variations sur un sujet* and *Prose pour des Esseintes*, in *Oeuvres complètes*, ed. H. Mondor (Paris: Pléiade, 1945), pp. 361 and 56.

35. Descartes clearly indicated that the privilege of the object (therefore of the phenomenon) of a mathematical sort derives from its character "purum et simplex," which supposes nothing that experience would render uncertain (*Regulae ad directionem ingenii*, AT X, 365, 16ff), that is to say, so poor in intuition that no givenness would ever be able to seize it in default since it consists only in this very default. Such a privilege of certainty is purchased with an equal poverty of intuitive given, that is to say, of "matter," insofar as it procures a real content and at the same time an irreducible uncertainty. This too is why the *intuitus* ensures certainty only for objects without material such as mathematical or quasi-tautological idealities such that "uniusquisque intueri se existere, se cogitare" (see ibid., III, 368, 21ff). The *cogito*, at least in its classic formulation, also remains a phenomenon poor in intuition—certain because empty.

36. *Kritik der reinen Vernunft*, A 290–92/B 347–49 and A 220/B 268 [English trans., pp. 294–96 (modified) and 240]. See G. Granel, "Le *nihil negativum* en son sens kantien," *Philosophie* 14 (1987), included in *Ecrits logiques et politiques* (Paris: Galilée, 1990).

37. I propose speaking of a saturated and not saturating phenomenon, as has sometimes been suggested to me. Actually, intuition saturates every concept or signification in such a way that this phenomenon is indeed manifest in a saturated mode by means of saturating intuition. Moreover, the intuition that saturates it saturates it solely in the name of givenness: the saturated phenomenon is so first with givenness. To be sure, such a phenomenon saturates next, and as a consequence, the gaze to which it gives itself to be seen and known. It therefore can also be called, rigorously, saturating. However, the saturation that it exerts in the field of knowledge only results from that which it receives in the field of givenness. Givenness always determines knowledge and not the inverse.

38. *Kritik der Urteilskraft*, §57, note 1, Ak. A., vol. 5, p. 342 [English trans., p. 218].

39. Ibid., §49, p. 314 [English trans., p. 192]. It should not be objected that the aesthetic idea is here named "representation of the imagination" and unrelated to intuition, seeing as several lines later intuition is itself purely and simply assimilated to the "representation of the imagination" ("Begriff, dem keine Anschauung [Vorstellung der Einbildungskraft] adäquat sein kann," ibid.). Elsewhere, there are other

confirmations: "die Einbildungskraft, als Vermögen der Anschauung" (§39, p. 292 [English trans., p. 172]); "Eine Anschauung (der Einbildungskraft)" (§57, n. 1, p. 342). There is nothing surprising about this assimilation, since the second edition of the *Critique of Pure Reason* already specified it explicitly: "*Imagination* is the faculty of representing in intuition an object that is *not itself present*. Now since all our intuition is sensible, the imagination, owing to the subjective condition under which alone it can give to the concepts of understanding a corresponding intuition, belongs to *sensibility*" (§24, B 151 [English trans., p. 165]).

40. *Kritik der Urteilskraft*, §57, n. 1, twice "inexponible Vorstellung," ibid., pp. 342–43 [English trans., pp. 218, 219]. For the positive use of this rare term, see "exponible Urteile," *Logic*, §31, p. 109.

41. [*Invisable*, from *viser*, designates that which cannot be aimed at, meant, or intended.—Trans.]

42. [*Irregardable* designates what cannot be looked at or gazed upon. The verb *regarder* has most often been translated "to gaze" while the noun form, *regard*, is rendered as "the gaze."—Trans.]

43. *Kritik der reinen Vernunft*, A 163/B 204 [English trans., p. 199].

44. *Passions de l'âme*, §73, AT XI, p. 383, 7–10 [English trans., p. 354]. See §78: "When it is excessive and makes us fix our attention solely on the first image of the objects before us without acquiring any further knowledge about them" (ibid., p. 386, 14–17 [English trans., p. 355]). See the perfect commentary by D. Kambouchner: admiration (connected to amazement) "which has a corporeal thing for its object has this thing as its object only *inasmuch as it appears*, and only with its 'new,' 'rare,' 'extraordinary,' unexpected character does its apparition become an event. . . . It has as its object *the phenomenon of a thing or the thing in its phenomenalization*" (*L'homme des passions: Commentaires sur Descartes* [Paris, 1995], vol. 1, p. 295, my emphasis).

45. *Ethica III*, appendix, definition IV [English trans., p. 142].

46. *Kritik der reinen Vernunft*, A 169/B 210 [English trans., p. 203].

47. Paul Claudel, *Tête d'or*, in *Théâtre I* (Paris: Pléiade, 1956), p. 210. Glory is weighty; Hebrew says this with just one word: *kavod*. Obviously, I am here quite close to J.-L. Chrétien, *L'inoubliable et l'inespéré* (Paris, 1991).

48. Plato, *Republic*, 515c and 517a. The term *marmaryge* originally designates vibration (for example that of a dancer's feet, *Odyssey* 8.265), then the vibration of overheated air, therefore that of the mirage, which provokes bedazzlement.

49. Plato, *Republic*, 517bc and 518a.

50. J.M.W. Turner, at the National Gallery (n. 498) and at the Clore Gallery of the Tate Gallery (for *The Decline of the Carthiginian Empire* and *Venice with Salute*, n. 5487). Here I am indebted to an as yet unpublished study by C. Monjou. See J. Gage, *J.M.W. Turner: A Wonderful Range of Mind* (New Haven: Yale University Press, 1957), chap. 4.

51. *Kritik der reinen Vernunft*, B 218 (see B 219) [English trans., p. 208 (see p. 209)].

52. Ibid., A 177/B 220 [English trans., p. 209 (modified)].

53. Ibid., A 177–78/B 220 [English trans., p. 210].

54. Ibid., A 179/B 222 [English trans., p. 210]. See also A 665/B 693.

55. Ibid., A 182/B 224 [English trans., p. 213].

56. In the absolute without analog, we thus come upon bedazzlement, characteristic of the phenomenon saturated with respect to quality. There is no incoherence here, seeing as, by excepting itself from the analogies of experience, the absolute phenomenon can no longer be compared to another. It shows itself as such, by reference to itself alone. It therefore brings to the fore what individualizes it as such—its unbearable intensity, provoking bedazzlement. As for its characteristic of unforeseeability according to quantity, it is self-evident that the disqualification of external relations (analogies among phenomena) confirms the disqualification of internal relations (summation of the parts of the phenomenon), far from contradicting it.

57. Spinoza, *Ethics I*, §16: "Ex necessitate divinae naturae infinita infinitis modis (hoc est omnia, quae sub intellectum infinitum cadere possunt) sequi"— almost the correct definition of the saturated phenomenon. See §17, sc.: "A summa Dei potentia, sive infinita natura infinita infinitis modis, hoc est omnia necessario effluxisse."

58. Whence the importance of a rereading of the *Critique of Pure Reason* that would attempt, though *a contrario*, to define and do justice to the saturated phenomenon, alongside common or poor phenomena. It would be a question of interpreting it no longer in terms of the *Aesthetic* (grossly put, Heidegger), of the *Analytic* (Cohen), or even of the transcendental doctrine of method (J. Grondin), but of the *transcendental dialectic*—taking seriously the doctrine of ideas (aesthetic as well as of reason) and asking after their paradoxical phenomenality.

59. [*Irregardable* designates what cannot be looked at or gazed upon. The verb *regarder* has most often been translated "to gaze" while the noun form, *regard*, is rendered as "the gaze."—Trans.]

60. *Kritik der reinen Vernunft*, A 74/B 100, A 219/B 266, and A 234/B 287 [English trans., pp. 109, 239, 252].

61. Ibid., A 225/B 273 [*zusammenshänge*] and A 220/B 267 [English trans., pp. 243 and 239].

62. See the works of C. Chevalley, in particular his introduction to the French translation of N. Bohr, *Physique quantum et connaissance humaine* (Paris, 1991); and that of W. Heisenberg, *Philosophie: Le manuscrit de 1942* (Paris, 1997).

63. On *intuitus* according to Descartes, see my study in *Règles utiles et claires pour la direction de l'esprit en la recherche de la vérité* (The Hague, 1977), p. 295ff.

64. That givenness (*Geben*) shows itself inasmuch as it remains irreducible to its given (*Gabe*) was established perfectly by Heidegger in *Sein und Zeit*, p. 8 (see *supra*, Book 1, §3).

65. "Das Sich-an-ihm-selbst-zeigende"; Heidegger, *Sein und Zeit*, §7, pp. 31, 12. See "Das an ihm selbst Offenbare von ihm selbst her sehen lassen," *Prolegomena zur Geschichte des Zeitbegriffs*, §9, GA 20 (Frankfurt am Main, 1979), p. 117. The

"von ihm selbst her" indicates an apparition "of itself" in the strict sense of "on the basis of itself." What remains is to establish how a phenomenon can be ensured a "self," the ipseity of a *Selbst*. The hypothesis of the saturated phenomenon lets us do this better than Heidegger does, who limits the *Selbst* to the ipseity of Dasein.

66. AT VII, 371, 25, and 52, 15. The infinite is never in potential, but *actu*: 47, 19.

67. AT VII, 46, 8, 12.

68. "Nihil univoce nobis convenire," AT VII, 137, 22 (see p. 433, 5–6, and *Principia Philosophiae* I, §51); *attingere*, AT VII, 139, 12 (esp. pp. 52, 5, and 46, 21, which doubts even this mere "touching": "Nec forte etiam attingere cogitatione ullo modo possum").

69. AT VII, 114, 6–7. This is why here, and here alone, *intueri* does not contradict *adorare*. Emmanuel Levinas recognized the more than normal phenomenality of the idea of infinity so perfectly that he revived it in order to describe the face of the Other: *Totality and Infinity*, pp. 26, 48–50; *Of God Who Comes to Mind*, pp. 26, 62–65, and p. 69. But above all, "The Idea of the Infinite in Us," in *Entre Nous*, pp. 219ff.

70. *Kritik der Urteilskraft*, §25, p. 248 [English trans., p. 306]; *Formlosigkeit*, §24, p. 247; *Unordnung*, §23, p. 246; "Uber alle Vergleichung" and *schlechthin*, §25, p. 248 (and §26, p. 251) [English trans., p. 306].

71. *Kritik der Urteilskraft*, §23 [English trans., p. 245]; *Gefühl der Unangemessenheit*, §26, p. 252 [English trans., p. 135 (modified)]; *Ungeheuer*, §26, p. 253 [English trans., p. 136 (modified)].

72. *Kritik der Urteilskraft*, *Unbegrenztheit*, §23 [English trans., p. 128]. See "keine angemessene Darstellung," p. 245.

73. *Kritik der Urteilskraft*, §23, p. 245 [English trans., p. 129 (modified)]. See *subjektive Unzweckmässigkeit*, §26, p. 252; *Widerstreit* of the subjective end, §27, p. 258. Respect (*Achtung*) comes up in §27, p. 257. I here follow P. Lacoue-Labarthe, "La vérité sublime," and J.-L. Nancy, "L'offrande sublime" (in particular: "The sublime totality is beyond the maximum: which is as much as to say it is *beyond all*"), in *Du sublime*, ed. M. Deguy (Paris, 1988), p. 68.

74. *Zur Phänomenologie des inneren Zeitbewusstseins (1893–1917)*, Hua. X (The Hague, 1966), "ständiges Kontinuum," §10, p. 27 [English trans., p. 48 (modified)] (see "beständliger Wandlung," "stetige Modifikation," p. 63). The very concept of object-in-its-how (*Objekt in wie*) indicates the permanent and perpetual transformation of the object, that is to say, the relation between its (permanent) signification and the corresponding lived experiences (always other), which obey another intentionality, that of their temporal succession without object. This is why one can say, following R. Bernet, that it is, properly speaking, no longer an issue of intentional consciousness, but of a "passive consciousness resulting from an affection" (*La vie du sujet* [Paris, 1995], p. 196).

75. *Zur Phänomenologie des inneren Zeitbewusstsein*, §16, p. 40 [English trans., p. 62 (modified)]. See §32, p. 70 and §36, p. 75.

76. *Zur Phänomenologie des inneren Zeitbewusstsein*, n. 50, p. 334 (twice); §39,

p. 82. See "The original time [*Urzeit*], which is not yet really time" (ms. C 7 I, p. 17, cited by D. Franck, *Chair et corps: Sur la phénoménologie de Husserl* [Paris, 1981], p. 188).

77. *Zur Phänomenologie des inneren Zeitbewusstsein*, §39, p. 83. On the double intentionality of the flux, §39, p. 8off [English trans., p. 105ff].

78. *Zur Phänomenologie des inneren Zeitbewusstseins*, §§10 and 11, pp. 28 and 29 *et passim*; §31, p. 67; and finally *Beilage* I, p. 100 [English trans., pp. 48 and 50 (modified)].

79. On this "pulsional . . . primordiality," see *Téléologie universelle*, ms. E III 5 (September 1933), n. 34, Hua. XV, pp. 593–97; and the commentaries from E. Fink ("intentional self-constitution of phenomenological time"), *Studien zur Phänomenologie*, and D. Franck, p. 153.

80. See *supra*, Book 1, §6, Book 2, §12, Book 3, §18. That givenness can sometimes not come to pass in and through its intuition has already been seen in Book 1, §§4–5, and will be confirmed below (Book 4, §23).

81. Descartes, *Regulae ad directionem ingenii*, AT X, 365, 16, cited *supra*, §20 [English trans., p. 12].

82. Goclenius (R. Göckel): "Paradoxum est inopinatum et admirabile, quod praeter opinionem et expectationem offertur," *Lexicon philosophicum graecum* (Frankfurt, 1615), p. 963.

83. Maurice Merleau-Ponty, *Phénoménologie de la perception*, p. 426.

84. The phenomenology that broaches this type of saturated phenomenon was elaborated in an exemplary fashion by Paul Ricoeur, in particular in *Temps et récit III: Le temps raconté* (Paris, 1985).

85. The phenomenology that describes this type of saturated phenomenon, the idol, could be attributed to Jacques Derrida—it being understood that he has inverted it exactly. The difference resides in the on principle irreparable deficit of intuition to intention. But it thus belongs all the more within the thematic of degrees of intuition and saturation: "Hear aright the chance and the necessity of a 'that's sufficient.' It's *enough*, but without satisfaction; and which does not saturate. Nothing to do with sufficiency or insufficiency. The verb *to suffice* will teach you nothing about such a 'that's sufficient'" (*La vérité en peinture* [Paris, 1978], p. 284 [English trans., p. 206], concerning G. Titus-Carmel).

86. One must, without question, attribute the elaboration of a phenomenology appropriate to the paradox (saturated phenomenon) inasmuch as absolute to the remarkably steadfast thought of Michel Henry, from *L'essence de la manifestation* (Paris, 1963) to *Phénoménologie matérielle* (Paris, 1990) and *C'est moi la vérité* (Paris, 1996).

87. Aristotle, *Categories*, 7, 8 a 14–15. To be sure, this phrase belongs to the formulation of a question, but it immediately receives a positive response, at least concerning the first *ousia*.

88. It goes without saying that we owe it to Emmanuel Levinas to have ingen-

iously reconfigured phenomenology so as to let it finally reach the Other as saturated phenomenon. I understand the icon (as previously the idol) in conformity with its phenomenological meaning, laid out in *Dieu sans l'être* (Paris, 1981), chap. 1.

89. This superlative, attested by the Septuagint in Wisdom 16:17, is used, rarely it is true, by Athanasius (PG 25 696 *d*), Gregory of Nyssa (*Life of Moses*, §24, p. 44, 406 *c*), and Evagrius (p. 86, 2753 *b*). See, even if he uses *paradoxōtaton* only in common usage, the occurrences of *paradoxon* in Cyril of Alexandria: M. O. Boulnois, *Le paradoxe trinitaire chez Cyrille d'Alexandrie: Herméneutique, analyses philosophiques et argumentation théologique* (Paris, 1994), pp. 574ff and 696ff.

90. Phenomenology describes possibilities and never considers the phenomenon of revelation except as a possibility of phenomenality, one that it would formulate in this way: If God were to manifest himself (or manifested himself), he would use a paradox to the second degree. Revelation (of God by himself, *theological*), if it takes place, will assume the phenomenal figure of the phenomenon of revelation, of the paradox of paradoxes, of saturation to the second degree. To be sure, *R*evelation (as actuality) is never confounded with *r*evelation (as possible phenomenon). I will scrupulously respect this conceptual difference by its graphic translation. But phenomenology, which owes it to phenomenality to go this far, does not go beyond and should never pretend to decide the fact of Revelation, its historicity, its actuality, or its meaning. It should not do so, not only out of concern for distinguishing the sciences and delimiting their respective regions, but first of all, because it does not have the means to do so. The fact (if there is one) of Revelation exceeds the scope of all science, including that of phenomenology. Only a theology, and on condition of constructing itself on the basis of this fact alone (Karl Barth or Hans Urs von Balthasar, no doubt more than Rudolf Bultmann or Karl Rahner), could reach it. Even if it had the desire to do so (and, of course, this would never be the case), phenomenology would not have the power to turn into theology. And one has to be completely ignorant of theology, its procedures, and its problematic not to imagine this unlikeness.

91. A magnificently untranslatable text. In effect, the formulation *egō eimi* means first: "It is me!" in answer to the question "Who are you looking for?—Jesus of Nazareth." But more radically, it means literally "I am," through a phrase that declines the very identity that Jesus claims in John 8; but these two translations can be added to one another in a subtle and secret dialogue: Who are you looking for? Jesus of Nazareth. / It is me. / But it is me because I am "I am." / By this redoubling, Here I am, the one who is always there for you to take ("Here I am") / and to take me for what I am, namely "I am." Whence the last meaning: "I am" equals, in the dialogue at Gethsemane, "I am he who says I am," therefore I am He from Exodus 3:14; and it is precisely on account of this claim (a blasphemy according to Matthew 26:65) that he will be put to death.

92. Husserl, *Ideen I*, §58, Hua. III, p. 139 [English trans., pp. 133–34] (cited *supra*, Book 2, §7).

93. A position that we had assumed in *God Without Being*. We owe this objection, in comparable terms, to Didier Franck and Thomas Carlson. See Carlson's *Indiscretion: Finitude and the Naming of God* (Chicago: University of Chicago Press, 1999); especially pp. 232–36.

94. See *supra*, Book 1, §§4–5, and Book 2, §11.

95. See *supra*, Book 5, §30.

BOOK V

1. ["Receiver" here translates the French *attributaire*.—Trans.]

2. *Kritik der reinen Vernunft*, §16, B 131ff [English trans., pp. 152–53].

3. Ibid., B 277 [English trans., p. 246]. We know that Kant defines this accompanying thought by the "I think" as well as by the "I am" (here, in B XL, etc.) since the latter adds nothing (no intuition) to the first, except for the tautology that I am a unity—absolute, but logical and therefore empty—inasmuch as I am thinking (A 354–55).

4. Ibid., §16, B 131ff [English trans., p. 153].

5. Ibid., §16, B 131ff (my emphasis) [English trans., p. 153]. This reversal would, for that matter, lead only to recognizing the ultimate consequence of the anteriority of "the synthesis of apprehension in intuition" to those of "reproduction in the imagination" and "recognition in the concept"—namely, the anteriority of givenness in and through intuition, therefore of the receiver "to whom/which" it comes forward.

6. Ibid., A 355, B 132; B 134 [English trans., pp. 337, 153, and 155].

7. Ibid., A 355 [English trans., p. 337].

8. Ibid., A 158/B 197 [English trans., p. 194].

9. Ibid., §24, B 155–56 [English trans., p. 167].

10. *Meditatio III*, AT VII, 42, 30. See my commentary in *Questions cartésiennes*, chap. 4, §3, p. 125.

11. See my *Réduction et donation*, chap. 3, §2.

12. *Sein und Zeit*, §65, p. 323 [English trans., p. 370].

13. Ibid., §9, p. 41 [English trans., p. 67].

14. Ibid., §60, p. 297 [English trans., p. 343].

15. Ibid., §40, p. 186 [English trans., p. 231 (modified)].

16. Ibid., §56, p. 273 [English trans., p. 318].

17. Ibid., §51, p. 252 [English trans., p. 296].

18. Ibid., §54, p. 267 [English trans., p. 312].

19. Ibid., §64, p. 322 [English trans., p. 369].

20. Ibid., §64, p. 322 [English trans., p. 369 (modified)]. In this sense, see Paul Ricoeur, "Heidegger and the Question of the Subject," in *The Conflict of Interpretations* (Evanston: Northwestern University Press, 1974); Dominique Janicaud, "L'analytique existentiale et la question de la subjectivité," *Etre et temps de Martin Heidegger: Questions de méthode et voies de recherche*, ed. J.-P. Cometti and D. Janicaud (Marseille, 1989), p. 51ff; and Jacques Derrida, "'Il faut bien manger' ou le calcul du sujet: Entretien (avec J.-L. Nancy)," in *Confrontation* 20 (Paris, 1989), p. 93;

see p. 99 [English translation as "'Eating Well,' or the Calculation of the Subject: An Interview with Jacques Derrida," in *Who Comes After the Subject*, ed. Cadava, Connor, and Nancy (New York: Routledge, 1991)]. These three opinions agree and, for the most part, I assume them. See *Réduction et donation*, chap. 3, esp. pp. 106–7.

21. *Metaphysics*, D, 1, 1012 b 34ff [English trans., p. 1599], for example: "It is common, then, to all to be the first point from which a thing either is or comes to be or is known" (1013 a 17–19 [English trans., p. 1599]).

22. ["The gifted" here translates the French *l'adonné*. A more literal, though awkward, translation would be "he who is given over." In everyday French, *l'adonné* means, roughly, something like "the addict" or the "devotee." The related verb *s'adonner* will be translated as "gives himself over."—Trans.]

23. Descartes thematizes this dichotomy, among others, in *Regula XII*, AT X, 413, 3–20, *Le Monde I*, AT XI, 3, 1, and *Dioptrique I* and *IV*, AT VI, 85, 13, and 112, 5. See my commentary (in particular on the notion of the "code") in *Sur la théologie blanche de Descartes*, §12, p. 231ff.

24. Leibniz: "The intelligent soul, knowing what it is and being able to say this 'I' which says so much" (*Discourse on Metaphysics*, §43, ed. Gerhardt, vol. 4, p. 459 [English trans., p. 44]).

25. Kant, *Prolegomena zu einer jeden künftigen Metaphysik*, §46, note, which goes on to say: " . . . and is only the representation of that to which all thinking stands in relation (*relatione accidentis*) [*worauf alles Denken in Beziehung . . . steht*]" (Ak. A., IV, p. 334 [English trans., p. 75]). One can also think of Rousseau here: "The flux and reflux of the water . . . sufficed to make me feel my existence with pleasure, without taking the trouble to think"; or: "What is the nature of one's enjoyment in such a situation? Nothing exterior to oneself, nothing except oneself and one's own existence. . . . The sentiment of existence, deprived of all other affections" (*Rêveries du promeneur solitaire*, in *Oeuvres complètes*, ed. B. Gagnebin and M. Raymond, vol. 1 [Paris: Pléiade, 1959], pp. 1045 and 1047 [English trans., pp. 111 and 113–14]). But as Michel Henry demonstrated (*Généalogie de la psychanalyse*, chaps. 1–2), and I remarked in *Questions cartésiennes*, chap. 5, §§2–3, we must acknowledge a Cartesian origin for the determination of thought of self and its existence as originally a feeling.

26. Kant, *Kritik der reinen Vernunft*, B 422, note [English trans., p. 378, note]. This text is cited and clearly explained by J. Benoist, *Kant et les limites de la synthèse: Le sujet sensible* (Paris, 1996), p. 314ff, whose overall thesis I share.

27. See my *Réduction et donation*, chap. 6, §6. Must I say again that I did not, in this analysis, play one call (that of the Father, for example) against another (Being)? This is true not only because both qualifications are Heideggerian ("Letter on Humanism," GA 9, p. 319ff), but above all because I already tried, with this pure phenomenological "model of the call," to articulate what comes after the "subject" in terms of givenness and because every assignation of any "caller" whatsoever was ruinous to this enterprise.

28. [*Interloqué* could be translated either as "the addressee" or "the one taken

aback or surprised." *Interloqué*, therefore, in the sense that one is surprised and taken aback in being addressed. I retain the French here since its usage has already been established in a translation titled "L'Interloqué," in *Who Comes After the Subject*, ed. Cadava, Connor, Nancy (New York: Routledge, 1991).—Trans.]

29. Emmanuel Levinas, *Autrement qu'être, ou au delà de l'essence* (The Hague, 1974), pp. 61 and 67 [English trans., pp. 47 and 53]; "Un Dieu-homme," in *Entre-nous* (Paris, 1991), p. 75 [English trans., p. 58]. Let me just call to mind a passage that juxtaposes the two meanings: "Intentionality means that all consciousness is consciousness of something, but *above all that every object calls forth and as it were gives rise to the consciousness through which its being shines and, in doing so, appears*," *En découvrant l'existence avec Husserl et Heidegger* (Paris, 1949), p. 134 (emphasis in the original) [English trans., p. 119].

30. Levinas, *Autrement qu'être*, p. 180 [English trans., p. 141].

31. For example, in *Erfahrung und Urteil*, §17, emphasizing "the stimulus exercised by the intentional object in its directedness toward the ego," which in turn "abandons itself to it [*gibt nach*]" indeed "gives itself over to it [*Hingabe*]" (ed. Classen, p. 81ff [English trans., p. 77 (modified)]). With regard to "objects invested with spirit (spiritual objects)," Rudolf Bernet has already offered a pertinent description of what I would like to establish definitively: "Their presence [that of things of the cultural world] for the subject is distinguished from that of objects by the fact that they are in effect 'given' to it in the true sense of the word. *The subject then becomes he to whom* this gift of the pre-given is destined, and *the intentionality* that inhabits his life *is defined by his capacity to receive such a gift* and make fruitful use of it. *The originary response* required by the gift is therefore less an activity of constitution than a confident acceptance" (*La vie du sujet*, p. 318, my emphasis). Similarly, see D. Franck, evoking "a change in the orientation of the gaze. . . . The emergence of the flesh as an alternative to consciousness" ("L'objet de la phéno-ménologie," *Critique*, no. 502 [March 1989], p. 195).

32. Here I am only resuming the thesis of §22. The same goes for the nonin-tentional traits of the four types of paradox (or saturated phenomenon).

33. *Passions de l'âme*, §53, AT XI, 373, 5–13 (my emphasis) [English trans., p. 350].

34. *Principia philosophiae* I, §7, AT IX-1, 7, 5–7 [English trans., p. 195]; *Discours de la méthode*, AT VI, 33, 4–5 [English trans., p. 127].

35. For a more detailed examination of this point, readers are referred to *Questions cartésiennes*, II, chap. 1.

36. This formulation, which we know was privileged by Heidegger (from *Sein und Zeit*, §82, p. 433, until "Ueberwindung der Metaphysik" in *Vorträge und Auf-sätzem* [Pfüllingen, 1954], vol. 1, p. 66), was explicitly challenged by Descartes, AT VII, p. 559, 5–7. See my clarification of this issue in *Questions cartésiennes*, p. 99ff.

37. AT VII, 25, 11–13 [English trans., p. 17], repeated at AT VII, 27, 9.

38. See J. Hintikka, "*Cogito ergo sum*: Inference or Performance?" *Philosophical Review* (1962). See my commentary in *Sur la théologie blanche de Descartes*, §16, p. 380ff.

39. AT VII, 24, 19–26; IX-1, 19, 17–22 [English trans., p. 16].

40. AT VII, 25, 6 [English trans., p. 17 (modified)].

41. AT VII, 24, 26–25, 5 [English trans., p. 16].

42. AT VII, 25, 5–10 [English trans., p. 17].

43. AT VII, 25, 10–13 [English trans., p. 17].

44. In Kantian terms, one could suggest that in the formulation of *Meditatio II*, only the "empirical self" is operative while the transcendental I is left in the anonymity either of the one who "deceives me" or the one who "persuades me," or the one who "utters." But as I have noted elsewhere (§25), it is the very duality of the "subject" (and the aporia that it betrays) that is here put into question. Let me note finally that elsewhere Descartes invokes the hypothesis of a thought in me that would not be my own (AT VII, 39, 10–14; 77, 23–27, and 79, 10).

45. AT VII, 10, 13–14 [English trans., p. 8].

46. AT VII, 27, 16–17 [English trans., p. 18], which closes the sequence dedicated to the essence of the ego, opens with the declaration: "Nondum vero satis intelligo, quisnam sim ego ille, qui jam necessario sum [I do not yet have a sufficient understanding of what this 'I' is, that now necessarily exists]" (AT VII, 25, 14ff [English trans., p. 17]).

47. AT IX-1, 21, 18ff: "Cela est certain; mais combien de temps? A savoir autant de temps que je pense"; AT VII, 27, 13, confirmed by 36, 16: "Quamdiu me aliquid esse cogitabo," and already by 25, 12: "Quoties a me profertur."

48. AT VII, 25, 20 (diluted by AT IX-1, 20, 5: "Avant que je n'entrasse dans ces dernières pensées"); 63, 9; AT IX-1, 50, 19; and 67, 20; AT IX-1, 53, 32–33. See "Casu quidem incidam in vertitatem [Cela n'arrive que par hasard]" (60, 2–3; IX-1, 47, 35).

49. AT IX-1, 28, 25–30; AT VII, 36, 15–17 [English trans., p. 25 (modified)]. For the interpretation of this text obscured by the discussion, see *Questions cartésiennes*, II, chap. 2, "La 'règle générale' de vérité," §6, p. 74ff.

50. AT VII, 36, 8–9; AT IX-1, 28, 21–22 [English trans., p. 25]. Quite logically Descartes emphasizes that this first thought come from an Other "compels me— non possum non fateri."

51. AT IX-1, 41, 12–40; AT VII, 51, 21–52, 9. Gilles Deleuze opposes to what he believes is the Cartesian ego a "passive subject which represent [*sic*] that activity to itself rather than enacts it, which experiences its effect rather than initiates it, and which lives it like an other within myself," in short, "a passive self issued from a groundlessness that it contemplates" (*Différence et répétition* [Paris, 1968], pp. 117 and 354 [English trans., pp. 86 and 300 (modified)]). In fact, Deleuze very nearly describes the original figure of Descartes's ego—*persuasus* evoked by a call.

52. See *supra*, §25, aporia (b), and §26.

53. Kant, *Kritik der praktischen Vernunft*, I, 3: "The Incentives of Pure Practical Reason," Ak. A., t. V, p. 73 [English trans., pp. 75–76 (modified)]. Likewise: "The propensity to self-esteem . . . is one of the inclinations which the moral law demolishes. Therefore the moral law strikes down self-conceit" (ibid.). And: "The moral law, which alone is truly, i.e., in every respect, objective, completely excludes

the influence of self-love from the highest practical principle, and it contributes an infinite demolishing [*unendlichen Abbruch*] in regards to the presumption [*Eigendünkel*], which decrees the subjective conditions of self-love [*Selbstliebe*] as laws" (ibid., p. 74 [English trans., p. 77 (modified)]).

54. Ibid., p. 76 [English trans., pp. 78–79]. Likewise, in *Grundlegung zur Metaphysik der Sitten*, I: "Respect is regarded as the *effect* of the law on the subject and not as the *cause* of the law. Respect is properly awareness of a value which demolishes my self-love [*meiner Selbstliebe Abbruch tut*]" (Ak. A., t. IV, p. 402 [English trans., p. 69 (modified)]).

55. *Kritik der praktischen Vernunft*, I, 3, pp. 72 and 73 [English trans., pp. 75 and 76].

56. The *Groundwork of the Metaphysic of Morals* makes this clear: "Although respect is a feeling, it is not a feeling *received* through outside influence, but one *self-produced* [*selbstgewirktes Gefühl*] by a rational concept, and therefore specifically distinct from feelings of the first kind, all of which can be reduced to inclination or fear" (Ak. A., t. IV, p. 402, note [English trans., p. 69 (modified)]). This feeling produces itself without and counter to the one who feels it because it produces itself on the basis of the moral law alone.

57. *Kritik der praktischen Vernunft*, I, 1, §7, pp. 31 and 32 [English trans., pp. 31 and 33].

58. See *supra*, §26.

59. *Kritik der praktischen Vernunft*, I, 3: "The Incentives of Pure Practical Reason," pp. 76 and 73 [English trans., pp. 79 and 75].

60. *Kritik der praktischen Vernunft*, I, 3, p. 74 [English trans., p. 77] (see: "But in relation to [this humiliation's] positive ground, the law, [this feeling] is at the same time respect for the law," p. 75 [English trans., p. 78]). "Humiliation, *Demütigung*" appears throughout pp. 73–80 [English trans., pp. 75–83], to the point of obsession.

61. *Metaphysik der Sitten*, II, introduction, XII (d), Ak. A., t. VI, p. 403 [English trans., p. 162 (modified)].

62. *Kritik der praktischen Vernunft*, I, 3: "The Incentives of Pure Practical Reason," pp. 79–80 [English trans., p. 82]; *Metaphysik der Sitten* II, introduction XII (b) Ak. A., t. VI, p. 401 [English trans., p. 161]. See *Kritik der praktischen Vernunft*, I: "Analytic of Pure Practical Reason" (t. V, p. 98 [English trans., pp. 101–2]).

63. The first panel of the triptych dedicated to the life of Saint Matthew, left side of the Contarelli chapel in the church Saint-Louis des Français in Rome (oil on canvas, 322 x 340 cm, June 1599–July 1600); see M. Cinotti and G. A. Dell'Acqua, [*Michelangelo Merisi detto il*] *Caravaggio: Tutte le opere* (Bergamo, 1983), n. 61, pp. 525–35 (an erudite but trivial commentary). The scene is constructed first of all according to the Synoptic Gospels—Matthew 9:9, Mark 2:13–14, and Luke 5:27.

64. There are good examples in Sartre: "We can see the use which bad faith can make of these judgments which all aim at establishing that I am not what I am. If I were only what I *am* [I would say rather: what *I* am], I could, for exam-

ple, seriously consider an adverse criticism which someone makes of me, question myself scrupulously, and perhaps be compelled to recognize the truth in it. But thanks to transcendence, I am not subject to all that I am" (*L'être et le néant* [Paris, 1943], p. 96 [English trans., p. 57]).

65. 1 Samuel 3:4; 9:19. See the analysis by Hans Urs von Balthasar, *Herrlichkeit*, III, 2/1 (Einsiedeln, 1966) [English trans. as *The Glory of the Lord*].

66. *Autrement qu'être*, p. 190 [English trans., p. 148 (modified)]; *L'appel et la réponse* (Paris, 1992), p. 42. Rousseau also showed, though in his own way, that the voice of the call consists first in the response: "Conscience, conscience! Divine instinct, immortal and celestial voice. . . . If [this guide] speaks to all hearts, then why are there so few of them who hear it? Well, this is because it speaks to us in nature's language, which everything has made us forget. . . . It no longer speaks to us. It no longer responds to us. And after such long contempt for it, to recall it costs as much as banishing it did" (*Emile* IV, "La Profession de foi du vicaire savoyard," *Oeuvres complètes*, vol. 4 [Paris, 1969], pp. 600–1 [English trans., pp. 290–91]). But before being amazed that the voice no longer responds, one must first explain why its call should respond.

67. See *supra*, §26.

68. See *supra*, §26.

69. J.-L. Chrétien: "Infinite excess, first of all, of the call over and above the response" (p. 31).

70. Descartes, *Meditatio III*, AT IX-1, p. 40, 24–28; VII, p. 50, 25–28 [English trans., p. 35] (my emphasis). See in contrast Emmanuel Levinas: "Birth, non-chosen and impossible to choose (the great drama of contemporary thought) which situates the will in an anarchic world, that is, a world without origin" (*Totalité et infini*, p. 199 [English trans., p. 223]), and also Jean-Louis Chrétien, p. 99.

71. See Michel Henry: "I forever hear the bustle of my birth" (*C'est moi la vérité*, p. 283; see pp. 79 and 92). This extraordinary text is one of the best examples of the interest, belated but now general, in a "phenomenology of birth" (Paul Ricoeur, Stanislas Breton, etc.).

72. Of course, the project of changing one's family name or given name changes nothing in this analysis. In these cases, I simply pretend to place myself in the position of the others (parents, etc.); therefore (i) I admit that I depend on them since it is their choice that I must correct, and (ii) far from denying the call, I merely try (and in vain) to repeat it. I am not contradicting the conclusions of Saul Kripke, since he admits that "rigid designators" can nonetheless deploy their necessity a posteriori, in the role of "contingent a priori truths." That is, "those who claim that the notion rigid designator supposes that of 'criteria of identity that count universally' put the cart before the horse. It is because we speak of him and of what could have happened to him, that 'identification that counts universally' does not pose a problem in the examples of this type." This exactly confirms my point. ("Naming and Necessity," in *Semantics of Natural Languages*, ed. D. Davidson and G. Harman [Dordrecht, 1972]).

73. In this sense, I will not speak of a "responsibility for the Other, older than any commitment . . . " (*Autrement qu'être*, p. 67 [English trans., p. 52 (modified)]) —precisely because no "commitment" (not even for the Other) would be thinkable without responsibility, taken in its phenomenological radicality.

74. See, for Heidegger, *supra*, Book 1, §3; for Levinas: "The dialectic of time is the dialectic of the relation with the other" (*De l'existence à l'existant*, p. 160) and my study "A Note Concerning the Ontological Indifference" in *Graduate Faculty Philosophy Journal* 20, no. 1 (1998): 2–21.

75. Jacques Derrida, "La différance" in *Marges de la philosophie* (Paris, 1972), pp. 8 and 10 [English trans., pp. 8 and 10].

76. One can pose the same question to Emmanuel Levinas: Temporalization is equivalent to the relation to the Other, but is it "the lapse of time irrecuperable" that produces the difference between the Saying and the said and also "the absolutely passive synthesis of aging" or the inverse (*Autrement qu'être*, pp. 66 and 67 [English trans., pp. 53 and 54])? In short, does temporality flow from alterity or alterity fom temporality? Does the ethical difference differ originarily or temporally? A fortiori, doesn't Deleuze leave undetermined, or rather too well determined, the conditions under which repetition (therefore difference) arises, since he confirms *in fine* its temporality—"Are not all the repetitions ordered in the pure form of time?"—in order to assign it still and always to Being following the most classical essence of metaphysics: "The only realized Ontology—in other words, the univocity of Being—is repetition" (*Différence et répétition*, pp. 376 and 387 [English trans., pp. 294 and 303]).

77. Here I resume, but transposed from the question of the gift to that of the given phenomenon, the discussion of §§7 and 12.

78. Charles de Gaulle, *Mémoires de guerre*, I, 2, vol. 1 (Paris, 1954), p. 67.

79. Gustave Flaubert, *L'éducation sentimentale*, in *Oeuvres complètes*, ed. B. Masson (Paris, 1964), vol. 2, p. 9 [English trans., p. 6]. We might also think of Petrarch:

> Full of that sweetness indescribable
> that my eyes drew from such a lovely face
> the day on which I gladly would have closed them
> to never look again at lesser beauty,
> I left what I want most; and so accustomed
> my mind is to the thought of her alone
> that it sees nothing else—what is not she
> out of old habit it still hates and scorns. (*Canzoniere* 66)

80. See Heidgger: "The peculiar indefiniteness of the caller and the impossibility of making more definite what this caller is, are not just nothing; they are distinctive for it in a *positive* way. They make known to us that the caller arises solely in its calling to . . . , that it means to be heard, without supplemental chatter, *only as such*" (*Sein und Zeit*, §57, p. 275 [English trans., p. 319 (modified)]). I also want to note here a passage from Jean-Louis Chrétien: "This being called is first, and this

affection precedes all determination of the identity of what calls me. Supposing that this identity can be assigned, it will be so only in and through a subsequent interrogation. Initially the being called leaves open all possibilities concerning the nature of the caller" (*L'appel et la réponse*, p. 60). This counts not only for the "Platonic call . . . neutral and impersonal par excellence" (p. 27), but for every call.

81. Paul Claudel, *L'annonce faite à Marie*, I:1, in *Théâtre II* ed. J. Madaule and J. Petit (Paris: Pléiade, 1965), p. 32.

82. Descartes, *Meditatio IV*, AT VII, 59, 2–4 [English trans., p. 41 (modified)]; *VI Responses*, AT IX-1, 233, 3–5 (the Latin reads: "Quam ejus voluntas se determinarit ad efficiendum ut id tale sit," AT VI 432, 4–5 [English trans., p. 291 (modified)]; *Meditatio IV*, AT VII, 58, 21–23 [English trans., p. 40].

83. See *supra*, §24.

84. Descartes, "Letter to X," 4 April 1648, AT V, 138, 6; March 1637, AT I, 353, 13 [English trans., pp. 331 (modified) and 55].

85. M. Scève, *Délie 77*, in *Poésie de XVIeme siècle*, ed. A.-M. Schmidt (Paris: Pléiade, 1964), p. 100.

86. See *supra*, Book 4, §22.

87. Descartes, *Dioptrique IV*, AT VI, 109, 8 [English trans., p. 164].

88. Nietzsche, *Wille zur Macht*, §1060 [English trans., p. 545]; *Thus Spoke Zarathustra* III, 14, 1 (*Werke*, ed K. Schlechta [Münich, 1966], t. 2, p. 462 [English trans., p. 328]); and *Wille zur Macht*, §1057 [English trans., pp. 544–45].

89. Rimbaud, "Aube," *Illuminations*, in *Oeuvres complètes*, p. 194 [English trans., p. 147].

90. Nietzsche, *Untimely Meditations* II, §§5–7 (*Werke*, t. 1, p. 237ff).

91. Thus Solzhenitzin, upon leaving the Gulag and entering a hospital: "All that, how could I tell it to the sick who surrounded me, and who were free? If I had to speak of it, they would not have understood" (*La main droite*, in *Oeuvres complètes*, vol. 2 [Paris, 1982], p. 577).

OPENING ONTO A QUESTION

1. *Grundprobleme der phänomenologie*, GA 58, p. 185.

ENGLISH EDITIONS CITED

Aristotle. *The Complete Works of Aristotle.* Ed. Jonathan Barnes. Princeton: Princeton University Press, 1984.

Augustine, *De Civitate Dei. The City of God.* Trans. Henry Bettenson. London: Penguin Books, 1972.

———. *In primam Epistulam Ioannis. The Fathers of the Church.* New York: CIMA Publishing, 1948.

———. *Soliloquia. The Fathers of the Church.* Vol. 1. New York: CIMA Publishing, 1948.

Bergson, Henri. *Evolution créatrice. Creative Evolution.* New York: Henry Holt, 1913.

Caputo, John D., and Michael Scanlon, eds. *God, the Gift, and Postmodernism.* Bloomington: Indiana University Press, 1999.

Chrétien de Troyes. *Le conte du Graal ou le roman de Perceval. Arthurian Romances.* Trans. D.D.R. Owen. London: Everyman's Library, 1987.

Davidson, Donald. *Essays on Actions and Events.* Oxford: Oxford University Press, 1980.

Deleuze, Gilles. *Différence et répétition. Difference and Repetition.* Trans. Paul Patton. New York: Columbia University Press, 1994.

Derrida, Jacques, *Donner le temps: 1. La fausse monnaie. Given Time: 1. Counterfeit Money.* Trans. Peggy Kamuf. Chicago: University of Chicago Press, 1992.

———. *Marges de la philosophie. Margins of Philosophy.* Trans. Alan Bass. Chicago: University of Chicago Press, 1982.

———. *La vérité en peinture. The Truth in Painting.* Trans. Geoffrey Bennington and Ian McLeod. Chicago: University of Chicago Press, 1987.

Descartes, René. *Discours de la méthode. Discourse on the Method.* In *The Philosophical Writings of Descartes.* Vol. 1. Trans. John Cottingham, Robert Stoothof, and Dugald Murdoch. Cambridge: Cambridge University Press, 1985.

———. *Letters.* In *The Philosophical Writings of Descartes.* Vol. 3. Trans. John Cottingham, Robert Stoothof, and Dugald Murdoch. Cambridge: Cambridge University Press, 1985.

———. *Meditationes et Responsiones. Meditations and Responses.* In *The Philosophical Writings of Descartes.* Vol. 2. Trans. John Cottingham, Robert Stoothof, and Dugald Murdoch. Cambridge: Cambridge University Press, 1985.

————. *Passions de l'âme. Passions of the Soul.* In *The Philosophical Writings of Descartes.* Vol. 1. Trans. John Cottingham, Robert Stoothof, and Dugald Murdoch. Cambridge: Cambridge University Press, 1985.

————. *Principia Philosophiae. Principles of Philosophy.* In *The Philosophical Writings of Descartes.* Vol. 1. Trans. John Cottingham, Robert Stoothof, and Dugald Murdoch. Cambridge: Cambridge University Press, 1985.

————. *Regulae ad directionem ingenii. Rules for the Direction of the Mind.* In *The Philosophical Writings of Descartes.* Vol. 1. Trans. John Cottingham, Robert Stoothof, and Dugald Murdoch. Cambridge: Cambridge University Press, 1985.

Fink, Eugen. *VI. Cartesianische Meditationen. Sixth Cartesian Meditation: The Idea of a Transcendental Theory of Method.* Trans. Ronald Bruzina. Bloomington: Indiana University Press, 1995.

Flaubert, Gustave. *L'education sentimentale. Sentimental Education.* In *Complete Works.* Vol. 5. G. P. Magee, 1904.

Heidegger, Martin. *Prolegomena zur Geschichte des Zeitbegriffs. History of the Concept of Time: Prolegomena.* Trans. Theodore Kisiel. Bloomington: Indiana University Press, 1985.

————. *Sein und Zeit. Being and Time.* Trans. John Macquarrie and Edward Robinson. San Francisco: Harper and Row, 1962.

————. "Summary of a Seminar on the Lecture 'Time and Being.'" In *On Time and Being.* Trans. Joan Stambaugh. New York: Harper and Row, 1972.

————. "Der Ursprung des Kunstwerkes," in *Holzwege.* "The Origin of the Work of Art." In *Poetry, Language, Thought.* Trans. Albert Hofstadter. New York: Harper and Row, 1971.

————. *Zeit und Sein. On Time and Being.* Trans. Joan Stambaugh. New York: Harper and Row, 1972.

Henry, Michel. *Généalogie de la psychanalyse: Le commencement perdu. The Genealogy of Psychoanalysis.* Trans. Douglas Brick. Stanford, Calif.: Stanford University Press, 1993.

Husserl, Edmund. *Cartesianische Meditationen. Cartesian Meditations.* Trans. Dorion Cairns. Dordrecht: Kluwer Academic Publishers, 1993.

————. *Erfahrung und Urteil. Experience and Judgment.* Trans. James S. Churchill and Karl Ameriks. Evanston: Northwestern University Press, 1973.

————. *Die Idee der Phänomenologie. The Idea of Phenomenology.* Trans. William Alston and George Nakhnikian. Dordrecht: Kluwer Academic Publishers, 1990.

————. *Ideen I. Ideas Pertaining to a Pure Phenomenology and to a Phenomenological Philosophy. First Book: General Introduction to a Pure Phenomenology.* Dordrecht: Kluwer Academic Publishers, 1998.

————. *Ideen II. Ideas Pertaining to a Pure Phenomenology and to a Phenomenological Philosophy. Second Book: Studies in the Phenomenology of Constitution.* Trans. Richard Rojcewicz and André Schuwer. Dordrecht: Kluwer Academic Publishers, 1989.

————. *Ideen III. Ideas Pertaining to a Pure Phenomenology and to a Phenomeno-

logical Philosophy. Third Book: Phenomenology and the Foundations of the Sciences. Trans. Ted Klein and William Pohl. The Hague: Martinus Nijhoff, 1980.

———. *Die Krisis der europäischen Wissenschaften und die tranzendentale Phänomenologie. The Crisis of European Sciences and Transcendental Phenomenology*. Trans. David Carr. Evanston: Northwestern University Press, 1970

———. *Logische Untersuchungen. Logical Investigations*. 2 vols. Trans. J. N. Findlay. London: Routledge and Kegan Paul, 1970.

———. *Pariser Vorträge. The Paris Lectures*. The Hague: Martinus Nijhoff, 1964.

———. *Philosophie als strenge Wissenschafte. Philosophy as Rigorous Science*. In *Phenomenology and the Crisis of Philosophy*. Trans. Quentin Lauer. New York: Harper & Row, 1965.

———. *Zur Phänomenologie des inneren Zeitbewusstseins. The Phenomenology of Internal Time Consciousness*. Trans. James S. Churchill. Bloomington: Indiana University Press, 1964.

Janicaud, Dominique. *La puissance du rationnel. Powers of the Rational*. Trans. Peg and Elizabeth Birmingham. Bloomington: Indiana University Press, 1994.

Janicaud, Dominique, Jean-François Courtine et al. *Le tournant théologique de la phénoménologie française*. In *Phenomenology and the "Theological Turn": The French Debate*. Trans. Bernard G. Prusak and Jeffrey L. Kosky. New York: Fordham University Press, 2000.

Kandinsky, Wassily. *Concerning the Spiritual in Art*. Trans. M. T. H. Sadler. New York: Dover Publications, 1977.

Kant, Immanuel. *Grundlegung zur Metaphysik der Sitten. Groundwork of the Metaphysic of Morals*. Trans. H. J. Patton. New York: Harper and Row, 1964.

———. *Kritik der praktischen Vernunft. Critique of Practical Reason*. New York: Macmillan Publishing Co., 1956.

———. *Kritik der reinen Vernunft. Critique of Pure Reason*. Trans. Norman Kemp Smith. New York: St. Martin's Press, 1965.

———. *Kritik der Urteilskraft. The Critique of the Power of Judgment*. Cambridge: Cambridge University Press, 2000.

———. *Metaphysik der Sitten. The Metaphysics of Morals*. Trans. Mary Gregor. Cambridge: Cambridge University Press, 1996.

———. *Prolegomena zu einer jeden künftigen Metaphysik. Prolegomena to Any Future Metaphysics*. Indianapolis: Hackett, 1977.

Kripke, Saul. "Naming and Necessity." In *Semantics of Natural Languages*. Ed. Donald Davidson and Gilbert Harman. Dordrecht: Kluwer Academic Publishers, 1972.

La Fontaine, Jean de. "La mort et le bûcheron." In *The Fables of La Fontaine*. Trans. Marianne Moore. New York: Viking Press, 1954.

Leibniz, G. W. *Discours de métaphysique. Discourse on Metaphysics*. In *Leibniz: Philosophical Writings*. Ed. G.H.R. Parkinson. London: Dent, 1973.

———. *Monadologia. Monadology*. In *Leibniz: Philosophical Writings*. Ed. G.H.R. Parkinson. London: Dent, 1973.

———. *New Essays on Human Understanding.* Trans. Peter Remnant and Jonathan Bennett. Cambridge: Cambridge University Press, 1981.

———. *Principles of Nature and of Grace.* In *Leibniz: Philosophical Writings.* Ed. G. H. R. Parkinson. London: Dent, 1973.

Levinas, Emmanuel. *Autrement qu'être, ou au-delà de l'essence. Otherwise than Being, or Beyond Essence.* Trans. Alphonso Lingis. Dordrecht: Kluwer Academic Publishers, 1991.

———. *De Dieu qui vient à l'idée. Of God Who Comes to Mind.* Trans. Bettina Bergo. Stanford, Calif.: Stanford University Press, 1998.

———. *De l'existence à l'existent. Existence and Existents.* Trans. Alphonso Lingis. The Hague: Martinus Nijhoff, 1978.

———. *En découvrant l'existence avec Husserl et Heidegger. Discovering Existence with Husserl.* Trans. Richard A. Cohen and Michael B. Smith. Evanston: Northwestern University Press, 1998.

———. *Entre-nous: Ecrits sur le penser-à-l'autre. Entre Nous: On Thinking-of-the-Other.* New York: Columbia University Press, 1998.

———. *Totalité et infini. Totality and Infinity.* Pittsburgh: Duquesne University Press, 1969.

Maimonides. *The Guide of the Perplexed.* Trans. Shlomo Pines. Chicago: University of Chicago Press, 1963.

Mallarmé, Stéphane, "Un Coup de dé." In *Collected Poems.* Trans. Henry Weinfeld. Berkeley: University of California Press, 1994.

Marion, Jean-Luc. *Dieu sans l'être. God Without Being.* Trans. Thomas A. Carlson. Chicago: University of Chicago Press, 1991.

———. *Réduction et donation. Etudes sur Husserl, Heidegger, et la phénoménologie. Reduction and Givenness: Investigations of Husserl, Heidegger, and Phenomenology.* Trans. Thomas A. Carlson. Evanston: Northwestern University Press, 1998.

———. *Sur le prisme métaphysique de Descartes. On Descartes' Metaphysical Prism.* Trans. Jeffrey L. Kosky. Chicago: University of Chicago Press, 1999.

Mauss, Marcel. *Essai sur le don. The Gift: The Form and Reason for Exchange in Archaic Societies.* Trans. W. D. Halls. New York: Norton, 2000.

Merleau-Ponty, Maurice. *L'oeil et l'esprit. The Eye and the Mind.* In *The Essential Writings of Maurice Merleau-Ponty.* New York: Harcourt, Brace & World, 1969.

———. *Phénoménologie de la perception. Phenomenology of Perception.* London: Routledge & Kegan Paul, 1970.

———. *Le visible et l'invisible. The Visible and the Invisible.* Trans. Alphonso Lingis. Evanston: Northwestern University Press, 1978.

Molière. *L'avare.* "The Miser." In *The Miser and Other Plays.*, trans. John Wood and David Coward. New York: Penguin Books, 2000.

Nietzsche, Friedrich. *Thus Spoke Zarathustra.* In *The Portable Nietzsche.* Trans. Walter Kaufmann. New York: Penguin Books, 1954.

———. *Wille zur Macht. The Will to Power.* Trans. Walter Kaufmann. New York: Random House, 1967.

Pascal, Blaise. "De l'esprit géométrique." "The Mind of the Geometrician." In *Great Shorter Works of Pascal.* Trans. Emile Cailliet and John C. Blankenagel. Philadelphia: Westminster Press, 1948.

———. *Pensées.* Trans. A. J. Krailsheimer. New York: Penguin Books, 1966.

Petrarch. *Canzoniere. Canzoniere.* Trans. Mark Musa. Bloomington: Indiana University Press, 1996.

Proust, Marcel. "Du côté de chez Swann." *Remembrance of Things Past: Swann's Way.* Trans. C. K. Scott Moncrieff. Vintage Books, 1970.

Racine, Jean. *Bérénice.* In *The Complete Plays of Jean Racine.* Vol. 1. Trans. Samuel Solomon. New York: Random House, 1967.

Ricoeur, Paul. *Temps et récit. Time and Narrative.* Trans. Kathleen McLaughlin and David Pellauer. Chicago: University of Chicago Press, 1984.

Rimbaud, Arthur. *Illuminations. A Season in Hell, The Illuminations.* Trans. Enid Rhodes Peschel. New York: Oxford University Press, 1973.

———. *Une saison en enfer. A Season in Hell, The Illuminations.* Trans. Enid Rhodes Peschel. New York: Oxford University Press, 1973.

Rousseau, Jean-Jacques. *Emile. Emile, or on Education.* Trans. Allan Bloom. New York: Basic Books, 1979.

———. *Rêveries du promeneur solitaire. The Reveries of a Solitary.* Trans. John Gould Fletcher. New York: Lenox Hill Publishers, 1971.

Sartre, Jean-Paul. *L'être et le néant. Being and Nothingness.* Trans. Hazel Barnes. New York: Philosophical Library, 1956.

———. *Vérité et existence. Truth and Existence.* Chicago: University of Chicago Press, 1992.

Shakespeare, William. *Macbeth.* In *The Yale Shakespeare.* New Haven, Conn.: Yale University Press, 1993.

Spinoza, Baruch. *Ethica. Ethics.* Trans. Samuel Shirley. Indianapolis: Hackett, 1992.

Thomas Aquinas. *De aeternitate mundi contra murmurentes. On the Eternity of the World.* Trans. Cyril Vollert, Lottie H. Kendzierski, and Paul M. Byrne. Milwaukee, Wisc.: Marquette University Press, 1964.

———. *De ente et essentia. On Being and Essence.* Trans. Armand Maurier. Toronto: Pontifical Institute of Medieval Studies, 1968.

———. *Summa theologiae.* New York: McGraw Hill, 1976.

INDEX NOMINUM

Cultural Memory | *in the Present*